LEADERSHIP
in Instructional Technology

MATTHEW M. MAURER
Butler University

GEORGE STEVEN DAVIDSON
Butler University

Merrill, an imprint of Prentice Hall
Upper Saddle River, New Jersey   Columbus, Ohio

Library of Congress Cataloging-in-Publication Data

Leadership in instructional technology / Matthew M. Maurer, George Davidson
        p.   cm.
    Includes bibliographical references and index.
    ISBN 0-13-239849-4 (pbk.)
    1. Educational technology. 2. Computer-assisted instruction. 3. Instructional systems—Design. 4. Educational leadership.   I. Davidson, George Steven. II. Title.
    LB1028.3.M383   1998
    371.33—dc21

96-50444
CIP

Cover photo: Laurie Bayer/International Stock
Editor: Debra A. Stollenwerk
Production Editor: Patricia S. Kelly
Photo Coordinator: Anthony Magnacca
Design Coordinator: Julia Zonneveld Van Hook
Text Designer: Anne Flanagan
Cover Designer: Russ Maselli
Production Manager: Pamela D. Bennett
Electronic Text Management: Marilyn Wilson Phelps, Matthew Williams, Karen L. Bretz, Tracey B. Ward
Director of Marketing: Kevin Flanagan
Marketing Manager: Suzanne Stanton
Advertising/Marketing Coordinator: Julie Shough

This book was set in Schneidler and Humanist 777 by Prentice Hall and was printed and bound by R.R. Donnelley & Sons Company. The cover was printed by Phoenix Color Corp.

 © 1998 by Prentice-Hall, Inc.
Simon & Schuster/A Viacom Company
Upper Saddle River, New Jersey 07458

Photo credits: pp. 2, 54, 71, 74, 100, 122, 166, 227, 295, 304, 307 by Matthew M. Maurer; pp. 32, 35 Courtesy of IBM Corporation; p. 224 by Tom Watson, Merrill; pp. 250, 280 by Anthony Magnacca, Merrill.

Printed in the United States of America

10 9 8 7 6 5 4 3 2 1

ISBN: 0-13-239849-4

Prentice-Hall International (UK) Limited, *London*
Prentice-Hall of Australia Pty. Limited, *Sydney*
Prentice-Hall of Canada, Inc., *Toronto*
Prentice-Hall Hispanoamericana, S. A., *Mexico*
Prentice-Hall of India Private Limited, *New Delhi*
Prentice-Hall of Japan, Inc., *Tokyo*
Simon & Schuster Asia Pte. Ltd., *Singapore*
Editora Prentice-Hall do Brasil, Ltda., *Rio de Janeiro*

DEDICATED TO
Carol Bowman and Kathy Zenz

FOR
**Ben, Joe, Alexander, David, Jason, Jonathan,
Michael, Zachary**

Foreword

Leadership in Instructional Technology is a welcome addition to the literature on the symbiotic junction between leadership and instructional technology—the linchpin in an organizational process that exploits new mechanisms for effective learning. The book's virtue lies less in the explication of bold new theories than in a visionary and insightful coalescence of concepts that create a persuasive argument for the adoption of technology. In so doing, it demonstrates a longstanding pattern wherein paradigmatic breakthroughs stem not from a brilliant flash of newborn perception, but rather from the imaginative arrangement of new and old conceptions that illuminate promising new paths.

The thirteen chapters in this book lead the reader through the central corpus of leadership, the essential interplay between soft and hard technology in meshing disciplines, and pragmatic matters such as evaluating outcomes, enhancing staff capability, and facilitating reinforcement.

Through this unfolding, several pivotal considerations emerge: the need to eliminate old habits of mind and accept new perspectives—"getting out of the box;" the utilization of diversified leadership to tap the collective talents of an organization's personnel; employing technological mechanisms to enhance knowledge integration; viewing the technological frontier not merely as new approaches to conventional practice, but as a powerful force which can revolutionize teaching and learning; converting data into information and information into knowledge; and aligning technologies with instructional objectives that foster cognitive engagement. The book is valuable and praiseworthy in its amalgamation of sound learning principles, technological theory, and practical application, reiterating Seymour Papert's contention that "the most important skill determining a person's life patterns has already become the ability to learn new skills . . . this will be increasingly true in the future. The competitive ability is the ability to learn."*

Such a nexus, however, creates a number of critical demands, among them: synchronizing procedures in the most advantageous manner, guarding against the temptation to substitute convenience for quality, and insuring that interactive discussion does not dissolve into uninformed conversation. A growing danger is that educational entrepreneurs, most interested in decreasing overhead and increasing

---

* *Source:* Papert, S. (1993). *The children's machine: Rethinking schooling, the age of the computer.* New York: Basic Books.

profit, will deploy technology as shortcuts rather than artful instructional tools, and thereby bring about an intensification of poor teaching.

Moreover, since codified knowledge is easily communicated electronically to unlimited numbers of students, thus permitting self-choice in content, pace, and utilization, a considerable peril is that, without sustained interchange among learner, subject matter, and teacher, excessive autonomy can easily distort and even offset intended benefits. The increasing accessibility of new research findings, furthermore, will make teachers who do no more than convey information increasingly archaic. Hence, where learning is formally certified through grade, credit, or other recognition, learner independence must be attached by some connective tissue to criteria standards. It is for this reason, perhaps, that this book consistently emphasizes the profound need for evaluative attention to "integration-interaction and personalization."

Complicating this calculus, much has been made, in recent times, of schools' liabilities. As with other issues arising in a culture of dissent, divided opinion invariably gives rise to contention. Some believe we are in the midst of authentic crisis, while others maintain the alleged difficulties are plainly counterfeit—fiction fabricated to serve private agendas. Be this as it may, educational leadership consistently has been held as an indispensable virtue in effective schooling, and in governing the riptides of reform. When leaders succeed, so does some additional consequence, whether good or bad.

Leadership is neither power, authority, nor status. Instead, it is the responsibility to envisage intelligent action. As with other skills, it develops through reflective, analytical practice. One cannot lead without understanding an organization's system, but such knowledge, in itself, is insufficient. Additionally, human talent must be discovered and utilized effectively. The cultivation of initiative and authority in others, as the authors of this book repeatedly suggest, occurs in a "community of leadership," wherein direction shifts with the changing locus of dominant expertise and improvement becomes a collective accomplishment.

Whitehead once noted that the art of progress is to preserve order amidst change and change amidst order. Modifying an organization's culture can indeed be precarious. Given the human penchant for security, stability, and the comfort of routine, some teachers feel threatened by even minor reorganization, however sensible. Still, conventional lore holds that whereas followers tend to fear new ideas, leaders generally are more troubled by old ideas. Hence, when attitudinal alteration is prohibitive, leaders may focus on circumstances in the work environment and, by modifying these, accomplish their purpose indirectly.

Staff development, in addition, is moving from the global and general to the focused and specific. In place of random workshops and institutes directed toward some general theme, predetermined objectives are set and the emphasis is on best-practice utilization—advance organizers, evaluation benchmarks, constructivist teaching, and so on. Of even greater moment, staffs are less likely to be viewed as subordinate personnel in need of reprocessing, but rather as autonomous agents who must be involved in the conceptualization, design, operation, and assessment of reforms. The blessing of this turnaround is that teachers and administrators can use their own insight and experience in restructuring goals.

A technological surge in educational enterprises is inevitable. In time, technology will revolutionize pedagogical procedure, learner individualization, interface between tutor and student, and teacher education. *Leadership in Instructional Technology* captures the spirit and essence of this coming metamorphosis, points us in the right direction, and initiates our exploration of uncharted waters.

Louis J. Rubin, Ph.D.
Professor of Curriculum and Instruction
University of Illinois at Urbana-Champaign

Preface

We wrote this book for all of us—principals, teachers, school board members, and parents—who are leaders of instruction and technology in our schools. We describe these participants as the *community of leadership*. It is our ultimate hope that by reading this book you will become instrumental in improving teaching and learning, and that children will benefit.

Inherent in this text are many connections and juxtapositions. We, the authors, come to this topic from our respective specializations, one from administration and the other from instructional technology. Yet we share some strong beliefs, the most important being the value of children and the importance of a caring, concerned community to guide their development. As we planned the text, we saw the power of our different and varied backgrounds. What we did not envision was the conflict that would arise in the completion of the project. A simple word like *follower*, for example, created discussion, argument, and conflict between and within us. Our resolution of these conflicts, we believe, will stimulate thought and discussion that, in turn, will benefit children.

Two important concepts frame the ideas in the text. Some scholars in educational administration write about *leadership*. The concept of the community of leadership derives from considerations of school culture, vision, mission, shared goals, roving or ad hoc leaders, and power and authority. The *instructional* foundation of the text evolves from student-active, teacher-facilitated, constructivist principles and cognitive psychological learning theory. We argue for teaching and learning environments incorporating developmentally appropriate concept and skills acquisition and multi-aged grouping in nongraded environments. Additionally, we advocate instructional principles grounded in schema theory and metacognition. Only by explicitly explaining the conjunction between the community of leadership and instructional technology and by providing strategies for successful implementation can we improve learning systemically.

During the course of writing this text we argued extensively about specific issues being "out of the box." In the box means being so strongly influenced by your field and your training that you cannot see issues in ways that those outside the field see them. We each accused the other of being in the box and subsequently challenged each other to get out of the box. When we challenged closely held beliefs and found they did not hold, we climbed out of the box. Unfortunately, we immediately faced the corollaries to those beliefs and found ourselves in another box. We offer this text as our best effort to help educators get out of the box and view leadership in instructional technology from a fresh perspective. We challenge you to climb out of more boxes.

ORGANIZATION OF THE TEXT

This book helps leaders create and expand their responsibilities and strategies as they establish technology-rich teaching and learning environments. The first part describes the intellectual and philosophical basis for ideas about the community of leadership and for quality teaching and learning. The second part describes technology tools, their uses, and implications for the community of leadership. This section describes basic hardware and software, explains how to support teaching and learning with technology, and offers sample lesson ideas. These chapters focus on word processing, spreadsheets, databases, hypermedia, the thinking curriculum, and telecommunications. The third part details strategies for the community of leadership to ensure academic success. These chapters guide the community of leadership through a successful change process to a technology-based curriculum including unique perspectives on staff development; techniques for strategic, curricular, and operational planning; and specific recommendations for internal and external funding. The last chapter speculates on the future of the community of leadership and the direction of instructional technology.

NOTE TO THE READER

We have chosen to use feminine pronouns throughout this book both to avoid the awkward "he or she" construction and to celebrate the advancement and achievement of women in leadership and instructional technology.

SPECIAL FEATURES

Leadership in Instructional Technology advocates ideas that we believe will improve instruction and student achievement in the classroom. Following are some of the features of this text.

- A theory-practice perspective that describes our values and beliefs about constructivist and developmentally appropriate teaching and learning
- A theory-practice perspective that establishes our values and beliefs about the community of leadership
- Instructional technology as a repertoire of tools to support a quality academic program
- A series of teaching and learning strategies that guide students to turn data (facts) to information (categories and organized data) to knowledge (the effective use of information) to wisdom (knowledge and experience influenced by values and beliefs and shared goals)

- Suggestions and recommendations about the integration of traditional curriculum areas and a specific discussion about the thinking curriculum
- The tools to develop student experts and encourage brilliance in children
- A student coaching model and classroom management ideas for classrooms with computers
- Suggested lesson plan ideas for each technology tool
- Planning models
- Funding models
- Staff development model designed to increase the transfer of knowledge, skills, and dispositions to the classroom
- Suggestions and insights about controversial telecommunications, InterNet, and World Wide Web concerns
- A presentation about equity issues and access to technology with emphasis on the InterNet

ACKNOWLEDGMENTS

We acknowledge and appreciate all of the people who contributed to the completion of this text. First, we thank the reviewers of the manuscript who helped us get out of our box: Dale L. Brubaker, University of North Carolina, Greensboro; John C. Daresh, Illinois State University; Carl H. Rinne, University of Michigan, Flint; Caryl Cook Schunk, Educational Consultant; and Nancy Harper Vick, Longwood College.

We also thank the faculty, staff, and students of the Butler University College of Education who supported and influenced our work; our friends and colleagues at Merrill who believed in the project and made quality recommendations, especially Debbie Stollenwerk, acquisitions editor, and Patricia Kelly, production editor; the individuals at the Iowa State University and the University of Illinois at Urbana-Champaign who prepared us for our journey; and, finally, to Louis Rubin, who encouraged us and graced the text with his foreword.

Brief Contents

Contents

CHAPTER 3
Software: Finding the Power   54

PART II
Instructional Applications   73

CHAPTER 4
Supporting Language and Literacy Development with Technology   74

CHAPTER 5
Mathematics and Technology   100

CHAPTER 6
Data Base Management: Turning Data into Information into Knowledge   122

PART III
The Community of Leadership　223

CHAPTER 10
Staff Development: A Community of Learners, A Community of Leaders　　224

CHAPTER 11
Planning Today, Insuring Tomorrow　　250

CHAPTER 12
Funding Technology Projects   280

CHAPTER 13
Toward a Brilliant Future   304

Foundations of Leadership in Instructional Technology

CHAPTER 1

Building a Community of Leadership

Leadership in Instructional Technology is a book for instructional leaders. The values and beliefs on which this book is based reflect an emerging view of leadership connected to a constructivist transformation of teaching and learning. Effective leadership practices based on theories and ideas about vision and mission, power and authority, reflective practice, moral leadership, school culture, organizational change, and the power of passion create a new paradigm: a "community of leadership."

The community of leadership are the stakeholders in children's education. The formal leader facilitates the community of leadership but is joined and supported by teachers, parents, students, school staff, and interested community and business leaders. Membership in the community of leadership demands that each participant contribute her expertise to the organization. The community of leadership's interests are threefold: (1) organizational—managing the school, (2) governance—directing the school, and (3) instructional—framing, implementing, and assessing a quality academic program supported by the wise use of instructional technology.

The community of leadership manages changes in instructional technology through the influence of its own instructional experts. For example, the teacher who has knowledge about word processing and process writing assumes a role of expert, *ad hoc* or "roving leadership" (DePree, 1989, p. 45), while the principal who does not have a foundation in language and literacy becomes an able follower. If that same principal has expertise in mathematics education, then she assumes the expert role in incorporating spreadsheet applications into the primary school curriculum, while the process writing expert assumes the follower role.

The community of leadership's unique recognition of change in school organizations and quality instruction can move a school into the Twenty-first Century. The infusion of a critical thinking, problem-solving curricula connected to a variety of integrated content areas, supported by instructional technology applications such as *Logo* and *HyperMedia*, meet the community's leadership and instruction needs. Schools of the Twenty-first Century no longer regard technology as a solution in search of a problem. The solution is powerful instructional methods and strategies that support quality academic programs, internalized and implemented by the community of leadership.

Constructivist instructional models favor student-active, teacher-facilitated learning environments; developmentally appropriate acquisition of concepts and skills; multi-age grouping in non-graded learning families; teaching and learning in a social context; teaching and learning that explores whole ideas and reduces them to parts; teaching and learning based on student observation, hypothesis generation and testing, and reflection; and teaching and learning based on established cognitive psychological learning theories, such as schema theory and metacognition.

The first section of this chapter explores a perspective of instructional technology based on constructivist and cognitive psychological learning theory. The second section explores a new leadership paradigm: the community of leadership.

THE CONSTRUCTIVIST PERSPECTIVE: TEACHING AND LEARNING IN INSTRUCTIONAL TECHNOLOGY

Clark (1983) provides a useful analogy for exploring the constructivist perspective of teaching and learning:

> The current best evidence is that media are mere vehicles that deliver instruction but do not influence student achievement any more than the truck that delivers our groceries causes changes in our nutrition. (p. 445)

The essential argument of this book is that the quality of instruction—the groceries—can be improved through the effective use of instructional technology—the delivery truck—and that instructional technology can be re-engineered by a new organizational and governance paradigm: a community of leadership.

Additionally, the change toward a community of leadership serves to reorganize the school so that it is governed with the child at the center and not for the convenience of adults. Under the new paradigm, teaching becomes a process of facilitating and providing interesting and challenging learning situations and environments. Learning becomes active, engaging, and a shared responsibility of the learner. The shared goals of the community of leadership demand a shift from the traditional knowledge-transmission models to constructivist perspectives and learning theories. These are important cultural changes in the school's values and beliefs.

Introduction to Leadership: A Connection to Teaching and Learning

The main theme of this section is that schools must change their learning culture from the current emphasis on school and teacher effectiveness research implemented by traditional knowledge-transmission teaching strategies. *Leadership in Instructional Technology* advocates research-based, student-active, teacher-facilitated, developmentally appropriate models of instruction—constructivism and cognitive learning theory, including schema theory and metacognition.

The ultimate purpose of instructional technology's support of an exciting, quality learning curricula explicitly is to encourage children to discover basic *data* (facts), to integrate and interpret those data into *information*, and to apply that information into action to create *knowledge*. Instructional technology supports the conversion of data to information to knowledge. Applications such as word processors, spreadsheets, and databases provide alternative approaches to the collection of data, interpretation of information (for example, creating a variety of graphs and charts), and application of that information into knowledge. Throughout the remaining chapters, we will expand upon this fundamental concept and purpose for instructional technology.

Definitions: Deconstructing Constructivism

Children construct reality from observation, hypothesis generation and testing, and reflection. For them, errors are not mistakes but new bits of data that help construct their emerging mental models and are incorporated into their existing schemata. Constructivism holds that children's representations of reality differ from those of adults (Elkind, 1971). Hence, learning is an active process, and teachers can facilitate the process but cannot effectively transmit facts or data. Additionally, children's developing construction of reality does not fall into neatly segmented areas of study, such as botany, geography, or history, but represent a more integrated view. Constructivist theory holds that content-area learning is an adult's social construction of reality, not a child's mental model.

Implications: How Constructivists Think

Young children see concrete objects as having human-like qualities such as purposes and emotions. To children, thoughts and dreams have reality and have the power to act. Elkind (1971) suggests that young children think that people built the world for man's benefit. Children's unexpected egocentricity and lack of empathy becomes a focal point in Piaget's developmental or stage theory: that children grow from the concrete to the abstract.

How, then, do young children construct realities that differ so significantly from adults, from teachers? Boyer and Semrou (1995) describe a child's constructed reality as a function of her experience, which includes observation, hypothesis generation and testing, and reflection. We recognize the physical signs of an 8-month-old infant confronting a new experience. We can almost see the mental processes the child uses to compare her new experience to her incomplete mental model of reality. Children's early experiences with drawing programs such as *Kid Pix* help them manipulate concepts and ideas and incorporate them into their emerging mental models.

The child constructs mental models or pictures of reality through observation, hypothesis generation and testing, and reflection from her sensory experiences. Both Piaget's constructivist perspective and cognitive psychology's learning theories support the concept of mental models or schemata.

The definitions and interpretations of Piaget's constructivist model expand to include the idea that the learner is an active participant in her learning from the earliest age. Constructivist learning emphasizes effort, observation, hypothesis generation and testing, and reflection more than it demands ability. In constructivist learning, both the teacher and the child have responsibilities. The child has responsibility for engaging in the learning and making connections, and the teacher has responsibility for facilitating or scaffolding developmentally appropriate learning strategies. Introducing children to writing applications such as *Kid Works II*, giving them minimal instruction, and letting them explore makes more instructional sense than directly teaching students to mimic a teacher's idea of children's writing. We find the groundwork for instructional technology in Piaget, with his ideals of developmentally appropriate teaching and learning and the relevance of cognitive development (Perkins, 1992).

The definitions and descriptions of a constructivist philosophy seemingly appear to leave little for teachers actually to do. Teachers, most certainly, would reject a perspective that leaves the construction of reality or learning exclusively to the child. In Chapter 8 we explore the thinking curriculum beginning with *Logo*. *Logo* asks children to move a "turtle" (the cursor) around the screen using a series of directional commands. The turtle's movement produces lines which draw graphical representations that demonstrate children's thinking. To create a square or a triangle, children must test assumptions about directionality, distance, shape, sequence, and fundamental mathematical and geometric principles. As we review several principles of constructivism, we see an almost one-to-one correspondence to the objectives and strategies of *Logo*.

Forman (1987) describes several constructivist beliefs:

> First, a constructivist believes that knowledge can never be reduced to what we learn from our senses. . . . Second, a constructivist believes that development is marked by an improvement in how well the child can reflect on his or her own thinking. . . . Third, a constructivist believes that meaningful learning results only when the learner can ask his or her own questions. . . . Fourth, the constructivist believes that we teach others by providing them with opportunities to experiment. Teachers design rich problem-solving environments. (pp. 71–72)

Perhaps nowhere else does the difference between constructivist and traditional models confront the teacher's values and beliefs about teaching and learning more than the act of children making errors—the process of observation, hypothesis generation and testing, and reflection. In traditional models, errors are mistakes. In constructivism, errors are redefinitions of mental models, of evolving schemata; in other words, errors are learning opportunities.

Instructional technology can support children's efforts to construct their reality. Word processing is used to support process-writing strategies that ease students' composition, editing, and publication. Problem-solving applications, such as spreadsheets and *Logo*, help children construct and test hypotheses and make judgments.

Traditional Models: Getting Better and Better at Doing the Wrong Thing

Principals and teachers recognize that the constructivist perspective is not the instructional model used in most schools. Many of us were taught to use a knowledge-transmission or a skill-based model in which the teacher is active and the student is passive, with lecture or lecture-demonstration being the preferred instructional strategy. Surely, this model dominates in today's schools. Much of the challenge in educational leadership is to encourage teachers to understand both models and to help teachers use both models responsibly. Au (1993) describes the differences between constructivist models and traditional knowledge-transmission models. In constructivist models:

1. The child is an active participant in her own learning.
2. Learning is based upon wholes and is reduced to parts.

3. Learning has a social element—children can learn by cooperation.

4. The child is asked to explore the purposes of literacy or of knowledge.

5. Teaching and learning is student-centered, and learning respects individual differences.

6. Learning supports observation, hypothesis generation and testing, and reflection.

7. Teaching and learning profit from individual and group differences.

In knowledge-transmission or skill-based models:

1. The teacher actively transfers her knowledge to the child, who accepts learning passively.

2. Learning is based upon decontextualized parts, and the child is expected to grasp the wholes.

3. Teaching and learning are abstract and do not rely on any social context, not even on authentic teaching materials.

4. Skills and knowledge are taught for their own inherent value, not for any special purpose or function.

5. Teaching and learning are skill and knowledge based, and children are assumed to be more alike than different.

6. Teaching and learning are product-centered, that is, based upon the completion of assignments without regard for the child's prior knowledge or schema elaboration.

7. The values associated with teaching and learning are those of the mainstream, usually of the principals and teachers, and the values deny contribution of diversity and difference to teaching and learning.

Our premises about the effective use of instructional technology are based, in part, on the ability of technology to support a quality instructional program. Teachers using constructivist and cognitive learning theories may use applications of technology to support quality instruction. Word processing applications can reinforce children's process writing; spreadsheets can assist children to manipulate numbers—to turn data into information and information into knowledge. Telecommunications, the InterNet, and the World Wide Web help children build and test hypotheses with volumes of multimedia-based data. Constructivist technology strategies contrast sharply with weaker traditional knowledge-transmission models described by Brooks and Brooks (1993):

First, the American classroom is dominated by teacher talk. . . . Second, most teachers rely heavily on textbooks. . . . Third, although there exists a growing interest in cooperative learning in America's schools, most classrooms structurally discourage cooperation and require students to work in relative isolation on tasks that require low-level skills, rather than higher-order reasoning. . . . Fourth, student thinking is devalued in most classrooms. . . . Fifth, schooling is premised on the notion that there exists a fixed world that the learner must come to know. (pp. 6–7)

Of all teacher behaviors, these beliefs are the most troublesome. They imply that the teacher's knowledge is the only knowledge, and that children's knowledge, however incomplete, is wrong. Additionally, this notion has at its core a hidden message that the teacher's knowledge is mainstream knowledge, and that knowledge derived through diversity and/or divergent thinking is inappropriate and wrong. As we argue in the second section of this chapter, systemic change, even change in teaching and learning, will happen only with a concurrent change in the school's culture. The movement from traditional knowledge-transmission models to constructivist/learning theory models is a major restructuring of the vision and mission in an emerging school culture.

Skill Development: The Standardized Test

Thorough and well-meaning principals and teachers, concerned about the pressures of accountability and standardized test scores, may point to constructivism's perceived lack of emphasis on skill development. The constructivist teacher does care about children's essential skills and their ability to demonstrate knowledge on standardized achievement tests. However, the constructivist teacher sees skill development as an integrated part of the learning model and treats essential skill development as another way children construct their own reality.

Indications of children's thinking—reading, writing, computing, and other content area skills—have conventional forms. In constructivist teaching and learning, the child is encouraged to demonstrate these forms as they naturally occur in her learning. For example, in knowledge-transmission models the scope and sequence chart dictates the curriculum. Many reading and language arts basal series suggest a point in the second grade for the teaching of quotation marks. However, because of the range of developmental readiness among second-graders, many struggle to learn the new skill. Constructivist skill development strategies suggest that the appropriate time to teach quotation marks is when the child begins to use dialogue in her writing. Skill development is authentic, using real learning materials, such as trade books or a local newspaper, thus connecting to the child's own reality. The skill or concept is taught explicitly when the child is most receptive.

Unfortunately, constructivist thinking and teaching strategies are considerably more amorphous and ambiguous than those of knowledge-transmission models. Principals and teachers also have the experience of having been taught, and having taught, the knowledge-transmission model. We may or may not like it, but we surely know it. Learning constructivist thinking and teaching strategies requires creating new teacher schemata or mental models and engaging in reflective practice. Integrating instructional technology strategies in a quality academic program based on constructivism and cognitive learning theory—for example, word processing and process writing—may ease the transition from the traditional knowledge-transmission model. Technology is the symbolic expression of an explicit change in a school's culture. It is not enough that we now know how to change, but that we now know where to begin. We suggest that the best place to begin is at the keyboard and the monitor.

In the next section we review learning theory as rediscovered and reinterpreted by cognitive psychologists and language and literacy specialists. Constructivist values and beliefs integrate theories of learning to offer a more comprehensive view of the relationship among teaching and learning, curricula, instructional programs, and technology.

Values and Beliefs about Teaching and Learning

The following paragraphs describe the values and beliefs about teaching and learning that form the foundation for this book.

Teaching and learning are more effective when schema-based.   Schema theory is the theoretical foundation of constructivist thinking and the intellectual base of comprehension and learning-remembering strategies. Schema formation and schema elaboration are the prime strategies for children's construction of knowledge and reality. Schema theory states that learning is a process of systematically attaching new information or knowledge to what children already know. Schemata are mental models or mental pictures of learning that, when activated or reinforced in the learner, help her remember and learn both details and concepts. For a schema to be effective, it must be activated explicitly. Both information storage and retrieval are necessarily active processes. Examples of schemata or mental models are: Thanksgiving dinner, the commutative property of addition, a standardized achievement test, and the Industrial Revolution (Anderson & Pearson, 1984).

The expert use of instructional technology by children and adults depends upon an emerging and increasingly sophisticated understanding of the possibilities and capabilities of technology's support of a quality academic program. To operate hardware and software, teachers and learners must access their background and current knowledge to construct patterns. For example, observers of young children note that teaching a young child how to maneuver within the *Kid Pix* program often leads to the child's understanding of more sophisticated programs. The Macintosh platform is particularly helpful because of the consistency of commands among applications; for example, the keyboard command for print is universally Command + P. Just as children learn these simple patterns, they construct evolving schemata or mental pictures of other application processes. Papert's (1971) *Logo* application is based instructionally upon a schema concept of building increasingly complex processes to demonstrate the child's thinking. Moving from simple rules—"mind sized bites" (Papert, 1980, p. 135)—to variables to procedures to recursion, children and adults activate their schemata and connect new knowledge to existing knowledge.

Teaching and learning are more effective when students evolve strategies to understand how they learn.   Metacognition is the child's ability to understand how she thinks and her ability to use strategies to monitor and correct her learning. Metacognitive activity occurs in clusters:

1. Reflection: The child thinks about how she thinks.
2. Monitoring: The child monitors her own learning for understanding.
3. Correction: The child creates strategies to repair problems of misunderstanding.

Metacognitive theorists understand that an effective learner knows when her learning fails: when she does not understand. Additionally, an effective learner creates strategies to repair her misunderstanding. An ineffective learner does not know when her learning fails and does not have, or even recognize, strategies to learn.

The application of instructional technology to interesting and exciting learning situations is an excellent example of metacognitive theory put into practice. Open-ended and complex learning tasks, such as plotting trends in a particular stock or commodities market, involves the integration of several intellectual disciplines and requires the technology user to create personalized applications within programs. The clever integration of a "hot" data base and spreadsheet, in which information altered in one program automatically changes in the other, can aid students' interpretive and problem-solving strategies. The goal is not to create children capable of pyrotechnic application processes but to help children turn data into information and information into knowledge.

The teacher's role is to teach metacognitive strategies explicitly and directly to learners. These strategies include: clarifying the purpose of learning, identifying the important ideas, focusing on main ideas, monitoring learning, self-questioning, and corrective or fix-up strategies (Baker & Brown, 1984).

Teaching and learning are more effective when they are active processes.   Active learning processes legitimize the child's use of learning strategies which support constructivist models. Exploration, inquiry, and other active strategies—for example, reading comprehension strategies, higher order thinking skills, and computer applications such as *Logo* or the *Carmen San Diego* series—represent the basis of constructivist teaching and learning. The learner interacts with the teacher, the author, or the learning program to construct her own meaning. Active learning is the child's individual or metacognitive act of observation, hypothesis generation and testing, and reflection.

Teaching and learning are more effective when skills are mastered and become automatic.   In an era in which considerable emphasis is placed on school accountability, often measured by professionally published or state-mandated standardized achievement tests, skill development is fundamental to any philosophy or model of teaching and learning. Children must be competent in essential skills: reading, writing, speaking, listening, and computing. Whatever our opinions of standardized achievement tests, there is no question that students, teachers, and schools must be accountable for children's mastery of essential skills. The question, then, is not whether children have mastered the skills, but how they learn them. Samuels (1988) states that skills become automatic when children are accurate in their use and when children's recognition occurs quickly. The teachers' responsibility, explicitly and directly, is to teach automaticity, to instruct students to become accurate, and to provide practice time to become quick. More significantly, the teacher must motivate students to become accurate and automatic.

If there is an educationally appropriate use of drill-and-kill learning games, then it is for the advancement of children's automaticity, to increase their speed using essential skills. The use of computer drill applications must be tempered with applications that encourage accuracy and provide motivation to practice. The process writing and arithmetic challenges involved in spreadsheets, for example, help children achieve accuracy and reach automaticity.

Teaching and learning are more effective when seen as a developmental or emergent process.   How we think about things directs how we behave. As educators we have many philosophical opinions about teaching and learning. These opinions represent opposite ends of a continuum. The traditional knowledge-transmission model is at one end of the continuum. The constructivist model, in which children learn authentically and at their appropriate developmental level, is at the other end of the continuum. Whichever side of the continuum educators endorse, they operationally define and implement their vision of knowledge and pedagogy.

The authors of this book value and believe in the efficacy of constructivist practices. One of technology's adaptive processes which enhances developmental learning is the availability of a variety of similar applications designed for children of various abilities and motivation. Educators can start young children on a continuous progress of critical thinking and problem solving with the introduction of *Logo*. Educators can then increase the learning stakes by moving to more sophisticated and complex learning applications with broader, more content-integrated learning objectives. The *Sim* series (*SimCity, SimEarth, SimTower*) and other thinking curricula programs (*The Decision Series* and *ABC News Interactive*) help teachers organize children to learn through schema building and elaboration and metacognitive strategies that refine children's thinking.

Teaching and learning are more effective when experienced and assessed in natural contexts using authentic learning materials.   Natural contexts are teaching and learning environments in which children uses authentic learning materials—literature, primary sources, real scientific and mathematical problems, and so on—which are relevant to their own experience. Natural and real learning materials and assessments are based on the proposition that effective learning is grounded in contextualized rather than decontextualized teaching. Constructivist-based, contextualized skill development and assessment depends upon strategies that integrate skills and use real learning materials for practice. Instead of relying upon artificial spelling lists and language arts scope-and-sequence tasks taught independently from children's experience, teachers can rely on process writing, journals, content-area essays, and problem-solving projects to elicit spelling mistakes and grammatical errors that form children's authentic spelling and language arts programs. No longer should 12-year-olds learn to spell "penguin" simply because a publisher's scope-and-sequence chart demands it; children now learn to spell "penguin" as they use the word in their own writing. No longer should 7-year-olds learn to read a clock in the third month of second grade just because the publisher's scope-and-sequence chart recommends it; children now learn to read a clock when they accept responsibility for controlling their time (Davidson, 1992).

The authors believe that constructivist practices and their teaching and learning strategies will develop the children's schemata and comprehension or remembering skills and increase children's ability to turn data into information into knowledge. When appropriate constructivist models and cognitive learning theories are used, children's learning will become increasingly more sophisticated and standardized achievement test scores will increase.

THE NEW LEADERSHIP PARADIGM

The essential argument of this text is that instructional technology fundamentally changes the notion of school, which in turn changes the organization of its leadership. The use of technology to support an effective and quality academic program is a revolutionary change, not an evolutionary path. Effective use of instructional technology becomes systemic change, that is, a change in the school's culture. Technology causes learners to do things differently. Technology causes teachers to change their methods and strategies. Technology causes the school community to adapt its shared goals and its values and beliefs about teaching and learning to accommodate a new culture. The traditional leadership function, based on formal leaders and followers who exist in an environment of differential power, is inconsistent with a change in the school's culture. A new paradigm of shared leadership must emerge to organize, govern, and implement the new learning. Nothing short of a community of leadership based upon expertise and respect can lead schools into the Twenty-first Century.

We believe that the traditional beliefs of leadership no longer meet the demands of schools and the need for change. A community of leadership, with inclusive participation, true empowerment, and expert or *ad hoc* leadership, will succeed. The current traditional conception operates through legitimate or position power and authority supported by reward and coercion. The new paradigm—the community of leadership—has at its core authority derived from expert and referent power. That is, participants with special knowledge—expert power—and participants with extraordinary reputations and influence—referent power—guide decisions about the school's organization, governance, and instructional practices.

The Community of Leadership

The current conventions of leadership, whether autocratic, democratic-collabora-tive, or *laissez-faire,* are no longer consistent with the goals of education. Under the traditional leadership model, administration had a strong principal who deter-mined the direction of the school. Formal leaders have seen the world through the lens of the principal's office. As important as formal leadership has been and con-tinues to be, systemic change—a change in the school culture—requires a new vision of school governance and quality learning. As important as teachers, staff, parents, students, and the community are, their traditional power and authority differences inhibit systemic change. The community of leadership is the collabora-tive exemplar for long-term change. The fundamental values and beliefs of contem-porary power-based, formal leadership and traditional or transmission models of teaching and learning are no longer relevant. The alliance between traditional lead-ership and traditional instructional models will not serve schools in the Twenty-first Century. They are evolutionary dead ends.

Since the mid-1970s, with the emerging research of the school-effectiveness scholars, formal leaders have been consolidating power and authority while permit-ting limited empowerment and decentralization. Historically, Taylor's scientific management (1947), Fayol's (1949) administrative management, Gulick and Urwick's (1937) fourteen principles of management, and Mayo's (1945) manage-ment of human resources evolved into a system of formal leaders with a rich description of their role. With their strong management background, many formal leaders now base their practice upon tenets of effective schools and effective teach-ing research. In this view, the principal is a manager and visionary leader who mobilizes others, and the teachers, staff, students, and parents are the principal's followers. At the principal's discretion, followers occasionally accept responsibility for accomplishing one or more of the leader's goals; they are temporarily elevated to the rank of an informal leader whose power and authority for action are teth-ered to those of the formal leader.

In some form or another, even in schools with decentralized governance or with empowered faculties and staffs, an inflexible, hierarchical barrier separates formal leaders, informal leaders, and followers. Whatever the organizational varia-tion, regardless of the individuals and in spite of the faculty's dedication, educators are so connected to a hierarchical, bureaucratic power model that almost all organi-zations, and most attempts at systemic school reform, are destined to fail. The problem is not with the roles, the duties, the responsibilities, the division of labor, or the people, but with a notion of systemic change that depends on current assumptions about power and authority. Simply put, the existing paradigm is wrong.

Conventional Power and Authority   The current view of power and authority within an organization or a school invokes the traditional description of five types of power and authority. Razik and Swanson (1995) reviewed the literature on power and authority and concluded that formal leaders derive their control from five types of power and authority: legitimate, reward, coercive, referent, and expert. The power to reward and the power to coerce are both examples of the legitimate power of the formal leader. Legitimate power is the individual's position within the school's organization (for example, principal) and the followers' belief in the leader's right and responsibility to lead. Thus, only formal leaders have the power to coerce and reward.

Referent power is collaborative leadership built on trust and personal beliefs, and expert power is the followers' belief that the leader possesses unique skills and special knowledge. Leadership whose authority comes from referent power and authority—influence—and from expert power and authority—knowledge—will be more successful than leaders who rely upon the power and authority of reward and punishment. The power and authority to accomplish the school's goals—that is, the power and authority of the community of leadership—derive from expert knowledge, belief, and participants' faith in shared leadership.

In our current administrative models we conceive of schools as organized around the principle that the formal leader has legitimate or position power supported by the authority to coerce and reward. The principal's power and authority comes from her position, which is legitimized by the state's school code, the school board, the superintendent, teachers, and school community. Position power and authority inevitably create superordinate (boss) and subordinate (worker) relationships. It is this difference in power and authority that limits an organization's ability to adapt and change. The insidiousness of dysfunctional, power-based relationships in schools is that the school community has normalized this distinction. Educators are so accustomed to hierarchical, bureaucratic power and authority that we accept differential relationships as the natural order and seldom question their efficacy.

An Effective Paradigm of Power and Authority   The new paradigm of leadership seeks not to destroy or devalue the concepts and ideas that define leadership: vision and mission, power and authority, moral leadership, organizational culture. Instead, the new paradigm seeks to redefine the power and authority relationships around which the school is organized. Looking through our conceptual lens, effective leadership, formal or otherwise, comes best from expert and referent power and authority. Additionally, members of the organization accept responsibility and direction based on their own sense of knowledge and influence. Schools of the Twenty-first Century will not reflect hierarchical, bureaucratic organizations dependent upon formal leaders, informal leaders, and followers. The new paradigm of school governance will be a community of leadership.

On the surface the differences between the characteristics of traditional conceptions of leadership (hierarchical, bureaucratic, power-based) and the community of leadership paradigm seem minor. Yet our understanding acknowledges the narrow theoretical differences between current leadership characteristics and the wide cleft in leadership effectiveness. In simple terms our basic value and belief is that the community of leadership, operationally defined, is a school participant's commitment to new processes of organization, governance, and instructional improvement. The individual's contribution is a special responsibility within the community of leadership based not on her legitimate or position power and authority, but on her expertise and influence, and defined by her obligation to the school community.

For example, when the librarian accepts of the responsibility to manage the school's instructional technology, she assumes the new role of media specialist as her direct contribution to the community of leadership. The shift in role works because the new media specialist has developed expertise in technology along with her expertise and influence in instruction. The acceptance of this responsibility has evoked respect and admiration—referent power and authority—from the rest of administration, faculty, students, and staff. Everyone benefits: the administration, the faculty, the students, and the media specialist herself. A new and cherished member has joined the community of leadership.

Instructional technology–rich learning has created new centers of power based upon expertise and influence. Schools of the Twenty-first Century will continue to expand these new centers of power and will require increasingly wise and sophisticated communities of leadership. Notions of power will fade as commitment to expertise grows.

How Traditional Leadership Evolves into a New Paradigm

To understand the functioning of the community of leadership in our emerging technology oriented schools, we first must understand the existing leadership paradigm. Traditional perspectives of leadership support the idea that the school's administration rests on four foundations: (1) formal leadership; (2) informal leadership; (3) participants in the internal school community: teachers, students, parents, and individuals who have a direct interest in children's education; and (4) participants in the external school community: individuals with indirect interests in children's education. These participants merge to establish the conventional leadership triad of formal leaders, informal leaders, and followers.

Conventional Leaders   Schools traditionally organize leadership so that formal leaders decide what is taught, why it is taught, and how it is taught. These are the people who guide teachers' teaching and influence learners' learning. They occupy a variety of roles within the school's organization and hierarchy. The formal leaders are the administration, and the followers are the faculty, staff, students, parents, community members, and other stakeholders in the children's education. The roles that all these participants play are necessary. The leadership convention is not. Without the diversity that the community of leadership brings to the process, there will be no change and no improvement. Traditional formal leadership induces either maintenance of the status quo or entropy, the inevitable slide toward decay. Neither is acceptable.

The traditional view of leadership also differentiates leader from follower. No matter how well intentioned, the term "follower" can be bothersome, even irritating, to committed participants. Teachers may argue strenuously that they are not mere followers, but professionals who get things done. The term "follower" suggests a more passive, less influential role, and a lesser degree of respect. Conversely, the term "doer" suggests active involvement, strong self-esteem, participation in meaningful decision making, and a high level of respect. In this book, therefore, except in cited definitions and direct quotes, followers are called doers. All members of the community of leadership are doers.

Conventional Instructional Leaders   The traditional premise about instructional leaders is that leadership has a fundamental hierarchical structure and a moral basis. The leaders' foremost goal is the improvement of teaching and learning. In this book we describe these ideas. We also suggest classroom skills and strategies designed to help leadership move toward effective instructional practices reinforced by instructional technology. We believe that the establishment of an effective instructional program, supported by technology, is the obligation of all participants in the educational process—of everyone in the community of leadership. We value the leadership that each participant exerts in the creative planning, implementation, and assessment of teaching and learning. However, we recognize and advocate that the school's community of leadership has an explicit responsibility to design, implement, and assess quality instructional programs.

Conventional Leaders: A Baseline Definition   To understand the leader in an emerging technology-rich school, the concept of leadership demands definition. Yet leadership is ambiguous, amorphous, contextual, and idiosyncratic. Leaders must create definitions of leadership for themselves that are consistent with their own values and beliefs. Every author, leadership expert, and theorist has a personal definition of leadership which stresses at least one special characteristic or attribute. Our vision of leadership includes Owens' (1995) perspective of leadership as a group process and leadership which influences the actions of other participants.

Garry Wills, in his book *Certain Trumpets* (1994), suggests a definition of leadership from which all personal definitions may evolve. Wills, however, seems bounded by a conceptual framework of traditional bureaucratic, hierarchical, power-based relationships. Nevertheless, the elements of his definition may contribute to understanding the community of leadership. Wills argues that leadership must contain three elements: a competent leader, willing and able followers, and worthwhile, shared goals. For Wills, leadership can come from individuals who occupy both formal and informal roles within the school, with either the principal or followers accepting informal responsibility. An example would be a process-writing teacher who mentors a novice teacher in the use of word processing.

The first element in Wills' definition of leadership, then, requires a formal or informal leader capable of action. Capable leaders are visionaries who guide the organization's future, its vision and mission, and its goals and objectives. The formal or informal leader believes in her ability to ensure that her view of the organization predominates.

The second element in the baseline definition of leadership is individuals who are capable of doing. Participants in the school must have the ability to support the leader's vision and mission. To do this, they need faith in the leader, a clear understanding and acceptance of the instructional tasks, and the skills and strategies necessary to reach a shared goal. Participants prepare for followership through empowerment and the decentralization of power and authority. Facilitating followers' willingness to act and enhancing their opportunities to make decisions affecting the nature of their work builds their skills, strategies, and experiences as participants and increases their confidence. These are Wills' able doers.

The third element in the baseline definition of leadership is worthwhile, shared goals. Both the leader and followers must believe that the goals are important, ethically just, and shared by the entire school community. Consensus among participants is the necessary element for achieving worthwhile, shared goals. The process can range from a polite discussion to "slugging it out in the values arena" (Ellsberry, 1995). Additionally, the decision-making process must arise from consensus rather than simple majority vote. When a leader coerces or manipulates a faculty into adopting her predetermined goal (for example, mathematics and science curricula supported by spreadsheets), the change is temporary at best and often causes mistrust. Lacking worthwhile, shared goals, leadership and followership become mere exercises, interesting for their potential but ineffective in their accomplishments.

The community of leadership must be visionary, must be capable of action, must be able to complete tasks, and must believe in worthwhile, shared goals. The difference between the less effective current conception and the new paradigm is egalitarian power and authority relationships and an expanded view of participation. Participation and expert knowledge shared among equally valued and committed members of the community of leadership represents a systemic change—a change in the school's culture.

Reflective Practice: A Strategy for Leadership Development

Reflective practice, or "thinking in action" (Schön, 1983), is the way that the community of leadership assimilates new knowledge about technology, formatively assesses technology's usefulness in learning, and directs its staff development. Reflective practice is the best strategy for making the transition from the old tradition to the new paradigm. Although reflection is an individual process, the collective wisdom generated from reflection eases the transition to technology-rich learning environments. Many reflective methods are idiosyncratic, formulated to meet each member's unique situation and personality.

These formative conversations or dialogues, whether they are recorded in written journals or are simply conversations, are the basis of reflective practice. Reflective practice may be described as the constant challenging of values and beliefs. Old values and beliefs that are held dear, as well as those which have emerged only recently, must be scrutinized, assessed, accepted, denied, or changed. It is less important that these values and beliefs be affirmed or rejected than that a leader continuously challenge her values and beliefs. Reflective practice is a successful strategy for improvement. The reflective leader who shares ideas with the community of leadership becomes a powerful model for the improvement in learning.

In the recent past, reflection required individual thinking in action, either through monologues or reflective journals. Reflective practitioners might converse in small *ad hoc* groups as time permitted. New telecommunications and word processing technology allow reflective practices never before available. Practitioners can participate in bulletin boards and e-mail lists (for example, the Middle Level and The American Educational Research Association's Section A, Administration lists) to think in action about their practice. E-mail lets practitioners confer privately and individually with peers and other specialists who are struggling with important issues or merely needing to vent. The World Wide Web has reflective potential. Web pages describing various schools' projects, lesson plans, policies, action research, and decision-making and problem-solving practices may transform an individual school's community of leadership into a "metacommunity" or "consortium of leadership."

The challenging of our individual values and beliefs as a reflective practice strategy has another outcome. Each member of the community of leadership must establish her set of bottom-line values and beliefs—her "moral minimum" (Boles, 1994) below which she will not negotiate or compromise. For many individuals, a moral minimum may be harm done to a child's self-esteem. For others, a moral minimum may be truth and integrity. Whatever each individual's moral minimum, its acceptance, through reflection, focuses the community of leadership's vision and mission and underlies the moral foundation of the school's culture.

Leadership: Doing the Right Thing

The foundation of the community of leadership depends on a qualitatively different view of power and authority. Traditional or current conceptions rely upon dysfunctional, hierarchical, bureaucratic, power-based relationships. A community of leadership is based on an egalitarian commitment to school governance and the improvement of teaching and learning. Many of these theories and ideas are important to any vision of leadership.

Since leadership cannot exist in isolation, we must consider several elements that distinguish effective communities of leadership. We must make a connection between the purpose of the community of leadership and the creation of technology-rich educational programs. Bolman and Deal (1994) help make that connection. They propose a basis for organizing and governing communities of leadership:

1. *"Leadership and management are different"* (p. 78). Bolman and Deal (1994) suggest that management is the accomplishment of routine administrative tasks. Bennis and Nanus (1985) describe management as "doing things right" and leadership as "doing the right things" (p. 21). The "right" in doing the right thing is the connection between leadership and the group's shared goals—its vision and mission. A definition of leadership, then, is a statement of what it means to be a participant in the school. Managing a computer lab so that the hardware and software work in concert is doing things right. Constructing a computer lab that supports

students' writing and encourages critical thinking and problem solving is doing the right thing.

2. *"Leadership and position are not synonymous"* (p. 81). Bolman and Deal (1994) propose a differential, power-based relationship among participants. DePree (1989), in his essays on leadership, suggests that *ad hoc* leadership is necessary for the accomplishment of all the school's goals. He calls these participants "roving leaders" (p. 45). Roving leaders respond to the needs of the school when formal leaders cannot or do not act. Roving or *ad hoc* leaders are essential to systemic change.

3. *"Leadership is inevitably political"* (p. 82). Political, in this sense, means that the community of leadership allocates limited resources to those competing special-interest groups that exert the most influence. In any organization, special-interest groups, such as teachers, parents, and the student council, compete for precious, limited resources. The community of leadership's role, in a political situation, is to determine who receives limited resources. The criteria should be how well the interest groups connect with the vision and mission of the school rather than how well they exercise their political clout.

4. *"Leadership is inherently symbolic"* (p. 83). Symbolic leadership mobilizes the organization's values and beliefs, vision, and culture. The symbolic value of leadership, based on values and beliefs, vision, and culture, overcomes political power with the message that the entire community may share resources.

5. *"Leadership calls primarily on intangible human qualities"* (p. 85). Bolman and Deal (1994) reject the traditional view of charismatic leadership which is tenuous and uncertain and inevitably leads to an entrenched bureaucracy (Weber, 1930). Instead, referent and expert power are the leadership behaviors of choice.

Moral Leadership: New Roles for Formal Leaders

The call for a community of leadership does not deny the existence or necessity of formal leaders, of principals. The new paradigm extends the formal leader's opportunities for improvement of instruction and organizational change. The principal retains several special responsibilities for organization and governance in the school's new system.

First, the formal leader is responsible for guiding the community toward worthwhile, shared goals. Second, the formal leader becomes the keeper of the vision and mission, supported by the work of the community. Third, the formal leader, by virtue of her expertise in management, absorbs the responsibility for completing or delegating activities not directly related to the instructional program. Fourth, the formal leader remains the symbolic intersection between the internal and the external school community. She represents the school at formal functions, acts as the conduit for communication from the organization to the public and from the public to the organization, and protects instructional time so that members can optimize learning. Lastly, the formal leader accepts the ritual responsibility for school-based problems. She accepts initial internal and external criticisms, answers or delegates responses, and acts to correct inaccurate perceptions of the school. The formal leader's role is important and irreplaceable. However, under the new leadership paradigm, her role is new, different, and constantly emerging.

The Formal Leader in the Community of Leadership: What Do I Do?

The change in the role of the formal leader within a community of leadership challenges the leader's sense of self, of who she is in the community. Under the old paradigm, her roles and responsibilities were clear. In the community of leadership, the leader must stake out her new roles and responsibilities while fulfilling her obligations to her profession and her responsibilities to her school. Sergiovanni (1996) delineates nine tasks which are important to the formal leader in the community of leadership. He characterizes each of these roles as "ministerial" (pp. 88–89).

Purposing   The first responsibility of the formal leader in a community of leadership is to assist the school community to create and align the shared goals of the school. The goals must be ethical and worthy of the community's commitment. DePree (1989) states that "the first responsibility of a leader is to define reality" (p. 11).

In the world of the practitioner, the leader must guide the community to articulate its values and beliefs. The formal leader can direct the community through a clarification process to adopt and publish its vision—a short statement of the community's values and beliefs. The vision statement is a projection of accomplishments; it describes the school after the shared goals have been met. If a vision statement exists, then the leader should facilitate revisiting the vision by asking the community to operationally define each important word and reach consensus on the meaning of the vision. Occasionally, spirited discussions ensue, with meaningful debate about individual values and beliefs. Consensus rather than majority vote, with respect for individual differences, is the preferred decision process. Then, shared goals can emerge.

Review your school's vision to decide whether there is consensus about its meaning and direction. The following are 10 characteristics of a vision. Use these ideas to guide and assess your school's vision statement.

Ten Elements of Vision   Following are the ten elements of vision described in *The Handbook of the Indiana Principals Leadership Academy* (IPLA), a staff development program of the Indiana Department of Education. Your school's vision statement may integrate many or all of the elements.

1. *As, not as is*. Set the vision as the new reality, as if all of the shared goals have been met.

2. *Run a movie of the mind*. Describe a mental visual or image of how the school will appear at its best.

3. *Sensory perceptions*. Sense the sights, smells, and feelings that define the new reality. The creation of metaphor works well.

4. *Knowledge based*. Understand the theories and ideas that when acquired will help reach the vision. Since the formal leader might have the strongest administrative knowledge base, she may become the connection between the theory and practice.

5. *Future oriented*. Focus the vision in the future, write the vision in present tense. The formal leader should assist the school's community of leadership to imagine the school once the shared goals have been reached.

6. *Best you can imagine*. Ask all participants to grow. The IPLA's unofficial motto is, "Good as we are, what would it take to make us even better?" Create shared goals and strategies to encourage or guarantee continuous improvement. Clinical supervision and peer coaching are two successful strategies; intense evaluation is not.

7. *Does not include barriers*. Think about quality and excellence without considering barriers to success. However, vision statements must reflect reality and must be attainable. When goals are shared and become part of the school's commitment, previous barriers to success are less problematic. Consensus works.

8. *Broad in scope*. Keep the vision general and expansive. Write and publish the vision so that every participant will understand the language and the ideas and believe them worthy.

9. *If we fail*. Measure the possibility of failure against the benefits of having tried. Is the school better for having tried and failed than not having tried at all? In constructivist theory we learn from our own errors. As adults, we have the same opportunity. Keep assessing, planning, and implementing.

10. *Needs to be achieved*. Recognize that the values and beliefs that support the vision are important and worthy of our effort. The vision should reflect a spiritual quality as if the community were "called." Do not fear being emotional. Our sense of the vision's moral dimension may be its most powerful connection to the community of leadership.

Maintaining Harmony   The second responsibility of the formal leader in a community of leadership is to create consensus among participants and to describe how the individual roles and responsibilities of individuals merge into a collective. A subcommittee may present a simple problem such as, "Does the faculty want a deli lunch or pizza?" Model the democratic process by taking a majority vote, then note how many of the faculty believe that they "lost." Next, model consensus-building so that no participant feels defeated or rejected—Covey's (1989) "win-win" result.

Institutionalizing Values   The third responsibility of the formal leader is to convert the shared goals into tactical and operational plans for accomplishment. The leader guides the establishment of the community's norms. Strategic plans define the school's values and beliefs. Tactical plans clarify values and beliefs and creates goals. Operational plans redefine goals into attainable objectives. Many planners believe change occurs only through operational plans that are based on attainable objectives. (See Chapter 11, "Planning Today, Insuring Tomorrow.")

Motivating   The formal leader's fourth responsibility is to contribute to the participants' needs. Needs may be stated according to Maslow's (1970) hierarchy: physiological, security, social, esteem, and self-actualization. They may also be stated as "basic cultural needs of members to experience sensible and meaningful school lives" (Sergiovanni, 1996, pp. 88–89). Leaders can help participants find meaning in their work. Teachers thrive when they have control over the conditions of their work (Herzberg, 1966). Leaders should encourage participants to accept increasing responsibility for making decisions about their work. Examples may be choosing basal or literature-based reading programs, block scheduling, or secondary school teaching and learning teams.

Managing   The fifth responsibility of the formal leader is to manage or regulate the daily operation of the school without interfering with instructional time. Additionally, effective management suggests that the formal leader accomplish the routine tasks of the building with minimal interruption of the participants' teaching and learning responsibilities. Leaders should not burden participants with unimportant managerial decisions in the name of decentralization. An empowered, collaborative committee need not order fish sticks for the cafeteria.

Explaining   The formal leader's sixth responsibility is to explain the rationale for the community's actions, both internally to participants and externally to the community's constituency. The leader stands squarely between the internal and external community. Her task is to define the school to each constituency (DePree, 1989; Mintzberg, 1979). She must be the symbolic representation of the school's values and beliefs, shared goals, and culture.

Enabling   The seventh responsibility of the formal leader is to provide the opportunity and the mechanisms for the community to achieve its shared goals. Initially, the leader may have to eliminate barriers to success. The leader must represent and defend the school's moral minimum and resist externally mandated obstacles to success.

Modeling   The eighth responsibility of the formal leader is "accepting responsibility as head follower of the school's covenant [shared goals] by modeling purposes and values in thought, word, and action" (Sergiovanni, 1996, p. 89). This, in a sense, reflects the first responsibility—purposing—or redefining reality through commitment and action. The most powerful modeling tool is to present and demonstrate new teaching strategies in a teacher's classroom with her students.

Take a few hours to master the progressive writing, the potato exercise, or preparing student journals on the word processor, then model the strategy to both the teacher and students. In this way the leader gains immediate credibility and instant respect.

Supervising   The ninth and final responsibility of the formal leader is to apply formative assessment strategies to find out whether the vision is being met, and to make adjustments to keep the vision healthy. Evaluation—deciding whether the participants and the shared goals are right or wrong, good or bad—is eliminated or reduced. Evaluation involves participants' egos, which inhibits success. The leader should guide the community of leadership in a continuous formative review of its progress, facilitating "corrections in flight."

The Formal Leader and Technology

One worthwhile shared goal which we advocate is the inclusion of technology as a support for established, effective, child-centered instructional programs. The role of formal leadership is to begin or encourage an existing dialogue about technology and instructional change. Additionally, formal leaders must guide the community of leadership through the maze of bureaucratic and political obstacles, both philosophical and financial. Once on the path, the formal leader may withdraw and focus on assisting the community of leadership in accomplishing systemic change through the use of instructional technology. Schools throughout the country have stockpiled hardware and software that lies unused because leaders and doers have not agreed on the worthwhile, shared goal surrounding technology and have not overcome their fear of change and made technology a part of the school's culture. Members' training with technology is seldom the determining issue. (See Chapter 10, "Staff Development: A Community of Learners, A Community of Leaders.")

Moral Leadership: Taking the High Road

Another important argument for a community of leadership in instructional technology is the community's absolute responsibility to take the high road: to practice and model moral leadership. Moral leadership depends upon the community's ability to reflect upon and make public their values and beliefs about teaching and learning. Moral leadership requires that the community adequately prepare its members for leadership, and that the community adequately prepare itself for doership. Experts in *Logo*, whether adults or children, must model the value of this thinking program to the thinking curriculum. Experts in *HyperCard*, a data-organizing program, must demonstrate how nonlinear thinking supports the curriculum. (See Chapters 8 and 9.)

Moral leadership is concerned with the establishment and maintenance of the school's vision and mission. It considers nonacademic issues only as they relate to an individual's belief about spirituality. Owens (1995) identified three conditions of moral leadership. The first condition is that the relationships among the community of leadership are not based upon position, reward, or coercive power, but upon referent and expert power and a genuine commitment to shared values and beliefs. The second condition is that leadership communication is a two-way process. The notion of leadership considers that for given situations, some members will become roving leaders while others will become doers. In other situations, based upon expert and referent power, different members will become roving leaders and doers. Leadership encourages members' responses to their ideas and practices, to their vision and mission. The third condition is that leadership must deliver the promises made to the school community reflecting its worthwhile, shared goals and its vision and mission. We view Owens' conditions of moral leadership as a justification or indication of the power of the new community of leadership paradigm.

Moral Leadership: Current Thinking

To understand strategies that promote moral leadership, we must look back to Burns' (1978) seminal work on transactional and transformational leadership. According to Burns, transactional leadership is a power-based relationship between a formal leader and doers. Doers accept scarce resources in exchange for allowing the leader to lead. Transformational leadership is based upon empowerment and collaboration. Transformational leadership induces a community of leadership to coalesce around moral issues, issues which are motivated fundamentally by values and beliefs and are stated as visions and missions. Transformational leadership is a theoretical precursor for the new community of leadership paradigm. The differences between transactional and transformational leadership are significant. Under the old paradigm, the formal leader might demand that technology be introduced into the instructional program. Under the new paradigm, the community of leadership gradually introduces technology into the school's instructional culture as part of its moral commitment—its vision and mission.

Sergiovanni (1995) supports the responsibility of the community of leadership to practice moral leadership. Although reflecting a different paradigm of formal leaders and doers, Sergiovanni states: "Leader and led develop a set of shared values and commitments that bond them together in a common cause" (p. 113). A community of leadership adds a moral dimension to the vision and mission of the school and socializes new participants into the community. Leadership's new paradigm represents a commitment by members to make the inclusion of technology a part of the school's culture: a worthwhile shared goal.

School leaders can find programmatic strategies for the improvement of teaching and learning from these ideas. Tucker-Ladd, Merchant, and Thurston (1992), although referring to formal leadership, suggested that the community of leadership's involvement in the school's culture created connections to the school's teaching and learning processes. They found that four leadership behaviors marked the shift to moral leadership and school culture. We believe these behaviors are the precursors to those essential to improving leadership in instructional technology:

1. Leaders for change are *transformational* in nature, engaging in a relationship with followers that inspires them to accept and accomplish values-driven, higher level goals beyond their own self-interest.

2. Leaders for change use *collaborative*, inclusive structures in the decision-making processes related to school improvement.

3. Leaders for change believe that school needs and the answers to those needs are defined by the school's *context* [culture].

4. Leaders for change *evaluate* the effects of improvement efforts in terms of a variety of student outcomes. (p. 402)

The importance of this connection to the community of leadership is that incremental change toward creating a school culture improves the outcomes of the school's teaching and learning program. Leadership, however, cannot generalize change strategies from one school's unique culture to another's. Much of leadership and instruction is contextualized: individualized for each school.

Moral Leadership: Effecting Change

Goodwin Watson (1967) studied the effects of change in schools and suggested several ways to ease change. Sensitivity to the issues of change may influence the shift toward leadership in instructional technology. Ignoring these admonitions will slow or end the movement toward technology-rich learning environments. The important message is that to achieve change, the community of leadership must honor the participants' legitimate fear of change.

Watson (1967; Wiles & Bondi, 1991) found that members changed more willingly when they:

1. accepted the change as their own, not conceived by outsiders;

2. understood that the central office supported the change;

3. believed that the change would reduce their workload;

4. recognized that the change represented their values and beliefs;

5. valued the outcomes of the change;

6. realized that their security was not at risk;

7. helped determine the problem that initiated the change;

8. accepted the change through consensus;

9. had a feedback loop or formative assessment; and

10. accepted the necessity for change when change was consistent with the school's vision, mission, and culture.

School Culture: What It Means to Be a Participant

In the name of reform and school improvement, leaders, scholars, and politicians have manipulated unsuccessfully many of the structural-organizational elements of the school and the school district. Structural change considers environmental factors, such as organizational charts. Structural elements do not promote change. Structural change often is dependent upon formal leadership and legitimate, reward, and coercive power and authority. It seldom meets the conditions of worthwhile shared goals evolved by the community of leadership. Structural change is often made hastily and does not meet the criteria of "transfer of learning" (Joyce & Weil, 1992, p. 472). Structural change does not last. Without continuing interest and staff development, changes in organizational behaviors quickly revert to the school's traditional practice. Student learning remains unaffected. Structural change is insensitive to the participant's legitimate fear of change. Finally, reform, especially changes in roles, organizational patterns, classroom management, and teaching and learning, should evolve from the culture, from the shared values and beliefs of the school's internal and external communities.

In building our argument for a community of leadership by presenting a set of ideas, strategies, and practices that will optimize the community's commitment to leadership in instructional technology, we have operationalized a definition of leadership, described issues that clarify the definition, and outlined five conditions of leadership. Just as Sergiovanni and Carver's (1973) book, *The New School Executive*, led principals to a new administrative perspective bounded by humanistic priorities, we suggest a unique change in the concept of formal and informal leadership energized by a community of leadership and framed by moral issues and the school's culture.

Culture: Social Relationships

We believe that the school should be governed by its moral dimensions—its vision and mission—and must be considered as a series of social relationships. We agree with Deal (1990), who stated: "At the very least, we need to treat educational organizations as complex social organisms held together by a symbolic webbing rather than as formal systems driven by goals, official roles, commands, and rules" (p. 7). Deal suggested that a reliance upon worthwhile, shared goals will change the behavior of the community of leadership positively and encourage loyalty among the external community.

Deal (1985) defined culture: "Although there are many definitions of the term, culture in everyday usage is . . . 'the way we do things around here.' It consists of patterns of thought, behavior, and artifacts that symbolize and define the workplace" (p. 605). The community of leadership represents a new paradigm for "the way we do things around here." Deal and Kennedy (1983) predicted the emerging idea of the power of school culture in reform. When the school's cultural values and beliefs are focused on the improvement of instruction with the support of instructional technology, then students and teachers will achieve success.

Culture: Definition and Action

The above definition of culture as "the way we do things around here" is simplistic. Several characteristics of culture form a system of beliefs and strategies for behavioral change. The school's shared values and beliefs set the school's cultural moral minimum: the point beyond which the members will not compromise. The culture also defines the school's moral maximum: the top-most purpose to which we dare to strive. Deal (1984) eloquently described the elements and characteristics of a school's culture:

> Culture is an evolving human invention that shapes behavior and gives meaning to any social collective. Core values define the essential character. . . . Where the elements of culture are consistent and mutually reinforcing, productivity, continuity, morale, and confidence are assured—as long as the culture fits the requirements posed by the external environment. (p. 129)

An overarching argument of this chapter is that positive changes in the culture can produce effective changes in the school's teaching and learning, structural components, organizational and governance processes, and participant behavior. Peters and Waterman (1982, pp. 13–15) described eight cultural outcomes of quality which become cultural goals for the community of leadership: (1) a bias toward action; (2) close to the customer; (3) autonomy and entrepreneurship; (4) productivity through people; (5) hands-on, value-driven effort; (6) sticking to the knitting; (7) simple form, lean staff; (8) simultaneous loose-tight properties.

A tenet of this book is that creating a meaningful school culture will produce greater academic gains than reforming the structural elements of the organization. The cultural change that we advocate is that the community of leadership inspire a quality instructional program based upon the school's vision and mission and constructivist, cognitive psychological learning theory. The appropriate use of technology is to support a quality instructional program. In schools with powerful formal leadership, the purposes of instructional technology are often ambiguous. Unfortunately, without adequate expertise, a clear vision, and effective leadership, computer applications remain a solution in search of a problem. One purpose of the community of leadership is to match the use of technology to the existing instructional program. Through commitment to moral leadership and the school's culture, and through reliance upon the school's vision and mission, the community of leadership can reverse the lesser outcomes of technology, such as drill-and-kill applications and problems of equity, to a more effective use of technology. The community of leadership can help the instructional program get "better and better at doing the right things" (Davidson, 1994).

Theory and Practice: Improvements in Teaching and Learning

We suggest that with the internal and external community's emphasis on technology, schools may begin with the implementation of instructional programs supported by technology. All of the precursors to implementation—planning, purchasing, installation, and staff development—can happen together. The important question is always, "How do we want the instructional program to change?" This is the salient question, the question of substance and quality in instructional programs.

The Power of Passion: The Changing of the Guard

In recent years, the selection criteria for principals seems to have moved toward increased professionalism. The community of leadership should not tolerate a principal who is selected because of her athletic reputation, her ability to maintain control of students, or her autocratic nature. Colleges of Education and Departments of Educational Leadership have the obligation to shape the new guard through principal preparation programs which are modern, exciting, and challenging. To accomplish this, preparation programs must be able to discuss management and leadership theory in the context of a community of leadership. Preparation programs must encourage excellent translations of administrative practice. Programs for the preparation of principals and assistant principals must reflect the change from the old formal leadership functions to the new community of leadership paradigm. Administrators prepared to commit to a community of leadership paradigm will contribute to both the speed of change and the increase in instructional quality. Principal preparation programs are of primary concern to the candidates and to the members of the community of leadership.

If Deal (1985) is correct in his definition of culture, "how we do things around here," then principal preparation informs the actions of the community of leadership. Administrators who are prepared to use empowerment and decentralization strategies will encourage autonomy, risk-taking, and life-long learning in their community of leadership. Additionally, we believe that what individuals think and know determine how they behave. Administrators who are prepared to consider change from a cultural perspective will solve problems by helping members develop instructional and technological knowledge and expertise. Thus, principals will mentor promising members, will use formative, clinical supervision rather than summative evaluation, will provide opportunities for roving leadership, and will show a genuine personal interest in encouraging the activities of the community of leadership.

It is our belief that no skill should be taught in isolation. Neither should the movement of schools from a structural-organizational perspective to a cultural perspective be made in isolation. There are many available environments for cultural transformation: language and literacy instruction, integrated curriculum models, and staff development programs. However, leadership in instructional technology combines a series of important educational reforms while changing the community of leadership's fundamental values and beliefs. Systemic change—that is, a change in the school's culture—can redirect teaching and learning toward consistency with the new community of leadership paradigm. We ask you to join the new paradigm and redefine the school's organization, govern the school using the metaphor of community, and empower quality academic programs supported by instructional technology. Use your leadership skills to create meaningful, systemic change in the school's culture, in its values and beliefs.

SUMMARY

This chapter offers the reader an elemental perspective of the theories, concepts, and strategies that create a community of leadership: our values and beliefs about organization, vision and mission, reflection, moral leadership, and emerging school culture. These are the significant intellectual ideas that form the foundation upon which *Leadership in Instructional Technology* rests. The first section of the chapter similarly declares our values and beliefs about teaching and learning. We have begun to integrate these ideas into more pragmatic applications that contribute to quality academic programs supported by the effective use of instructional technology. In the next chapters we consider a variety of specialized programs and their application to the curricula. In Chapter 2 we apply the principles of the community of leadership, constructivism, and learning theory to constructing models that reflect teaching and learning wisdom.

REFERENCES

Anderson, R. C., & Pearson, P. D. (1984). A schema-theoretical view of basic processes in reading comprehension. In P. D. Pearson (Ed.), *Handbook of reading research*. New York: Longman.

Au, K. H. (1993). *Literacy instruction in multicultural settings*. Fort Worth, TX: Harcourt Brace Jovanovich.

Baker, L., & Brown A. (1984). Metacognitive skills and reading. In P. D. Pearson (Ed.), *Handbook of reading research* (pp. 353–394). New York: Longman.

Bennis, W., & Nanus, B. (1985). *Leaders: The strategies for taking charge*. New York: Harper and Row.

Boles, J. (1994, January 12). Personal communication.

Bolman, L. G., & Deal, T. E. (1994). Looking for leadership: Another search party's report. *Educational Administration Quarterly, 30*(1), 77–96.

Boyer, B. A., & Semrou, P. (1995). A constructivist approach to social studies integrating technology. *Technology and Social Studies, 7*(3), 14–16.

Brooks, J. G., & Brooks, M. G. (1993). *In search of understanding: The case for constructivist classrooms*. Alexandria, VA: ASCD.

Burns, J. M. (1978). *Leadership*. New York: Harper and Row.

Clark, R. E. (1983). Reconsidering research on learning from media. *Review of Educational Research, 53*(4), 445–459.

Covey, S. R. (1989). *The 7 habits of highly effective people*. New York: Simon & Schuster.

Davidson, G. (1992). Beyond direct instruction: Educational leadership in the elementary school classroom. *Journal of School Leadership, 2*(3), 280–288.

Davidson, G. (1994, April). Personal communication.

Deal, T. E. (1984). Educational change: Revival tent, tinkertoys, jungle, or carnival. *Teachers College Record, 86*(1), 124–137.

Deal, T. E. (1985). The symbolism of effective schools. *Elementary School Journal, 85*(5), 601–620.

Deal, T. E. (1990). Reframing reform. *Educational Leadership, 47*(8), 6–7, 9, 11–12.

Deal. T. E., & Kennedy, A. A. (1983). Culture and school performance. *Educational Leadership, 40*(50), 14–15.

DePree, M. (1989). *Leadership is an art*. New York: Dell.

Elkind, D. (1971). Giant in the nursery: Jean Piaget. In J. C. Stone & F. W. Schneider (Eds.), *Readings in the foundations of education commitment to teaching* (Vol. II, pp. 254–267). New York: Crowell.

Ellsberry, J. (1995, April 12). Personal communication.

Fayol, H. (1949). *General and industrial management*. Paris: Pitman.

Forman, G. (1987). The constructivist perspective. In J. L. Roopnarine & J. E. Johnson (Eds.), *Approaches to early childhood education* (pp. 71–84). Upper Saddle River, NJ: Merrill/Prentice Hall.

Gulick, L., & Urwick, L. (Eds.). (1937). *Papers on the science of administration*. New York: Columbia University.

The Handbook of the Indiana Principals Leadership Academy. (n.d.). Indianapolis, IN: Indiana Department of Education.

Herzberg, F. (1966). *Work and the nature of man*. New York: Crowell.

Joyce, B., & Weil, M. (1992). *Models of teaching*. Boston: Allyn & Bacon.

Maslow, A. (1970). *Motivation and personality*. New York: Harper and Row.

Mayo, E. (1945). *The social problems of an industrial civilization*. New York: Ayer.

Mintzberg, H. (1979). *The structuring of organizations*. Upper Saddle River, NJ: Prentice Hall.

Owens, R. G. (1995). *Organizational behavior in education*. Boston: Allyn & Bacon.

Papert, S. (1971). *Teaching children thinking*. Boston: Massachusetts Institute of Technology.

Papert, S. (1980). *Mindstorms: Children, computers, and powerful ideas*. New York: Basic Books.

Perkins, D. (1992). *Smart schools from training memories to educating minds*. New York: Free Press.

Peters, T. J., & Waterman, R. H. (1982). *In search of excellence: Lessons from America's best run companies*. New York: Harper and Row.

Razik, T. A., & Swanson, A. D. (1995). *Fundamental concepts of educational leadership and management*. Upper Saddle River, NJ: Merrill/Prentice Hall.

Samuels, S. J. (1988). Decoding and automaticity: Helping poor readers become automatic at word recognition. *The Reading Teacher. 41*, 756–760.

Schön, D. A. (1983). *The reflective practitioner: How professionals think in action*. New York: Basic Books.

Sergiovanni, T. J. (1995). *The principalship: A reflective practice perspective*. Boston: Allyn and Bacon.

Sergiovanni, T. J. (1996). *Leadership for the schoolhouse*. San Francisco: Jossey-Bass.

Sergiovanni, T. J., & Carver, F. D. (1973). *The new school executive: A theory of administration*. New York: Dodd, Mead.

Taylor, F. W. (1947). *Scientific management*. New York: Harper and Row.

Tucker-Ladd, P., Merchant, B., & Thurston, P. (1992). School leadership: Encouraging leaders for change. *Educational Administration Quarterly, 28*(3), 397–409.

Watson, G. (Ed.). (1967). *Change in school systems*. Washington, D.C.: Cooperative Project for Educational Development.

Weber, M. (1930). *The Protestant ethic and the spirit of capitalism*. (T. Parsons, Trans.). New York: Scribner. (Original work published 1904)

Wiles, J., & Bondi, T. (1991). Supervision: A guide to practice. Upper Saddle River, NJ: Merrill/Prentice Hall.

Wills, G. (1994). *Certain trumpets*. New York: Simon & Schuster.

Hardware: What Is It and What Should We Do with It?

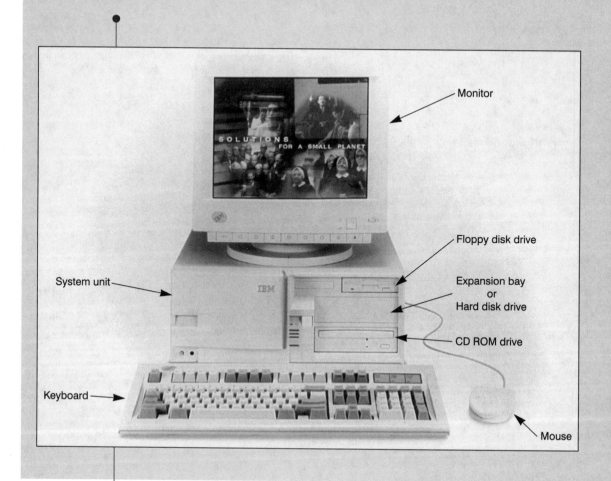

Monitor

Floppy disk drive

Expansion bay
or
Hard disk drive

CD ROM drive

System unit

Keyboard

Mouse

The two basic elements of computer technology are hardware and software. Hardware is the machines that control the computer's actions: the processor, memory, drives, input tools, plug ins, monitors, printers, networking electronics, CD ROM drives, video disks, scanners, boards, and modems. Software is the programs or applications–the directions–that permit the hardware to work.

One of the most difficult tasks that instructional leaders face is deciding what hardware to buy and how to use it. All hardware is not interchangeable. Instructional technologists have to make decisions about Windows versus Macintosh systems, computing power, peripherals and accessories, printers, and connections to other computers. This chapter introduces hardware, its purpose, the parts, selecting hardware for the school, and trends in hardware innovation. We suggest that the instructional technologist first ask three questions before purchasing hardware: What quality academic goals and objectives will be supported by the hardware? Who will use it? Where in the classroom or school will it be used?

INTRODUCTION

The computer is the center of the computer learning station, so it is a worthwhile endeavor to gain an understanding of its useful features. Although students do not directly interact with the computer's electronics, these components are the essence and power of the system. Other non-computer hardware systems are used in schools. For example, distance learning applications currently are in vogue. In this chapter we concentrate on computer hardware because it is so prevalent in schools.

Most schools have some computers for instruction. However, many schools are struggling for ideas for computer use. Our way is to use computers to support an existing quality academic program. When planning for computer implementation, one should always start by creating an excellent curriculum. The goals and objectives of the curriculum should dictate the instructional purposes of computers, not the other way around.

Computer usage always presents puzzles for technology leaders. Should each classroom have a few computers, or should computers be made available in a computer lab? Equity is another issue: Who gets computer time, to do what, and for what reason? Do urban schools have an advantage over rural schools in telephone rates and other resources? Does the teacher's knowledge or disposition to use a computer present an instructional advantage for certain groups of students? Should the teacher facilitate children's instructional use of computers or delegate that responsibility to a computer teacher or aide? These difficult questions are best answered by a coalition of interested and knowledgeable participants. The community of leadership is an appropriate interest group to begin these deliberations. Our vision is that computers should be used to help students turn facts into information and information into knowledge. Another way to view computer use is as a mechanism to display each child's individual brilliance.

WHAT IS HARDWARE?

The term *hardware* encompasses all the physical parts of a computer system. It includes processors, monitors, printers, disk drives, modems, scanners, expansion boards, and other specialty devices. It is separate from the software, which is the programs that make the hardware useful. We discuss software in detail in Chapter Three. Firmware is software that the manufacturer permanently incorporates into the hardware to start the machine and handle its basic functions. Another term, coined by satirists, is *vaporware:* hardware or software that the manufacturer has promised but does not yet produce, or that may never exist.

THE PURPOSE OF HARDWARE

The purpose of hardware in instructional technology is to enhance the teaching and learning environment. This may seem patently obvious, but it is a concept that we frequently forget. We label many new school buildings "technology schools." By doing this, we tend to make technology the primary focus, when the children and the learning always should be our primary concern. Technology is merely a means to an end. That end is to support a quality academic program—in other words, to ensure children's learning.

Much of the hardware on the market today is very impressive. We must guard against being blinded by gizmos with lots of flash, and instead keep children's learning as our primary focus.

HARDWARE: THE PARTS

CPU

The central piece of hardware you will need to consider is the computer. Other terms you might hear applied to this device are the CPU (central processing unit) and the system unit. The CPU is the computer in isolation from its other parts, such as the monitor and the printer.

Inside the computer is the "guts" of the machine, the mother board, which holds all the various integrated circuits that make the computer function. Attached to the mother board are memory chips, chips that control the screen, chips that operate the disk drives, and the main processor chip, which is the actual central processing unit. The main processor chip largely defines the speed of the computer.

You can buy computers with different processors. Some new models design the mother board so that you can replace the processor chip. As new processors become available, you can take out the old one and replace it with a newer, faster, and better processor. There are also different styles of processors. The processor is one of the main elements that defines the difference between a Macintosh and an IBM-compatible machine.

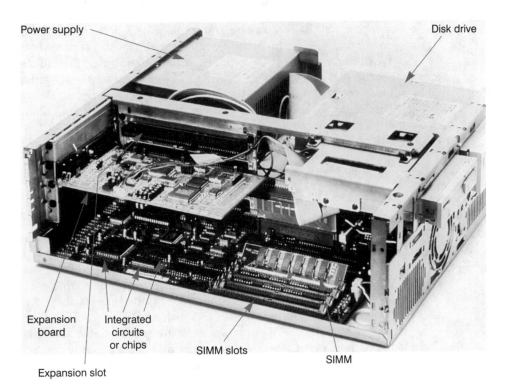

Internal components of a computer.

For the most part, the speed of the processor in a new machine is not an issue in education. The speeds of current processors are sufficient to support most educational applications. There are exceptions, however. Applications that involve massive data manipulation or excessive calculation, such as multimedia development using extensive graphics or computer-aided design, require fast machines. You usually will be able to recognize these exceptions in advance. The rule is, the faster the processor the better, but also the more expensive.

Processors get faster with every new generation of machines. Also, the style of the processor changes rapidly. This means that the way the chip operates internally changes. Typically, the chip can do more things, or it can operate more efficiently. These changes only indirectly affect educational computer users. The indirect effect, however, is that we need to keep current. Over time, a style of chip becomes so outdated that you cannot find any useable software.

Random Access Memory

Every computer comes with some amount of random access memory, or RAM—the CPU's working memory. The amount of RAM determines how big a program you can run and how many programs you can run at the same time. Every new version of software tends to get larger and more complex, so that RAM requirements continually increase. Along with the processor's style and speed, the amount of RAM is another feature that causes a computer to become obsolete. When purchasing a new computer, adding extra RAM may increase its usable life span. With every new generation of computers, the standard amount of RAM tends to increase. At the time this book is being written, most computers come with 8 megabytes of RAM. (A megabyte is equivalent to a million characters.) The standard 8 megabytes of RAM is inadequate for most situations and would limit severely the machine's operations. Most applications require twice that amount: 16 megabytes. It is important to note, however, that RAM requirements are likely to continue to increase.

Disk Drives

A modern computer will have at least one floppy drive and one internal hard drive. The disk drives are where you store your software, and where teachers and students will save the files they create. The hard drive is large and fast, but the data is not portable. The floppy disk drive is slower and much smaller but offers portability. The term "floppy" refers to the type of disk that is used in the drive. There are two main types of floppy disks, 3½ inch and 5¼ inch. The 3½ inch floppy disk is now the standard. The 3½ inch disks are more durable and reliable because they have a rigid case that covers the entire disk surface. Many people mistakenly call a 3½ inch disk a hard disk and a 5¼ inch disk a floppy disk because of the case.

There are two main types of 3½ inch floppy drives, double-density and high-density. A high-density disk stores more information than a double-density disk. New computers always have a high-density drive, but older machines may have a double-density drive. The newer high-density drives can read and create both high-density disks and double-density disks, but the older double-density drives can only use double-density disks.

All modern computers have an internal hard drive. Additional hard drive space is necessary if the learning community plans to store several large programs on a single computer. The creation of large files requires additional hard drive space. High-resolution graphics, digital movies, and digitized sound are the most common large files. Standard text files, such as word processing files, are considerably smaller.

There are two ways to add hard disk space. The school's technician can install an additional internal hard drive in an open disk drive bay. Or, if the computer lacks an additional bay, then the school's technician can add an external hard drive. An external hard drive will cost more and may operate more slowly, but it is an effective solution to an information storage problem.

There are two additional considerations when purchasing a hard drive. Size is the most obvious. The larger the drive—the more megabytes of storage it contains—the more it will cost. However, the larger the drive, the less expensive the cost per megabyte. For example, if a 500 megabyte drive costs $500, each megabyte of storage costs a dollar. A one gigabyte drive—1,000 megabytes—may cost $800, but its cost per megabyte of storage is lower: $.80 per megabyte.

Speed is a second consideration when purchasing a hard drive. All hard drives are fast, but some are faster than others. The faster the hard drive, the faster the computer can move data from the drive (permanent memory) to RAM (working memory) or conversely. The speed of a hard drive is not important for applications that work with relatively small files, such as word processing. However, as files get larger, the speed of the hard drive becomes more important. Multimedia is an application that requires a fast hard drive. If students will be working with large files, such as high-resolution picture files, sound, or video files, then their work will be accelerated with a fast hard drive.

Input Tools: The Keyboard and Mouse

Modern computers also include a keyboard and a mouse, although retailers often sell these items separately. Most keyboards are quite similar. The old typewriter keyboard pattern remains the standard. The standard keyboard is often called the QWERTY keyboard, after the upper left-hand alphabetical keys. There are three main types of keyboards. The first type of keyboard has 101 keys—all the standard keys along with some special keys and a numeric keypad. This keyboard has everything built in, but it is relatively large. Manufacturers also offer a second, smaller version which has fewer special keys and omits the numeric keypad. This smaller keyboard is nice for tight spaces. The third type of keyboard is ergonomically designed to reduce fatigue and pain so as to be physiologically friendly. The main purpose of ergonomic keyboards is to put the typist's hands in a more natural position to avoid wrist problems such as Carpal Tunnel Syndrome. There are several versions of the ergonomic keyboard. Some styles bend in half so the hands can more easily reach the keys while angled inward. These keyboards use elevation to keep the wrist straight, since using the keyboard with bent wrists may cause wrist problems after extended use.

The mouse is a pointing device that allows you to place the cursor efficiently on the screen and do something to it. A mouse has become a standard device on modern computers. There are three types of mice available, identified by the number of buttons on them: a one-, two-, or three-button mouse. Macintosh computers uses a one-button mouse. IBM-compatible computers use a two-button mouse. The three-button mouse adds a third, programmable button for special purposes. The mouse requires desk space to move, and space can sometimes be a problem. Additionally, the frequent and repeated use of the mouse can cause wrist problems. For these reasons, other types of devices for pointing to the screen have been developed. The most common is the track ball, which resembles a mouse turned on its back. With a track ball, the user manipulates the ball to point to the screen; the device itself remains stationary.

Other devices that manufacturers have experimented with to eliminate the problems with the mouse include the touch pad and a track button. A touch pad is a small, flat area that uses finger movements to point to the screen. The track button is a button in the middle of the keyboard that you put your finger on and tilt to point to the screen. The mouse is still the dominant "point and click" device, but the track pad is gaining popularity on portable computers.

Ports, Bays, Slots, and SIMMs

A number of features inside the computer's box determine its versatility. These features include ports, bays, expansion slots, and SIMM slots. Ports, to which devices such as the keyboard, printer, external hard drive, and modem are attached, are usually located on the back of the box. Macintosh computers and IBM-compatible computers have different types of ports, but the concept is identical.

The most common type of port is a serial port. Most printers and modems are connected to a serial port, although on IBM-compatible computers the printer may be connected to a parallel port. Both IBM-compatible and Macintosh computers have serial ports, and they work identically; the only difference is the connector on the end of the cable. Most computers come with two serial ports, allowing connection of two printers or a printer and a modem. If you want to connect more devices, you will need to expand your system.

Another type of port is the SCSI (Small Computer System Interface) port, pronounced "scuzzy" port. You use the SCSI port for devices that require a faster, more interactive connection to the computer than the serial port provides. You can connect some printers, and most scanners and external hard drives, to the SCSI port. The nice thing about a SCSI port is that it allows "daisy chaining." This means that you can plug the first SCSI device into the SCSI port. If you have another SCSI device, you plug it into the first SCSI device. You can have several SCSI devices on a single SCSI port.

The bays in the computer are open places for new devices. The most common thing you will put in a bay is a disk drive. There are 3½ inch bays which can hold a 3½ inch hard drive or a second 3½ inch floppy drive. There are 5¼ inch bays that can hold a 5¼ inch hard drive, a 5¼ inch floppy, or a CD ROM drive. Typically the manufacturer provides standard connectors for each bay to connect the new device(s). You probably will not add hardware to the bays of most school computers. However, you may want to consider available bays in specialty machines, such as those you intend to use for multimedia development systems or library reference systems.

Expansion slots are places inside the machine which hold expansion cards or boards. Expansion boards let you add different hardware functions to the computer. Examples include a board for video digitizing and a board with additional ports. Computers come with up to 8 expansion slots. As with bays, you will probably not add boards to most school machines; however, specialty machines may require several expansion slots for boards that contain special functions.

SIMMs (System In-line Memory Modules) are memory chips grouped on a small board which plugs into a special slot inside the computer. SIMMS are the preferred way to expand a computer's RAM. Different computers use SIMMs of different sizes and speeds. The most common SIMMs have 1, 2, 4, 8, 16, 32, or 64 megabytes of RAM.

When you want to expand the internal memory, you have to know two things: which type of SIMM you need and how many SIMM slots your computer has. If you want to add 4 megabytes of RAM and you have 4 slots, then you have several options. If you only have a single slot, then your options are limited. In addition, some machines require that SIMMs be added in groups, so you cannot put in a single SIMM. The retailers of SIMMs are usually helpful in seeing that buyers get the right SIMMs for their computers.

Manufacturers base the price of a SIMM on the module's size. Larger SIMMs cost more but are less expensive per megabyte. The price tends to fluctuate based on supply and demand. Although the standard rule is the more memory the better, memory is not cheap. A 64-megabyte SIMM easily can cost more than the computer, which is expensive for an item about the size of an open match book.

Monitors

The monitor is the device that teachers and students will use to see the results of their work. The monitor is the one piece of hardware that the students will interact with most often, since so much of their time will be spent viewing the screen. Choosing the right monitor for a specific type of work station is an important purchasing decision.

There are several choices to be made when selecting a monitor. The first choice is between monochrome or color. Monochrome monitors are cheaper, but color has an integral role in most applications. Color monitors are almost a necessity in today's highly graphical computing environment.

The next choice is the monitor's size. The bigger the monitor, the more you can display at one time. As with RAM, the standard size of a monitor has increased over time. The standard monitors today have 14- or 15-inch screens. Larger screens are considerably more expensive. The standard 14-inch color monitor is sufficient for most classroom applications. Special work stations, such as those used to produce the school newspaper or carry out computer-assisted design, will require larger monitors. A video editing station which requires students to display several different views simultaneously also necessitates a larger monitor.

A third decision is whether stereo speakers should be built into the monitor. Standard monitors typically do not have any sound capability, but the new audiovisual (AV) monitors have speakers with a built-in volume control. These monitors are essential on an AV work station, since this type of station needs sound amplification and including it in the monitor saves the expense of buying external amplified speakers. The ability to control the volume without changing the operating system is helpful. Additionally, built-in speakers save desk space. Although an AV monitor is more expensive, the cost should decrease as this type of monitor becomes standard.

Printers

Many computer buyers underspend when purchasing their printer. They only consider cost and often purchase the least expensive printer available. The output of most computer tasks is a printed copy. Therefore, the quality of the printer should match the quality of the computer system.

In addition to cost, there are six main considerations when selecting a printer: print quality, speed, durability, black-and-white or color, supply and maintenance costs, and the ability to network. The quality of print is determined by the type of mechanism by which the printer prints: inked ribbon (ImageWriter), ink cartridge (ink jet), or toner (laser). The original dot matrix printer used a series of pins that poked an inked ribbon and made an impression on paper with a series of dots. Most of us are familiar with the look of dot matrix output. In today's world, dot matrix printers are no longer adequate. Today's standard is "laser quality." Both ink jet and laser printers produce laser-quality output. Both types of printers produce an impression as a series of small dots. If the dots are large, ragged edges of curved printed surfaces are apparent when one looks at the output; if the dots are small, the curves look smoother. The more dots per square inch (dpi), the higher quality the output.

Printed words are the most common printer output. For the output to be considered laser quality, it should be almost impossible to determine whether the page came from a computer printer or a high-quality typewriter. The new printers available today transfer graphics from the screen to the paper with virtually no loss of visual quality. However, schools often buy low-cost, used printers. The older dot matrix printers are not a good purchasing decision due to their poor print quality. Although for most applications the print quality of any modern printer is sufficient, certain situations, such as graphic arts and computer-aided design, call for spending extra money to get better print quality.

A printer's speed—measured in pages printed per minute—is not important if you will use the printer only for short runs. You will need a faster printer for printing large documents or for networking several computers to a single printer. Several excellent, inexpensive ink jet printers are available for applications which do not require high speed. A laser is a better option when speed is a consideration. Laser printers operate at different speeds and come with a variety of features. Although additional speed and features increase the price, remember that underspending on the printer limits the output of the entire system. Students and teachers should be engaged in meaningful teaching and learning activities, not waiting for the printer to work.

A printer's durability is as important as its speed. The computer industry measures durability by the average number of pages a printer produces before replacement. If an application requires speed, then the school should probably purchase a durable printer. Faster speed and greater durability add to the purchase price.

Color output was once a luxury reserved only for high-end computer users. Color printers are becoming less expensive and more reliable, and each new generation of color printers produces better images. Color printers will be the standard in the near future. Today, the majority of printed output is still black and white. Color is not necessary for many applications but it does add an important dimension to the work. Without access to a color printer, students cannot take advantage of this dimension in their work. Fast, durable color printers are available but are quite expensive. A good compromise is to provide several monochrome printers and one or two color printers for color-based work.

The school not only should consider the initial cost of the printer but also the cost of supplies. In choosing between the two most popular printer designs—an ink jet and a laser printer—the costs may be a surprise. Both use plain paper. The differences are in the medium used to create the image. The laser printer uses toner and the ink jet printer uses ink. If a toner cartridge costs $100 and an ink jet cartridge costs $30, the ink jet cartridge may appear to be less expensive. However, if the toner cartridge prints ten times the number of pages as the ink jet cartridge, then the toner cartridge is cheaper. Both cartridges need to be refilled, and the purchaser should factor these costs into the purchase price.

Networking is another issue that needs to be considered when deciding which printer to buy. Some printers can attach only to an individual machine, while other printers are "network capable"—able to be linked to several computers. Network-capable printers are relatively fast and durable but are more expensive.

CD ROM Drives

A CD ROM drive is a disk drive that reads disks that look like the compact disks used to record and play music. The advantage of a CD ROM drive is that it holds hundreds of megabytes of data—many times the memory of a floppy disk. As programs continue to get larger, and as more audio and video is added to software, the CD ROM has become the preferred storage medium. Some of the most exciting software is or will be CD ROM based. With the growing popularity of CD ROM, the drives will soon be standard on any new computer system. They add to the cost of a new machine, but are well worth the price for their additional functions. The school also can buy drives to add to the computer. If the computer has an available bay, you can install an internal CD ROM drive. Otherwise, you can connect an equally effective external CD ROM to a board in a slot or to a SCSI port.

Video Disk Players

Some software uses video from a video disk. The video disk looks like a large CD ROM disk, and the player resembles a larger CD ROM drive. The player connects to the computer through a serial port, and the software operates the player using commands. The student can select a command on screen, such as play or fast forward, and the computer will initiate that video command.

The beauty of a video disk is direct access. Moving from one piece of video to another on a standard VCR is impractical because of the time required. The user can access video from a video disk in a few seconds. Video disk players also tend to have better still frames. Some video disks have video on one side and others have video on both sides. One side of a video disk can hold more than 50,000 still pictures. Some software producers use a video disk like a huge slide tray; *The National Gallery of Art,* which displays an art gallery on video disk, is an example.

Video has a powerful potential for education. It is a highly realistic communication medium and therefore has strong possibilities for improving learning. For example, realism in instruction is related strongly to affective change, and the realism of video is a powerful medium for achieving affective objectives.

A video disk player requires an external monitor. A video disk based work station includes a computer, keyboard, computer monitor, video disk player, and video monitor. The computer monitor and the video monitor are two attention points, which can be confusing to some students. A CD ROM application can eliminate the need for an additional video disk player and monitor. As CD ROM players become faster, software producers are likely to replace video disk applications with equivalent CD ROM based applications. In addition, the software can focus the learner on a single attention point.

Scanners

A scanner is a copying device that attaches to a computer. Scanners look and operate like a photocopier and can reproduce the same input as a photocopier. However, instead of producing a paper copy, a scanner creates a highly realistic digitized picture. Students can use these images in a variety of computer applications; for example, they can put them in word processing documents as illustrations. A scanned illustration has better image quality than a similar illustration created with a graphics program. Authors can include scanned images in their written documents and print them in the same way as text-only documents. Students and teachers also can include digitized pictures in other applications, such as a hypermedia presentation. Realistic pictures can enhance presentations by teachers or students. A teacher can use pictures to inspire and motivate students. For example, a teacher might scan an interesting picture and distribute it as a topic for a creative writing exercise.

Several options need to be considered when buying a scanner. The first is the scanner's design. There are two types: flatbed scanners and hand-held scanners. Flatbed scanners fit on a desktop and operate much like a conventional photocopier. The user places a document on the scanning surface, closes the cover, and initiates the scanning process through software commands. A hand-held scanner is smaller. The user passes it over the document by hand. Most flatbed scanners have at least an 8½ by 11 inch scanning surface. Most hand-held scanners capture a width of about 5 inches, which means that an 8½ by 11 inch piece of paper must be scanned in two sections. Most hand-held scanners come with software that automatically joins scanned sections, but the result usually is less satisfactory than that achieved with a flatbed scanner. The flatbed scanner is easier to operate. A hand-held scanner is usually less expensive and can be more efficient if teachers and students will use the scanner throughout the school.

The next decision is whether to purchase a black-and-white or color scanner. The trend in the computer industry is toward more color. In the near past, a color image was often wasted because most printers were black and white. As color printing gains popularity, so does color scanning. Black-and-white scanners are becoming increasingly rare on retailers' shelves.

Expansion Boards

The issue of expansion is a controversial one and is discussed frequently in the hardware arena. The opposing arguments have to do with issues of acceleration or upgrading. Some computer users want to buy the unit cheaply and add functions later. Other users do not want to change the "guts" of their computer; when they need more power or different features, they are ready to buy a new model.

Some of the earliest models of personal computers were easy to expand, as manufacturers provided space and receptacles for expansion. Then, many models were designed with less concern for expansion; they contained less space and were more difficult to access. Lately, manufacturers returned to creating machines with built-in expansion capabilities.

Specialty Boards or Cards

Another way to expand a computer is to add a specialty board, sometimes called a card. A number of cards are available. Sound cards were popular for a while, but they have become standard features in recent computer models. Today, video digitizing cards are popular. These expansion boards provide the capability to plug in a video source, such as a camcorder or a VCR, and create a digital movie directly on the computer. Many audio-visual computers have this capability built in, making an additional specialized board unnecessary. Some recent developments are TV and radio cards. These cards contain the receivers that allow you to listen to the radio or watch TV on a computer screen.

Another popular expansion board is an accelerator card, which increases the speed of the computer. There are several ways an accelerator can operate, depending on the constraints of the model. Most often, an accelerator card has a faster processor chip which bypasses the original processor on the mother board. As additional features become popular, they often become standard; this is a long-standing trend in the personal computer market.

Modems

A modem is an option that allows you to connect your computer to other computers using telephone lines. The modem electronically translates the computer's language into telephone language and back again. When connecting two computers, a modem must be on each end of the telephone line to translate for each computer. In essence, the two modems "talk" to each other over the phone line and relay messages to their respective computers. Most modems use regular voice lines. High-speed modems may need matching high-speed data lines.

A modem's speed is measured in units called baud. Modem speed has been continually increasing. Early modems were 300 baud. Later models were 1200 baud—four times faster than earlier models. Today's models operate at many times the earlier speeds, in the thousands of baud or kilobaud (Kbd) range. Modem speed is usually the limiting factor of telecommunications interactions. Faster modems make communication happen faster. As communication techniques and demands change, faster modems are needed. For example, downloading a large video file with a 1200 baud modem can take three hours. Downloading the same file using a 28.8 Kbd modem can take only eight minutes. Telecommunications conventions also necessitate faster modems. Newer communications software uses more graphically oriented screens that represent more data than older text-oriented screens. A faster modem transfers these newer, more complex screens of information more smoothly. In the modern world of telecommunications, the faster the modem, the better the modem.

Many computer users find initial modem connections to be one of the most troublesome aspects of setting up a computer work station. This is probably because the system has so many elements, any of which can cause a bug in the system. All of the elements must be working correctly, and working together, for the system to work. Following is a list of parts and instructions for connecting an external modem.

Parts List

- a modem
- the modem power supply (usually separate from the modem)
- a computer with an available serial communication port
- a serial cable
- a standard telephone cable
- an available, live, telephone jack
- communications software loaded on the computer
- telephone hand set (optional)

Steps to Connect an External Modem

- Plug the power supply into the modem on one end and into an electrical outlet on the other end. A port for the serial cable is on the back of the modem.
- Plug the serial cable into the port on the back of the modem and plug the other end into an available serial port on your computer.
- On the modem will be one or two RJ11 receptacles (phone jacks). If there are two phone jacks, one is for a hand set (a regular telephone). Plug the hand set into the modem to use a single line and single phone jack for both the modem and for voice.
- Plug the other jack into the wall using regular telephone cable.

The last piece is the software on the computer. The software must be compatible with the specific modem. Although there are many industry standards for modems, each model has idiosyncrasies. For that reason, virtually all modems come with the correct connection software. Although most modems will work with any computer, the software may not. The software and the computer must match. Modem software will operate the modem correctly, but it may not be the most convenient software for the task. Most "Works" type programs contain telecommunications software. This software may be more convenient because the learning community is already using the program for word processing, spreadsheets, and data bases. Thus, the access and the learning curve are better. However, this software may or may not be able to successfully operate your modem. If you are using the software that comes with the modem, you will have to make several decisions. At the very least, you have to set the modem's software port and the modem's speed.

Any one of the parts that are not working properly can cause the entire system to fail. For example, if the telephone cable has a bad connector on one end, the entire system will not work. If the software is not communicating properly with the modem, it will not connect with the other system. Many problems can cause the system not to work. The most common problems involve cables. Since several cables are involved, improper installation can cause the whole system to fail. Another common problem involves the telephone line. If the phone line is not working, the whole system will fail. It is easy to check for a working telephone line with a hand set: Simply pick up the receiver and listen for a dial tone.

There are a number of ways to connect the learning community to the rest of the world. With a modem, students and teachers can connect to data services to get information. They can send messages to other individuals around the world. At one time, a modem was a luxury reserved for only the most zealous computer users. Today, the modem is a common feature. The world of computer technology increasingly is becoming an interconnected world. The modem is the device that brings truth to the song, "It's a Small World After All."

SELECTING HARDWARE FOR A BUILDING

When selecting hardware for a building, the main issue is functionality. Ask this question: What does the community of leadership want the hardware to do? An even better question is, What does the curriculum ask students to do with the hardware? It is tempting to get too specific when selecting hardware. The problem with this approach is that hardware changes so quickly that the decision maker may not know the best computer configuration. When selecting equipment, decision makers should focus on the proposed use of the hardware. When it comes time to purchase the equipment, you may find that newer technology can accomplish the task.

A disconcerting set of choices needs to be made when purchasing hardware. Computer purchasing choices resemble the choice between buying fresh and "day old" bread. The older equipment will be cheaper and often will include an appealing variety of software. However, buying older equipment is seldom a wise decision. A year-old model is already a year closer to obsolescence.

Networks

Networking computers is a difficult hardware issue. A computer network lets the computers in your building communicate with one another. If the computers can communicate, so can the people using them. A network also allows more options for organizing software (see Chapter 3). Networking hardware is a wise decision, as the advantages are substantial. The application of e-mail is enough to justify the expense. If teachers have e-mail in the building, they have one more powerful way to communicate. To have community, individuals must communicate. E-mail aids communication, helping to form a community of learners and a community of leadership.

The crux of the networking problem is that networks are not trouble free, regardless of vendor claims. Networking experts use the term "architecture" to describe the way a network operates and is organized. Some network architectures are more complex than others. The complexity of a network should be in direct proportion to the time and expertise that the school can devote to its maintenance. If little expertise is available and the community plans to devote little staff time to maintenance, then keep the network simple. If the community plans to hire a network manager instead, then the school can build a complex and powerful network.

Some schools have compromised by delegating network maintenance to district-level technicians or to private organizations. Experience suggests that neither option is satisfactory. Many schools have networks that school personnel do not understand, cannot troubleshoot, and cannot repair. When these networks go down (cease to function), they seem to stay down for a long time. Instructional programs that depend on the network cease when the network stops.

One function of the community of leadership may be to organize individuals to be responsible for the management of the network. The capabilities of your in-house or local network should fit the ability of the personnel. A photocopier machine is an excellent analogy: When a photocopier runs out of paper, everyone can fix the problem. When a paper jam occurs, several people can clear the jam. When special problems occur, such as changing toner, only trained personnel can fix them. The community of leadership should maintain the network the same way. By using the community of leadership's expertise, outside maintenance people become less important.

Hardware Organization

Hardware organization has implications for hardware selection. When buying computers for classrooms, the cost of each unit is important because of the quantity. When buying a work station for the media center—a one-of-a-kind machine—the school may be able to spend more since that one work station will serve students throughout the entire building. The same is true when organizing a few specialty work stations—for example, multimedia development stations—for a lab or work area. If the number of units is small, you can include additional features more easily than if you are buying several computers for each classroom.

Managing and Maintaining Hardware

Computer purchasers often focus strictly on hardware costs. However, hardware costs are only a fraction of the total cost of a computer system. Schools must also consider software costs. Another cost that many organizations ignore is the human cost. When purchasing hardware and software, consider who will install and service the hardware.

Teachers usually are not required to manage software. This function is not a wise use of their expertise. Schools need someone whose defined duties include the management and maintenance of hardware and software. Simple issues such as hardware maintenance can become troublesome if schools do not have a responsible technology manager. As mentioned earlier, a local network will require someone who can manage it.

Often it is the simple problems that keep the system from working and the students from learning. For example, on a network it is possible to store files on a central file server. Ignoring the network is similar to ignoring classroom wastebaskets.

Staff development is a cost related to both hardware and software maintenance. One of the biggest problems with advancing technology is keeping current. As hardware and software improve, the faculty and staff may need to learn more about hardware and software operation, and about how new features are useful to the curriculum. It is important to have someone in the building who can keep teachers aware of changes. The school also may need to release faculty and staff from teaching duties to attend a staff development experience. These expenses belong in a realistic hardware purchasing budget.

Hardware Innovation

In addition to the people who will manage and maintain the hardware, other issues need to be considered. One is a schedule for updating hardware. In light of rapid obsolescence of computer hardware, the community of leadership must have a plan for upgrading. Three years is the practical life span of most computer hardware.

There are two approaches to updating hardware, each of which has advantages. The first approach is to equip the school with one standardized hardware platform initially and later replace it all at once. The other approach is to buy new hardware and update systems continuously. The first choice is easier to manage because all the equipment in the building is the same. However, this choice strains the budget. The school must allocate enough money to replace the hardware every three years. This is often impossible. The second choice is easier on the budget but may increase hardware maintenance problems. If the school is buying new hardware continually, then it will have a variety of equipment in the building. This can be problematic when upgrading software; for example, the newest word processor may not run on an older computer.

A PERSPECTIVE ON HARDWARE

The history of modern computing may help us understand its current state and may help us predict how things will change in the future. The history of computing devices begins as far back as the abacus. Electronic computers originated during the late 1930s and early 1940s. The microcomputers emerged in the late 1970s. Modern computing has a short but intense history.

Trends in Computing

Several trends have occurred during the history of computing. Knowledge of each trend can enlighten the community of leadership and contribute to its decision making.

Decreases in Size   One of the most obvious trends in computing is the change in the physical size of computers. The early computers were room-sized devices that were less effective than modern calculators. The computing power that sits on desks today would stun the computer professional only a few years ago. The major condition that helped computers become smaller is technological invention. The vacuum tube was the major defining element of the size of early computers. When transistors replaced vacuum tubes, computers became considerably smaller. A computer that used vacuum tubes was too big, bulky, and delicate to be sent into space. When the transistor was invented, computers became small enough that scientists could put them in a spacecraft and use them to guide a space capsule to the moon and back. The development of the integrated circuit was the next major technological advance that contributed to decreases in the size of computers. The integrated circuit reduced the computer to a size that would fit on a desk.

With each of these major technological advances have been smaller innovations that also allowed computers to continue to shrink. A device that a few years ago would use a sizable portion of a desk is today on a single chip that can balance on the end of a finger. It is difficult to predict what new invention will make computers even smaller.

Increases in Computing Power   Continual increases in computing power followed the diminishing size of computers. The computing power of a typical desktop computer today would have stunned a computer professional a decade ago. As computers became smaller, the capacity or the power of CPUs increased. If the size of the components keeps shrinking, then the amount of computing that fits in an equivalent space is likely to increase. Each model is more capable than the last.

Increases in Processor Speed   Increases in speed is another trend that correlates with smaller, more powerful computers. Year by year, personal computer processors run faster. Manufacturers increase processor speed in two ways. One is by running a family of chips (for example, the PowerPC, which includes the 601, 603, 604) faster. The other is by designing faster chips.

To understand processor speed, an analogy is useful. You can think of processor speed as water through a pipe. If you want more water to flow, you can do it in two ways. You can push the water through the pipe faster by increasing pressure, or you can use a wider pipe. A faster or greater flow of water relates to more processor speed. If you want a faster computer, you can run a processor at faster speed, or you can design a processor that operates faster. The unit for measuring processor speed is megahertz (MHz). The MHz rating on a chip is like the speed of water flowing through the pipe. However, just like water through a pipe, there are natural limits on how fast you can "turn up" any family of chips. When the current chips have reached that limit, typically a new chip is introduced.

Intel is one of the major processor manufacturers, and their line of processor chips serves as a typical example. Their first major chip in the personal computer market was the 8088 chip that drove the original IBM PC. This chip was later replaced by the 80286 (called the 286 for short), then the 386, the 486, and most recently, at this writing, the Pentium. Within a family of chips there are a variety of speeds; the faster the speed, the more expensive the chip.

The trend toward faster processor speeds has not been incremental. The speed of processors increased gradually (20 or 30% at a time) as chips ran at faster speeds. Then, when Intel or Motorola introduced a new chip, processor speeds took a large leap, doubling or tripling speed. It is likely that this trend will continue.

Decreases in Costs   Computers have gotten less expensive over time. Manufacturers have tended to maintain a price point while adding more power. Eventually, however, the price point is broken and manufacturers establish a new, lower price point. In the early years of personal computers, a reasonably priced desktop system cost about $5,000. A few years later, a new computer system still cost $5,000 but was more powerful. Eventually this $5,000 price point was broken and resettled at about $3,000; each year this price brought more power. This price point was broken again in recent years; complete systems now cost as little as $1,000.

Decreases in cost have meant that the public is more willing to replace an older computer with a newer one. This is particularly true of business users. Accountants used to designate computers as capital expense. Capital expense items are expensive outlays with long life spans, like buildings. Today, accountants consider computers a regular expense, meaning that computers are considered more like paper and pencils than buildings.

Decreases in Development Time   At one time a new line of computers took several years to develop. Development time has decreased so that new models appear continuously. This can be frustrating to purchasers because it is difficult to know when to buy. When one compares computers to cars, the cause of this frustration becomes clear. With new cars, the model year begins and ends regularly. The buyer knows what the difference means in price and features for a car bought at the end of the model year. There is no equivalent model year for computers, nor is there a standardized season for the introduction of new models. New models arrive at retail outlets continuously.

Increases in Number of Features   Another trend is the continual increase in the number of features that computers contain. New features are continually being developed, and features that were optional in past models become standard in new models. For example, the standard monitor used to be monochrome (black and white, black and green, or black and amber). Color monitors were rare and expensive. Today, color monitors are standard and are relatively inexpensive, and monochrome monitors are considered specialty monitors. Disk drives are another example. Floppy disk drives were optional with early personal computers. Today, manufacturers include floppy drives as standard features. Later, hard disk drives were initially an option but eventually became a standard component. Likewise, CD ROM drives began as an option and are now included in the majority of new computer systems. The list of standard features grows with each new model.

The same trend has occurred with printers. A few years ago only a few printers were capable of color printing, and they were complicated and expensive. Today, several color printers are available at a reasonable price. Although the black-and-white printer is still standard, color printing technology is likely to improve and become less expensive.

Animation, sound, and video capabilities were rare in early computer systems. Today, these features are common and are continually improving. We expect to see computing and video become more interactive in the near future.

Pervasiveness of Computers   Another trend is the extent to which computers have been integrated into our daily lives. A computer in the home was once rare. Now it is common. Analysts who previously estimated the home market thought in terms of a single computer in the home. Many homes today have more than one computer. Some even have a computer for each family member.

As computers get cheaper, manufacturers can integrate them into more devices. Most automobiles use at least one internal CPU to monitor performance. Specialized CPUs are now part of most VCRs and thermostats. This means that the devices that make our lives easier are becoming more intelligent. There is no telling where that intelligence will next appear. Someday we may be able to buy an inexpensive toaster that consistently and accurately toasts a piece of bread . . . but we are optimists.

Expanded Marketing Channels   The marketing of computers also has changed over time. In the early years of computers, buyers had to purchase hardware from the manufacturer. It was an important day when a computer system was first sold in a retail store. From that point on, customers were able to test and compare computer systems. Today, computers sell in many places: in computer stores, discount stores, and department stores. Mail order marketing has moved from being a minor player to a major one in the computer retail business. With most mail order houses, a new device ordered at noon on one day is delivered by noon on the next day. The expansion of marketing channels continues. Soon, computer hardware may be sold even in grocery and movie rental stores. Tomorrow's users may be able to go to the corner for a tank of gas, a pack of gum, a loaf of bread, and a new hard drive.

Increased Standardization   The last trend is toward increased standardization of hardware. Computers once varied a great deal according to type. For some years the two main choices were IBM-compatible machines (using DOS and Windows operating systems) and the Macintosh. As these machines developed over time, they became increasingly similar. Today, an IBM-compatible system with the most recent version of the Windows operating system looks and operates like a Macintosh. Further, many software packages have a version that will run on both hardware platforms. Many new CD ROM based applications include software for both platforms. Most of the standard software tools (for example, word processors and spreadsheets) have translation programs that allow the transfer of files from a Macintosh to an IBM-compatible or the reverse. This trend is likely to continue; eventually a computer user will not need to consider the platform.

Implications for the Community of Leadership

How can schools make good decisions about hardware purchases using the information from these considerations? One clear indication is that we will need to think of computers as short-term purchases. A computer's life span is somewhere between that of art supplies and a textbook. Schools probably cannot afford to replace their computers sooner than every three years. Regardless of economic conditions, we cannot afford to keep them for much more than every three years for teaching and learning reasons. The potential learning benefits of a new computer are much greater than that of a three-year-old computer. The academic advantages are enough to warrant the purchase of new equipment.

Another implication is the recognition that teachers and students must use modern technology. No longer can schools argue that "we have always done it that way." Every day computers offer a new capability, a new way of doing something. If schools are to take advantage of new capabilities, the curriculum must be fluid and adaptable enough to accommodate new ways to reach instructional objectives.

We believe a disclaimer is necessary here: The trends clearly tell us that the list of what is possible will continue to grow. However, just because something is possible does not necessarily mean it is the best choice for children's learning. An example is the virtual field trip. With current technology, a virtual field trip can replace the annual trip to the zoo. This means that rather than taking the children to the zoo, we can use technological means to "visit" the zoo from the school. At first glance this may seem like a good idea. The cost may be lower, safety may be easier to ensure, and discipline may be better. In our estimation, however, this is clearly a bad idea. Our students cannot realize the richness of the real experience of the zoo by going on a virtual field trip. The smells alone are a large part of the experience. Children can experience many important learning objectives at a real zoo that they cannot experience at a virtual zoo. The virtual zoo becomes useful only when teachers wish to enhance and reinforce the real learning experience.

SUMMARY

The most critical element of the role of the community of leadership remains making good decisions about the learning experiences we provide for children. Good hardware decisions provide computers that are easy to use, flexible, expandable, and capable of multiple uses. Better hardware decisions promote the ability of the computers and accessories to support quality academic programs. The best hardware decisions connect the power of the computer to the brilliance of the children and adults.

3

Software: Finding the Power

This chapter has three purposes. The first purpose is to introduce the software described in later chapters. We introduce and define the terminology necessary to become a leader in instructional technology. This chapter prepares the reader for the six chapters that follow, which cover word processing, spreadsheets, data base management, hypermedia, thinking software, and telecommunications.

The second purpose of this chapter is to help technology leaders manage software in schools. Although we consider management functions of lesser priority than teaching/learning activities, we also recognize that all the benefits of technology in schools depend on efficient and expert management of hardware and software. In this chapter we suggest concepts underlying software evaluation, distribution of software to labs and individual computers, and multiple uses for applications.

Our third and most important purpose is to inspire the community of leadership to move beyond mere management—"doing things right"—to leadership—"doing the right things." The right thing is an interconnected chain of encouragement: leaders helping doers helping children to learn. The beauty of the encouragement chain is that it is interactive: children helping doers helping leaders. This is an exciting aspect of the community of leadership.

INTRODUCTION

Software comprises the programs that make the computer useful. There are two types of software: system software and application software. System software is the programs that operate the computer and provide the "user interface." The user does not manipulate system software directly, but the system software is necessary to make the other software function. System software boots up the computer when you turn it on and coordinates all the parts (e.g., the printer and the mouse). The user interface defines what the screen looks like and how the user interacts with the computer. Examples of system software include MS DOS, Windows 95, and System 7.5.

Application software describes all the programs that you will use to accomplish a task. They include: word processors, spreadsheets, graphics programs, telecommunications programs, data base management systems, games, utilities, and a variety of educational programs.

Without software, a computer is not useful. Many people overlook or underbuy software when they purchase a computer. An initial purchase should include enough computing power and software power to complete your tasks now and in the future. It makes little sense to purchase a high-powered hardware with weak software.

CATEGORIZING SOFTWARE

The arena of application software is so large that several people have organized methods of categorization. In education we traditionally talk about four software categories: drill-and-practice, tutorial, simulation, and tools.

A drill-and-practice program provides students with opportunities to practice a skill previously learned. Drill-and-practice programs typically are not preferred in the educational community. These programs have been called "electronic flash cards" or "electronic ditto sheets." These terms describe drill-and-practice programs at their worst. At their best, drill-and-practice programs offer two features that are difficult to accomplish with flash cards and ditto sheets: They can enhance student motivation through animation, color, immediate reinforcement, and a game format, and they can give students immediate feedback. The importance of this is obvious to the teacher who hands out a ditto sheet with 100 math problems, only to find that some of the students give the wrong answers because they have practiced the skill incorrectly. Common examples of drill-and-practice programs include drills for math facts and spelling skill. Information about specific drill-and-practice programs is given in Chapters 4 and 5.

A tutorial is a program that teaches new information. Tutorials are not condemned by the educational community as much as drill-and-practice programs, but early examples of "electronic lectures" have maligned this application. At their worst, tutorial programs are little more than text-heavy electronic page turners. At their best, they include engaging interactive lessons utilizing techniques such as high-quality sound and video. The powerful second- and third-generation tutorial programs are learner controlled, making them more useful for teachers and students. Tutorial programs are available in virtually all curricular areas but are popular particularly in the disciplines of music, science, and social studies. More information on tutorials is given in Chapter 7.

Simulations allow a student to interact in a situation that would otherwise not be possible. These programs overcome cost, risk, convenience, and practical obstacles. A powerful simulation allows a student to learn the desired objectives by engaging in an activity. Early simulations were very simple (for example, *Lemonade Stand*) and thus not terribly engaging. Students had control of only a few elements. Today, the best simulations closely rival arcade games. They are more sophisticated and are designed to engage the student at both the cognitive and the affective levels. It is thrilling to see children as engaged in a learning activity as they are when playing an arcade game. Good simulations are available in a variety of curricular areas. In addition to their primary focus (for example, social studies or science), most simulations involve the practical use of many different mathematics skills. They also require the implementation of problem-solving strategies, thus providing a platform for the development of critical thinking.

Tool software encompasses programs that help us accomplish a task. The most common tools are word processors, spreadsheets, data base management systems, telecommunications systems, and graphics programs. There are also specialty tools: music composition programs, grade book programs, desktop publishing programs, graphics design programs, and others. Although tools may be perceived as a mundane category of classroom software, that may be a misconception. Seeing a student who is actively and effectively using tool software is truly exciting. Is there anything more thrilling than seeing children actively engaged in word processing, capturing and refining their ideas? Many people consider their tools to be their partners. Few modern authors write without a word processor. Imagine where modern accounting would be without spreadsheets.

Software programs can fit strictly into one category or can embody many categories. For example, many tutorial programs also include drill and practice. Many simulations include a tutorial on critical or complex aspects of the simulation. Many tool packages come with tutorials that help the new user learn to use the tool.

Another method of categorizing software is offered by Taylor (1980). Rather than focusing on how the software worked, Taylor focused on how the learner interacted with the software. He divided software into three categories: tutor, tool, tutee. In the tutor category, the computer acts as tutor. Included in this category are drill-and-practice and tutorial software. The tool category comprises tool software and simulations. The final category, tutee software, is unique. Software that the students use to program the computer belongs in this category. This category includes hypermedia development programs.

USING SOFTWARE IN SCHOOLS

Tools for Teachers

One of the most obvious uses of computers in schools is as a tool for teachers. Teachers can use word processing for all their formal communications. They also can use it to plan instruction. They can use the computer to help with student evaluation—to record grades, for example. They can use the computer to prepare instructional materials, both standard printed lessons and interactive lessons. If the school provides a telecommunications connection, then teachers also can use computers to locate and acquire instructional materials, in the form of software or text documents, from the vast archives of various telecommunications networks.

In some instances, the computer can help the teacher become more efficient. Greater efficiency with tasks such as grading and formal communications allows the teacher to spend more time working with students. In other instances, the computer will help the teacher do things that would be difficult or impossible to do otherwise, such as downloading information from the InterNet or developing a hypermedia lesson. The computer enables teachers to acquire and create better instructional materials, thus supporting their goal of enriching and enhancing the teaching/learning environment for students.

Student Use

The ultimate goal of using computers in school is to help students learn effectively. Adding software to the instructional environment supports this goal in many ways. Educational games can engage students, tools can help students work and learn more efficiently, simulations can offer novel experiences and teach thinking strategies, and telecommunications can connect students with the world outside the classroom.

Students are capable of using software, and they are motivated to use it. So, how should students use software in schools? A broad answer to this question is: Children should use software that supports or enhances an excellent instructional program. The role of the teacher is to guide children's learning. This involves setting expectations for students and monitoring students' progress in achieving them. It also involves matching students' learning styles with the proper learning strategy. In addition, teachers must strive to meet the social and emotional needs of children. If a hug is what is needed, even the best software cannot do the job.

Many adults believe children need copious instruction on the manipulation of the computer and on each piece of software. Although some instruction is necessary, adults have a strong tendency to overdo direct instruction on the operation of hardware and software. Children need less help than adults might predict. In fact, the operation of hardware and software is natural and predictable to children when it is often foreign and unpredictable to adults. Often, the best way for us to help children benefit from the use of computers is to step aside and let them explore on their own.

Another mistake many teachers make is to assume that they need to know everything there is to know about a software program before they can teach their students to use it. Rather than teacher-centered lessons, student exploration and informal peer tutoring are effective ways for students to learn software use. Teachers often find that they learn a great deal from their students. This is an example of how technology changes our traditional teaching and learning roles. These changes benefit all the school's stakeholders.

Although children may come to our classrooms with prior knowledge of software use and may be capable of learning to use new software independently, that does not mean that we should allow them to work unsupervised. As stated above, the teacher must establish the learning outcomes, monitor the student's progress, and consider the children's affective and social needs. Although, many software programs lend themselves to independent work by individuals or small groups, the teacher still needs to play a supervisory role. If students are unsupervised, then the results will be less predictable than if the students were guided in reaching desired learning outcomes. Software does not replace the teacher but instead makes her role far more powerful.

The use of various software tools also may support different ways of organizing our children to learn. An example is multi-age grouping. A young child can dictate a story to an older child using word processing skills. Older children can use a hypermedia development system to create interactive "reports" for use by younger children. In these examples, both the younger children and older children are engaged in important learning activities.

One aspect of computers in schools that should not be overlooked is children's affinity for the computer. Children will engage in an activity on the computer simply because they like to work with the computer, whereas they might not do a very similar activity in another way. This phenomenon may be due to the relative newness of computers in schools, but it is real nonetheless. As instructional leaders we need to acknowledge this phenomenon and use it to our learners' advantage.

EVALUATING SOFTWARE

Every school has limited funds and must use its money wisely. If we preview software and evaluate it carefully before we buy, we will make better financial decisions. Most descriptions of software evaluation focus strictly on issues of quality, when in fact quality issues are the final step in software evaluation. Focusing strictly on quality dooms us to making poor use of the limited funds we have available for software. If we were to use the same model to select an animal, we might end up with a proposal like this:

> I want to buy Bebe the Elephant for my classroom. Bebe is a relatively small elephant so she will fit in the corner of my classroom. She is calm, so her disruption of the learning environment will be minimal. Bebe effectively demonstrates elephant behaviors of trumpeting and manipulation of objects with her trunk. I have examined all the available elephants in our geographic area and Bebe is certainly the best buy for the money.

Obviously, even the best elephant we can find would not support the instructional program and would distract students from other important learning opportunities. This is also true of many high-quality educational games.

Evaluation of software is a three-step process. First, teachers must be aware of what is available. Second, they must determine how the software meets the learning outcomes of the instructional program. Third, they must make quality decisions about individual pieces of software, answering questions such as:

- Will the students want to use the software?
- Is the learning outcome worth the price of the software?
- Is there a better program that can reach the same outcome?
- Is there a cheaper program that can reach the same outcome?
- Is the outcome appropriate for the computer, or can it be achieved in some other, cheaper way?
- Are there features that will detract from the learning environment, either for the learner using the software or for others in the room?

Teachers first must learn the capabilities and possibilities of educational software. Only then can they determine whether those capabilities and possibilities fit their instructional program. Only after the teacher has laid this groundwork should she begin to select individual pieces of software and examine them for quality in terms of how well they match her defined learning outcomes.

Learning about Software

One quick and easy method to help teachers learn what is available is place software catalogs in the teachers' lounge and professional library. Software publishers and mail order retailers will gladly send multiple copies of their catalogs to schools.

Another method is to place instructional technology journals in teacher areas. These journals have articles on the effective use of software, as well as software reviews and advertisements for new software. Many classroom teachers are featured in articles about successful classroom projects. These journals not only inform but also inspire teachers.

Another way that teachers keep current with the newest software is by attending local, regional, or national conferences. Most states hold a yearly conference for teachers in instructional technology. These conferences have sessions on the effective use of software. They typically have a vendor room in which software publishers display and demonstrate their latest products. Possibly the most powerful reason to send teachers to technology conferences is to get them informally interacting with their colleagues. Ideas that teachers share with one another are often the most valuable result of attending a conference. It is seldom possible to allow all the teachers to attend a conference, so the leader must make judicious selections. When making the selection, it is common to choose the most technologically savvy teachers. The experience of attending a technology conference is important for them, but other, less high-tech teachers should not be overlooked. All teachers can benefit from exposure to completely new information and the enthusiasm of the presenters and attendees at conferences.

A fourth way to help teachers keep up with new software is to hold short workshops on the possibilities and capabilities of various software. Local experts can deliver these sessions. Consider local vendors, instructional technology professors, or the school's own experts. The leader might even consider the teachers themselves, especially those who are doing new things or have recently had new experiences, such as attending a technology session at a conference. More information on how to organize a workshop is given in Chapter 10.

Evaluating Possible Learning Outcomes of Software

The school should begin looking for software when the community of leadership members identify an instructional need. Perhaps there is an objective that the students are not attaining. Perhaps a particular lesson is difficult, time consuming, or expensive to deliver. Perhaps there is a particular element of learning that students simply dislike. All these issues can prompt a teacher to investigate improving instruction with technology. When teachers express a desire to improve their instruction, the school should investigate the efficacy of a software solution.

A teacher needs to answer two questions about any particular piece of software: "Will it meet my instructional need?" and "Will it enhance the learning environment?" The teacher is in the best position to answer the first question. She answers it many times a day by making decisions about her children's learning experiences. As to the second question, software can enhance the learning environment in many ways, including:

- Providing additional information.
- Enhancing student engagement.
- Providing more accurate or realistic information.
- Providing additional capabilities.
- Allowing different ways of organizing children to learn.
- Providing additional modalities of learning.
- Allowing improved individualization of learning.

If the software meets the learning need, supports the instructional program, and enhances the learning environment, then we are ready to move on to the next stage, evaluating software. Only after we decide that a piece of software will benefit our learners do we consider the issue of the quality of the software.

Evaluating the Quality of Software

The final issue when evaluating software is the quality of the program. As educators, we are not in the business of evaluating the technical quality of software, but of evaluating the software's ability to improve learning. Many elements of quality are situationally specific. A program that is useless for one teacher may be precisely the right tool for another. Questions a teacher might want to consider when evaluating the quality of software include:

- Is the software appropriately engaging for my students?
- Are the possible learning outcomes worth the expense?
- Is the software relatively free of distractions?
- Does the software provide enough "on-task time" to achieve my desired objectives?
- Does the software fit with the way I want to organize my children to learn?
- Does the software fit with my educational philosophy?
- Can the software be used to enhance learning in multiple ways?

Evaluators of software quality can tend to get sidetracked by technical bells and whistles. Although high-quality graphics, color, sound, and animation are impressive, we know, from many years of media research, that technical quality alone does not improve learning (Clark, 1983). Slick features do not necessarily make a quality learning product. The questions listed above subsume issues of technical quality. A program can have high-quality graphics, beautifully crafted animation, clear digital sound, spectacular digitized video stills, and motion clips, but if it does not engage students and does not help them learn, then it is not a quality program.

Television cartoons serve as a good example of this principle. Cartoon shows such as *The Simpsons, Beavis and Butthead,* and *Ren and Stimpy* capture children's attention, yet the quality of the graphics and animation of these shows are poor when compared to a Disney cartoon. In spite of the strangely drawn, two-dimensional characters in these programs, youngsters become engaged with the stories.

SELECTING SOFTWARE

Tool Software

The first and most important software selections are the basic tools: the word processor, spreadsheet, and data base. It is highly beneficial if all the teachers in the building are using the same basic tools so they can share learning outcomes from classroom to classroom. Teachers want a versatile word processor with a good reputation. The other tools also are important, but students and teachers will use the word processor most often.

Because of cost, most schools select one integrated package. An integrated package includes a word processor, a spreadsheet, a data base, a telecommunications program, and some limited graphics capabilities. Three packages that have gained wide acceptance are *Microsoft Works, ClarisWorks,* and *WordPerfect Works.*

The power of each of the pieces of an integrated package is less than a similar stand-alone software program. The word processor and the spreadsheet are typically the strongest elements of the integrated packages. The other features are functional but are less well developed. Considering that the cost of an integrated package is typically less than the cost of a high-quality, stand-alone software program, it is no wonder the packages are popular in schools. The power that is surrendered in creating an integrated package is seldom a significant limitation. For instance, the features omitted from the word processor are more suited to professional writers than to students, and the features omitted from the spreadsheet application are more suited to accountants than to students.

There are typically three ways to buy popular software packages for a school: single copies, lab packs, and network versions. The most expensive way to buy software is to purchase single copies. The cheapest way usually is to purchase network versions of the software. This option is not available for all software titles, nor can every school afford to take advantage of this option. Often a viable compromise is to purchase a lab pack. A lab pack contains individual copies of software and one or two copies of the manuals. The network manager can install the individual copies on each machine and maintain the manuals in the media center or library. Software manuals are notorious for being difficult to understand and use, so many people opt for purchasing third-party software instruction books.

Classroom Software

Once you have selected the standard tools for the building, you should consider specialty software for the classroom. A common approach to the selection of classroom software is to take a top-down approach, whereby the selection is made by an administrator, librarian, or media specialist. The top-down approach is ineffective. If teachers cannot find a positive use for a software application, they either will not use it, or worse, will use it poorly. Poor use of software is not only financially wasteful but also a waste of student's limited learning time.

Teachers must have input into the selection of specialty software. Leaders should give individual teachers, departments, grade levels, or other organized teams a portion of the software budget and allow them to select the software they need. This ensures that teachers will use the software more effectively.

When teachers are asked to choose software, it is important that they know what is available. School leaders should see that teachers know about available software, and should encourage them to evaluate the several possibilities. For suggestions, see the earlier section entitled "Learning About Software."

Media Center Software

A third type of software to consider is software for the library or media center. Every modern library or media center should have access to an electronic encyclopedia. This tool is rapidly replacing the traditional row of books. Not only is an electronic encyclopedia cheaper to buy and easier to maintain, but typically it is easier for students to use. Electronic encyclopedias offer capabilities that are not available in print versions. For example, they allow multiple term selection; the student can ask questions such as, "Give me every article that contains the words gold, silver, and copper, but not lead." They also let students cut and paste text. But be careful—plagiarism has never been so easy.

Several other electronic reference works are available for students to use. Some examples include interactive dictionaries, atlases, history resources, biology references, and other resources.

Another software application for the media center is software that is too expensive for the individual classroom, or software that requires the use of specialty equipment not available in the classroom. This includes most multimedia software. Modern multimedia software is some of the most exciting and potentially most engaging software available today. Most multimedia programs require a CD ROM drive. Some programs use video disks, which require a special player. Although many of these software packages are expensive for individual classroom use, a single copy may be within a school's budget. The primary advantage of most multimedia software is learner control; look for this feature when selecting multimedia software. More information on multimedia software is given in Chapter 7.

Lab Software

If you have decided to organize the computers in your building into one or more computer labs, then you will have to consider lab software. All of the computers will need tool software, and the computers in the lab should be consistent with the other computers in the building. There are two main ways the students can use a computer lab. Each has implications for software selection and purchase.

One way to use a computer lab is for whole-group instruction. In this case you will want all the computers in the lab to have the same software. The teachers determine which activities require whole-group work in the lab, and the activities determine the necessary software. Many whole-group activities involve standard tool software; examples are writing activities with a word processor and math activities using spreadsheets. However, there may be other whole-group activities that require special software, such as an activity in which the whole group works on the same simulation program.

Keyboarding is one whole-group activity that almost justifies a specialized computer lab. The primary method of interacting with the computer is through the keyboard. Until this changes, which it most certainly will over time, we must help students learn to use the keyboard efficiently. One of the most powerful uses of the computer is as a way to capture and refine our thoughts. A student who can type 60 words a minute can capture more of her thoughts than a student who has to hunt and peck to capture five words a minute.

A second way to use a computer lab is as a drop-in center or exploration center. A lab set up for this purpose would have a variety of equipment. Each computer station could afford a different specialized capability. Specialty hardware and associated software is essential in this situation. For example, you may have a computer-aided design (CAD) station with a scanner and CAD software. You may have a publication station with all the necessary hardware and software to do desktop publishing. Another possibility is a multimedia development station. This station would have a CD ROM drive, a video disk player, video capture hardware and software, and multimedia development software.

When establishing a drop-in lab, it is difficult to know in advance which stations students will use most. A way to handle this problem is to make selections based on teacher and student feedback, track the use of the various stations, and then duplicate the stations that students use most. Keep in mind, however, that the novelty of an activity may be a factor; students may investigate a new offering, then lose interest after it becomes a standard part of the school's applications.

SOURCES OF SOFTWARE

When we speak of software, most people think exclusively of software purchased from a commercial vendor. But there are two other sources of software. Software created by other educators can be obtained at little or no cost. This method of distributing software is called shareware or freeware. Another way to get software for classroom use is for the teacher or the students to create it.

Commercial Software

Commercial software is purchased from a software publisher or software retailer. Although apparently expensive, commercial software may be the most economical option. Retailers sell popular educational and tool software in large quantities, which means that the unit price stays relatively low. The main advantage of commercial software is its quality. Commercial software usually is well developed, well tested, and has strong user support. In addition, it offers the possibility of sharing outcomes and strategies among a network of people who use that software; for example, a student can share a data base created in Microsoft Works with a student in another school who also uses Microsoft Works. Commercial titles intended specifically for the educational market have another benefit: Many come with teacher's guides, student materials, or other associated tools that benefit the teaching/learning environment.

A negative aspect of most commercial software is its inflexibility. Commercial software is mostly a "what you see is what you get" world. If a teacher is unhappy with the way software developers organized the learning, or dislikes the exact content of the software, there is rarely anything she can do. For example, *Where in the World Is Carmen San Diego?* is a popular program about geography. A screen from this program is shown in Figure 3–1. However, the designers of the program have predetermined the geography clues, and the clues may have minimal connection to a teacher's predefined learning outcomes.

Shareware and Freeware

Shareware and freeware are programs that an individual or small company has produced and distributed through nontraditional channels. As its name implies, shareware is distributed through sharing among individual computer users. The programs can be shared but not sold, and the producer or author of the program expects users to voluntarily pay a small fee. Freeware, also as its name implies, is free; the producer or author does not expect users to pay any fees.

The most common source for shareware and freeware is through electronic networks or user groups. Virtually all telecommunication services, such as America

Figure 3–1

Screen from *Where in the World Is Carmen San Diego?*

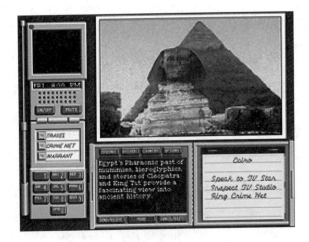

Online, Prodigy, and CompuServe, offer archives of shareware and freeware that subscribers can download and use. Vast collections of shareware and freeware are also available on the InterNet.

Although you do not have to pay for shareware, it is sensible to do so. Shareware producers or authors try to make at least part of their living producing software. If you find the software useful, then it makes sense to support the individual or company so as to contribute to the continual improvement and support of the software.

One advantage of shareware and freeware is price. Even if one pays the asking price for shareware, that price usually is less than comparable commercial software. Another advantage of shareware and freeware is that the user may find programs that are not available on the commercial market. Often, shareware producers and authors are individuals with specific interests. They often market their products through shareware channels because the commercial market has rejected their ideas. You, however, may be able to put those ideas to good instructional use.

A disadvantage of shareware and freeware is that the programs are seldom as well developed and tested as commercial software. This means that the programs may have bugs or problems that cause minor disruptions. They may not work at all on your specific configuration of equipment. The organizations that produce most shareware and freeware are small, so they do not have the resources to produce programs that can compete with large commercial software publishers. However, exceptions exist. Some shareware offerings are better than comparable software produced by commercial developers.

Some vendors use freeware as a marketing tool. To market a series of programs, the vendor makes the first program available for free, in hopes that users will like it and will buy the rest of the series. These freeware programs are usually of high quality because they are, essentially, free versions of commercial software.

Home-Grown Software

Teachers can create their own software. The main advantage of doing this is complete control of the content and instructional methods. The main disadvantage is the time and effort involved. Producing a small piece of sound educational software can take a teacher hundreds of hours. In light of the worth of a teacher's time, this is by far the most expensive way to acquire educational software. Hypermedia development tools make software development much easier, since much of the work is handled by the development program. Even so, it is not reasonable to expect any individual teacher to produce much software. One mitigating factor is that collecting all the software that teachers have produced and making it available as freeware is a way to collectively publish effective and tested software. This process happens through the use of telecommunications.

ORGANIZING SOFTWARE IN A SCHOOL

There are four methods for accessing software within a school building: operation from a floppy disk, operation from a hard disk, a simple file service, and network software from a file server. Any of these methods can be employed individually or in combination.

Software on Floppy Disk

If software is maintained on floppy disks, it can easily be shared from classroom to classroom. The software can be maintained in the school media center and checked out by teachers or students. This method is economical and convenient but is becoming less practical as programs get ever larger. Many of the best programs are completely impractical to run from a floppy disk. Speed is another disadvantage. Floppy disks are much slower to access than hard disks, and so are not practical for applications requiring significant disk access time.

Software on Individual Hard Disks

Hard disks have become a standard feature in modern computer systems, and thus most software is run directly from the hard drive. This method is fast and convenient, especially when running large programs. One negative aspect of loading all your software onto individual hard disks is the cost of hard drive space. Another problem is the management of the software: If the software needs to be changed for some reason, such as upgrading to a newer version, the program must be changed on every machine. Further, the school must have legal rights to use as many copies as it has computers loaded with that program, even when a program is used only infrequently.

Software from a File Server

A school that has a school-wide network with a file server can share software over that network. This can be done in two ways. The first is to place one or more individual copies of a program on a network file server so that it can be accessed by any computer that has access to that file server. Note, however, that a school that has purchased only a single copy of the software only has the right to use a single copy of that software at any one time. Some license agreements even specify how purchasers may use the software in a network environment. Be aware of your legal rights and responsibilities.

A problem with network software is speed. If the network is relatively slow, or if it is busy, then students and teachers could find that accessing software from a file server is slow. A slow or inconsistent network can frustrate students and may even diminish the quality of the learning environment.

A second method for sharing software over a school-wide network is to purchase network versions of software. Network versions give users the right to have a certain number of people use a single program simultaneously. For example, the school can have the right to have 15 simultaneous users on one application. Network software is usually the most economical choice when multiple copies of the software are needed. Network versions of software also are the easiest to manage and upgrade. Since there is only one copy of the program, when it needs to be changed the process is quite simple. Several problems exist with this format, however. A software publisher may offer a network version for 50 users, and a school only needs 20; or the publisher may offer a 20-user network version and the school needs 22. A second problem with network versions of software is if that software is damaged for any reason, everyone is "out of service." This is also the case when a network problem occurs. Any of several problems can bring down a network and render all its software inaccessible. The potential for all users to be unable to access software should give school leaders pause for consideration.

Compromises

The choice between using a network file server and purchasing software individually for each machine is a difficult one. As a result, a few compromises have been designed. Some schools standardize all their software in order to minimize the maintenance headache that results from having all the software loaded on individual machines. Every classroom hard drive will have the same software. A copy of what each hard drive contains is maintained on a file server, and all the machines are reloaded periodically from the file server. This means that any changes made to a single version on the file server can be transferred by the server to the individual computers.

A second compromise involves the use of a key server. This compromise solves the problem of speed of access. Individual copies of software can be "keyed" and loaded on all the hard drives in the building. A network key server is maintained to keep track of how many copies of the program are available and how many are in use. When a user begins a program, the key server is checked; if a copy of the program is available, the program is allowed to install. If all available copies are already in use, the key server notifies the user that use of the program is denied. The beauty of this system is that the actual software is on the hard drive, so the only portion of the operation that is dependent on the network is the initial start-up.

The negative aspect of both of these compromises is that they add complexity to the maintenance and management of the computer network. To use either of these methods, the school must have a roving leader who can manage the complexity of the network. That establishes yet another technological dependency.

MANAGING SOFTWARE

Personnel Issues

After the software is purchased, the school has several ongoing software management responsibilities:

1. Maintaining a software inventory.
2. Making and archiving software back-ups.
3. Managing the network file server.

4. Maintaining records of software purchase and license agreements.

5. Installing software.

6. Ordering software.

7. Interacting with hardware and software vendors.

These are not trivial responsibilities. They usually fall to a roving leader, such as the school media specialist. In some schools, software management responsibilities are split among several people.

It is important that whoever is identified to complete these tasks be knowledgeable, capable, and well prepared. Many people currently doing this work are self-trained and have learned on the job. Recently, schools of education have begun to improve the preparation of leaders in software management.

It is important that the roving leaders responsible for the hardware and software have access to experts in the field. Most states have active organizations for technology in education. Members of the community of leadership should join these organizations. Partnerships with nearby universities also may be an important part of the relationship with instructional technology. When users are stumped by problems with technology, as will happen from time to time, it is important that they have someone to call besides consultants who charge hourly fees.

Updating Software

Schools will need to purchase new software when teaching staff changes, when instructional needs change, and when new software becomes available. Some resources should be budgeted every year to allow teachers to upgrade their instructional software. The media center, and the computer lab if one has been established, also must purchase software yearly.

Just as hardware tends to change and improve quite rapidly, so does software. Some software changes are ongoing and minor, such as upgrading from version 3.0 to 3.1 to 3.2. Software also undergoes major overhauls which involve incorporating small changes and adding major new features—for example, upgrading from version 3.0 to version 4.0. Approximately every year, producers of top-selling software issue a new major version. New versions add features that make the software more powerful and easier to use. With each new version, software inevitably becomes more complicated and sophisticated and has greater system requirements, such as more RAM and more hard drive space. Software publishers offer upgrade licenses for newer versions of software at slightly reduced prices. These software upgrades account for a greater share of a software producer's income. The newest upgrade tends to come close to the purchase price of the original software. Eventually publishers cease support for older versions of their software.

Schools should upgrade software whenever possible and whenever necessary to remain consistent with instructional objectives. You do not need to upgrade software every time a new version is published, but if the school falls too far behind, the power available to the students and staff is significantly diminished. The school risks not being able to get support for an old version of the software when problems occur, and not being compatible with other schools using the same software.

Schools tend to budget for computer software when they purchase computers. This is not sufficient. The school must add new software applications yearly to benefit the instructional program. Tool software should be upgraded at least every other year. This is costly and must be a regular, budget item.

IMPLICATIONS FOR THE COMMUNITY OF LEADERSHIP

The community of leadership becomes the facilitator for change. Change requires that the community of leadership diminish the prevalence of transmission instructional strategies and encourage and model constructivism and learning theory. Change requires the movement from summative evaluation of professionals to formative assessment using clinical supervision and peer coaching. Change requires strategic, tactical, and operational planning. Change requires massive staff development efforts. Change requires that schooling reflect developmentally appropriate practice built upon a foundation of caring and trust. Change depends on the community of leadership's accepting and articulating its values and beliefs, stated as a vision and mission and formalized as a shared culture.

Change also requires a shift in management practices, to doing things right. Great leaders must be good managers. In managing technology, the community of leadership and formal leaders must establish effective strategies to manage the selection, purchase, and distribution of hardware and software. Effective leadership must model the appropriate instructional and managerial applications of hardware and software. Effective leadership must affirm and celebrate the community of leadership and students' learning. Finally, effective leadership must contribute strategies to guarantee lifelong learning.

What school leaders should know about software cannot possibly fit in a single chapter. Therefore, the following six chapters provide more detail describing specific software applications and suggesting ways they can be used effectively in the classroom. Each chapter focuses on helping students turn data into information into knowledge.

CONCLUSION

It is our belief that software can enhance the teaching/learning environment. One way we believe it helps children learn is by taking the unorganized bits and pieces of their world—the data—and organizing that data into information. Words, for example, are simply data. When we organize them into meaningful sentences and paragraphs, they take on a higher level of meaning; they become information. After students take the data from their world and convert it into information, the task of teaching and learning is only half completed. The next step is to turn the informa-

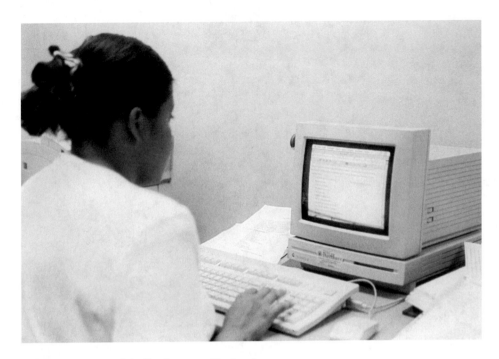

Formal leaders model effective use of technology.

tion into knowledge. This step implies that the information is internalized, that it is used. Information must be activated to have any value to students.

Following this example, when our paragraphs inspire, persuade, or emotionally move the reader, we have turned information into knowledge. When we have used knowledge to construct a reality or promote a social good, we have succeeded. This theme of turning data into information and information into knowledge is repeated throughout the subsequent chapters. We believe one effect software can have on children's learning is to help them increase their content and process knowledge.

REFERENCES

Clark, R. E. (1983). Reconsidering research on learning from media. *Review of Educational Research*, 53(4), 445–459.

Taylor, R. (Ed.). (1980). *The computer in the school: Tutor, tool, tutee*. New York: Teachers College Press.

Instructional Applications

4

Supporting Language and Literacy Development with Technology

anguage and literacy are reading, writing, listening, and speaking. Instruction in language and literacy is a part of all students' curricula from pre-kindergarten through twelfth grade. The focus of primary students' instruction is on essential skills. Students learn how to form sounds from letters and learn the conventions of formal language—punctuation, spelling, style. From middle school, language and literacy instruction is content based. Students learn comprehension strategies—summarizing, main idea, questioning—in a specific content area—for example, math or geography—or in a inter-disciplinary or thematic environment—for example, dinosaurs, community, aging in America.

There is a strong relationship between reading and writing. Reading and writing should occur together. Children should use writing to learn to read and should use reading to learn to write. This chapter presents several computer applications that support a strong language and literacy instructional program. Educational, tool, and tutorial software connected to explicit instruction in essential skills, using constructivist and cognitive learning theory, will help children learn to read and write.

Whole-language instruction is an approach grounded in constructivist and cognitive learning theory. In this chapter we describe whole language and its writing counterpart, process writing. Additionally, we connect the mastery of essential skills to automaticity, a strategy to instantly recall essential skills. We suggest two strategies to introduce and expand natural or process writing: progressive writing and the potato exercise. Finally, we describe the community of leadership's responsibility to support language and literacy development with technology.

INTRODUCTION

Some time ago, we were working with a group of first-graders, showing them how to create a journal on a word processor. We asked each teacher to identify two students who were competent with the computer to act as the class experts. We taught the experts the necessary journal entry steps, and they tutored each of their classmates. In a classroom one of the experts was a boy who had often seemed sullen and withdrawn. However, when we involved him in this activity his whole attitude changed. He was excited, engaged, and seemed happy. He spent a lot of time working with individual students during the first day. Before school the next day, he ran up to one of us and asked excitedly, "Can I do that again today?"

Often teachers get so caught up in the cognitive side of education that they forget the affective side. School ought to be a place where children want to spend time. They need more experiences that prompt them to ask, "Can I do that again today?" Technology can play an important role in achieving that goal. The story above gives us insight into the mechanisms of making that happen. It is not so much the technology itself that is important, but its power to assist us in organizing our children to learn better. In our quest to recapture the excitement of teaching and the joy of learning, teachers can connect language and literacy instruction and technology. Although one can argue that the connection is possible in any content area, there is a strong relationship between language and literacy and research in learning theory. Learning theory in language and literacy nurtures the development of instructional wisdom in teachers and excitement about learning in students.

AN OVERVIEW OF THE SOFTWARE FOR LANGUAGE AND LITERACY DEVELOPMENT

There are several software applications that can help develop language and literacy: educational programs, drill-and-practice and tutorial programs, tool applications, and programs that incorporate both. In addition, a number of software programs developed for other disciplinary areas are applicable to language and literacy. Tool software that may not be language and literacy oriented also can have strong application, especially if language and literacy instruction happens in an integrated curriculum approach.

Educational Software

Several educational programs exist specifically to help with the development of language and literacy. For young children, the most popular of these are primarily drill-and-practice programs. *Reader Rabbit* and *Word Munchers* are common in schools. Although many young children seem to enjoy these programs, their value to the learning process is questionable. From personal observations we believe that the children who enjoy these programs most are those who need drill and practice least.

Several literature-based programs have great potential for improving the teaching/learning environment. Many books on compact disk (CD-ROM) have become popular. These CD-ROM books involve translating the books to electronic media and enhancing them with interesting technology. One of the most popular is the *Living Books* series, written specifically for early readers. A screen from this program is shown in Figure 4–1. The number of titles in the series grows year by year. An electronic computer voice can read the entire book to the child or assist an early reader with individual words. The pictures are interactive—that is, the child can click on an image with the mouse, and something interesting happens; for example, a language development or sequencing activity may appear.

A similar series written for intermediate readers is the *Scholastics Smart Book* series. These books are enhanced with activities designed specifically for intermediate and middle school children. This software has the potential to increase learning by adding context to the reading environment using interactive pictures, by giving computers the ability to "read" to children, and by adding meaningful follow-up activities to the reading process. At the same time, this software has potential for abuse, and thus potentially weakens the teaching/learning environment. If children

Figure 4–1
Screen from *Living Books* Series

are allowed access to these programs without supervision or purpose, they will only play. Shooting a picture of an umbrella in the air 50 times in a row, for example, has little value to the development of children's language and literacy. As we continue to integrate this software with quality instructional strategies, we need to be concerned with the issue of real improvement of the teaching/learning environment. Given the students' affective needs, socialization needs, and the comfort many children need, the day a computer replaces children sitting on the laps of adults with books will be a sad day indeed.

A number of more sophisticated software programs are available for older children. Some programs involve the analysis of literature, such as the *Literature For Mastery* series. A number of multi-media programs either focus specifically on language and literacy development or have multiple curricular objectives, such as *Cultural Reporter*. In addition, many software packages that are written for specific disciplines can be used as reading and writing activities with older children, such as the interactive video disk series from National Geographic, *Rain Forest* and *Human Body,* or ABC News's *In the Holy Land* and *Powers of the Supreme Court.*

Tool Software

The two main tools for language and literacy development are word processing and desktop publishing programs. Word processing can be a significant element in the teaching/learning environment. Desktop publishing programs are designed specifically to prepare written work for publication. There are programs produced for young children, such as *The Writing Center* and *Storybook Weaver.* Applications for more mature writers include *PageMaker* and *Quark XPress.* The main feature of desktop publishing programs is the ability to integrate pictures and words conveniently. They also simplify features such as multiple columns and banner pages. The more sophisticated programs allow the user to do all the things a professional publisher can do to prepare material for publication. For example, users can import text from multiple word processing programs, scale and crop pictures, and rotate text and graphics. Desktop publishing programs can help students publish professional-looking documents.

Adult desktop publishing programs have a reputation for being difficult to learn. However, if children learn to use desktop publishing programs designed for them, and begin early, children can use some of the more rudimentary functions of desktop publishing, such as placing pictures and making words flow around pictures. Then, as children understand the patterns and operations, and as their thinking and writing become more sophisticated, teachers can introduce them to higher level programs and features. If this strategy is implemented, then by high school students will be proficient at using sophisticated, professional desktop publishing programs. Many small-town newspapers are completely formatted using standard desktop publishing programs.

In addition to the traditional language and literacy development tools, we need to consider how other tools enhance reading, writing, speaking, and listening. Hypermedia allows our students to publish their ideas in a relatively new way. Rather than the traditional final step of producing a paper product, students produce multimedia presentations. The final product, then, is electronic. We must not overlook these opportunities to increase students' writing skills. The inherent motivation that hypermedia programs have for many children can be the "hook" we need to get children writing. (For more detail on hypermedia, see Chapter 7.)

Telecommunications is another example of a set of tools that we might use for language and literacy development. Electronic mail (e-mail) has enormous potential for children's reading and writing in a context-rich environment. E-mail allows us to connect our students electronically to almost any person or group. We can connect them to other children in our country or in other countries. We can connect them to individuals in government, individuals with special expertise, or individuals of different ages. All the interaction happens through written language, so all e-mail connections make an important contribution to language and literacy development. (For more detail on telecommunications, see Chapter 9.)

Some of the relatively new telecommunications opportunities play a powerful role in encouraging children to read, write, and publish. As a child "surfs the net," she must read text. Furthermore, some of the latest tools, such as the World Wide Web, allow our students to publish their writing for readers throughout the world. These latest tools make creating pages on the web within the capability of a teacher or child. Children benefit from publishing their writing in many ways. One exciting and challenging strategy is creating home pages. It is one thing to ask a child to write an essay on what she thinks is the most interesting thing to do in her city or state; it is quite another to make that child's essay available to children around the world. With these opportunities, we again realize that it is not so much the technology itself that will improve our students' learning, but the opportunities that technology provide us, the community of leadership, to enrich children's learning environment, to encourage them to care about the quality of their writing, and to stay engaged in the learning process. We must keep them asking, "Teacher, can I do that again today?"

Blending Tools and Tutorials

A new group of programs blends the concept of tools and tutorials. A popular example is *Writer's Workbench*. These programs analyze writing and offer suggestions for improvement. For young writers, the program can be used to address simple structural elements. With more experienced writers, complex writing issues, such as subject/verb agreement, use of passive voice, or misplaced modifiers, are the appropriate focus of instruction. As with many productivity tools, using this software does not relieve us of the necessity to teach the skills explicitly, nor does it relieve us of the job of reading and analyzing student writing. This tool gives the teacher time to work with more sophisticated skills and strategies. The software can only make suggestions about mechanical changes; it cannot make suggestions about the content or artistry of the writing. The teacher still is responsible for students' clarity, beauty, and power.

Our language is so complex that modern software that analyzes writing is not always correct in its analyses. A student must know when a suggested improvement is appropriate. She also must know when an identified problem is really a problem or merely has been misidentified by the software. For instance, a missing comma can cause a program to misinterpret a phrase and diagnose a problem where none exists.

Another benefit of this software is that it can assist students when a teacher is not available. Once we have children routinely writing with word processors, the next step is to have them routinely analyzing their writing with grammar-checking software. This can establish a different teaching strategy for developing young writers. We can significantly tighten children's thinking about their writing quality. Normally, a child will write a piece, hand it in, and wait for a grade; only when she receives the grade does she consider the quality of the writing. With the aid of grammar-checking programs, once a student finishes writing a piece, she can immediately analyze it for routine mechanics. For many young writers, this process can improve their writing habits.

We must still teach our children what constitutes good writing. We also must spend time reading, analyzing, and discussing their writing. However, with the aid of programs that analyze writing, we might help students develop better writing strategies. Also, teachers can have more time to interact with students about their ideas in a nurturing way, and thus help students improve their writing.

Essentials Skills

As students' writing habits improve, they will become more effective writers. The demand for accountability and for better scores on standardized tests questions the efficacy of progressive, constructivist instructional strategies, including process writing and invented spelling. Constructivism and learning theory advocate mastery of essential skills specifically in the content areas. Efficiency or automaticity (Samuels, 1988) allows students to spend less time on mechanics and devote more time to capturing ideas.

Automaticity

Samuels (1988) describes the procedure that learners use to master an essential skill. He terms this process "automaticity" (p. 756). Our task as educators is to help the child become automatic in the use of her skills. We have extrapolated the notion of writing as a specialized skill to the learning of all essential skills. Samuels argues that the learner only has so much psychic or cognitive energy to devote to comprehending a piece of text or learning a concept. The more energy that she expends trying to understand a skill, such as how to use quotation marks, the less energy she can devote to comprehension or learning.

Automaticity is as much a goal as it is a process. The goal is to elicit responses quickly and correctly. To achieve mastery of essential skills, children must accomplish three tasks. First, children must become accurate at the skill. Accuracy demands that the students get the facts right. For example, they must recognize the appropriate use of quotation marks in a dialogue. Second, children must have time to practice their accuracy so that these essential skills become habits. Not only must the children recognize the need for quotation marks in a dialogue, they must do so instantly. Third, the teacher must facilitate the children's motivation to become automatic, to be both correct and immediate. Students must have many different successful experiences with automaticity in general, and with individual skills specifically. Silent reading for pleasure increases a child's automaticity.

Word Processing in Schools

Over the last 15 years, word processing has become a standard part of our writing culture. The vast majority of writers, both professional and amateur, use word processors. Word processing has become so pervasive that when most people think of writing, they envision a writer sitting at a computer. Although many of us grew up using a typewriter, the new generation takes features like word wrap, cut and paste, and spell-checking for granted.

Two aspects of word processing are important to schools: word processing as a teacher tool and word processing as a means to support the development of student writers. The use of word processing by teachers is an important modeling strategy. However, we consider the second aspect to be the most important and hence give it the greatest consideration. Word processing may play a small but important role in improving students' ability to read, write, speak, and listen. Word processing also may add to the professional image of schools.

Word Processing as a Teacher Tool

Word processing is the standard for formal written communication in today's world, yet many teachers resist its use. Parents who bring their children to the school in the late summer for the "school roundup" still pick up a hand-written, photocopied list of supplies for the year. Teachers still send home hand-written notes about field trips, special school events, and classroom news. There is certainly nothing wrong with hand-written notes for more personal communications, such as "Judy did a nice job on her science report." But when the communication is formal, the presentation should be as well. If we strive to be more professional as educators, we may find that we are treated more professionally and afforded more respect. This form of professionalism can be an asset to educators as we gain deference from other professionals and the school community.

Word processors should be readily available to teachers, and teachers should know how to use them. School leaders should encourage, if not demand, that word processors be used for all formal communications. A good rule of thumb would be that no hand-written document should be photocopied, especially if the communication is to be disseminated outside the classroom. Office personnel can model the use of word processing for teachers and support the teachers' transition to the word processor.

If we are to demand that teachers use word processing, then we also must make sure they have their own computers. Thus, when teachers have computers in their classrooms, a computer also must be installed at the teachers' work space. If we expect behavioral change, the teacher must believe that she has ready access, even ownership, of word processing.

Another reason a teacher should have ready access to a word processor is to enhance student learning. Teachers need to be role models, and children need to see their models writing. When the group is writing together, the teacher also needs to be writing with the children. Seeing the teacher writing, having the teacher involved in whole-group writing activities, and reading the teacher's published work are important elements in the development of children's writing skills.

THE RESEARCH ON LITERACY DEVELOPMENT USING TECHNOLOGY

A discussion of relevant research is a critical element in establishing our theory base. If we are to establish instructional wisdom in language and literacy development, then we must study current theory, add to it our collective experiences, and filter it through our value system. The resulting instructional wisdom can guide our future teaching and learning culture. It can guide our practice, inform the future interests of researchers, and even help us establish a connection between research and practice through teacher-initiated action research.

The body of research in language and literacy development with the aid of modern technology is neither as focused nor as useful as we might hope. The statements below illustrate the problem:

> I was asked by the editor of this column to investigate the topic of reading and technology. As I began my search of the literature, I was immediately dismayed at the lack of current research that effectively dealt with those topics. (Thompson & Montgomery, 1994, p. 6)

> Despite intense research into the effects of computers on writers and writing over the last several years, we have not received a clear perception of the complex issues involved, including the role the computer plays in the teaching of writing and the impact it has had on writing classrooms. (Herrmann, 1990, p. 124)

It is important to explain why the findings of a large body of research are so ambiguous and often contradictory. At least four areas of concern arise from the existing research on technology and language and literacy development.

One issue is that much of the research does not adequately reflect natural reading and writing environments. Literacy development happens in a rich and complex environment in which students learn skills in context. Rigidly controlled research studies eliminate many of the environmental elements. The result is that we know how literacy develops in a research study, but we may not know how literacy develops in emergent literacy contexts, often before children enter school. This limitation probably accounts for much of the conflicting findings reported in the literature. Findings such as the following are common:

> These results are contrary to that portion of the literature that suggests that performance improves when word processing is used. (Langone, Willis, Malone, Clees, & Koorland, 1994, p. 181)

A second issue with the research literature is that it lacks an appropriate focus. The bulk of the studies simply measure the difference between results obtained using technology and those obtained using a traditional approach. This series of investigations may be useful, but since schools do far more than simply provide the tools for literacy development, this line of inquiry only tells part of the story. We need answers to more complex questions, answers that shed light on the relationships between the tools (technology) and our responsibilities (teaching and learning).

A third issue stems from how we define the word "better." Many studies report improvements of writing, but does technology make children's writing better? What the research means by "better" is uncertain. It may mean that children who use computers write more words than students who use paper and pen, or it may mean that children who use computers make more attempts at revision. "Better" may relate only to the final product, without considering the process. In addition, the way researchers measure "better" also varies from study to study. Variation in what research means by "better" writing, along with variation in how researchers measure better writing, may account for the conflicting findings of the research.

A fourth issue is the time required to publish a research study. It is not unusual for a study to be published two to three years after its completion. Given the time required to write and revise a manuscript, the time to get information indexed, and the ever-present issue of procrastination, many studies that we might use to inform our practice are ancient in "computer years." This means that by the time a teacher applies the findings of a study, the technology has become obsolete.

Much of the available research on language and literacy and technology is from studies using mainframe computers and early microcomputers with word processors. Today's technology does not resemble those early tools. The ease, convenience, and power of today's tools far exceed those of early tools. If, indeed, we consider technology as a tool we can use in the development of language and literacy, then we must consider the nature of the tools that were used in the research that guides practice. Failing to do so is like trying to judge the contribution of the hammer by observing a carpenter driving a nail with a rock.

With these issues in mind, what insight does the research literature offer? Researchers have conducted a number of reviews of the literature on children's writing and word processing technology. Cochran-Smith, Paris, and Kahn (1991), recognizing the research issues, suggested:

> The findings in the literature on word processing, as well as the questions and assumptions that underlie these findings, are complex and varied. They defy global generalization and require, instead, careful consideration of nuances in terminology, research methods, and pedagogical contexts. (p. 23)

In light of these problems, Cochran-Smith, Paris, and Kahn offer significant guidance for instruction. They tell us many ways our students might benefit from using the word processor: writing longer texts and performing more revisions. They also remind teachers about the importance of instruction in the development of student writers. If we only give children a powerful tool and do not teach them what the tool should be used to accomplish, we are only helping them get better and better at doing the wrong thing.

Cochran-Smith, Paris, and Kahn also address the social impact of using word processing in the classroom. They suggest that possibilities exist to improve classroom management—how we organize children for learning and the "feel" of the classroom—using word processing:

> It must be noted, however, that the only proposition that all who examined this research agreed upon seemed to be that students using word processors tended to

write longer texts; the children wrote more words. Other research germane to this topic contradicted one or more of these suggestions (Bangert-Drowns, 1993; Hawisher, 1989; Russel, 1991). Each reviewer, however, seemed to offer some unique piece of insight. Hawisher (1989) suggested that word processing may be more beneficial to the basic writer as opposed to the advanced writer. Russel (1991) suggested that the positive effects found in many studies may be more attributable to classroom management strategies used in computer labs rather than to the technology they used. This may seem a disparaging suggestion, but upon further consideration it focused our efforts in precisely the proper direction. As we have suggested repeatedly, one important contribution of technology is the possibility it offers to organize learners in more developmentally appropriate ways.

TEACHERS, CHILDREN, AND WORD PROCESSING: WHAT WE KNOW

Bangert-Drowns (1993) suggested that the literature implied that, "The word processing experience has a motivational impact on basic writers, encouraging all to engage in writing tasks more wholeheartedly" (pp. 87–88). This was a rather bold statement given the variation in the literature, but nonetheless it does give us some instructional direction. The word processor can contribute to our students asking, "Teacher, can I do that again today?"

Researchers conducted a number of studies investigating technology and writing in a social context. An interesting example which suggests several valuable ideas is Snyder's (1994) eight-month observation of a group of eighth-year girls in Australia. Snyder observed one group of girls writing with pen and paper in a classroom and another group writing in a computer lab. He noted that the teacher in the computer classroom was "a learner in a learning community, modeling the processes of learning" (p. 155). Snyder concluded:

> Writing with computers, while initially more difficult than pen for almost all of the computer students, evolved for many of them into an increasingly engaging process. The computer setting seemed to invite writing. Writing with computers developed into an engrossing, interesting and enjoyable activity. Although there was always some noise, even if only the sound of the computers, the word-processing students were not easily distracted: they were intently focused on the writing and kept on writing. (p. 156)

Snyder also reported that the learning was significantly more student-centered and student-initiated.

These observations again illustrated the power of technology to offer opportunities to change the way we organize our students for learning. More thought was focused on the social aspects of the changed learning environment than on the technology itself. This was exactly as we believe it should be.

Several reviewers (Bangert-Drowns, 1993; Cochran-Smith, Paris, and Kahn, 1991; Snyder, 1993) either suggested or stated the importance of the connection between teaching and the positive benefits from word processing. According to Snyder (1993):

When an "effective" teaching model is employed, writers using word processing have achieved at a higher level than similar writers not using word processing. (p 61)

The literature suggests that when we teach good writing strategies, the word processor helps our students put those strategies into action.

DEVELOPING STUDENT WRITERS WITH WORD PROCESSING

The literature gives us broad direction in organizing children to use technology in the development of language and literacy. Rather than focusing on how students' writing will be better using technology, we should focus on how to improve the teaching/learning environment and, as a result of that change, how students' writing will improve. The first and easiest step in changing the teaching/learning environment is to give students more powerful applications with which to capture their thoughts.

Many writers consider their word processor to be their writing partner. Their statements range from the practical: "A word processor makes the connection between your mind and the manuscript stronger, more efficient and more responsive" (Krajewski, 1983, p. 54) to the poetic: "The cursor is your pointer, yet you can never catch it. It always stays one step ahead of you" (Latamore, 1983, p. 106). There is little mystery about these feelings. The word processor is such a powerful tool for a writer that it is surprising that some writers still do not use it.

The power of the word processor should be modeled and practiced in the writing process in schools. Word processing should be used across all grade levels and across the curriculum. When children begin learning to develop and improve their writing skills, they should have a word processor as one of their tools. As future adults, students should be using a word processor regularly, and teachers should model its use for their students.

Learning Benefits

Although the research literature gives us less direction than we would like, we can blend our theories of learning with our practice to invent effective instructional practice for an appropriate curriculum for developing language and literacy. In practice, having children write using a word processor has a number of benefits. One benefit is that children do not have to recopy their work when using a word processor to edit. Writing can be thought of as having two parts, capturing thoughts and refining thoughts. The word processor has only limited benefits in the process of capturing thoughts. Once those thoughts are captured, however, the word processor greatly facilitates the process of refining them.

When children edit using paper and pencil, their primary task is to form the letters, and the actual editing becomes a secondary task. The word processor lets the learner focus specifically on the editing task. For example, if the emergent writer is working on placing capital letters at the beginning of a sentence and periods at the end, the word processor allows her to focus directly on those two skills.

In several upgraded versions of word processors, capital letters at the beginning of a sentence can be inserted automatically. The more advanced writer may be focusing on getting the most important ideas into the topic sentence of the paragraph. Here, the word processor lets the writer focus exclusively on the main ideas.

Children's affinity for computers is an additional benefit of using the word processor for writing. Young children seem to like the computer and to like doing things with it. It could be that the computer gives children a feeling of control, or that it offers an element of excitement. This phenomenon may dissipate over time, but until that happens, we can take advantage of it. Children experience a strong and exciting attitudinal boost when writing with a computer, as illustrated by the story we used to introduce this chapter. The story suggests children's excitement at using the computer, and the possible benefits in self-esteem they realize from making the computer do what they want.

Organizing Children to Word Process

The day will come when organizing children to write with a word processor will be much simpler than it is today. The present stage in the development of computer hardware and software is reminiscent of colonial times, when few students had access to paper and pencil. When word processors become as ubiquitous as calculators, organizing children to write will be more effective. Until then, we need to work on giving children ample opportunities to write using word processors.

There are two significant methods for organizing children to write with a word processor: whole-group learning activities and ongoing, individual activities. Each method has its respective instructional rationales. In the early history of computers in schools, the focus was on computer labs. More recently, instructional leaders recognized that computers can be effective in the classroom. Today, computer labs are being dismantled and moved into the classroom. It seems reasonable to predict that, eventually, each child will have her own computer. Until then, we will need to provide computer labs for whole-group activities and classroom computers for ongoing, individual work. An answer to this temporary concern may be making computer stations portable and accessible for teachers' instructional purposes: computers on wheels.

One useful whole-group activity is to help children develop keyboarding skills. The speed at which children type determines the speed at which they can capture their thoughts. The time to begin teaching keyboarding skills is when children start working with computers: pre-kindergarten. They must first become familiar with the arrangement of the keyboard. Later, in second or third grade, children should learn to touch type. The ability to touch type enables children to capture more of their thoughts more quickly. That outcome is certainly worth the time to teach a child touch typing. Although keyboarding may eventually be replaced by audio input technology, until then we must continue to emphasize keyboarding skills.

Other whole-group activities can be beneficial to a child's language and literacy development. For instance, some process-writing activities require that all the children write together. With other activities, whole-group writing affords a more convenient organization of the instructional day. For instance, if we wanted all of our children to write their reactions to a field trip, it might take too long to route all the children through one or two classroom computers; by the time the last child has had her turn, the experience will have "grown cold." In both of these cases we have two choices: Either we can maintain computer labs so children can write as a whole group, or we can give up all the benefits of writing with a word processor and return to paper and pencil.

One possible compromise is to have the children jot down their ideas with paper and pencil and do their actual writing on the word processor. We do not recommend a standard practice of having children write on paper and copy onto the computer; this weakens the power of the word processor and simply teaches the children to use inefficient methods. If a child chooses to do some or even much of her writing using paper and pencil, then that is acceptable, but we do not want to teach children less effective, intermediary techniques. Although some adults still prefer paper and pencil, we must remember that adult experiences differ from children's experiences in schools. Today, the way we write is with a word processor. The words you are reading now began with an outline that was composed at the keyboard, followed by a first draft composed at the keyboard, followed by several stages of editing at the keyboard. Thus, the thoughts you are reading were captured and refined solely on a word processor; none were written with pencil and paper. This should be our goal for our children.

Word Processing in the Classroom

When each child has a computer, organizing children to word process is a relatively simple task. When only one or two computers are available, the task is much more difficult. If you believe, as we do, that it is important for children to write every day, and if you want that writing to be a powerful learning experience, then you will want children to be word processing often. This may mean that management of classroom time will have to change. In the elementary classroom, "seat work" may include a schedule of word processing time. Reading group also may be a time when some children write. We must keep the children cycling through the computer continuously throughout the day. Only when classrooms are engaged in activities that require whole-group participation will the word processor be idle. Changes in classroom management may not only maximize the power of the children's writing time, but also may benefit the learning environment in other ways.

As children prepare to write, it is important that we consider issues of equity. If our method of allowing children time on the computer involves free choice, it is likely that we will see the boys dominating the machines. We also may see those children who need computer time the least dominating the computer. Our systems for organizing children's equitable access to computers require knowledge of the research on the effects of gender and race in classroom participation. All students, especially girls and children of color, should have equal opportunity to use the word processor.

In middle and high schools, time schedules often organize subject areas, so the chance for frequent and productive use of word processing is tenuous. In most schools, the use of word processing in writing classes is becoming the norm, but is less typical in other classes, such as science, math, and social studies. The availability of computers is limited, while the need is great. For example, in mathematics, the limited time a teacher can use for computer lab is customarily spent on tools other than word processing, such as spreadsheets or drill-and-practice programs. This not only defeats the effort to "write across the curriculum"—an effort most educators strongly favor—but also puts some math students at a disadvantage. We believe that writing about math is important for certain students to be able to integrate the concepts of math. Children's own words, however, can be more compelling than the voice of experts (Burns, 1995).

Math and Writing

What writing does for me is it unlocks my brain and it lets me think. But if I didn't write, I would be getting nowhere. I wouldn't learn anything. I mean I wouldn't think so hard if I didn't write. I would just play the game even if I didn't know how because I wouldn't have to write. But when you write it just makes you think.

When you write about your work, you ideas lead to other ideas, which lead to other ideas etc. and you can use that noledge for games which lead you to new thieries about the game, which solve problems nobody's ever thought of. Plus whos going to stop you? You can write so much, you can change your perspectie about probability so you can use it every day. (Burns, 1995, pp. 43-44)

The children's words offer sophisticated thinking about the writing and math connection. Traditional math classrooms that teach symbolic math without a writing component may be losing an entire group of students. The ability to write about math on a regular basis may recapture those students. Adding word processing to this powerful strategy can strengthen that connection by helping children refine their thinking about math by revising their writing.

Writing in math classes is simply one example of how we organize children for instruction. Other strategies, such as block scheduling, setting up teams, and involving families, may help us provide more opportunities for children to integrate word processing into their normal learning day.

CHILDREN AS WORD PROCESSING EXPERTS: REWARD FOR KNOWLEDGE NOT BEHAVIOR

Developing a team of student word processing experts allows the teacher more time to work with individual students. The "experts" are children who have demonstrated mastery of the computer and the word processor. They can offer assistance to children who are having problems with saving and printing, simple spell- and grammar-checking, and even complex formatting.

In elementary schools, children perform many classroom duties. The teacher can add various computer-related jobs to the daily list. In the upper grades it may simply be a matter of identifying children who have the aptitude or expertise and then striking a bargain with these children to act as consultants. This activity can be the students' service to the school-community.

This approach not only benefits the teacher and the other students, it benefits the "experts" in a number of ways. We saw a clear indication of the power of this approach in our work in one elementary school:

> Frank was an obviously bright fifth-grade child who was labeled "behaviorally disordered." He was somewhat big for his age, and although it was clear that he could behave appropriately, he acted immaturely at times. He might, for example, imitate an ape while walking down the hallway. More disturbingly, Frank would get in serious fights with his male classmates. Frank was suspended for fighting on a number of occasions. One of the indications of Frank's intelligence was his ability to manipulate the computer. In conjunction with a project we were doing with the school, Frank was identified as a technology leader among his peers. He had a specific role to fill and met his responsibilities well. In this context, Frank displayed none of his frequent troublesome behavior. Although he had to work closely with most of his male classmates, and that work naturally evoked minor confrontations, all the interactions with the other boys were handled appropriately.

Frank's story is another indication of the power of technology to organize children for instruction. The technology itself did not teach Frank appropriate behavior. However, the technology did play a significant role for Frank. His computer expertise gave him affirmation and an opportunity to be brilliant.

LITERACY DEVELOPMENT PROJECTS USING TECHNOLOGY

The Power of Journal Writing

Journal writing is an application of metacognition that encourages children to think and to practice language and literacy. Our experience with children writing journals using a word processor is so positive that we believe this should be a regular part of the writing experience. We believe children should begin keeping an electronic journal in first grade and continue throughout their lives.

Using the computer to create journals is convenient and efficient. However, the main benefit we see is not so much the capturing of thoughts and ideas, but what happens with those thoughts afterwards. We believe journals should be a private affair, a writing environment in which the child can feel confident, comfortable, and able to express some of their closely held thoughts and feelings. That does not mean that children cannot use their journals for other purposes. For example, when a teacher assigns a creative writing project, the journal may be the first place that student looks for ideas. If the child's journal contains material the child wants to use, she can simply cut-and-paste it into a new document and use it as a starter for the creative writing exercise.

A Recipe for Electronic Journals with First-Graders

Beginning electronic journal writing with first-graders may seem premature, but our experience has shown that it has benefits. We believe journal writing is so important to developing language and literacy that we provide the following recipe for starting an electronic journal with first graders:

First, create a word processing document named for each child. Second, place all the files in a single folder or directory that is easily accessible, such as on the computer's desktop. Choose two children from the classroom who are adept at using the computer to be student experts. Work with the student experts on the steps of opening a document, adding to it, saving it, and putting it away until you are satisfied that they can help other children through the steps. Organize the remainder of the class to work with the student experts on the first journal entry. Observe the student expert's work with the first two or three children. When necessary, coach the student experts in proper tutoring behavior. This is a necessary step with younger children. After the children have made their first journal entry, have them continue with further entries on their own, conferring with the student experts as necessary.

The biggest problem we observed with journal writing is not how to write on the computer, but what to write. With first-graders, our expectations for their writing were modest. We had children begin each entry with the date and then write two or three sentences. The first day we had them begin by recounting the most important thing that had happened to them the night before. When a few children had trouble thinking of anything, we suggested they write something that happened to them that day in school. Through the next few journal entries, we found that children wrote without assistance from the teacher.

For many children, the writing became a "formula," for example: "Last night I went home and watched Power Rangers." To remedy this problem, we asked the teacher to suggest topics, for example: "Today, write something about yesterday's trip to the park" or "Today, try to use at least two of your spelling words in your journal entry." This seemed to work effectively. However, as you might expect, some children needed more prompting and prodding than others.

As we looked at the children's journals, we always respected their privacy by asking them for permission first. Almost without exception, the first-graders were willing to share their writing and at times were quite aggressive in doing so. One little girl hunted us down in another part of the building just to show off her journal. The pride she displayed in sharing her work is an indication of the importance of writing.

Examples of Published Projects

Sources for projects related to technology and language and literacy development abound. Journals such as *Learning and Leading with Technology* (formerly *The Computing Teacher*), *Instructor*, *The Reading Teacher*, *Reading Research Quarterly*, and *The Journal of Reading* regularly include reports of projects from professionals who have developed and implemented worthwhile projects. Books also contain descriptions of technology projects for literacy development (Knapp, 1986; Monroe, 1993; Russel, 1991; Solomon, 1986). Many of these projects can be used as presented, adapted to a specific learning environment, or used as inspiration for new projects. Making practice-oriented journals and books available to teachers is an important element in facilitating powerful instruction. We can all benefit from strategies used by good teachers in good schools. Following are two summaries of published project descriptions related to word processing.

Project 1: Life Stories   In this project (Simms & Simms, 1994), elementary school students published biographies of a senior citizen. The students were connected to their seniors through telecommunications, although the authors make the point that other means are equally effective. The children were prepared for the project by their teacher. In the process of gathering information about their senior and writing the person's biography, the students learned both technology skills and interviewing skills. They also got involved in a number of ancillary content areas, such as map reading, graphing, and library research. The final product used a variety of computer-based tools that helped the students publish professional-looking documents. The short article description ends with these statements:

> Our students and seniors met in person for the first time at a publishing party. As students present biographies to their partners, exchanging smiles and hugs, it's clear that the value of this project reaches beyond the books. "You'll never know how easy it's been for me to get up in the morning," said one senior. "This project has made me feel needed." Seniors have an equally profound effect on students; more than one has said: "I'm going to write a biography about my grandparents." (p. 51)

Project 2: Multimedia Memoirs   This article (Reissman, 1994/1995) describes a writing lesson with an inner-city sixth-grade class. The lesson was based on the book *Parallel Time* (Staples, 1994), a memoir of a youth in the inner city. The book opens with a graphic description of the author viewing the body of his younger brother, the victim of a gang shooting. The teacher read the passage to her class, in hopes that it would stimulate her students to talk about their own feelings and experiences living in a violent urban neighborhood. Instead of having them discuss the passage, "which would only have involved eight of them (about a quarter or so)," she asked them to respond using a word processor. The results were dramatic, with all but two of the students reacting to the piece. Some of the children's responses are both insightful and touching:

> That stuff about the wound and the stitches. I have an uncle who likes to pick up his shirt to show his "trophies" too. They are all thick ugly scars. My uncle thinks they show how strong he is, but I don't buy that. (p. 33)

The teacher continued the lesson with more reading and asked the students to expand their writing using the word processor or graphics tools. The students became engrossed in the activity. The initial writing lesson blossomed into a full multimedia project for which the students used a variety of tools to illustrate scenes and events in the book. The varied activities, such as video and multimedia authoring programs, encouraged additional writing. Many students wrote about their neighborhood memories and those of their close relatives. Culminating activities created completed memoirs. Reissman (1994/1995) described them as lengthy and containing different media, and concluded:

> Based on this successful introduction of memoir excerpts into the sixth grade core language arts experiences, I have decided to use other excerpts from both "adult" memoirs and those written specifically for juvenile audiences with my classes. I feel that the multimedia-supported memoir study can move its audience forward.
>
> Preteens gain greater insights into the deep meaning of common experiences and the impact of children's places and events on adult life. While middle school students may not fully grasp the affective content of memoirs, the integration of actual photos, recordings, sound effects and video do make memoirs meaningful to young students. Multimedia offers a venue for making memoirs accessible and engaging for young students who can use these productivity tools to give meaning and form to their evolving memoirs. (p 35)

Many of these students found their medium of expression somewhere in this project. Some students do not consider class discussion a safe way to express themselves. Asking students to write using a word processor allows them to open up. Often, the results are stunning.

WHOLE LANGUAGE

Whole-language approaches to language and literacy instruction focus on students' use of language in a natural context rather than in isolation. Basal reading series often teach skills, strategies, and text in isolation, decontextualized from real learning environments. Whole-language instruction closely complies with our constructivist, cognitive psychology values and beliefs about teaching and learning described in Chapter 1. Froese (1990, cited in Piper, 1993) defined whole language simply and elegantly:

> We define whole-language as a child-centered, literature-based approach to language teaching that immerses students in real communication situations whenever possible. (p. 2)

The exciting aspect of the whole-language concept is that the teaching and learning is child centered, must be literature based, and uses real communication situations.

The whole-language philosophy is not without its detractors. Any teaching method which is taught incorrectly or used only partially may not teach essential skills and strategies, is too labor intensive, and weakens students' learning. Piper (1993) warned language and literacy teachers about misuse:

When the tenets of whole language are implemented in a sensible manner, it has been a successful approach. Unfortunately, some educational malpractice also has been perpetrated in the name of whole language. Teachers or educational administrators who have not fully understood the concepts supporting whole language practice have sometimes used it as an excuse for a pedagogical *laissez-faire* which has not improved children's learning. But where whole language practice has been consonant with its definitions and principles, the result has been beneficial to children's language development in school. (p. 275)

Process Writing

Donald Graves (1983) connected language and literacy with whole-language tenets. He advocated a writing method similar to the way real authors write. His process-writing strategy is a systematic method for writers to capture their ideas and create clearly written documents. According to Graves, process writing has five basic processes:

Planning or pre-writing stimulated ideas through interaction, gathering materials from the writer or the external world, organizing ideas (what will work, text structure, personal goals). *Drafting* or composing was turning thoughts into written words, deciding what needed to be said. Drafting emphasized meaning not mechanics. *Revising* or getting perspective from yourself and others and considering new ideas helped the writer's ideas not her mechanics. The writer made changes in the text and developed new thoughts. *Editing* or rethinking was rearranging, changing, and refining the writing. The writer applied form and accepted writing conventions. The editing stage demands excellent use of children's essential skills. Finally, *publishing* made the work public and accessible to others (Graves, 1983).

Process-writing teachers advocate teaching skills and strategies as the need arises in students' natural writing. When students need to edit their writing into standard English conventions for publication, the teacher exploits the students' sense of purpose to teach the skill or strategy. For example, at the editing stage the teacher can show novice writers that sentences end with a period because it tells the reader when to stop. Teachers also can discover several common mistakes in children's writing, form an *ad hoc* group, and explicitly teach the skill. Teachers also can correct consistent writing errors (for example, split infinitives) proactively by requiring the correct use of several infinitives in the students' subsequent writing assignments.

This is a different and more sophisticated approach to teaching essential skills development than using a scope-and-sequence process which is independent or decontextualized from children's writing. In many basal reading and basal language arts series, skill development is organized in isolation from children's writing and their natural environments. To see a perfect description of this process in action, review the scope and sequence chart of any basal series. The teaching and learning begins with the notion that children can and should master certain skills at predetermined years and months. For example, students often are asked to master the meaning and use of verbs in the second or third grade. We understand that this is a developmental skill that is gained when children are ready. Also, telling time often is not connected to any real or meaningful learning situation, such as reading or writing about the chronology of a mystery story. We discourage the teaching or learning of any skill or strategy in isolation or decontextualized from children's natural learning.

Successful Word Processing Lessons

We have worked with children and word processing for many years and through our experiences, we have used a number of learning activities with varying success. Each of these activities is consistent with the whole-language philosophy and process writing. Progressive writing and the potato exercise represent a part of the process-writing strategy. These activities can be used to get children started writing with word processors, or, if your students are experienced, the activities can be used as a motivational boost for ongoing writing activities.

Progressive Writing   Progressive writing with a word processor is an activity in which a small group of children take turns writing a complete story. The teacher can give the students a story starter, for example: "I was holding that $10,000,000 winning lottery ticket, basking in my great luck, when a big wind blew it out of my hand. . . . " Or, the teacher can solicit a story starter from the participants. Students, each working at their own computer, copy the story starter and continue creating the story. After a few minutes, the students are asked to move to the next computer and continue writing until every student writes a part of every story. After writing, the students share their stories and talk about their writing processes.

We have used this activity successfully with writers from first grade through graduate school. Modifications are necessary to meet the needs of the specific writers involved. Some young writers have problems reading what another student has written. To solve that problem, we have the children write in pairs. Only one of the pair rotates to the next computer, and the child expert reads the story to the new writer. Also, young children need more time to write because it takes them longer to capture their thoughts using the keyboard. With more mature writers, this activity moves smoothly and can be used periodically as a writing boost.

Progressive writing can meet a large number of learning objectives depending on the developmental age and ability level of the writers. The most obvious objective of this lesson is to help students believe that they can write creatively. Many students have difficulty knowing what to write when asked to write creatively. This activity always motivates students' writing, and the results frequently are humorous and engaging.

This activity also can be used as a beginning step in working on specific writing skills. After the initial activity is completed, the document can be edited in a number of ways. It can be used as a punctuation exercise, wherein children examine comma placement or find opportunities to use semicolons. It can be used to work with modifiers: students can underline all the adjectives and italicize all the adverbs, or add five more adjectives and three more adverbs to strengthen the descriptive element of the text. The document also can be used for higher level writing activities designed to achieve clarity of expression or persuasion.

Progressive writing also can have learning objectives tied to the word processor. Students can use the activity to practice their keyboarding. After the document is complete, the students can format the document using specific features of the word processor including tabs, styles, and pagination.

One learning objective we always include is to help students appreciate the act of writing by having fun being excited and challenged. The choice of story starters is important for this objective. Also, reading the writing at the end of the activity is an important part of helping students enjoy the act of writing. We always have at least three or four student volunteers read their final product, and since all the writers contributed to those stories, all of them share some of their own writing. All good writing teachers participate in the activities, share, and publish their writing with their students.

Although this activity has never failed, some precautions need to be taken. If children in the group have vastly different keyboarding skills, the slow keyboarders will only get a word or two entered while the faster ones will contribute more. This is another indication of the importance of keyboard training for young writers. Another serious problem is that sometimes a writer will try to sabotage the activity by interjecting pornography, racism, sexism, or other inappropriate text into the stories. This is controlled easily by observing what the students write. Some writers are nervous about having someone watch them write, but teachers must ensure that the final products are appropriate for the writers. Large groups present another management problem. If a teacher is working with more than about seven or eight students, she will have to regroup the students into several subgroups. This involves more management of the students' rotation, but it gives everyone a chance to contribute to every group story without taking too much time. Subdividing a large group also helps the activity's pacing. Progressive writing may become tiresome after seven or eight rotations. Teachers should experiment with progressive writing with a small group to rehearse the strategy before using it with a whole class.

The Potato Exercise   The potato exercise is a writing activity to introduce and practice descriptive writing. The teacher provides a bag of potatoes and asks each writer to select one. The teacher then instructs the writers to "get to know your potato, commune with it, find its essence." After a few minutes, the students move to their computer stations and write a creative, descriptive paragraph about their potato. The students are told not to alter their potato's appearance. They cannot, for example, plunge their pen into the top and describe the pen-shaped hole. They are encouraged to use more creative descriptions. For example, "Mine is an old potato. Its skin is loose and wrinkly. It appears sad and lonely. Toward the top of my potato's head is a beret that keeps the wind from his hair."

After the paragraphs are printed, the potatoes are placed in a pile on a table. The teacher shuffles the paragraphs and gives one to each student. The students now must read the paragraphs and find the actual potato from the writer's description. Students volunteer to read the paragraph, display the selected potato, and ask if the choice was correct. This activity inevitably encourages laughter and an interesting variety of optional ideas for describing the potato. Emphasizing this aspect of the exercise is an excellent way to infuse problem solving into the writing curriculum.

IMPLICATIONS FOR THE COMMUNITY OF LEADERSHIP

Vision and Mission: Building a Culture

We believe that the community of leadership has a long-term responsibility to set the vision and mission of the school. Using an encompassing definition of leadership, we expect the participation of the internal community—administration, teachers, students, and parents—and the external community—citizens, community leaders, key communicators, business and industry representatives, and unique individuals with special knowledge.

We believe that the entire school community will set the moral minimums and the moral maximums for the school and monitor the school's course toward meeting the vision and mission. Using the philosophical, psychological, and spiritual values of the community, we believe that the participants of the school will evolve the norms, rituals, and roles: the culture of the school. In the best traditions of vision and mission, school culture, and moral leadership, the responsibility to complete this task falls to community of leadership. The most difficult activity will be when members of the community sit together, begin talking about what they value and believe, and reach consensus.

Teaching and Learning: The Daily Trust

We believe that all participants, at various times in the school year, will become leaders and doers. In our conception, the participants who have the most expertise and influence will be the roving leaders for an activity, skill, organizational plan, or staff development. The leaders with less expertise and influence in this particular set of teaching and learning will shift into the role of doer. As doers gain expertise and confidence, they also accept roving leadership by helping other doers to learn and apply skills or strategies with children. At some point during the school year, all educators can and should accept roving leadership and doership. The hierarchical leader, the principal, may be a doer in language and literacy instruction, and a novice teacher may be a leader in using trade books to enhance reading instruction. Leadership has much less to do with hierarchical power and authority than it does with expertise, influence, and the disposition to act and to accept responsibility.

Language and Literacy Instruction

The most significant responsibility of the community of leadership is to guide, facilitate, and model appropriate learning strategies for teachers and children. Leaders must be excellent teachers capable of demonstrating strategies to the best faculty in the teacher's classroom with her students. The task of the community of leadership in language and literacy education and technology is to explicitly teach the definition, characteristics, strategies, and assessment of these approaches and to model expert practice.

Formal and roving members of the community of leadership must become responsible for modeling and mentoring teachers and students. For example, essential skill development may be an expertise of a roving leader. She may assist teachers who are struggling with teaching essential skills, or she may tutor students who need help developing essential skills. Her task may involve demonstrating to teachers the limited utility of drill-and-practice strategies. She may suggest strategies relating to the student's real experiences, using trade or library books and basing instruction on developmental issues instead of scope-and-sequence chart demands. Finally, the leaders must create formal and informal assessments that measure the student's dispositions: what the student has learned and how she uses that learning.

For a community of leadership which is beginning or struggling with technology integration, we believe that leaders must encourage children's writing. Training teachers and students to do elemental word processing activities is relatively simple. (This is discussed further in Chapter 10.) The community of leadership should model simple writing activities for teachers. Teachers only need to learn the computer functions; they should already know the writing strategies.

Of all the options, we find daily journal writing to be the most engaging starting point. Individual children with minimal expertise can train other students with only the minor involvement of the teacher. The adults can concentrate on solving more complicated technical problems and, more importantly, facilitating children's writing. Even in classrooms with only one or two computers, students can write journal entries throughout the day. The one computer that often sits idle can now become a powerful tool. Buoyed by their success with journal writing, teachers and students can progress to creative and expository writing using journals as a starting point. The leadership must help teachers to "jump in the deep end." Journal writing, supported and modeled by leadership, can be an exciting and inviting beginning.

DePree (1989) reminds the community of leadership that "the first responsibility of a leader is to define reality" (p. 11). Reality in language and literacy instruction is connecting excellent instructional strategies and instructional technology. DePree also reminds us of the community of leadership's final responsibility: "The last is to say thank you. In between the two, the leader must become a servant" (p. 11).

REFERENCES

Bangert-Drowns, R. L. (1993). The word processor as an instructional tool: A meta-analysis of word processing in writing instruction. *Review of Educational Research, 63*(1), 69–93.

Burns, M. (1995). Writing in math class? Absolutely. *Instructor, 104*(7), 40–47.

Cochran-Smith, M., Paris, C. L., & Kahn, J. L. (1991). *Learning to write differently*. Norwood, NJ: Ablex.

DePree, M. (1989). *Leadership is an art*. New York: Dell.

Froese, J. C. (Ed.). (1990). *Whole-language practice and theory*. Scarborough, Ontario: Prentice-Hall Canada.

Graves, D. (1983). Writing: Teachers and children at work. Portsmouth, NH: Heinemann.

Hawisher, G. E. (1989). Research and recommendations for computers and composition. In G. E. Hawisher & C. L. Selfe (Eds.), *Critical perspectives on computers and composition instruction* (pp. 44–69). New York: Teachers College Press.

Herrmann, A. W. (1990). Computers and writing research: Shifting our "governing gaze." In D. H. Holdstein & C. L. Selfe (Eds.), *Computers and writing theory, research, practice*. New York: Modern Language Association.

Knapp, L. R. (1986). *The word processor and the writing teacher*. Upper Saddle River, NJ: Prentice-Hall.

Krajewski, R. (1983). A writer's guide to word processing software. *Writer's Digest, 63*(9), 54.

Langone, J., Willis, C., Malone, M., Clees, T., & Koorland, M. (1994). Effects of computer-based word processing versus paper/pencil activities on the paragraph construction of elementary students with learning disabilities. *Journal of Research on Computing in Education, 27*(2), 171–183.

Latamore, G. B. (1983). A fluid well for your words. *Personal Computing, 7*, 106.

Monroe, R. (1993). *Writing and thinking with computers*. Urbana, IL: National Council of Teachers of English.

Piper, T. (1993). *Language for all our children*. Upper Saddle River, NJ: Merrill/Prentice Hall.

Reissman, R. (1994/1995). Multimedia memoirs. *The Computing Teacher, 22*(4), 33–35.

Russel, R. G. (1991). *A meta-analysis of word processing and attitudes and the impact on the quality of writing*. Paper presented at the Annual Meeting of the American Educational Research Association, Chicago.

Samuels, S. J. (1988). Decoding and automaticity: Helping poor readers become automatic at word recognition. *Reading Teacher, 41*, 756–760.

Simms, J., & Simms, B. (1994). Life stories. *Instructor, 104*(4), 50–51.

Snyder, I. (1993). Writing with word processors: A research overview. *Educational Research, 23*(1), 49–68.

Snyder, I. (1994). Writing with word processors: The computer's influence on the classroom context. *Journal of Curriculum Studies, 26*(2), 143–162.

Solomon, G. (1986). *Children, writing and computers: An activity guide*. Upper Saddle River, NJ: Prentice-Hall.

Staples, B. (1994). *Parallel time*. New York: Bantam.

Thompson, V., & Montgomery, L. (1994). Promises, problems, and possibilities: Reading and writing with technology. *The Computing Teacher, 22*(3), 6–8.

RESOURCE LIST

Adobe PageMaker, Adobe

Cultural Reporter, Tom Snyder Productions

In the Holy Land, ABC News Interactive

Literature for Mastery Series, Bradford Publishing

Living Books, Bröderbund

Powers of the Supreme Court, ABC News Interactive

Quark XPress, Quark Inc.

Rain Forest, National Geographic Society

Reader Rabbit, The Learning Company

Storybook Weaver, MECC

The Human Body, National Geographic Society

The Writing Center, The Learning Company

Word Munchers, MECC

Writer's Workbench, EMO

CHAPTER 5

Mathematics and Technology

The underlying assumption of the software application chapters remains technology's use as a support to a quality academic program. Additionally, many software applications, notably integrated programs containing word processing, spreadsheet, data base, graphics, and telecommunications applications, assist students to construct their knowledge through the process of collecting data, converting data into information, and applying information into knowledge. Spreadsheet applications are the quintessential program for changing data into information. The numerical and graphical capabilities inherent in spreadsheets help learners apply instructional strategies to complete the art of turning data into information and information into knowledge.

This chapter presents several mathematics-related applications, including drill-and-practice programs, tutorials, and simulations. We present the terms and definitions and model the use of spreadsheets. We suggest several lessons for leaders to model in classrooms, and offer several ways to sharpen spreadsheet skills. Finally, we discuss how the community of leadership can improve teaching and learning through the use of spreadsheets to support a quality mathematics computation and concepts curriculum.

INTRODUCTION

The public seems to have enormous concern for children's mathematics ability. School reform is driven by concerns about students' declining SAT scores and lack of essential skills. The concerns of many critics of our educational system often are exaggerated and misdirected. However, we cannot deny the importance of children's competence in mathematics. All of our schools can improve in this area.

We will improve children's math skills only by improving mathematics instruction. Two ways we can achieve this are by using better teaching materials and by improving the way we organize children to learn. Technology can play a central role in both these instructional strategies.

Mathematics-Related Software

A number of software programs that support the development of mathematics' knowledge and skills are available. There are drill-and-practice programs that help students gain automaticity (Samuels, 1988) with basic mathematics facts. There are tutorial programs that help students develop knowledge and understanding of mathematical principles. Tutorials also include tool applications with features such as graph construction and statistical output. In addition, many simulation programs, such as *Lemonade Stand*, have an underlying mathematical structure. Much of what happens in simulations is controlled by algebraic formulae. By concentrating on the mathematical elements of simulations, we can support children's development of mathematics knowledge and skills.

Many standard software tools—word processing, spreadsheets, and data bases—also can help students develop mathematics knowledge and skills.

The spreadsheet is a mathematics tool that has enjoyed wide acceptance in the business world. We believe that the spreadsheet is the most underutilized software tool in schools. In this chapter we explore how spreadsheets can help educators build students' computation and conceptual knowledge.

Mathematics Drill-and-Practice Programs

A common program found in schools is the arithmetic drill-and-practice program. *Number Munchers* and *MathBlaster* comprise a major share of this market, although many other popular titles are available. Most mathematics drill-and-practice programs use a game format and are quite popular with children. There are drills that are appropriate for all grade levels, from pre-K *(Millie's Math House)* through secondary school *(Alge-Blaster)*.

Although these programs can enrich the teaching and learning environment and help children learn necessary skills, we believe mathematics drill-and-practice programs often are misused in today's schools. The main problem is that the children who need practice with a particular skill—that is, children with automaticity problems—are not the children who typically spend time playing these games. Teachers frequently use mathematics drill-and-practice programs as a reward for fast workers ("Those who finish their ditto sheet early can go to the back of the room and play XYZ mathematics game") or as a substitute for recess ("Since it is raining and you can't go outdoors, you can play computer games"). These approaches do not help the children who need help the most. The speediest children have already mastered their mathematics facts. The children who choose to play a mathematics game at recess are seldom the children who need the extra practice.

Nevertheless, mathematics drill-and-practice programs are not inherently bad. They can be a positive element of the teaching and learning environment if used appropriately. First, we must make sure that students who need the practice are the students who use the applications. Second, we need to make decisions about the effective use of teacher and student time. Since most drill-and-practice programs use a game format, the children spend part of the time playing a game and part of the time practicing mathematics skills. The purpose of game element is to maintain student motivation, but it takes time away from skill development. We need to increase the quality of the motivation for individual children.

For example, in *Turbo Math Facts,* the reward for success is a car race. Not all children will find the car race rewarding or stimulating, and thus will lose the motivational boost. *MathBlaster* uses a "shoot 'em up" theme. The teacher may believe that students spend too much time "blasting" and not enough time "mathing." If we make good decisions about who needs practice, if we make good decisions about which programs to use in our classrooms, and if we make good matches between our students and the available programs, then mathematics drill-and-practice applications will enrich the teaching and learning environment.

Mathematics Tutorials

Most mathematics tutorials also include a drill-and-practice component, so the distinction between the two programs often is blurred. Tutorials include the means for students to learn new skills and develop automaticity with existing skills. Like the drill-and-practice programs, tutorials are available for all age groups, from programs such as *Coin Critters* (grades K–6), to *What Do You Do with a Broken Calculator?* (grades 4–8), to *The Geometric SuperSupposer* (grades 8–12). A teacher can organize children to learn in several ways: in whole groups, using a large-screen display, in small groups, or individually. The tutorials' primary advantages are to pace students through the learning and to offer appropriate practice time.

Most tutorials focus on one specific mathematics' area, and each has limited use during the school year. For example, you would use *Clock Shop* only while you are working on telling time. Therefore, if a teacher, department, or grade level is going to use mathematics tutorials, then schools will need to make a variety of programs available to students.

Software publishers are producing a small number of multimedia tutorials, including ABC News' *Wide World of Mathematics*. These are powerful pieces of software, but they are expensive. These programs often include a significant amount of video and audio information. The high level of realism not only adds a strong motivational boost but also adds context to the mathematics concepts, thus aiding learning. When this software becomes more available and more economical, it will be more practical for the classroom.

Simulations

We generally think of simulations as being for disciplines other than mathematics. Several simulations which are available for science *(SimEarth* and *G-Netix)* and social studies *(SimCity* and *Oregon Trail)* also have connection to mathematics. In *Oregon Trail,* for example, students begin with a certain amount of money and must manage that money, as well as their bullets and their food, throughout their travels.

Beyond the obvious mathematics involved in simulations, many programs have underlying formulae that control the simulations. In *SimCity,* for example, all the student's money comes from taxes. The student can set the tax rate, but that rate and other variables affect the number of people who can move into the city. Population dynamics is a complex formula. Students might investigate the factors in the formula that determine the city's population. They also might determine the relationships between these variables. These activities not only help students understand the functioning of cities but also give them context-rich mathematics' principles to manipulate. A sample screen from *SimCity* is shown in Figure 5–1.

As students work with simulations, their mathematics abilities can benefit in two ways. Mathematics frequently are involved in the simulation, such as the amount of money available for supplies in *Oregon Trail*. This gives students more practice working with numbers in a context-rich environment. Individual simulation experiences are controlled by mathematical formulae. *SimEarth* determines

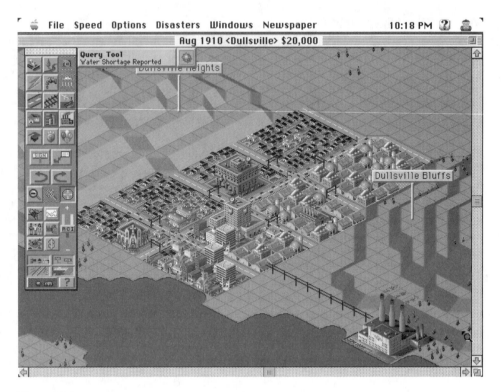

Figure 5–1

Sample Screen from *SimCity*

the ground temperature using the interaction between the ratio of atmospheric gasses, the dust in the air, and the distance from the sun. Understanding these formulae and their relationships is an engaging and meaningful way for students to interact with mathematics. Understanding involves not just mathematics skill, but also mathematical principles. The following story illustrates the power of this activity:

> At an educational technology conference, a teacher was presenting a project that involved the use of *SimCity*. She had two of her middle school students with her, and they were demonstrating the program for people who passed the display. I chatted with one of the children, and after a few minutes I decided to ask him what interested me: "So, do you know how to cheat it?" He knew immediately what I was talking about and became more animated. As one avid game player to another, we launched into a rapid-fire discussion of how to get extra money and what to do with it. We were talking in the shorthand language of content-area colleagues.

This story is a perfect example of our theme of converting data into information and information into knowledge. The student started with all the data the program contained. Then he organized it into information that had meaning for him. After that, he began to get involved, to care about it. He wanted to control it, to win it, to beat it. At that point, all the information he had created from the game became knowledge, because he was using it to achieve his desired outcome.

"Cheating" a simulation simply means understanding the underlying mathematical relationships and finding the holes in the simulation's logic. This is an activity that many children revel in, but to do it, they must have an understanding of the underlying mathematical relationships. This activity combines rich context with strong motivation. It is a powerful learning environment.

Tools

The few tools that are specifically available for use in mathematics—graph construction and statistical programs—have a strong basis in mathematics. Tools that include mathematics-related concepts are morphing software—software that incrementally changes one graphic image to another—and tessellation software—software that creates large patterns from small tiles. The most useful tools seem to be those that either allow students to visualize mathematical principles or perform mathematics-related operations. Another benefit tools have is that they ground students in the real world by adding context to mathematics learning.

Graphing programs are designed for all ages and for a variety of purposes. Some are designed specifically for use in the mathematics curriculum, and others can be adapted for mathematics. Programs used in business *(Harvard Graphics* and *Delta Graph)* and programs designed specifically for upper grades *(Graph Wiz* and *Zap-A-Graph)* are appropriate for older students. Several graphing programs are designed specifically for younger children *(The Graph Club* and *GraphPower)*. In addition, a number of tutorial programs have graphics elements that students can use as tools to actively manipulate numerical concepts graphically *(Mastering Calculus, Building Perspective,* and *Mathematics Shop)*. Graphics tools are important for developing mathematical concepts because of their ability to engage children and get them interacting with mathematical concepts. In addition, this activity may fit better with some children's ability to learn in visual modalities rather than through symbolic approaches.

Also available are several statistics-oriented programs that span the entire K–12 range. Some programs are designed specifically to help younger children develop mathematical concepts and skills *(Probability Toolkit)*. Other programs are designed to teach older children mathematics concepts *(Statistics Workshop* and *Taking Chances)*. Statistical programs which are commonly used by adults *(JMP* and *StatView)* can be used by older students to put their math skills into practice; in other words, they can use statistics programs to help them turn mathematics data into information and information into knowledge.

The spreadsheet is a mathematics tool relied upon in the working world. It is also a potentially powerful learning tool for children. We believe this tool is essential to developing children's mathematics knowledge and skills.

WHAT IS A SPREADSHEET?

Spreadsheets derive from the financial industry. A spreadsheet is, in essence, an electronic ledger (see Figure 5–2). An analogy that may help make the purpose of a spreadsheet clear is a comparison of spreadsheets to word processing. A spreadsheet is to numbers what a word processor is to words. A word processor helps people manipulate words and a spreadsheet helps people manipulate numbers. Taking this analogy further, a word processor offers little help with ideas. The writer must generate the ideas, choose the appropriate words, and decide how to organize those words. The word processor only helps with the construction and organization of words.

A spreadsheet is the equivalent application using numbers. The learner must know what the numbers are and how they interrelate. The spreadsheet only helps with the expression of those numbers and their relationships. Using budgeting as an example, the learner must know which categories she needs and how much money she plans to spend. She also must know the information she wants from each category. The spreadsheet helps organize the numbers and calculate the information according to the user's instructions.

A few years ago, people who worked with large numbers would not consider doing their work without a calculator. Today, those same people would not consider doing their work without a spreadsheet. In comparison, the mathematics curriculum has been slow to adopt electronic tools. Recently, the use of calculators in school was a topic of heated debate. Today, most mathematics educators accept the calculator as a tool and expect students to master its use. It is now time to take the next step and accept more powerful mathematics tools in the classroom. The spreadsheet is that next step.

	A	B	C	D	E
1			Personal Budget		
2		Jan	Feb	Mar	Q1 total
3	Rent	$350	$350	$350	$1,050
4	Gas	$150	$150	$100	$400
5	Elec.	$75	$75	$70	$220
6	Tele.	$150	$75	$75	$300
7	Food	$100	$150	$150	$400
8					
9	Total	$825	$800	$745	

Figure 5–2

Example of Part of a Personal Budget Spreadsheet

Spreadsheet Terms

The world of spreadsheets has its own vocabulary. Mastery of the jargon makes it easier to read and talk about spreadsheets. The community of leadership must master these terms and use them correctly to be a positive model for teachers. Similarly, if teachers model these terms correctly, the students will adopt that behavior.

Spreadsheet Definitions

We use the terms *column* and *row* to refer to the vertical and horizontal directions on the spreadsheet. The name of a column is usually a letter. The first column is called A, the second B, and so on up to Z. After Z, most spreadsheets start over with AA, AB, AC . . . AZ, then BA, BB, BC . . . BZ, then CA, CB, CC, . . . CZ, on so on up to the maximum number of columns, usually hundreds. The name of a row is usually a number. The first row in a spreadsheet is number 1, the second row is number 2, and so on up to the maximum number of rows, usually thousands.

The intersection of a row and column forms a *cell*. A cell is named first by its column letter and then its row number. For example, the name of the cell formed by the intersection of column B and row 7 is B7. You can think of the cell as the basic unit of a spreadsheet just as you think of a cell in biology as basic unit of life. A cell can contain one of four types of entries: a label, a value, a formula, or a function.

A *label* is any information that is not a number. Users often name row or column headers; examples are "Total," "August" and "Year To Date."

A *value* is a number. Values are used for data such as the cost of a single item, a score on a single test, or a frequency of a single variable.

A *formula* is usually a calculation involving values or numbers from the spreadsheet. For example, in a grading spreadsheet, a teacher may have values representing each graded item and a formula that totals all the grades. Formulae are the power of the spreadsheet.

A *function* is a built-in formula. All spreadsheets have many basic functions, such as summing and averaging. Examples of other functions include trigonometric functions such as sine and cosine, and financial functions that calculate loan payments or compute the value of annuities.

The following is a description of the spreadsheet shown in Figure 5–3. Notice how the spreadsheet terms are used.

In this grading spreadsheet, the students' names are entered in rows and the grades are in columns. Column A and rows 1 and 2 contain only labels. Cells B3 through F9 contain the values that represent the grades. Column G contains the total of the students' scores; this total was calculated using the sum function. Column H contains the students' average; this was calculated using the averaging function. Column I contains the students' percentage, calculated using a percentage formula. Row 11 contains the class average for each graded item.

	A	B	C	D	E	F	G	H	I
				Science Grades					
1									
2	Name	Quiz 1	Assgn 1	Quiz 2	Assgn 2	Test 1	Total	Average	Percent
3	Points Possible	50	100	50	100	100	400		
4	Judy Adams	45	80	48	88	67	328	65.6	82.0%
5	John Jones	31	95	36	100	75	337	67.4	84.3%
6	Alan Meyer	48	85	49	76	99	357	71.4	89.3%
7	Sharon Smith	50	97	50	96	100	393	78.6	98.3%
8	Cindy Stone	42	88	42	86	87	345	69.0	86.3%
9	Jack Taylor	0	45	49	100	99	293	58.6	73.3%
10									
11	Class Average	36.0	81.7	45.7	91.0	87.8			

Figure 5–3

Sample Grading Spreadsheet

The General Operation of a Spreadsheet

The operation of a spreadsheet at first may seem rather complicated because you are entering data in two places on the screen simultaneously. Notice the dark line around cell A4 in Figure 5–4. That dark line is the cell pointer. If you want to enter data in a cell, then you must first locate the cell pointer. When you type the data, it will appear in the command center at the top of the screen. Once you have finished typing the data, press enter and the information in the command center is transferred to the cell indicated by the cell pointer.

File   Edit   Formula   Format   Data   Options   Macro   Window

A4 | Bridge to Terabithia, The

Class Book Review Summary

	A	B	C	D	E	F
1	Book Title	Quality	Development	Clarity of	Quality	Total
2		of Plot	of Characters	Writing	of Writing	
3						
4	Bridge to Terabithia, The	10	10	10	10	40
5	Cay, The	10	10	10	10	40
6	Giver, The	9	9	10	10	38
7	Julie of the Wolves	8	9	9	10	36
8	One-eyed Cat	7	9	10	9	35
9	Pink and Say	10	8	10	9	37
10	Silver Chair, The	7	7	8	9	31
11	Wind in the Willows, The	8	7	9	10	34

Figure 5–4

Spreadsheet Showing the Command Center

A spreadsheet is large, so you only can view a portion at one time. You can view different parts of the spreadsheet by shifting the viewing window. There are several ways to shift the window. If you move the cell pointer past the last column on the screen using the tab key, then the window will automatically shift to show that column. Most spreadsheets also provide scroll bars for moving the window. Figure 5–4 shows the scroll bar at the right for shifting the window up and down and the scroll bar at the bottom for shifting the window left and right. We always suggest that you consult the software publisher's manual or a third-party instruction book for specific instructions for your particular spreadsheet.

To change data in a spreadsheet, move the cell pointer to the data you want to change; the existing data in that cell will be shown in the command center. Change the data in the command center and press enter, and the software will transfer those changes to the cell automatically.

Learning a spreadsheet requires mastering a few commands, formulae, and patterns. A schema-based approach (see Chapter 1) suggests that the user begin with a simple, one-operation application, such as a small budget, to learn new skills that apply to real-world spreadsheet applications.

The Power of the Spreadsheet

Our primary purpose in using spreadsheets in classrooms is to help students become interactive with authentic mathematical challenges. Spreadsheets offer many opportunities to enhance the authenticity of mathematics for our students. Spreadsheets also offer significant advantages to the design of instruction at all grade levels. Using a spreadsheet, we can predefine mathematical relationships by loading formulae into the spreadsheet, and then have students enter their data and interact with those relationships. The students can change the individual numbers and instantly see the effect of those changes. If they change any individual value— for example, the score on a test—all calculations that use that value also change. When students use the spreadsheet in this way, they quickly can see the exact mathematical results of the situation they are manipulating.

If the teacher has predefined multiple and complex mathematical relationships, then students can see high-level results of small manipulations of individual numbers. "What if" analysis is experimentation or "playing around" with the numbers. A spreadsheet is essential for students to do "what if" analyses.

In more specific terms, we want students to use spreadsheets in two situations. The most obvious is when they need to manipulate numbers. Examples include budgets, science lab experiments, grading, and estimation exercises (see Lesson 1 in the "Spreadsheet Lessons" section later in this chapter). A less obvious use of spreadsheets is to put information into rows and columns. Since the tool uses that format for data, it is useful for those situations when data is not numerical, but the teacher wants to represent it as a table or a matrix (see Figure 5–5). This operation is helpful for visual learners.

Figures 5–6, 5–7, and 5–8 show three views of spreadsheets that students might use in a physics laboratory. Figure 5–6 shows the spreadsheet with the for-

	A	B	C	D	E	F	G	H
1			State's Major Mineral Occurrences					
2								
3		Bauxite	Coal	Copper	Gold	Iron	Limestone	Silver
4	Alabama	Yes	Yes	No	No	Yes	Yes	No
5	Alaska	No	Yes	No	Yes	Yes	No	No
6	Arizona	No	No	Yes	Yes	No	No	Yes
7	Arkansas	Yes	Yes	No	No	No	No	No
8	California	No	No	Yes	Yes	Yes	No	Yes
9	Colorado	No	Yes	Yes	Yes	Yes	No	Yes

Figure 5–5

A Spreadsheet Used to Keep Track of State Minerals

mulae printed in the cells instead of the numbers. The option of displaying either the formulae or the resulting numbers is a built-in feature of most spreadsheets. Figure 5–7 shows the same spreadsheet after the student has filled in the values. The spreadsheet automatically calculates the formulae as the student enters the numbers. Figure 5–8 shows the spreadsheet after the student has entered new values. Notice that the spreadsheet automatically calculates the new values.

The Bells and Whistles

All spreadsheets allow you to change the format of the numbers. For example, you can round decimal places, show numbers as money, and make percentages easier to read. This option may seem like a frill, but it is important for understanding the information. For example, the meaning of the number 3214562 is different from $3,214,562. The first number is ambiguous and difficult to read; the second number is clearly three million two hundred fourteen thousand five hundred sixty-two dollars. Some students may have difficulty comprehending .97865, but 98% is clear.

Most spreadsheets include additional features. The most common are automatic chart and graph creation. The user can convert numbers in the spreadsheet into charts (see Figure 5–9). The chart feature has many curricular and interdisciplinary applications and is another way to convert data into information and information into knowledge.

The "hot spreadsheet" is another feature becoming popular in various integrated programs (see Chapter 3). Spreadsheet users often export and cut-and-paste the results into a word processing document. For example, a student might use a spreadsheet in a science experiment to perform various calculations, and then transfer the results of those calculations to a laboratory report that she wrote on a word processor. Without hot spreadsheets, if the student changed the values in the spreadsheet, she also would have to change the values in the word processing document. With a hot spreadsheet, a change in the spreadsheet would change the data in the word processing document automatically. This is a very useful feature, and a good example of how computer applications are getting "smarter" and "friendlier."

Figure 5–6

A Science Lab Spreadsheet
Showing Formulae

	A	B
1	**Specific Heat of a Metal**	
2	Mineral	
3	Mass of Water (g)	
4	Beginning temperature (C)	
5	Ending temperature (C)	
6	Change in temperature	=B5-B4
7	Specific heat of water (Cal/g x C)	1
8		
9	Heat gained by water (Cal)	=B3*B6*B7
10		
11	Mass of metal (g)	
12	Beginning temperature (C)	100
13	Ending temperature (C)	=B5
14	Change in temperature	=B12-B13
15		
16	Specific heat of metal	=B9/(B11*B14)

Figure 5–7

The Same Spreadsheet Filled
with Values

	A	B
1	**Specific Heat of a Metal**	
2	Mineral	Silver
3	Mass of Water (g)	300
4	Beginning temperature (C)	22
5	Ending temperature (C)	27
6	Change in temperature	5
7	Specific heat of water (Cal/g x C)	1
8		
9	Heat gained by water (Cal)	1500
10		
11	Mass of metal (g)	387
12	Beginning temperature (C)	100
13	Ending temperature (C)	27
14	Change in temperature	73
15		
16	Specific heat of metal	0.053095

Figure 5–8

The Same Spreadsheet with Values Changed

	A	B
1	**Specific Heat of a Metal**	
2	Mineral	Copper
3	Mass of Water (g)	300
4	Beginning temperature (C)	23
5	Ending temperature (C)	27
6	Change in temperature	4
7	Specific heat of water (Cal/g x C)	1
8		
9	Heat gained by water (Cal)	1200
10		
11	Mass of metal (g)	182
12	Beginning temperature (C)	100
13	Ending temperature (C)	27
14	Change in temperature	73
15		
16	Specific heat of metal	0.090321

Most spreadsheets include a feature called macros. Macros are small programs that reduce several actions to a few simple keystrokes. Macros are particularly useful for repetitive tasks. Teachers can use macros to simplify the use of spreadsheets for students, or to create spreadsheet tutorials that illustrate for students the various features of the spreadsheet and strategies for interaction.

An example of the use of a macro involves simplifying a laborious task. The teacher might have a spreadsheet that she wants students to fill with sample numbers. Once they have done that, she might ask them to clear the numbers and enter a different set of values. The process of clearing the values without disturbing the formulae can be a tedious chore. The teacher can create a macro that allows students to clear the values automatically. Another use of macros in classrooms involves creating examples. Since a macro performs a series of simple keystrokes, a teacher might devise a series of "help macros." Each macro could perform a series of spreadsheet operations that model the operations the teacher wants the student to do.

SPREADSHEETS IN THE CLASSROOM

Although the spreadsheet has enjoyed wide acceptance in our society, few teachers have embraced it for classroom use. This may be because teachers see spreadsheets as complex and requiring significant mathematical ability. On the contrary, kindergarten children can use the spreadsheet effectively. The teacher can establish the mathematical relationships (construct the formulae) before instruction and have

Figure 5–9

Creating Charts from Spreadsheets

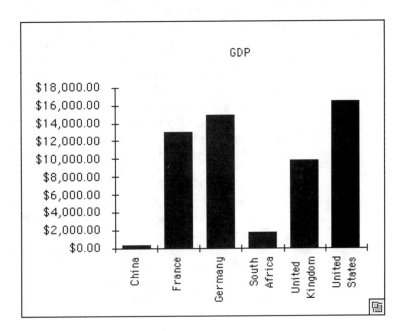

	A	B
1	**1986/1987/1988 Per Capita**	
2	**Gross Domestic Product**	
3	Country	GDP
4	China	$280.00
5	France	$13,020.00
6	Germany	$14,890.00
7	South Africa	$1,700.00
8	United Kingdom	$9,800.00
9	United States	$16,444.00

the children enter their data into the preloaded formulae. In this way, children do not have to deal with the mathematics, but can concentrate exclusively on the concepts. (See Lesson 1 in the "Spreadsheet Lessons" section later in this chapter.) Thus, by using a spreadsheet, the teacher can involve students interacting with ideas that are beyond their computational ability but not beyond their conceptual ability. As children mature and master more mathematical concepts and develop greater mathematical skills, teachers can add the mathematics to the spreadsheet in developmentally appropriate ways. As their mathematical ability develops, children can design progressively more sophisticated spreadsheet applications.

Teachers can organize the use of spreadsheets throughout the grade levels and curricula. Spreadsheets can be introduced in kindergarten and at the beginning of first grade as a way to organize data. Children can see data organized and can have limited computational interaction with the spreadsheet. This will familiarize young children with the basic entry functions of the spreadsheet and will help them see the transition of data into information.

In early elementary school, as students begin to develop an understanding of numbers and simple mathematical manipulations, they can begin using teacher-designed spreadsheets. The teacher should draw activities directly from the existing curriculum, rather than design lessons specifically to learn about spreadsheets. This will encourage students' understanding of the usefulness of the tool while teaching curricular concepts.

As students' mathematical abilities improve, the teacher should shift the design of spreadsheet applications to students. For example, in upper elementary school science classes, the teacher may design the first "lab report" spreadsheet and then ask students to design their own format for subsequent lab reports.

As students master the elements of spreadsheets, the teacher can introduce new features. By middle school, teachers can expect students to design spreadsheets that are easy to read and understand and to create charts and graphs from specific information. High school students can learn to perform complex functions using macros and to develop interactions among multiple documents. If students begin working with spreadsheets early and add to their skills incrementally throughout the grade levels, teachers can expect high school graduates to have the skills to complete sophisticated problem-solving tasks.

It is easy to imagine the use of spreadsheets in the mathematics and science curriculum. However, we should not limit their use to those curricular areas. Just as we stress the importance of having children read, write, and speak about mathematics, we should also stress a similar connection with other content areas. Subjects such as language arts and social studies often have underlying mathematical relationships. If students use spreadsheets in these content areas, then their concept knowledge should improve.

If we draw a parallel between spreadsheets and word processing, we might predict the increased use of spreadsheets in the curriculum. Remember the analogy: The spreadsheet is to numbers what the word processor is to words.

Spreadsheet Lessons

Following are lesson ideas that use spreadsheets. We present these lessons to illustrate some of the ideas described in this chapter, and to help school leaders begin to think in concrete terms about how they might use this powerful tool to improve children's learning.

LESSON IDEA 1:   Population Estimation for Primary Students

Begin the lesson by establishing the concept of population estimation using local events. For example, a large population of ducks lives in Indianapolis. Periodically, stories appear in the newspaper and on newscasts about the number of ducks that live in or pass through the city. We can use these stories to initiate a discussion about population estimation. The ultimate question is, "How do we know that there are 15,000 ducks living in the city?"

After a guided discussion about the local events, reading a story, and a writing activity, we take the students to the school yard and ask them to observe a specific parcel of grass. We ask them to guess the number of blades of grass in that area. The students write down their estimates. Next, we ask them to talk about how we might make our guesses better. The teacher guides this discussion toward methods of sampling, concluding with a clear description of the technique of sampling. Students then try sampling:

One group of students, working in pairs, is given index cards containing a one-square-inch hole. Two pairs of students are given a yardstick. The students with index cards throw their card onto the grass, count the number of blades of grass that appear in the one-square-inch hole, and write the number of blades on their card. The students with the yardsticks measure the plot of grass: One pair of students counts the number of yards the field is long, and a second pair of students counts the number of yards the field is wide. With all this information recorded, the students return to the classroom and enter their values into a spreadsheet. The teacher has the spreadsheet formatted to average the number of blades of grass per square inch, and to calculate the number of square inches in the school yard. As the students enter their information, the spreadsheet automatically calculates the total number of blades of grass in the school yard. The students publish the result by posting a temporary sign on the plot of grass, informing the community about their estimations.

Most first-grade students possess the mathematics skill needed to perform this lesson: the ability to count. The concepts are much more sophisticated, but are well within the children's capabilities.

LESSON IDEA 2: Make Your Own "Places Rated Almanac"

This lesson idea is appropriate for students from the upper elementary grades through high school. The content applies to mathematics, geography, language arts/English, sociology, and psychology. We believe in interdisciplinary teaching, and this is an example for a team of teachers.

In an interesting book called *The Places Rated Almanac,* Savageau and Boyer (1993) rate over 300 metropolitan areas in ten major categories: cost of living, jobs, housing, transportation, education, health care, crime, the arts, recreation, and climate. The authors assign the categories specific indicators or values and report each indicator as a number. For example, they count the number of golf courses, movie theaters, and fine restaurants in a city and use these figures to calculate a portion the city's score in the "recreation" category. Cities get additional points for special recreational activities such as zoos, theme parks, professional sports teams, and horse tracks. These factors are weighed and totalled to establish a city's overall recreation score. A similar process is used for each of the other categories, and the city is rated using the total scores in all ten categories. The reader can use the total score and the ten category scores to make comparisons among cities.

In the lesson, the students first are given an opportunity to examine the book. With guidance, they can see how the authors rate a city according to a collection of numbers.

Afterwards, the students "brainstorm" to arrive at a list of cities that they are familiar with and would like to compare. Once a list of cities is compiled, the students brainstorm to arrive at categories they believe are important about a city. Next, students define specific indicators within each category and make decisions about the relative weight of each indicator. This involves answering questions like, "Does a bowling alley count the same as a movie theater?" and "Does a theme park count the same as a golf course?" Once these decisions are made, the students can develop a spreadsheet. Older students who are familiar with spreadsheet design can create one themselves. For students who are less skilled with spreadsheets, the teacher can either design the format or help the students design one. A single spreadsheet application is needed to compare cities.

A teacher can use two approaches to entering data into the spreadsheet. The teacher can control the students' access to data; for example, the teacher can use the indicators that Savageau and Boyer used in *The Places Rated Almanac*. Or, the teacher can include variables related to data gathering: Groups of students (we prefer pairs) can pick a city or group of cities to research, collect all the data about their city(ies), and enter it into the spreadsheet. At this point they begin their analysis of their work—turning information into knowledge. The spreadsheet will calculate the total for each city and show the results of all the students' decisions.

Once students see the spreadsheet results, they can evaluate their decisions. Does their ranking of the cities seem to fit with what they know about those cities? Does the compilation of the numbers give them any new insight into the cities? Should they adjust some of their weighting factors? Several avenues of analysis are open for exploration. The use of the spreadsheet makes these manipulations possible. The students can do various "what if" analyses to manipulate different categories and different weighting factors.

For younger students with weaker schema or little prior knowledge about cities, the teacher can use a different theme: teachers' classrooms, the local neighborhood, or large stores. The process will be the same and will encourage the same problem-solving strategies and spreadsheet activities.

Follow-up activities for this lesson might include several writing projects. Students can publish their findings in the school newspaper, write a narrative description of their numerical findings, or write travel brochures based on their findings.

LESSON IDEA 3: Creating a Star System

This lesson idea can be used with a students from early elementary grades through high school. The main difference will be in the sophistication of the outcomes.

Our society uses a numerical system to rate many different categories: five-star restaurants, two-thumbs-up movie reviews, and top-ten books and songs. With guidance, children can select a category from their own lives and develop their own rating system for it. Questions the students must consider include:

1. How will the whole category be broken into component parts?
2. How will the individual scores be assigned?
3. What is the relative importance (weight) of each component?
4. How will the final ratings be reported?

	A	B	C	D	E	F
			Movie Ratings			
1						
2	* Rate each category using a number from 1 to 10					
3	Weighting Factors	50%	15%	15%	20%	
4						
5				Special	Acting or	Stars
6	Title	Story	Characters	effects	Animation	(1 to 5)
7	The Lion King	9	10	5	10	4.5
8	Angels in the Outfield	8	9	7	8	4
9	Power Rangers Movie	7	6	9	4	3.5
10	Indian in the Cupboard	10	8	9	9	4.5

Figure 5–10

Sample Movie Rating Spreadsheet

As students work with these ideas, the mathematics involved can easily overwhelm their ideas. This situation screams, "Use a spreadsheet!" In this lesson, the spreadsheet becomes a tool to convert data into information and information into knowledge. As the students talk about categories, they can enter them into spreadsheet along with data. They can estimate the relationships and adjust them to the situation and to their aesthetic taste.

Once they have made all the decisions and the spreadsheet is created, students can use the spreadsheet on an ongoing basis. The results can be published in the school, classroom newspaper, or PTA Bulletin. Figure 5–10 shows what a movie rating spreadsheet might look like.

PURCHASING A SPREADSHEET

Several different brands of spreadsheets are available, for all major hardware platforms. The most popular versions in schools are in integrated packages, often called "works" programs, which include several major tools: word processing, spreadsheets, data bases management, telecommunications, and graphics. The major brands are *Microsoft Works, ClarisWorks,* and *WordPerfect Works.* Popular stand-alone spreadsheets are *Lotus 1-2-3, Microsoft Excel,* and *Quattro Pro.* Software publishers now sell their individual tools in an "office" or a "suite" package; major offerings are *Microsoft Office, WordPerfect Office,* or *Lotus SmartSuite.*

For most situations, an integrated package will be sufficient for the needs of both teachers and students. An integrated package usually costs only slightly more than a stand-alone word processor or spreadsheet. This means if you buy an integrated program just for the word processor, you get the spreadsheet almost free, and the additional features—data base management, telecommunications, and graphics—are a bonus. Stand-alone programs typically offer larger spreadsheets, more special features, and easier operation. A stand-alone spreadsheet program may be necessary in some special situations, such as high school business mathematics.

IMPLICATIONS FOR THE COMMUNITY OF LEADERSHIP

Developing Your Skill with Spreadsheets

The community of leadership must use and model spreadsheets for two reasons. First, it should use the tool to manage the school—for preparing attendance records, budgets, and state and federal reports. The community of leadership needs sufficient skill to model and explicitly teach spreadsheet use in the classroom. If the community of leadership does not have this basic skill, then there are several ways to develop it. Larger school districts can offer workshops in spreadsheet use. Schools in large metropolitan areas can approach small businesses that specialize in computer training. Local computer stores frequently offer training classes on popular software. Additionally, trading knowledge and expertise with other community of leadership members is a useful and powerful way to learn. One leader can teach another about process writing in return for instruction on spreadsheets.

Several good third-party teaching manuals are available. The fact that software publishers' manuals are often difficult to understand has created a large market for third-party instruction books. Several books specific to any major software product are sold in book stores. Teachers also can use these books as a personal reference and for written tutorials.

Spreadsheets in the Classroom

Spreadsheets have been available and popular for several years, yet they commonly are absent in schools. Staff development needs proactive leadership. The community of leadership should promote spreadsheet use in the classroom. Many teachers have a significant level of mathematics aversion and computer anxiety. The potential for spreadsheets to help students is sufficient for school leaders to devote explicit time and effort to prepare teachers to use spreadsheets as an important instructional strategy.

The first step is to help teachers learn how to use the tool. The community of leadership can do this by offering traditional after-school workshops or teacher in-service days. It is important that this instruction be kept short and purposeful. The community of leadership must establish immediate expectations and required outcomes, or teachers will not transfer their learning. For information on other, more powerful methods of teacher in-service, see Chapter 10.

A second step is to require teachers to use spreadsheets for their own instructional management. The community of leadership can require and support the use of spreadsheets in the teacher's financial interactions within the school: classroom budgeting, grading, and recording attendance. Although this step will enhance the teacher's skill with spreadsheets, it is not sufficient to get most teachers to use spreadsheets in their instruction. Many teachers will not translate their personal use into classroom use unless we explicitly teach the transfer. Modeling classroom instruction is a powerful way to begin. The lesson ideas in this chapter serve as a possible starting point for the planning of model lessons. School leaders can use these ideas to co-plan and co-teach with teachers lessons that involve the instructional use of spreadsheets in the classroom. The community of leadership must scaffold teachers' use of spreadsheets in the curriculum.

Once teachers begin using spreadsheets in their classrooms, they will internalize the tool into their teaching repertoire. We believe that learning is easiest and transfer is strongest if teachers learn to use a software application in their classrooms with their students. We believe that staff development activities should happen with teachers and children in their classrooms using the teachers' own curricula. (For a more detailed description of a staff development model, see Chapter 10.) The ease with which the typical young student adopts spreadsheet applications is sufficient justification for continuing its use in the classroom. As with most applications of computers in the classroom, the children can be a powerful influence to encourage and teach the teachers.

REFERENCES

Samuels, S. J. (1988). Decoding and automaticity: Helping poor readers become automatic at word recognition. *Reading Teacher, 41,* 756–760.

Savageau, D., and Boyer, R. (1993). *Places Rated Almanac.* Upper Saddle River, NJ: Prentice Hall Travel.

RESOURCE LIST

Alge-Blaster, Davidson and Associates

Building Perspective, Sunburst Communications, Inc.

ClarisWorks, Claris Corporation

Clock Shop, Nordic Software

Coin Critters, Nordic Software

Delta Graph, Delta Point

G-Netix, ISM, Inc.

The Geometric SuperSupposer, Sunburst/Wings for Learning

The Graph Club, Tom Snyder Productions

GraphPower, Ventura Educational Systems

Graph Wiz, William K. Bradford Publishing Co.

Harvard Graphics, Software Publishing

JMP, SAS Institute, Inc.

Lotus 1-2-3, Lotus Development Corporation

Lotus SmartSuite, Lotus Development Corporation

MacStat, MECC

Mastering Calculus, William K. Bradford Publishing Co.

MathBlaster, Davidson and Associates

Mathematica, Wolfram Research

Mathematics Shop, Scholastic, Inc.

Microsoft Excel, Microsoft Corporation

Microsoft Office, Microsoft Corporation

Microsoft Works, Microsoft Corporation

Millie's Mathematics House, Edmark

Number Munchers, MECC

Oregon Trail, MECC

PerfectOffice, WordPerfect/Novell

Probability Toolkit, Ventura Educational Systems

Quattro Pro, WordPerfect/Novell

SimCity, Maxis

SimEarth, Maxis

Statistics Workshop, Sunburst Communications, Inc.

StatView, Abacus Concepts

Taking Chances, Sunburst/Wings for Learning

Touchdown Mathematics, Gamco

Turbo Mathematics Facts, Nordic Software, Inc.

What Do You Do with a Broken Calculator?, Sunburst/Wings for Learning

Wide World of Mathematics, ABC News Interactive

WordPerfect Office, WordPerfect/Novell

WordPerfect Works, WordPerfect/Novell

Zap-A-Graph, William K. Bradford Publishing Company

CHAPTER 6

Data Base Management: Turning Data Into Information Into Knowledge

Storing data is an effective use of instructional technology. This enables the computer to assist students in manipulating and changing data into information through graphics, organizational functions such as formatting, sorting and finding, and establishing relationships between concepts. Many applications can produce charts or graphs and thus depict data as information. More importantly, from the perspective of constructivist and cognitive psychological theories, students can use that information to construct knowledge. Student learning must become a disposition to create knowledge. Memorizing facts or organizing information is not learning. Learning is the willingness to construct and apply knowledge.

In this chapter we describe an important and overlooked instructional tool to help construct knowledge: the data base management system. We define terms, provide examples of authentic applications, and suggest other purposes. We demonstrate how to form a simple data base management system. We connect other tools to a data base management system. We present four easy-to-learn and easy-to-model classroom applications for data base management systems. We suggest several data base management systems found in the child's natural environment. Finally, we suggest the role of the community of leadership in the instructional application of data base management systems.

INTRODUCTION

Our world is flooded with data. We continually are finding more sources of data. We are reducing that data to finer details. We are combining existing data to create new data. To be useful, this data must first be turned into information. That process involves organizing and summarizing data for a specific purpose. For example, daily 10:00 A.M. temperatures collected by kindergarten students and entered into a data base are data. Information is the manipulation or categorization of the data, often by graph or chart. The next step is to turn that information into knowledge. That implies that we attach relevance to the information. For example, students can use the temperature graph to construct ideas about what clothes to wear, how often to water the lawn, or how much ice cream to buy.

The relevance we attach to data will determine our students' knowledge. Scholars talk about factual or declarative and procedural knowledge. Factual knowledge includes things we know; procedural knowledge includes things we can do. Students need both factual and procedural knowledge. In this chapter we argue that our students need both to understand data and its organization (factual knowledge) and be able to retrieve and manipulate it (procedural knowledge). Bransford, Burns, Delclos, and Vye (1986) offer another way to think about knowledge. These authors use the term *inert knowledge* to describe those things we know but cannot apply usefully. Instead, students need to develop useful knowledge—that is, knowledge that they can put to meaningful purposes.

As technology leaders, our first obligation is to improve our instructional programs. It is not enough to help our students turn data into information and information into knowledge. We must insure that students are developing both factual and procedural knowledge and that they can put that knowledge into action when necessary.

UNDERSTANDING THE WORLD OF DATA

We define data as a collection of isolated facts with no attached meaning. The popular belief is that we exist in a sea of information, (for example, the information age, the information explosion, or the information super highway) when, in fact, we are awash in a sea of data. To obtain useful information, we must find the relevant data and organize it purposefully. Organizing data into information is a technology process skill. Data with meaning becomes information. A student can enter the information age only when she has the necessary skills to turn data into information.

Information becomes knowledge when it influences our dispositions, when it affects our behavior, when we use it for our purposes. Metaphorically, data is a brick, information is a blueprint, and knowledge is a house. One instructional strategy within schools is to manipulate data using data base management systems to create information and to construct knowledge.

Common Vocabulary

The term "data base" is problematic because it refers to two different concepts. One meaning of data base is "the base of data"—a collection of data needed to carry out a particular function. Another meaning is a shortened form of the phrase "data base management system"—a program that manages a base of data. In common language we use a data base—a program—to access a data base—a set of facts. This language is unfortunate but is traditional. To avoid confusion, in this book we use the longer phrase "data base management system," but keep in mind as you hear and read about data bases, that this is not a common practice.

To ease understanding about the features of a data base and data base management systems, mastery of common terms is helpful. As defined above, a *data base* is the entire base of data that is necessary to carry out one particular function. Each type of data within that data base is called a *file*. A file is not only a conceptual organization of information but also a physical one. A file in a data base context is similar to a document in word processing. In word processing, a document can be a page, a chapter, a book. A file can be all necessary information or a subcomponent defined by any criteria. We might think of a file as an electronic "physical entity" that the users must decide how to organize. Computer experts use the terms *data base* and *file* interchangeably.

Within a file is a collection of similar items. Each individual item is called a *record*. For example, in a data base about U. S. Presidents, each President would be a record. The decisions about what will be in separate files and what will be contained in each record of each file is the essence of the creativity and problem solving in data base management.

Subcomponents of a record are called *fields*. In our example, the President's name would be one field, his political party another field, date of birth a third. Records can contain as many fields as necessary. Every record has the same fields. This consistency unites records into a cohesive file which becomes a part of the total data base and which allows a user to manipulate, sort, and select the data.

Some data bases also have *keys*. A key is the way to search a data base. If the data base is small, containing several hundred records, then a key is not necessary because users can quickly search an entire file for information. However, if the data base is large, then users need keys as a more efficient way to search the files. In the Presidents example, a key would probably not be necessary due to the limited number of records in the file. However, for a large file—for example, the electronic card catalog of public library—keys allow users to perform a search with greater speed and accuracy.

When deciding which keys to use, we must first decide how we want to access the data. Using the card catalog example, users commonly search the data base by author, title, or subject. To do that, the data base is organized with fields for each piece of data, and with those fields identified as key fields. Searching a data base using a key field, such as "author," is much faster than searching using another field, such as a significant word in the text.

An Example of a Data Base Management System: Motor Vehicle Registration

Motor vehicle registration is one example of a data base that readers understand. A description of this data base both illustrates the use of common terms and further defines the concept of a data base.

If you own a car, then you are listed in your state's motor vehicle registration data base. The main file in the data base contains information about all the owners and their cars. Other files involved might include a vehicle manufacturer's file, an insurance company file, and a driver's license file. The state's Department of Transportation keeps a file of information from automobile manufacturers on the approximate weight and cost of various vehicles; it uses that information to determine the cost of license plates. The Department usually keeps an insurance file to verify the owner's insurance before licensing the vehicle. It also may keep a driver's license file to make sure each applicant is a licensed driver and to check the applicant's accident record. It also has several smaller files, such as a file to track plate numbers available for new cars or a file for vanity plates.

Within the main file, each individual car becomes a record. If you have more than one car, then you have a record for each car. The fields in your record include all the data the Department of Transportation needs to know about you: your name, your address, and the data about your car, such as its make, model, and color. Most of the fields are printed on your vehicle's registration form.

As you pay for your license plates, you should consider the importance of individually unique records. You want to make sure that your check pays for your license plate and not your neighbor's. Files contain keys to access the correct record; keys allow faster, easier access to the correct record. Since the motor vehicle data base is used not only to collect the fee for your vehicle registration, but also by law enforcement agencies, access to the correct record is important. Several keys give quick access to the correct record in the data base. The plate number is a unique identifier and the most obvious key. However, since the data base is about cars, and a car's license plate may be missing, the data base also contains a key for each vehicle's unique vehicle identification number, or VIN. Most people do not know their plate number or VIN, so the driver's name and social security number serve as additional keys. Quick access helps minimize long lines of angry people at the Motor Vehicle Registration Bureau.

Data Bases in Our Society

The creation and manipulation of data is rapidly becoming a life skill. Our lives are organized through data bases. Many people believe that data bases rule our lives. Virtually every bill we receive comes from a data base, from the telephone company's huge data base to the dentist's relatively small data base. Each of us has experienced a "computer error" that resulted in a complicated and frustrating transaction. To correct such an error, we usually ask someone to search the data base for our record and change the "amount due" field. Knowledge of how data bases function and how they are organized helps us function in our growing, data oriented society.

We interact with other data bases that do not generate bills. As mentioned earlier, our driver's license and motor vehicle registration numbers are on a data base. All our memberships are on a data base. All our junk mail is labeled by data bases. Our college transcripts are stored on a data base. Our tax and social security information are maintained on a data base. The list continues to grow. Our relationship to most data bases is passive: We receive a bill, or we get a membership renewal notice. Only when a problem occurs—for example, when a bill is incorrect—do we change from a passive recipient of data to an active participant. Other data bases, such as a library catalog, require us to be active participants from the start. Such data bases require that we have a working knowledge of their operation. When we confront an inaccurate data base, we need more than factual knowledge; we also must have procedural knowledge. Just knowing about data bases is not enough. We have to be able to manipulate them.

Data Base Management Software

A number of data base management systems are useful for schools. The most common of these are included in integrated software packages, such as *Microsoft Works* or *ClarisWorks*. *FileMaker Pro* and *Fox Pro* are examples of stand-alone data base programs. The data base management systems in an integrated program typically are less sophisticated than stand-alone data bases, but for the majority of teaching/learning strategies, integrated packages are effective.

A data base management system allows students to create data bases to attach meaning to data. They can define fields and thus form a record. They can enter data, create records, and, as a result, construct files. They can change, revise, and update records. They even can create related files to form another data base; for example, they can add a state data base to the U. S. Presidents data base.

Once the data base application is purchased, created, or borrowed, the students can access the data and organize it into a meaningful report. This is the active process of turning data into information. The creation of a report is an important reason for creating any data base. Typically, students must make many choices when creating a report: They must decide which data to include in the report, how to organize the data, and how to format the report.

ORGANIZING DATA: HOW TO CREATE A DATA BASE

Although every data base management program is slightly different, in general, the procedures for operating most data bases are similar. The first step is to define the purpose of the data base. If students do not understand the purpose of the data base, then manipulating the data base is merely an intellectual activity, with little connection to authentic, real-world issues. Once the purpose of the data base is defined clearly, the second step is to plan its organization. The decisions require organizing the data. Will it be organized in one file or more than one file? If it is organized in more than one file, then how will the separate files interrelate? How will the data base be used? What information is needed in each file? What fields will each record contain? What data will each field contain?

When planning a data base, most beginning designers start with the question, "What will I put into the data base?" A better question is, "What do I want to retrieve from the data base?" Students who begin by considering what goes into the data base might omit critical elements. Once they try to use the data base, they will find that those omissions make the data base useless. If instead students begin by deciding what the data base will do, and use their information requirements to determine which data must be included, the final product will more likely serve its intended purpose. Professional data base managers, known as systems analysts, design a data base by first asking, "What is this data base supposed to do?"

Once students determine the organization, they can begin creating the data base management system. Most programs operate by having the students create a new file, much like they would create a new word processing document. Once the file is created, the students begin defining fields. Each field has a name. Often this is confusing to students because they tend to think about the information rather than the name of the field. Using the U. S. Presidents data base as an example, the data base should have a field for last name. The name of the field should be "last name." Many students, thinking about the data in the field, will name the field "George Washington." This misconception is easy to correct if the teacher catches it early and corrects it. Once learned, this distinction seldom is forgotten.

The creation of all the fields completes the record. Once the fields are defined, the student has a blank form or a record template. The next step is to enter the data into the template. Depending on the particular data base, this can either be a simple data entry task or a complicated procedure involving library research and other data collection techniques.

Once the data is entered, the data base management software has features to sort or select the records. These commands let students access the exact information from the data base. It is more important that students learn how to get data from a data base than it is to enter data. Once students can select the data from data bases and sort the data usefully, they have mastered an important learning objective: turning data into information.

A data base management system also has features that allow the student to print the records. Most systems help students print only the records and fields needed. For example, students may only wish to print the ages of the Presidents who were in office in the Nineteenth Century. To do that, they would select the records from the Nineteenth Century and print only the "name" and "age at inauguration" fields. The mastery of the combined techniques of sorting, selecting, and printing is how a student turns the data in a data base into information to, then, construct knowledge.

OTHER DATA TOOLS

In addition to creating their own data bases, students can access several data bases, including data bases on floppy disk, data bases on CD ROM, digital video data bases on video disk, and data bases accessible through telecommunications. Teachers and students can access an increasing number of data bases. Each of these is a beginning point in our effort to help students turn data into information and information into knowledge.

Commercial Data Bases

The advantage of purchasing a data base rather than creating one is that most commercial data bases are larger, faster, and more flexible. Although creating data bases is an extremely valuable activity, having students use larger, commercial data bases has certain learning advantages. In most cases, the larger the data base, the more valuable it is to the teaching/learning environment. For example, a data base of animals with only a few records would have limited value. A data base that contained thousands of records, encompassing animals from a wide range of biomes and representing a large number of animal families, is more useful.

Data bases available on floppy disk are less common because of the disk's limited amount of storage. CD ROM technology, on the other hand, allows for the storage of large amounts of data; hence, CD ROM data bases are increasingly common. Another type of data base is digital video, which has digitized still pictures and digitized video that look less like pictures and movies and more like data bases.

When the software producers add a computer connection to these video disks, thus making them "interactive," these programs truly become a data base.

Commercial data bases should be included in the classroom environment and integrated into the school curriculum. Commercial data bases represent data available to our students. We should be challenging our students, even requiring them to turn data into information. When possible, we should ask them to undertake the final task: to turn information into knowledge.

Data Bases on Floppy Disk

The data base management system, *Bank Street Filer*, was published originally for the Apple IIe computer. It is a data base management system that is simple enough to be used by first- or second-grade students. The producers of *Bank Street Filer* also provide commercially prepared data bases. The topics include Endangered Species and Whales.

A number of products which are essentially data bases are *PC Globe* and *Mac Globe* (geography), *Point of View* (history), and Davidson's *Zoo Keeper* (science). These programs are beneficial to students developing skills in the use of data bases.

Data Bases on CD ROM

Because a CD ROM disk can hold a large amount of data, many of the products that come on CD ROM are similar to data bases. Examples are *The New Grolier Multimedia Encyclopedia* and *Street Atlas USA*. These CD ROMs provide both the data and the procedures to access the data. CD ROMs are available for virtually every curricular area, and several that have cross-curricular or thematic possibilities. Examples of CD ROMs in science include *Animals!*, *Better Homes and Gardens Gardening*, *Hip Physics*, *The Way Things Work*, and *DinoSource*; in social studies, *Capitol Hill*; in geography, *U. S. Atlas* and *China: Home of the Dragon*; and in history *Time Traveler* and *Ancient Greece*. CD ROM data bases are available even for art, such as *The National Gallery of Art*.

Video-Oriented Data Bases

The recent popularity of digital video has brought about a new form of data. In the past we thought of pictures and motion video as separate and distinct from what we thought of as data. However, when video is digitized, it becomes indistinguishable from data. Certain types of educational materials are evolving that look more like data bases, with large collections of data and mechanisms for accessing, sorting, and selecting data. Several interactive video disk–based systems are data bases of still pictures; *Bio Sci II* and *The National Gallery of Art* are examples.

Several other interactive video disk systems involve the use of short segments of motion video. Two examples are the series from ABC News Interactive and the National Geographic Society. Although some might call these systems tutorials and others might call them multimedia based systems, they also are data bases of video segments. The ABC News Interactive series provides a standard tool to search the video library, to retrieve portions from that library, and to organize excerpts into a presentation. This is similar to the capabilities of a traditional data base system that allows searching, sorting, and report generation.

On-Line Data Bases

In addition to creating or buying data bases, students also can access data bases through telecommunications. On-line data bases have the advantage of being more fluid than commercial data bases. When you purchase a data base, the data is frozen in time. The information that the data represents may be changing; the data base may be out of date even before its purchase. A CD ROM atlas that at one time might have been satisfactory is less useful in today's environment of changing boundaries, the splitting and joining of nations, and fluid populations. An on-line data base can change as often as necessary, so that users always have access to current data.

The on-line environment adapts so quickly that the number and type of data bases available change almost daily. A variety of data is available on-line, including financial data, weather data, library card catalogs, sports statistics, TV listings, and airline schedules.

Environmental Data Bases

Just as we consider environmental print important to the development of language and literacy, we can consider environmental data bases as important to constructing knowledge. Our students experience these data bases in their lives outside school. We should be using these experiences to connect students' prior knowledge of data bases to new learning. Many retail stores have product directories that are available for customers to find items they wish to purchase. Many music stores have data bases that link to reviews of music on compact disk. Several grocery store chains have experimented with data bases accessible from a panel mounted on a shopping cart. Most public libraries have converted their card catalogs to electronic data bases. Sports fans have an increasing volume of statistics available as data bases. Television program listings are data bases. As teachers, we can use these resources to help our students understand the operation of data bases. Students can be assigned community-based data bases—for example, records of libraries and museums—to develop understanding (inert knowledge) and skills (useful knowledge) for meaningful purposes.

The increasing availability of data bases in our environment is not only another educational opportunity, but also an indication of the importance of skills related to data access. Accessing data, making sense of it, and using it for day-to-day purposes in our lives is not our future, it is our present.

Data Bases in the Classroom

The purpose of considering data in the classroom is to help students construct knowledge. There are two paths to this learning. The first path involves the data itself: the nature of data, the organization of data, and the access of data. The second path stems from the meaning of the data. When we have children working with a weather data base, we have learning objectives about weather and learning objectives about data. When we have students working with stock prices, we have objectives about finance and objectives about data base management. We want students to use increasing volumes of data that are available and turn them into information. This process brings content and process together.

To form data into information, students must not only understand the nature of data and be able to actively manipulate data; they must understand the underlying concepts about that particular data set. To predict tomorrow's weather, they must understand how to select the proper data from the data base, and they must understand what that data tells them about future events. To make intelligent stock purchases, they must be able to select appropriate past stock performance data, and they must understand what past performance tells them about future performance. These activities involve both subject matter knowledge and data knowledge. They also involve factual knowledge and procedural knowledge. The active use of data bases for practical purposes can assist students to construct useful knowledge.

We can actively involve students with data bases in two ways: by having them use data bases and by having them create data bases. A logical argument is that a child should first learn to access data before she learns to create data. In this way, the use of data becomes background information for the creation of data. The converse argument also can be made: The creation of data acts as the basis for a deeper understanding of data organization. We believe in a compromise approach that reinforces students' learning modalities. We believe that activities that involve using data should be merged with activities that involve the creation of data. Children come to us with some notion of data from their experiences outside school, and both activities help our students expand or elaborate their existing data schema. By interweaving these experiences, we give them the maximum opportunity to find appropriate and useful ways to connect new knowledge with their existing knowledge, to elaborate or expand their schema.

The creation of data bases has several learning outcomes. The activity requires students to make critical decisions about the nature of the data they create: decisions about the creations of files, decisions about the fields in a record, and decisions about which records to include or to omit. Thus, the creation of data bases is an active process important to the development of procedural knowledge.

For a concrete example of some of the decisions that must be made, consider again the creation of a data base about U. S. Presidents. The first decision students must make is how they will use the data. Students can brainstorm possible uses of the data base. The uses determine what should be included in the data base, a list of possible pieces of data. Next, the students can decide how the files will be organized. If it seems that students need only one kind of information, then one file may be sufficient. If the data seems to fall into more than one category—for example, information on presidents, information on vice-presidents, and information on first ladies—then students may decide to create more than one file and use the files together. The next set of decisions the students must make relates to the fields that will comprise each record. Discussion about the use of the data base should make this an exciting and challenging task, one that involves decision making and problem solving.

In this example, the creation of the records is easy: simply include all the Presidents. This is not true of all data bases. In a weather data base, the user must decide which years to include and how often to create a record. In a stock price data base, the user must decide which stocks to include.

Once the students have created the data base, they must use it. This creates a natural feedback loop. As students try to use the data base as intended—to answer various questions about the Presidency—they will see the strengths and weaknesses of the decisions they made when organizing the data. They can modify their data base and enter new data to meet their needs.

CLASSROOM LESSON IDEAS: CREATING DATA BASES

We offer specific classroom lesson ideas that involve the creation of data bases. These lessons are a starting place for teachers and classroom leaders who want more concrete ideas about where to begin using data bases. The lesson ideas offered here are only a few of many that are available in the published literature. A good source for other ideas are computer-oriented, practitioner journals such as *Learning and Leading with Technology* (formerly *The Computing Teacher*), *TechTrends*, *Electronic Learning*, and *Technology and Learning*. These publications frequently contain articles that describe lessons.

We call these lesson ideas rather than lesson plans because we believe it is impossible to create lesson plans independent of classroom context, without knowing the children, their special talents and needs, the school's vision and mission, the community, and the school culture. The teacher must write good lesson plans. We hope these lesson ideas can either form the basis for a good lesson plan or, at least, inspire creativity.

LESSON IDEA 1:   Class Information Data Base

A good starting point in working with data involves the creation of a class information data base. When we recommend a class information data base to teachers, a common objection is that it takes too much of the teacher's time and effort. However, by turning this activity into a lesson rather than a management task, teachers can fulfill both a management objective and a learning objective.

Two approaches can be used in the design phase, based on the students' developmental level. With more accomplished children, the teacher may involve the class in determining the use of the class data base. With less accomplished children, the teacher may simply explain its purpose. Either way, before the students begin using the data base, they should clearly understand its uses.

If the teacher defines the purposes of the data base, then she also may wish to design the files and records. This same design can be used and modified from year to year. However, if the students defined the purposes of the data base, they also should be involved in the design of the files and records. By knowing the purpose of the data base, students can engage in problem solving in establishing the fields.

To design a data base, the teacher can take the time to create it, or she can assign that experience to students as another learning activity. Creating a data base using a computer, an LCD panel, and an overhead projector models and displays decision-making and problem-solving strategies. Another approach is a tutorial experience, which is useful with an individual student or small group of students. Tutors might be students who need remedial technology help, or they might be the classroom technology leaders. Along with the jobs of watering the plants, feeding the animals, and acting as crossing guards, teachers can assign students the task of data base specialist. This is a real job title, one that carries a high salary in professional data processing organizations.

Once the data base is created, the teacher or students can print a blank record to use as a student information form. Students can complete this form at home. The students, then, can enter their own information in the data base. In this way, the classroom data base can be created with a minimum of teacher time and a maximum of student learning.

After the data base is complete, students can determine new learning activities. If personal information about the students is to be part of the information, then teachers can use "treasure hunt" activities to find the student who has blue eyes, is 4 feet 3 inches tall, and walks home after school. Another activity uses the data base as part of a safety simulation: "A student is hurt and we need to contact her parents. What do we do?" These activities help students develop the procedural knowledge to find desired information in large data bases using authentic student learning experiences.

LESSON IDEA 2:   Organizing Collections

Most students collect something—baseball cards, toys, books, coins, rocks, bugs, or mementos. Each collection is a physical data base that can be converted to an electronic data base. The general process is similar to the design suggested for the class information data base—that is, define the purposes of the data base, design files and records, create the files by establishing the fields, enter the data, and use the data base for specific purposes.

This activity begins with students bringing in their collections and sharing them with the class. This not only helps students think about the purpose of the data base, but also is a nice way to get students to share more about themselves—helping the class form a stronger learning community. This data base might be used as part of a unit about self-esteem or self-concept.

LESSON IDEA 3:   Science Identification Data Bases

We teach concepts of scientific classification several times in elementary school, again in middle school, and again in high school. The student reaction is frequently, "So what?" Rather than presenting concepts such as the periodic table of elements or the biological classifications of kingdom, phylum, order, family, genus, and species in a didactic format, we instead can use a more student-active approach. We can ask our students to generate their own classification system by creating a data base. We can ask students to examine a collection of individual items and organize them into a data base. In the process, students must make decisions about various aspects of the data set, which requires that they think actively about classification. This activity can be done in geology with minerals, in biology with plants or animals, and in chemistry with elements. As a specific example of this activity, we describe how students develop a tree data base.

The teacher describes the purpose of the data base: "We want a data base that allows us to name a tree by looking at its leaves." In other words, the purpose of this data base should be to assist the student to name a tree by recognizing its leaf.

The first step is to have students collect leaves and make a record of each leaf and the tree from which it came. The information on each leaf becomes a record in the data base. After finding the leaves, the students need to decide which features of the leaves are useful in telling them apart. Teachers may explicitly teach about forming groups or categories. The teacher can use an expository strategy—by telling—or use a more discovery-oriented strategy—by letting various groups of students explore categories. Working in pairs or in small groups (we prefer pairs), the students discuss various aspects of the leaves that separate them into useful categories. These categories become the fields in the data base.

Next, the students build the data base using the categories they have created for their leaves. Once they have created the data base and entered all the features of their leaves, they need to name their tree. They will need to use a tree identification data base, a tree book, or a tree CD ROM. These resources will have their own classification system for leaves, thus providing students feedback on their own decisions about their leaves' categories. When the tree names are determined and entered, students can test the data base. New leaf samples can be examined, and pairs of students can use their data base to name the trees.

LESSON IDEA 4:   Book Review Data Base

A trade book data base can be useful in language arts. A number of purposes can be generated for this data base, all connected to finding a good book to read. Students can use this data base to share their reading experiences with their classmates in different ways. The teacher can design the data base, and the students can enter the data. If the students design the data base, then the learning is more powerful. Using the data base, teachers initiate discussion of the characteristics of books by asking, "What features make a book good?" Younger students may consider illustrations and characters to be important, while older students may believe theme and setting to be important.

The students can create the data base as before. One difference is that the teacher will want one data base shared by the whole class and continued each year by subsequent classes.

Once the data base has been created and students have had time to enter data about their favorite books, the data base becomes important in the children's reading routine. When they want to find a new book, they can use the data base to find one that has been recommended by a fellow student, or one that has the characteristics they select. After a student has read a book, she can create a data base record instead of writing the traditional book report. The knowledge that this record will be used by other students adds publishing to students' thinking and writing about the books they have read.

ADDITIONAL DATA BASE ACTIVITIES

Using Environmental Data Bases

The number of data bases available in today's world is large and growing. These myriad data bases can be used as learning activities in several ways. The "find a product" kiosks that are in department stores can be used for data base access "treasure hunts." With the cooperation of the department store, we can send our students with specific criteria for finding a product and require that they use the store's data base to locate information about various merchandise.

Library card catalogs are another example of environmental data bases. Teachers can create learning activities using a library's card catalog. Most card catalogs use the keys of title, subject, and author. Each key could be used for data access activities. For example, the teacher might ask the students to find how many different authors have the last name "Gardener" and list all their first names. Or, the teacher might ask students to find how many book titles contain the word "yellow."

Data bases are so pervasive in our world that there are numerous examples of hard copies generated from data bases: driver's licenses, social security cards, membership cards, magazine labels, and junk mail. To help students understand the nature of data, the teacher might ask them to find several documents and examine them as data base reports. Students might identify the record in the data base, usually a single person, and the fields that comprise the record. Depending on the knowledge of the students, teachers might discuss uses for the data. For example, the teacher might ask students to name all the uses of a driver's license file. Or, the teacher might have students examine various pieces of junk mail and determine how a particular advertisement came to the addressee. Magazine labels contain a wealth of information; having students examine every character on a label could help them better understand how publishers organize data.

Mail order catalogs might generate an entire unit. Students could examine the three data bases that are involved with mail order catalogs. The customer data base generates the label on the catalog and is used when a customer places an order. The product data base has all the information about the various products. This data base usually uses keys for access. A key (the item number) is usually printed with every item in the catalog. The order data base operates once a customer places an order. This data base is used to keep track of what the customer bought, to generate a document that ships the product, and to print the bill. The teacher might model a catalog order telephone call so students can see how to place a catalog order and how the phone operator uses the item number to access the product data base.

Presentations About Data Bases

If your school is in a metropolitan area, or if corporate headquarters, large government offices, or data processing centers exist in your area, you have access to professionals who can speak to students about working with data. Data processing professionals work with data and design data bases as part of their jobs. Many professionals are willing to share their expertise with students. If the teacher gives a qualified speaker sufficient information about how students use data bases in her classroom, the resource person can tailor a presentation about classroom applications. This demonstration might be displayed in conjunction with other related activities. For example, if a teacher has had students examining their driver's licenses, a good follow-up to that activity might be a presentation by a local Department of Transportation employee about the state's driver's license data base. Using local speakers helps students in two ways: students obtain valuable information about the organization and use of data, and they might begin to think about a career in data base management.

IMPLICATIONS FOR THE COMMUNITY OF LEADERSHIP

The data base management system is the one application whose instructional and management purposes overlap. We even suggest that teachers and students learn the application by constructing a basic management tool: a classroom information data base. Creating this tool helps both teachers and students understand the purpose of a data base management system, learn definitions, and grasp the application's functions and procedures.

The community of leadership, using *ad hoc* leaders, should require that teachers and other educators use data base management systems to accomplish management tasks. For example, teachers must know how to enter and access data from the building data base: student name, medication, or reading group. Then teachers must be required to complete their classroom management tasks on a data base management system. For example, teachers must report attendance and grades, create missing homework assignments or weekly progress report letters, and produce individualized student learning and tracking data bases. Finally, roving leaders should assist teachers explicitly to transfer the management uses of data bases to instructional applications. It is relatively simple to move from a classroom information data base to constructing data base management systems such as "Books to Read," "Favorite Rainy Day Games," or "Careers."

Clearly, formal leaders must be able and willing to model both management and instructional data base management systems in teachers' classrooms using the teachers' children. Additionally, formal leaders must inform teachers and students explicitly and directly to transfer their data base management skills to instructional applications. By requiring, advocating, and supporting teachers' use of data base management systems, the community of leadership can move learning beyond memorization into turning data into information and information into knowledge.

CONCLUSION: PUTTING IT ALL TOGETHER TO IMPROVE INSTRUCTION

Individuals encounter data bases regularly in their everyday lives. As an educational issue, teachers must teach children how to relate to data bases, to understand the purposes of data bases, to recognize how data bases are constructed, and to engage in problem solving by determining the variables contained in data bases. Community of leadership members must explicitly model and teach doers how to use data bases constructively and how data bases support a quality instructional program.

The modeling of instruction is a powerful tool to teach children and to influence teachers. As community of leadership members model data base strategies in each classroom, teachers should become more accepting of the strategy. Teachers may need more than superficial staff development. We believe that the most effective staff development occurs in the teacher's classroom, during school, and with her students. The community of leadership must accept the modeling of appropriate teaching/learning behavior as one of its important missions. For a deeper understanding, see Chapter 10.

REFERENCES

Bransford, J. D., Burns, M. S., Delclos, V. R., & Vye, N. J. (1986). Teaching thinking: Evaluating evaluators and broadening the data base. *Educational Leadership, 44*(2), 68–70.

RESOURCE LIST

Ancient Greece, Queue

Animals!, Software Toolworks

Atlas Pack (1991–1992): U. S. Atlas, Software Toolworks

Bank Street Filer, Sunburst

Better Homes and Gardens Complete Guide to Gardening, Multicom Publishing

Bio Sci II, Video Discovery

China: Home of the Dragon, Orange Cherry/New Media Schoolhouse

ClarisWorks, Claris Corporation

DinoSource, Queue

FileMaker Pro, Claris Corporation

Fox Pro, Microsoft Corporation

Hip Physics, Tom Snyder Productions

Mac Globe, Bröderbund

Microsoft Works, Microsoft Corporation

The National Gallery of Art, Pioneer Video, Inc.

The New Grolier Multimedia Encyclopedia, Software Toolworks

PC Globe, Bröderbund

Point of View, Scholastic, Inc.

Street Atlas USA, DeLorme

Time Traveler, Orange Cherry/New Media Schoolhouse

The Way Things Work, Thompson Learning Tools

Zoo Keeper, Davidson and Associates

Developing Knowledge with Hypermedia

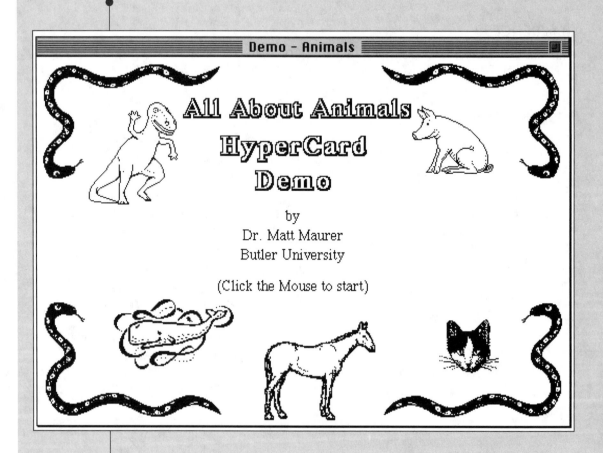

One of the difficult tasks of establishing a quality academic program is to help the adults "get outside the box," to see the world differently from the way their experience dictates. Hypermedia is an "outside the box" application. It is nonlinear, student-active, individually prescriptive, and useful for a student's construction of knowledge.

Developing knowledge with hypermedia connects *HyperCard* applications to constructivist and cognitive psychological learning theory. The notion of Hypermedia as nonlinear distinguishes this application from the three basic programs—word processing, spreadsheets, and data base man-agement systems. Hypermedia is a move toward student-active, individualized learning that supports different learning styles and intelligences. Hypermedia can be purchased, created by the teacher, or constructed by the student(s). Hypermedia is connected to constructivism and to the student's increasing competence in turning data into information and information into knowledge. In this chapter we describe hypermedia, illustrate how hypermedia applications work, and suggest ideas for classroom projects. We close the chapter by exploring the implications of Hypermedia for the community of leadership.

INTRODUCTION

Hypermedia: What Is It?

Technology frequently helps us improve what we do. Computers enable us to do things faster, do more than we were doing before, and do it more accurately. Hypermedia is an example of technology that supports teaching and learning by doing things differently.

Hypermedia is a unique computer application for presenting information. The advantage of Hypermedia is its ability to organize data. We perceive most traditional information as linear. A book is an example of a linear medium. All the elements of a book are in a line: One word follows another, one paragraph follows another, one page follows another. Although the reader can choose to skip around the book, it is difficult to do so effectively since the author meant the book to be read from beginning to end. Even if a book has a good index, if a reader wants to reorganize the text for her own rather than the author's purpose, that can be done only with significant inconvenience.

A reader can access a piece of Hypermedia differently depending on her needs and desires. The information is presented in a nonlinear format; that is, the reader easily can move from one idea to another according to her own purposes. She can access the information she wants and skip the unwanted or unnecessary information. She also can experience the material in an order that makes the most sense to her and that is most useful for her learning. Hypermedia technology provides and maintains the links that make this possible.

Compare a history lesson taught to a whole group in a traditional classroom to the same lesson organized using Hypermedia. Traditional classroom instruction is an example of a linear approach. The teacher assigns a chapter to be read and students read the chapter in the book. Then, in class, the teacher further expands and explains the ideas contained the chapter. Next, the teacher asks students to react to the ideas by writing an analysis or synthesis. The teacher closes the lesson with a short video that reinforces the learning. This lesson may have been a terrific learning experience or a total bomb; that is not relevant. The significance is that every student experienced the material in much the same way. Even though each of the learners is different, each has experienced the same instructional method.

If the same lesson were available in a Hypermedia format, a teacher would make all the elements of the lesson available to all the students, and each student could experience the lesson according to her particular learning needs and styles. For example, a student might begin reading and find she needs further explanation about an idea. With Hypermedia, the student can skip from the reading to further explanation and then return to the reading. Another student may find that the video intended for reinforcement is more understandable than the text. With Hypermedia, she can begin with the video and use the text for reinforcement. She may find the text is unnecessary after having watched the video and may choose to skip the text. Another student may read only a portion of the text because she already has mastered or learned some of the knowledge, skills, and dispositions. She can skip the unnecessary material and concentrate on the requisite information. Another student may decide to rearrange the writing assignment according to her learning style and objectives. Instead of doing all the writing at one time, she may learn better by writing sections as she constructs her ideas.

In short, Hypermedia allows students to reorganize material to meet their individual learning preferences and to accommodate their previous knowledge and experience. Each student gets the information in a way that satisfies her idiosyncratic learning strategies. Further, she does not have to interact with unnecessary text.

Hypertext is a special classification of Hypermedia. A hypertext document is a text-only document that includes "hot links"—nonlinear connections from one part of the text to another. For example, a hot link might connect a word in a description to the definition of that word. Other hot links might connect an idea conceptually. For example, a paragraph that describes animals in a rain forest might include hot links to detailed descriptions of each animal. A student who is reading about the rain forest might jump into specific detail of a particular animal. Another student might skip the discussion about the animal and instead select information about a plant that grows in the rain forest. Each student can access the text easily and in the order that is most useful and meaningful for her.

Hypermedia typically contains a variety of material besides text, including pictures, sounds, and motion. The variety of media contained in a Hypermedia product can span the scope of what is technically feasible. The media can be applied to existing technology. This means that month by month, the capability of Hypermedia products increases as new applications emerge. A few years ago, motion video was too difficult and too expensive to include in a Hypermedia product. Today, motion video, in small portions, is commonplace. In the future, software developers will include more and longer video segments of increasing quality.

What Should We Do with Hypermedia?

In the description above we have suggested implications related to learner choice. We imply that it is good teaching and learning practice for a student to choose the material she needs for her learning. Some educators may disagree with this premise. Some may say, "It is a teacher's job to make choices about the materials a learner should use and when she should use it." A teacher might speculate, "Students do not have enough knowledge or experience to make good choices about their learning; if they did, what would they need us for?"

Although we do not disagree completely with these concerns, we would like to redirect them. No teacher or team of teachers can ever have enough knowledge about their content or their learners, nor enough time to make every decision about learning that students make during a day. Leaders and doers cannot control all of the decisions that students make in a day. Leaders and doers must control the premises upon which children make those decisions. Constructivist practice is a premise that leaders and doers can control. Children make literally thousands of important decisions about their learning every day. The teacher's job is to provide a reasonable and useful set of choices that promotes learning, and to guide the student's choices. Rather than making all the learning decisions for our students, we should help them learn to choose for themselves, metacognitively. We should monitor their choices and make "in-flight" formative learning corrections. When necessary, teachers must teach students explicitly to construct these connections. If we help our students learn to make good choices about their own learning, then eventually students will learn more independently, which is a disposition of quality, constructivist education. We want our students to become independent, life-long learners.

We can use Hypermedia to reach our goals in two ways: by having students use Hypermedia and by having students create Hypermedia. Both approaches are important and both have different learning outcomes. If we want students simply using Hypermedia, we can either buy commercial products or create our own Hypermedia materials. Commercial products usually are high quality and include a variety of media in several formats. Compared to commercial products, the Hypermedia applications we create ourselves typically are of less quality and are less complete. On the other hand, teachers can create their own Hypermedia to focus their students' objectives more directly. When a teacher cannot find a commercial product that perfectly fits her instructional objectives, she can create her own instructional materials using a Hypermedia development program.

Regardless of who develops the Hypermedia, students should experience this application in school. Presenting material nonlinearly can make ideas more powerful. Also, students will find more nonlinear information outside the school. Many of our students come to school with previous experience making substantial choices about learning. Our materials should take advantage of that prior knowledge, not extinguish it.

Using Hypermedia requires that students make choices. Making choices requires more creative thinking or problem-solving activity than transmission methods. However, even the most exciting, professionally developed Hypermedia can become a relatively passive learning experience. Although we believe using Hypermedia is important for student learning, we believe it is even more important that students create their own Hypermedia.

When teachers ask students to create coherent Hypermedia presentations, those students become necessarily and purposefully involved in their own learning. Hypermedia is one application in which students can become brilliant. Most teachers have experienced the heartache and uncertainty of giving a student a low grade. Consider the following hypothetical scenario:

> I hated to give Billy a "D." He is a smart boy, but he just does not perform well on class work. The term paper was a large part of the semester grade, and he really did it badly. He might tell me all about his topic, but even with help, he just could not organize it into a coherent term paper.

In situations like this, many of us recognize that the fault lies with ourselves and our concept of learning as much as it does with the child. Often, we have not found a way for the child to demonstrate her brilliance. Creating Hypermedia can bring out the child's brilliance. For some children, nonlinear collections of information are much more sensible and understandable than linear ones. Many students can express themselves better with other media than they can with words. Hypermedia makes these students' full expression possible.

HYPERMEDIA AND CONSTRUCTIVIST THINKING: GETTING HYPER

We often use Hypermedia as a concrete illustration of schema theory. (Schema theory is reviewed in Chapter 1.) The information in high-quality Hypermedia software is a close analog of a mental model or schema. Hypermedia contains a variety of information, and that information is connected by divergent pathways. Teachers must purposely activate those pathways to retrieve important information. That activating or elaborating schema is important to learning has been well-documented by careful research (Anderson & Pearson, 1984).

If Hypermedia is an analog of schema theory, then it follows that the use of Hypermedia would be effective in activating or elaborating a student's schema. As students make choices about information, they are activating or elaborating their own schema.

Schema theory is the theoretical foundation of constructivist thinking and the intellectual base of memory and comprehension—remembering and learning strategies. Schema formation and building is the prime strategy for children's construction of knowledge and reality. Anderson and Pearson (1984) argue that a schema is a mental model of what the child understands about a concept or idea based upon her experience, observation, hypothesis generation and testing, and reflection. As children mature physically, their schemata—their mental pictures of their knowledge—become increasingly complex and sophisticated.

As children mature developmentally, their schemata shift from the concrete to the abstract. They are able to remember individual parts of a schema by recalling the entire schema; for example, a child remembers the princess by recalling the fairy tale. Conversely, children can understand an entire schema by recalling an individual part or parts. For example, when a storyteller mentions grandmother's house and the wolf, the children recall the entire plot of "Little Red Riding Hood." The process required to recall parts from the entire schema, or to remember the entire schema from individual parts, is fundamentally simple. A schema—a mental model or picture—begins construction of knowledge as children experience learning at an early age; hence the push for parents to begin reading to young children. As children mature, they connect new knowledge to what they already know; they continue to build increasingly complex and sophisticated schemata. If children are read several fairy tales, they begin to create a schema, a mental picture, of the genre called "fairy tales." When they encounter a new fairy tale, they are able to recall the schema and attach or connect the new information—plot, character, moral message—to their expanding fairy tale schema.

The pieces of the schema—the places where the children connect the new information to the existing knowledge—are called slots or nodes. The children make connections best when teachers actively, explicitly, and directly help them activate or recall their existing schemata. For example, when a teacher begins a lesson about electrons, she may ask the children to brainstorm what they already know about molecules, or she may read aloud a piece of text about electrons, or she may review what the children already know about atoms. This is the constructivist connection between schema theory and Hypermedia. The Hypermedia stack represents the mental model or mental picture of a concept or an idea. Each part of a stack, an individual card, resembles a slot or a node—a piece of information. The cards within the stack can be used both linearly and nonlinearly. In Hypermedia, the links that students create to organize the data into information and the information into knowledge are buttons.

Teachers have several important responsibilities in supporting children's construction of schemata. Teachers must explicitly and directly help children activate their schemata—that is, focus their understanding—before presenting new information. Often teachers refer to children's schemata as prior or background knowledge: the essential information that children must know to build their mental models. For younger children, examples of prior or background knowledge may include color names, letter names, the act of being read to, or going to the store. For older students, prior or background knowledge may include arithmetic operations, the Revolutionary War, the process of writing a research paper, or the classroom behaviors appropriate in a variety of learning environments.

When the teacher recognizes that children have incomplete schema or no prior or background knowledge, then she must provide those missing slots or nodes. The teacher explicitly may teach the missing concepts, provide experiential learning (field trips to the store, to downtown, or to the zoo), or compare an existing schema to a new schema ("Christmas" to "Thanksgiving"). In Hypermedia, the selection of data included in each card and the way the cards are organized within the stack help children learn missing prior knowledge or activate what they already know. Without knowing the children's prior or background knowledge, and without activating it, comprehension and learning are difficult and revert from the constructivist perspective to the transmission model.

Anderson (1985) describes six purposes of schemata in children's learning and remembering processes that also support the remembering and learning aspects of Hypermedia.

A schema provides ideational scaffolding for assimilating text information (p. 376). The slots or nodes make remembering and learning easier. They provide support for children's knowledge. New information that is connected to existing knowledge or placed into a slot or node is learned more easily and quickly.

A schema facilitates selective allocation of attention (p. 376).   One of the important purposes of schemata with their slots or nodes is to help the learner prioritize or determine the importance of the information in relation to the entire schema. This organizing function helps children concentrate on main ideas and sort relevant information. This process helps children remember and recall—a necessary function for all learning, even for standardized achievement tests.

A schema enables inferential elaboration (p. 376).   The information in most learning environments, including text, is not always explicit; that is, the information is not always stated. Often, children must make inferences about the intended meaning of the information. They must make predictions about where in an incomplete schema to connect the new information: where to add new cards and connecting buttons.

A schema allows orderly searches of memory (p. 376).   Schemata and slots or nodes allow two-way recollection of information. Recognition of the whole can activate recall of parts. Knowledge of a schema can help children remember slots or nodes within a schema. Either way, whole to part or part to whole, the learners improve their recall and increase their access to information.

A schema facilitates editing and summarizing (p. 377).   Because a process for determining important information is one purpose of schemata and of the process of stack creation, schema theory and Hypermedia will aid children's ability to prioritize and summarize important information, such as the main idea. The process also permits children to de-emphasize peripheral or less relevant facts.

A schema permits inferential reconstruction (p. 377).   The use of schema theory and Hypermedia can facilitate a learner's ability to recall forgotten information. Through hypothesis generation (prediction) and reflection, learners can recall forgotten information in one slot or node by remembering information in other slots or nodes. Inferential reconstruction, explicitly taught and practiced, may improve children's memory and performance on memory-based activities, including standardized achievement tests.

Clearly, constructivist, schema-based learning and Hypermedia benefit children at many developmental stages of comprehension and learning. The application of schema-based teaching strategies with Hypermedia will engage more students in remembering and learning and, when the learning is transferred appropriately, should increase their scores on standardized achievement tests.

CONSTRUCTING HYPERMEDIA

We have already described several benefits that students gain by creating Hypermedia. An additional advantage comes from learning to use Hypermedia development programs. To learn to use a Hypermedia development program effectively, a student must have a deep conceptual understanding of how the software works. So much of our learning is factual that activities that focus on conceptual learning are increasingly valuable in the curriculum.

A project detailed by Maurer (1995) makes the power of conceptual learning clearer. Every semester, Maurer has a group of elementary students teach his college students to use the Hypermedia program, *HyperCard*. These children use *HyperCard* in elementary school and have a thorough conceptual understanding and well-developed skills in using the program. This skill also produces a high level of self-confidence. After getting over initial jitters, these fourth- and fifth-graders effectively tutor the college students in the construction of a simple *HyperCard* stack. Over the life of this project, children who have been tagged with every conceivable label—learning disabled, behaviorally disordered, mildly mentally handicapped—have participated. A surprising result was that the college students could not distinguish these tutors, not even the mildly mentally handicapped ones, from the regular education tutors. The children's conceptual knowledge, skill, and confidence were sufficient to overcome the problems that had earned them an educational label. The Hypermedia environment was their way to be brilliant.

HYPERMEDIA TOOLS

Hypermedia Authoring Programs

Several Hypermedia authoring programs are available, each with its strengths and weaknesses. Three programs have been available for some time and have gained significant popularity: *HyperCard* for the Macintosh, *Linkway* for DOS computers, and *HyperStudio*, which has a version for both Macintosh and DOS. Several newer applications of Hypermedia development programs are offered, each with a particular focus. For example, *Macromind Director* has a particularly strong video component. *Digital Chisel* has a reputation of having a friendly learning curve. Teachers and students can use any of these programs effectively in the classroom.

Doers, teachers, and students should all be involved in the selection of software. Their involvement insures that the software will match not only the available hardware, but the intended objectives and learning needs of the teachers and students. We want Hypermedia programs that have strengths consistent with the intellectual needs of the students using them.

Following is a general summary of the strengths and weaknesses of the more popular Hypermedia authoring programs. The reader should remember that these strengths and weaknesses change as regularly as software producers release new versions or upgrades. To make informed decisions, users should supplement this information with evaluations that are specific to the particular version being considered.

In comparing the various programs, you must consider the issues of application power versus ease of use. Typically, the easier a program is to learn, the less power it has. More powerful programs are more difficult to learn, if for no other reason than that they offer more possibilities. *HyperStudio, Linkway,* and *Digital Chisel* are all relatively easy to learn yet they also have a reasonable level of power. *HyperCard* and *Macromind Director* are more difficult to learn but offer more sophisticated tools.

Another issue is the shape of the learning curve. Each of the programs has potential instructional power. To wield that power, a student must learn. Some programs, such as *HyperCard*, have a relatively smooth learning curve; that is, a student can learn some features, master them, learn other features, and continue to learn at a steady rate. Other programs, such as *Linkway*, have a shallow learning curve for the rudimentary functions of the program but have a much steeper learning curve for advanced features. Overall, we prefer a program that may be somewhat more difficult to learn at the outset, but that offers a steady growth curve for students over a long time. Programs with easy initial learning curves tend to encourage learners to master the simple functions; however, students seldom attempt to master more advanced features. *Digital Chisel* seems to offer a reasonable compromise: It has a wide range of multimedia capabilities which are easy to learn.

The Media in Hypermedia

When we talk about Hypermedia, the "hyper" portion of the word refers to the organization of the material, while the "media" portion suggests the variety of material authors can organize. Most Hypermedia authoring packages have ways of organizing various forms of text, pictures, audio, and video. The organization of text and crude pictures are typically lower level functions, while high-resolution graphics, audio, and video are higher level functions. This usually means that it is relatively easy to create Hypermedia with words and simple graphics, but more difficult to add high-resolution pictures, audio, and video.

Text   Text is the simplest form of media found in a Hypermedia presentation. All Hypermedia authoring programs detail several ways of incorporating text. Most have some simple word processing capabilities coupled with the ability to place and shape text within the presentation. Text, in its simplest form, is merely a description with no logical connections to anything else in the presentation. The steps necessary to create simple text is to form a text frame, adjust it to the desired shape, and process the words. If, however, that text has logical connections to other text or other media, such as pictures, video, or sound, then after the author enters the text, she must add the nonlinear connections to the other media. A word that acts as a connection to other media is called "hot text." The ease with which an author can create hot text depends on the authoring program. Some are easier than others.

Digital Pictures   Digital pictures permit more sophisticated presentations. The easiest way to describe digital pictures is to define them as images constructed of a series of dots. A low-resolution digital picture has relatively large dots and a high-resolution picture has relatively small dots. The smaller the dots, the finer the image's detail.

The easiest way to incorporate pictures into a Hypermedia presentation is to draw them. Hypermedia programs provide that capability, but the result is dependent upon the artistry of the author. Most Hypermedia drawing tools are rather crude, and they create low-resolution pictures. However, this approach is sufficient when a simple illustration is all that is necessary. If higher quality images are necessary, then authors will need additional hardware.

High-resolution digital images can be captured in several ways. A scanner allows you to digitize an existing picture. This device works much like a copy machine. The way the device works limits the type of material an author can scan. There are black-and-white scanners and color scanners. Scanners have specialized software to run them. Most scanner software allows you to control the level of resolution. When you scan a picture, you create a file, much like a word processing file. That file describes the dots or pixels. The file of a picture scanned at low resolution has fewer dots, so it is smaller than a file in high resolution, which has more dots. In addition, to scan a picture in color, the file must contain information about the color of each dot, thus increasing the file size. Scanned pictures can be large and therefore require a significant amount of disk storage space. When students begin working with multimedia, unless they will scan only low-resolution, black-and-white graphics, we must provide them with ample disk space to store the graphics.

Another way to get a digital picture is through a video source, such as a VCR or camcorder. You can digitize a single frame of video and thus create a digital picture. The advantage of this method is that it gives the author a wider range of digitizing possibilities. Students can take a camcorder on location, shoot a segment of video, and use it to create individual digital pictures.

The hardware determines the expertise necessary to create a picture from a video source. The process can be simple or complex. Older methods of digitizing video require a special video-digitizing device with accompanying software. The user connects the video source into the video-digitizing device, and connects the device to a computer. The software provides the capability to capture a single frame or picture from the video. Some newer multimedia computers offer a built-in video source. Multimedia computers usually come with software that makes digitizing a picture simple. At its easiest, the steps of digitizing a picture involve plugging in video-capture hardware, starting a program that displays the video, and copying a still picture from the video by clicking with the mouse.

Hardware manufacturers have created a new device that is important for digitizing pictures: the still video camera. Examples are Apple's Quick Take model and Canon's Zap Shot model. Although the devices differ significantly from manufacturer to manufacturer, they look and operate like a traditional camera but create a digital video image. Still video cameras are popular in schools because of their ease of use and the ease of incorporating the pictures into a multimedia presentation. The teacher can send students on a field trip with a still video camera, and then have them create a multimedia presentation using their own text and pictures.

Incorporating a high-resolution digital picture into a Hypermedia presentation is simple in some authoring programs and difficult in others. Several elements need to be included in a digital picture. The user must tell the program the name of the picture's file, place the picture on the screen, and specify the shape and size of the picture. The way the user tells the authoring program this information can be straightforward or extremely complex. As a general rule, the easier it is to do a task, such as placing a picture, the less power the user has to manipulate that picture. For example, the process of simply dropping a copy of the picture onto a screen is simple, but once the author places that picture on the screen, it is relatively static. The process of describing the name and position of the picture involves a complex set of commands, but the commands can be changed to do things such as animate the picture by moving it around the screen. Thus, ease and power act in opposition to one another.

Digital Sound   A strong analogy can be formed between digitizing pictures and digitizing sound. Like a digital picture, a digital sound is also a file. As with pictures, different levels of quality are possible, and the higher the quality, the bigger the file. When magnified, a digital picture is a collection of small dots. Analogously, sound is a collection of volumes and frequencies, each of which represents a moment in audio time. Moments in time, when placed end to end, produce the original sound. Quality depends upon the sound sampling rate—the size of the moments in time. If they are relatively large, then the sound is less like the original. If they are small, then the sound is a more exact copy.

To create a digital sound that is close to the original, each dot of time must be quite small. That means that a file for even a low-quality sound is rather large. A file for a high-quality sound can be much larger.

As with pictures, how digital audio is created depends upon the exact hardware and software available. Newer multimedia computers have built-in capabilities to create digital audio. Older computers, or computers lacking this capability, require a specialized sound device called a sound card or sound board. These devices come with software that makes the capture process relatively simple: The user simply plugs in a sound source, such as a microphone or a cassette player, and converts sounds to a digital file.

All Hypermedia programs have some capability to incorporate audio. Exactly how an author incorporates a digital sound is different within each program. Some have capabilities to capture the sound directly into the authoring program. In some cases, that can simplify the learning curve for students: Rather than learning a whole new program, they only have to learn a feature of the program they are already using. Other Hypermedia authoring programs operate better when you digitize the sound using external programs and simply incorporate the sound file after creating it. Either way, the incorporation of audio is well within the capability of upper primary-age students.

Video Disks   As mentioned earlier, files containing high-resolution pictures are large. In the case of video, crude pictures are not sufficient to make meaningful videos, so we must begin with high-resolution pictures. Motion requires the use of many of these pictures. The smallest number of pictures or "frames" that will produce smooth motion is about 15 frames per second. This means a single minute of video requires at least 900 pictures. Commercial video uses a speed of 24 to 30 frames per second; high-quality video uses more. If we think of high-resolution picture and audio files as large, then we must think of video files as an order of magnitude larger.

Because of the sheer volume of the digital data, the earliest attempts to connect video with Hypermedia used a totally external format. The software producers recorded video on a video disk, and the student would play it back on a separate monitor. The Hypermedia presentation itself started and stopped the video disk player. The disk format allowed fast, nonlinear access to any piece of video.

Activating a video disk player from a Hypermedia program is a standard feature, although the ease of doing so varies from program to program. To make the function work, the learner must connect a video disk player to her computer. Once connected, the process for making the video disk player run is simple. A helpful analogy is to imagine that the computer can operate the remote control for the video disk player. Besides the usual functions of a VCR, a video disk player also has a "Seek" function that allows the player to go to the start of any piece of video quickly.

Compressed Digital Video   The size of digital video files made the video disk viable for several years. This approach is not ideal, however, because schools need extra hardware—a video disk player and a television—and because the system presents two visual attention points: the computer screen and the video screen. However, recent developments in video compression afford other possibilities. The early digital video was essentially a process of describing every dot on the screen and giving a new description every 30th of a second. This process produces very large files, and those files contain redundant information. For example, within a single frame many dots are the same color, and from frame to frame only minimal change may occur in any single dot. This redundancy represents empty space in the digital description of a movie, and digital compression reduces that empty space from the digital description. As digital compression improves, it squeezes more empty space. At this writing, however, the size of digital video files is still quite large, even with the best compression tools.

To keep file sizes reasonable, a Hypermedia author has to use video sparingly. One way to do this is to keep videos short. Another way is to use small video windows; the smaller the window, the fewer the dots the digitizer must describe. This is changing rapidly, however, as digital compression helps make file sizes smaller and hard disk space gets less expensive. Just a few years ago, a few seconds of video filled a standard 40 megabyte hard drive. Now, with hard drives in excess of 500 megabytes and video compressed to almost one-tenth the original size, a Hypermedia author easily can incorporate several minutes of video into a Hypermedia presentation. Even so, video files are still very large, so video must be used sparingly.

For the most part, if a student can capture a still picture from a video source, she can create a digital movie. Although some video capture tools create still pictures only, most current tools can create either still or motion video. The difficulty and the artistry occur not in simply capturing video, but in capturing exactly the video wanted. This may involve complex video editing. Programs are available specifically for this purpose. Some Hypermedia development programs have built-in video editing capabilities, although this is a rather uncommon feature due to its complexity. Video compression is important, and most video-capture software is programmed into the application. Programs that compress video do it better; they generally create smaller files while maintaining the quality of the video.

USING HYPERMEDIA IN THE CLASSROOM: A DEVELOPMENTAL APPROACH

We recommend that if any teachers and students are to use Hypermedia, then the entire school must develop a general plan for use of Hypermedia technology. This plan will allow children to develop their abilities continuously using Hypermedia. Without a plan, any single teacher would have a difficult time managing the use of Hypermedia in the classroom because of the range of experiences the children may have. Three questions need to be answered in designing a plan to use Hypermedia in a school system: When do we start, how far will we go, and what path will we follow from the beginning to the end?

The first consideration is, when are children ready to begin using Hypermedia? Children must have reading and writing skills, and they must be able to conceptualize information in a nonlinear way. We believe that the upper primary grades are a developmentally appropriate age to begin. A teacher might choose to start earlier or later, depending on the nature of her children and the teaching and learning approach she uses.

For the first project, the children will learn to use Hypermedia to create a product. We do not believe students should learn to use any software tool out of context. However, teachers should keep the content of the first Hypermedia project rather simple and well defined so that students can devote sufficient mental energy to learning the software procedures. A good first project might be a whole-group activity in which the class contributes pieces of a Hypermedia project. Another possibility for the first project is one in which groups of students work on a small number of separate projects. In the early stages of learning about Hypermedia, we believe it is important that children work together and talk about the organization of information. The role of the constructivist teacher is explicitly to guide children's thinking.

The first project should start with the simpler features of the Hypermedia program, such as pictures and text. However, teachers should get to higher level features quickly because these are highly motivating for students.

A simple text-and-picture project is sufficient to begin creating nonlinear organizations of information. One way to help children see the organization of information is to create a web or graphical representation of a concept or an idea. Another way is to have children brainstorm elements of the presentation and put their ideas on note cards. The teacher can put the note cards on a bulletin board and connect the cards with pieces of yarn to show the nonlinearity of the Hypermedia connections.

Even when starting Hypermedia with older children, the teacher still must include some instruction of the nonlinear organization of information. Most children and adults who have never created nonlinear presentations will have a strong tendency to organize information linearly. They need to see directly how to organize information in a nonlinear way, and they need exemplars of nonlinear organization. Then, as with all instruction, the teacher needs to insure that they put this new information into action. This is the teacher's explicit task. For many students, the path to nonlinear representation of information is steep indeed.

THE DETAILS OF *HYPERCARD*

The reader may find the following example helpful to understanding the operation of a Hypermedia development program. To make the example as concrete as possible, we describe the beginning steps necessary to create a simple Hypermedia presentation using the *HyperCard* program. Although the language and the specific procedures relate to *HyperCard*, the concepts involved in putting together a Hypermedia presentation relate to any Hypermedia authoring program.

Definition of Terms

HyperCard contains five entities that its creators call objects: the stack, the card, the button, the field, and the background. The stack refers to the entire project. A stack is also a file. The card is essentially a single screen of information. The card can contain pictures, words, buttons, and fields. A button is an area on the screen that makes something happen. The most common use for a button is to go to another card; this is done by clicking on the button with the mouse. A field is a word processing area. It can be shaped to fit any rectangular area on the screen. The background can be thought of as existing behind the cards. The background can be seen through the card, and many cards in a stack can have a common background. The background can contain graphics, buttons, and fields.

Experimenting with *HyperCard* Tools

HyperCard's Tools menu is shown in Figure 7–1. Under the Tools menu is a tool box containing tools that the user can "tear off" and place anywhere on the screen. You will use the tool box often when creating a *HyperCard* stack.

A good place to begin learning about *HyperCard* is by experimenting with the graphics tools. Start with the pencil and all the other graphics tools below the pencil in the tool box. Each of these tools lets you put graphics on the screen. To select a tool, move the pointer to that tool and click it. Then, when you move from the tool box, you will notice that the pointer changes to an icon of that tool. Most of the graphics tools work by clicking and dragging—holding the mouse button down while moving the cursor. Experiment with the Pencil, the Paint Brush, the Spray Can, the Rectangle, and the Oval tool. The Eraser lets you remove graphics from the screen. The Paint Bucket lets you fill in enclosed spaces—that is, a space on the screen that is enclosed within a line. Be careful with the Paint Bucket, because if you leave a hole in the line around the space you are filling, the paint will "run out" and cover the whole screen. Don't spill the paint!

The last tool you should try is the Text tool. You use the Text tool to put simple, short pieces of text on the screen. The Text tool works differently than the other tools. You must move the text bar to the area where you want the text, click the mouse to activate a text cursor, and type the desired text. If the text is longer

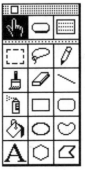

the **browse** tool ( ), the **button** tool ( ), the **field** tool ( ), the **select** tool ( ), the **lasso** tool ( ), the **pencil** tool ( ), the **paint brush** tool ( ), the **eraser** tool ( ), the **line** tool ( ), the **spray can** tool ( ), the **rectangle** tool ( ), the **rounded rectangle** tool ( ), the **paint bucket** tool ( ), the **oval** tool ( ), the **curve** tool ( ), the **text** tool (**A**), the **regular polygon** tool ( ) and the **polygon** tool ( )

Figure 7–1
The *HyperCard* Tool Box

than a few words, then there is a much better way to put text on the screen than using the text tool; this is the purpose of a field.

You use the Select tool or the Lasso tool to move and modify graphics. The Select tool lets you identify a rectangular graphic. The Lasso tool lets you identify other shapes. With these tools, a graphic can be moved, the size of a graphic can be changed, and a graphic can be copied.

The creation of a stack uses the top three tools in the tool box: the Browse tool, the Button tool, and the Field tool. Click the Browse tool when you want to use a stack, push buttons, or type in the field. The Button tool is used for the creation and modification of buttons. The Field tool is used for the creation and modification of fields.

Creating a *Hypercard* Stack

Begin a New Stack   To begin a new stack, pull down the File menu and choose New Stack. Next, name the file "Pets." Your new *HyperCard* stack now has one card. The stack also has a blank background.

Using the Text tool, type the title "All About Pets" and your name on the first card. This card will be the main menu for the stack. Later you will put buttons on this card. Buttons provide the nonlinear connections among all the cards in the stack. Your card should look something like the one shown in Figure 7–2.

Make a New Card and Name It   Pull down the Edit menu and select New Card. Now you have two cards, one with the title on it and one that is blank. Your cards have an order. The first card is always the one *HyperCard* creates when you

Figure 7–2

First Card in *Hypercard* Stack

select New Stack. Whenever you add a new card, *HyperCard* places it directly after the card on the screen.

Give the new card the name "Hamster." To do this, pull down the Objects menu and select Card Info. This gives you a window that lets you specify the characteristics of the card. The only thing you are interested in now is the name. Type the word "Hamster" in the box at the top of the window and you have named the card. When you have finished typing, click the OK button. You will use this name later when you want to move among cards.

Draw a Picture   Draw a picture of a hamster on this card using the Pencil tool. Put the drawing in the middle of the screen, leaving room for a title on the top and some information about hamsters on the bottom. Next, type the title "Hamster" at the top of the page using the text tool. You can change the look of the text—bold, italics, size, etc.—by double-clicking the text tool in the tool box. For more sophisticated stacks, you might want to include a commercially prepared graphic or a scanned image of a hamster.

Add a Field and Type On It   Put a field at the bottom of the card using the Objects menu. Select New Field from the bottom of the menu. Notice that the Field tool is automatically selected after you have created a new field.

Now, make the field the size and shape that you want by stretching it from the corners. To do this, place the cursor on a corner, hold down the mouse button, and drag the cursor outward. Then move the field by clicking on the middle of the field and dragging the cursor until the field is in the desired location. Once the field is the shape and size you want, and in the place you want, choose the Browse tool. You must have the Browse tool selected to type in a field. Type in the field some information about a hamster as a pet. Your card should now look similar to the one shown in Figure 7–3.

Make More Cards Using Cut, Paste, and Go Recent   Make a third card by selecting File and then New Card. Name this new card "Dog," just as you did the "Hamster" card by selecting Objects and Card Info. After you have named the card, type "Dog" on the top of the card in large, bold letters.

When you buy *HyperCard*, you usually get a clip art library—a collection of pictures that can be added to cards. Find pictures of dogs from the clip art collection and place them on your card using the Cut and Paste functions. There are several ways to open the clip art stack. One easy way is to use the Home stack that Claris provides with Hypercard. To get to the Home stack, select "Home" from the Go menu. On the Home stack there is a button called "Art Bits" or "Art Ideas." These are stacks filled with clip art that you are free to use in your stacks. When you find a picture of a dog, select that picture using the Select tool or the Lasso tool. Once the picture is selected, use the Edit menu to copy the picture. After copying the picture, go to your dog card. You can go directly to this card by using the Recent option in the Go menu. The Recent option shows small representations of all the cards you have seen recently. While looking at these cards, click the dog

Figure 7–3

Hamster Card with Information
Typed in Field

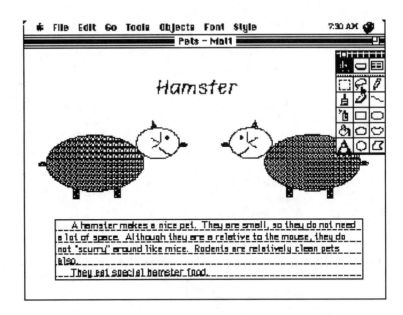

card. Paste the picture using the Edit menu. To move back and forth from your stack to the clip art stack, select Go from the menu at the top of the screen and then select Recent.

Now put a field on the card and type some information about dogs in that field. Your new card should look something like Figure 7–4.

Move Around the Stack Using the Go Menu   You can move among your *Hypercard* cards using the Go menu. Pull down the Go menu and select the First command. That will take you to the first card, the one with the "All About Pets"

Figure 7–4

The "Dog" Card

title. Pulling down the Go menu and selecting the Next command will take you to the next card, the hamster card. The Last command in the Go menu will move you to the last card in your stack. You can move easily around your stack using the First, Last, Next, and Prev commands.

Do It All Over Again   Make three more cards for three different kinds of pets, such as cats, birds, and ferrets. Put graphics and fields on each card. Remember to name each card using the Card Info command from the Objects menu. Remember the exact name used in the Card Info window. You will use that name later.

Create the Menu Buttons   Once you have all the information in your stack, you are ready to link all the cards. The first card is your main menu card. Go there. Pull down the Objects menu and select the New Button command. Notice that *HyperCard* automatically selects the Button tool in the tool box. Move the button to a convenient location by clicking in the middle and dragging. You will be using five buttons, one for each animal, so plan for all five buttons as you place the first one. Notice that the "Button Name" area has "New Button" as the name of the button. Double click the button and change its name by typing the word "Hamster." After changing the name, click the script button. This is how you make the button do what you want it to do. Type *Go to card "Hamster"* in the space between the On Mouse Up script and the End Mouse Up script. This tells *HyperCard* to display the hamster card when the student clicks on the button named "Hamster." If you click on the button named "Hamster," then the second half of a click, letting the mouse button up, will move to the card called "Hamster." Your screen should look like the one shown in Figure 7–5.

Go through the same process to create a button for each animal. Your main menu card should look something like the one shown in Figure 7–6.

Test Your Buttons   Make sure each of your buttons works. The name of the card, from the Card Info menu, must match what you typed in quotes in your script for the button. The most common reasons that a button does not work are that the author forgot to name a card or named the card differently from the name used in the script. For example, the author might put an "s" at the end of one and not the other.

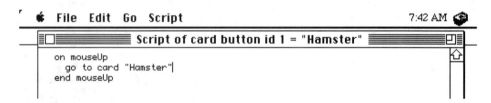

Figure 7–5

Simple *HyperCard* Script

Figure 7–6

Main Menu Card for Hypermedia
Stack

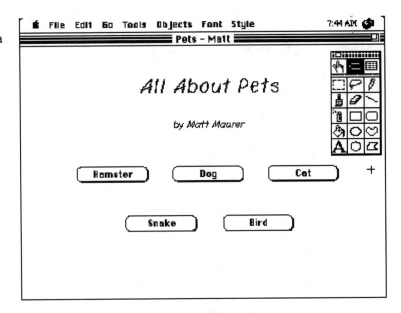

Jazz Your Buttons Using Visual Effects   You can add special effects to a button to make the change from one card to another more interesting. Using the Button tool, double click on a button. From the button definition window, click Visual Effects to see a list of the possible visual effects. Choose one, and try it!

Make a "Home" Button Using the Background   After you have installed the buttons on the main menu card, you have created a way to manage each card, but you do not have a way of returning to the main menu. What you need is a button on each card that takes you back to the menu card, the first card in your stack. Go to the Edit menu and select the Background command. You can tell that you are working with the background because the menu at the top is different; it looks as if there are stitches around it. As mentioned earlier, the objects on the background are on every card. This is a quick way to get a button on every card. It also works for graphics and fields.

Select the New Button command from the Objects menu. Since we are in the background, this button is on the background. Select the corner of the button and drag it to size it into a one-inch square. Next, move it to the lower right corner.

Double click the button. Go to the script, and type Go First. Click the OK command. This is how you activate the button.

Double click the button again. We are going to use an icon—a small picture—to indicate the function of the button, instead of its name. First de-select the Show Name command by clicking its box. Then, click the Icon button. This will allow you to select an icon. Choose one that seems to indicate returning to the main menu; the bent arrow or the house are common choices for this function. After you choose an icon, click OK, and you will return to the background.

Exit the background by selecting Background from the Edit menu. Notice that the new button is on every card. The stack should be complete. Test it to make sure everything works!

LESSON IDEAS

Following are several examples of Hypermedia projects children can create. We offer these not as specific ideas that we intend teachers to use directly in their classrooms, but instead as starting points. Teachers can adapt these lesson ideas or use them to help form their own stacks.

LESSON IDEA 1:   The "Me" Stack

Important objectives for children in the early grades are the development of self-concept and the strengthening of self-esteem. A common activity in that area involves having children tell their classmates about themselves, their experiences, and their lives outside school. This may include information about family, home, travel, extended family, toys, friends, neighborhood, and a number of other topics. A teacher can easily adapt this activity to Hypermedia by creating a predefined, nonlinear structure for a defined set of facts. The children tell about themselves and illustrate their stories with the graphics tools. The activity can include writing objectives if appropriate, or the children can dictate to a classroom helper, such as an aide, parent helper, or older student, and the helper can enter the data.

The "Me" stack is an easy yet helpful introduction to nonlinear information for children. They do not have to conceptualize the nonlinear organization of information, but they can see how it works. The nonlinear information also has personal relevance to them because it is about them. We have seen this approach used in a variety of early childhood classrooms with great success. An example of a "Me" stack is shown in Figure 7–7.

LESSON IDEA 2:   Science and Social Studies Reports

The standard report or term paper has many positive learning outcomes, but few students enjoy these assignments. The teacher can extend the outcomes of a report by having students use Hypermedia rather than plain text. Using this approach, the teacher can not only maintain the writing objectives, the content-related objectives, the critical analysis objectives, and creativity objectives, but also add objectives related to creative expression with other forms of media. In addition, many students find working with a good Hypermedia authoring program to be motivating intrinsically. Creating high-quality pictures, editing short video sequences, and adding audio tracks can help students make constructivist connections and enjoy a motivational boost. A report on whales, for example, may include whale songs, high-resolution pictures of whales, and even short video sequences showing whales in motion. A report on the Civil War can include scanned images of Civil War documents, songs from the era, and video sequences showing battle recreations.

Although teachers may fear that working with scanners and video digitizers will take children away from time on task, these activities can actually increase the time chil-

Figure 7–7

A "Me" Stack with Connections Among Cards

dren are engaged academically. Some children may have a greater interest in the content area if they have more ways to display their knowledge than only the printed word. We have seen many examples of Hypermedia presentations evoking a child's brilliance.

LESSON IDEA 3:   Classroom Data Bases

Another use of Hypermedia authoring programs is to create data bases. The difference between standard data bases and Hypermedia data bases is that they can contain more than just text. For example, a tree identification data base created with a Hypermedia program can include scanned pictures of tree leaves along with a verbal description of a tree or its digitized photo. A historical data base might include textual information along with digitized pictures of historical artifacts, videos of historical sites, and folk songs of the period. One of the exciting aspects of these classroom data bases is that students can use them from year to year, add to them over time, and over the course of several years create a large, rich collection of data.

ADHERENCE TO COPYRIGHT LAWS

Teachers and students should be aware of the limitations that copyright laws place on the creation of Hypermedia presentations. We should think of scanners and other digitizing devices as we do the photocopy machine. Material we can legally copy with a photocopy machine we also can scan and use in a Hypermedia presentation. It is technically possible, and it is even rather simple, to digitize many forms of copyrighted material. Students can even alter this material. For instance, children can copy sequences from commercial videos, scan photos from books, and digitize music from commercial tapes and compact disks. Most of this material is protected under copyright laws, so students should not copy it. Students can alter this material by re-editing a video using computer-based editing tools. They might change music using a variety of sound-altering programs. Neither of these practices is legal or ethical. Students seldom understand the importance of intellectual property, so teachers should include this topic in their instruction about the use of Hypermedia authoring programs.

STACKS FROM THE LITERATURE

Teachers can get many Hypermedia project ideas from the literature. We offer the following description of one project as an inducement for teachers to seek other examples in journals, such as *Electronic Learning, Creative Classroom, Technology and Learning,* and *Learning and Leading with Technology*.

In an article entitled *Learning HyperCard Through Story Writing*, Havice (1994) describes a project in which fourth- and fifth-grade students learned to create stories using *HyperCard*. The article contains a description of the materials and a day-by-day lesson plan for the unit. Havice includes an example of one of the student's stories. The author makes many observations about the students and their reaction to this tool. One observation was that students were active, constructivist learners and on a few occasions even helped their teachers learn. Havice observed:

> Even the students who were initially uninterested in participating in this project were eager to author a story of their own after observing their peers. Students learned to nurture and support one another, realizing that decisions they make can affect others. (p 26)

Havice concludes the article with these comments:

> Hypermedia provides students and teachers the means to revolutionize the classroom. I see authoring tools such as *HyperCard* as the creation tools or "the chalk

and slate" of the next century—tools that allow the student to write with text, video, photos, audio, and graphics. Activities such as the electronic story book activity will prove to be invaluable in the future. (p 26)

IMPLICATIONS FOR THE COMMUNITY OF LEADERSHIP

Two significant responsibilities of the community of leadership is to establish a quality academic program and to support it with instructional technology. Once the various participants have accepted the premises of the academic goals and objectives, the second, more difficult task begins. The community of leadership must explain, describe, model, and defend academic decisions. The formal leader and the community of leadership often stand between the internal school-community—the participants in the educational process—and the external school-community—the patrons of the school district who do not have children attending the district's schools. Misconceptions, rumors, and erroneous statements often plague an unprepared school administration. The community of leadership's responsibility is to intervene actively to communicate its goals and advocate the efficacy of its academic program.

Krug (1992, pp. 432–433), in the context of the effective schools movement, suggested five areas of involvement in the school's teaching and learning program for formal leaders: defining mission, managing curriculum and instruction, supervising teaching, monitoring student progress, and promoting instructional climate. Defining the school's mission and managing curriculum and instruction involve the process of promoting technology as a support to a quality academic program. Supervising teaching (clinical supervision), monitoring student progress, and promoting instructional climate are community of leadership process skills that support the leader's task of improving teaching and learning. As Krug (1992) puts it:

> The effective instructional leader is perceived as one who strategically applies knowledge to solve contextually specific problems and to achieve the purposes of schooling through others. (p. 434)

Modeling and Encouraging Powerful Instruction

If the community of leadership wants to help students garner the benefits that Hypermedia can provide, principals and Hypermedia specialists must first lead by example. We need to model the use of Hypermedia in our media centers, and where possible, bring Hypermedia into classrooms in powerful learning contexts. Leaders must model examples that support the curriculum. Although difficult to plan and hard to accomplish, modeling is a most effective teaching tool. The strongest examples are those that teacher-models connect to student learning within the curriculum. Teachers need strong examples to convince them that this tool can become part of their regular classroom work. Teachers are likely to consider Hypermedia activities which are unconnected to the curriculum as unimportant or as an enrichment activity.

Also, formal leaders must encourage teachers to take risks by having students use Hypermedia. Every attempt need not be successful or elaborate, but we must celebrate the courage to try. With support and guidance, Hypermedia projects can become as successful or more successful learning activities than many of our more traditional, transmission model approaches. In addition, such projects nearly always improve student motivation, and increased motivation can have a multiplicity of positive effects on individual students and on the school's shared culture. Hypermedia may be one strong component of the message that the school is an active and engaged learning community in which everyone is a life-long learner.

Two processes by which the community of leadership can teach novice teachers about Hypermedia and encourage them to use Hypermedia to support a quality academic program are peer coaching and teacher staff development or in-service education. Peer coaching is a method of formative assessment for the improvement of instruction. The process involves the teacher and the coach selecting an area of interest, planning a lesson, observing the lesson using an objective data-collection tool, analyzing the data, and sharing the learning. Teacher in-service education is a formal process which involves providing teachers with new information about teaching and learning. We elaborate upon both strategies in Chapter 10.

Availability of Hardware and Software

Another obligation and responsibility of the community of leadership is to provide appropriate hardware and software. A good Hypermedia development station can be quite expensive. Most schools must buy and place the stations with great care. As mentioned earlier, one issue with Hypermedia is its large hard disk requirements. Hypermedia computers must have large hard drives to allow students to store large digital media files. Each machine also needs sound capabilities so students can hear the sounds they have created. Each classroom probably does not need every specialty tool on every computer. A school may be able to function quite well with only one or two devices. One or two video digitizers and scanners will be sufficient in most situations. However, if Hypermedia development expands, then the community of leadership must be prepared to become creative at helping learners get the equipment needed to remain excited about learning.

The community of leadership also must consider how to achieve the maximum access for the children who will benefit most. The school media center is the logical place for several types of multimedia products intended for student use. However, other products may be better for classroom use. A typical solution is to put multimedia stations on wheels so teachers can move them from classroom to classroom. If teachers will use the stations for whole-group activities, then large-screen displays should be part of the stations so that the material can be displayed large enough for all to see. The school can distribute Hypermedia authoring stations in the same way. If your school can afford only a few Hypermedia stations, the community of leadership may decide to put the stations on wheels and have teachers schedule their use in blocks of time. This is one way to get the capability into the classroom without limiting the students' access.

Publishing Hypermedia: Making Learning Public

The community of leadership must encourage teachers to publish students' Hypermedia projects. Although this can be more difficult than publishing student writing, teachers should find ways nonetheless. A computer station near the school entrance that displays student projects can be a pleasant greeting for school visitors and can have a positive impact on school-community relations. Most importantly, students will see their work being used by others. A parent going through a student's Hypermedia project can benefit from the teaching and learning environment in many ways. Another way to publish Hypermedia projects is by having an older student create presentations for younger students. The younger students, then, become natural readers of the Hypermedia. Hypermedia projects also can be published by making them available through telecommunications. A huge volume of Hypermedia material is available on the InterNet and the World Wide Web. Students' work can become part of that growing collection.

CONCLUSION

Effective instructional strategies, with or without technology, rely upon schema theory. Schema are mental models of concepts or ideas that children use to connect new knowledge to what they already know to expand remembering and learning. Hypermedia is an instructional tool that supports this constructivist strategy. The creation of Hypermedia stacks and cards resembles the process of constructing knowledge that all learners use. Additionally, Hypermedia has a nonlinear or divergent thinking capability which most resembles how learners learn.

Just as schema theory is connected to Hypermedia as an instructional support, metacognition is connected to critical thinking and problem solving. In the next chapter we explore the basic elements of metacognition and how instructional technology can support a quality academic program that infuses thinking strategies into content areas.

REFERENCES

Anderson, R. C. (1985). Role of the reader's schema in comprehension, learning, and memory. In H. Singer & R. B. Ruddell (Eds.), *Theoretical models and processes of reading* (pp. 372–384). Newark, DE: International Reading Association.

Anderson, R. C., & Pearson, P. D. (1984). A schema-theoretical view of basic processes in reading comprehension. In P. D. Pearson (Ed.), *Handbook of Reading Research*. New York: Longman.

Havice, B. (1994). Learning HyperCard through story writing. *The Computing Teacher, 22*(1), 23–26.

Krug, S. E. (1992). Instructional leadership: A constructivist perspective. *Educational Administration Quarterly, 28*(3), 430–443.

Maurer, M. M. (1995). Elementary school students as college faculty. *Journal of Computing in Teacher Education, 12*(1), 7–10.

RESOURCE LIST

Digital Chisel, Pierian Springs Software

HyperCard, Claris Corporation

HyperStudio, Roger Wagner Publishing

Linkway, IBM Corporation

Macromind Director, Macromedia, Inc.

CHAPTER 8

Thinking with Technology

The thinking curriculum, unlike more traditional content areas, presents a challenge to educators. The thinking curriculum is difficult to observe, subject to disagreement about implementation, can appear frivolous or seem like play, and has serious, organized detractors. However, quality thinking goals and objectives support the existing curriculum while helping students gain sophisticated skills for the emerging world of work in the Twenty-first Century. Thinking curricula develop responsible and productive adults.

In this chapter we explain why thinking is important, establish a working definition, and relate the thinking curriculum to constructivism. We re-emphasize the value of a thinking curriculum and our belief that technology can enhance a quality instructional program. Next, we explore developmentally appropriate thinking software. We emphasize *Logo* as a thinking curriculum tool for young children. We describe the history of *Logo*, the ideas on which it is based, its components, the power of *Logo*, and research on *Logo*. We present a sketch of a thinking curriculum with sample *Logo* lessons, including the *Logo* house, polygons and stars, and the Total Turtle Trip Theorem. Finally, we investigate the values and beliefs of leading *Logo* scholars and suggest implications for the community of leadership.

INTRODUCTION

Why Is Thinking Important?

Teaching our students to think is perhaps our most important goal. Yet much of the available evidence indicates that our schools' thinking curriculum is not faring well. We periodically read shocking articles reporting the inadequacy of schools in teaching students critical thinking and problem solving. Although as educational leaders we may overlook the narrowly focused reports in the popular media, we cannot overlook carefully designed research that corroborates those reports (e.g., Ennis, 1980, Nisbett & Ross, 1980, Norris & King, 1984). It is important that our graduates be clear, effective, and correct thinkers. Clearly, some change is necessary in our approach to teaching and learning about thinking.

A Definition of Thinking

In education, the two terms most frequently used to refer to thinking are *problem solving* and *critical thinking*. Other terms are *higher order thinking* and *creative thinking*. John Dewey (1910) wrote about *reflective thinking*. Some scholars make distinctions between these various terms, but for our purposes we refer to thinking as a curricular area.

It is important to distinguish between remembering and thinking. One way is to view remembering and thinking as separate points along a continuum from data to information to knowledge. Remembering is an active process that begins with a reason to remember and ends with recall. Thinking follows recall and satisfies the original reason for remembering. Thinking is a process that involves the active mental manipulation of the things we remember.

To illustrate, the text in a simple story may state, "The boy went to the store. He bought milk." The student's purpose or motivation to remember may be the teacher's question, "What did the boy buy?" The answer, "milk," is simple recall or remembering. An excellent follow-up question, one that elicits critical thinking, would be, "Why did the boy buy milk?" Answering this question requires the student to combine information from the text with her own experience to construct a response that demonstrates her thinking strategies.

Some scholars call the example above a problem-solving event. We are interested in problem solving, but also in thinking that does not involve problems. For example, the evaluation of the quality of a piece of writing is difficult to frame as a problem, yet it involves the active mental manipulation of ideas that students remember (Bloom, 1956).

At this point some educators may suggest that remembering is not thinking. Thinking does not stop with remembering. Beyond remembering, thinking is the active manipulation of what a person remembers to arrive at a decision or conclusion. In Ennis' words, thinking is "deciding what to believe or do" (1985, p. 6).

For a student to engage in appropriate and effective thinking, she must have the skills necessary to engage in thinking and the desire or disposition to engage in thinking. These two elements represent the cognitive and affective aspects of thinking. We can think of no curricular area in which affect is more important. Since thinking is a largely intellectual process, it is essential that the disposition to think be present. So thinking is not simply "deciding what to believe or do," but also *wanting to decide* what to believe or do.

We suggest that a third element is necessary for effective thinking. Students also must know *when* to think. Thinkers combine a desire to think with their thinking skills and thinking strategies to produce intellectual products: decisions and ideas. Effective thinkers add judgments—judgments about when to engage in thinking and when to apply specific thinking skills and thinking strategies.

Constructivism and Thinking

We learned in Chapter 1 that basic constructivist philosophy and learning theory hold that children construct new knowledge and interpretations from connections with existing knowledge. We discovered that the process was observation, hypothesis generation and testing, and reflection. Children's recognition of their own thinking errors motivates them to generate and test revised hypotheses accompanied by reflection. The outcome of this process is the children's construction of increasingly sophisticated and elaborate mental models or schemata.

Another process supported by learning theory is metacognition: children actively learning about how they learn. It is through this learning theory that children move from creating and making connections (schema theory) to developing thinking strategies. The movement from schema generation to metacognition is the transition from data to information to knowledge. As Mason and Au (1990) observe, "Effective readers, unlike poor or beginning readers, are *aware* of what they are doing as they read [learn], and of what they need to do to meet their purposes. Awareness of one's own thinking or cognition is called *metacognition*" (p. 15).

Beyond mere awareness is children's ability to use successful strategies to meet their idiosyncratic purposes (Winograd & Paris, 1988). Children need to understand their own strategies to construct their purposes for learning and thinking and to adopt useful strategies to satisfy those purposes. The role of the teacher in fostering metacognition is to explicitly teach and model three basic approaches to metacognition: monitoring of learning, learning effective question-and-answer strategies, and reciprocal teaching. Mason and Au (1990) give an example of the latter strategy:

> Palinscar (1984) describes a program of instruction shown to be effective in improving children's comprehension monitoring/fostering activities. The program targets four activities: (1) self-questioning (asking main idea rather than detail questions), (2) summarizing, (3) predicting, and (4) evaluating (identifying and clarifying the meaning of difficult sections of the text). The basic procedure can be adapted for use with small groups of children from the first grade on up. (p. 59)

The reciprocal teaching aspect of this strategy requires that the teacher model each of the methods and that students mimic the process with scaffolding or support from the teacher until they demonstrate proficiency. Metacognitive strategies help create a process for cultivating children's thinking. According to Muth (1989):

> Part of the power and appeal of these strategies is that they are based on the theoretical delineation of a comprehension process. This delineation [thinking process] typically identifies the component, interactive processes of accessing prior knowledge [schema theory], inferring, and monitoring. (p. 245)

A RATIONALE FOR THINKING AS A DISTINCT CURRICULAR AREA

Just as scholars in the area of thinking argue about the definition of thinking, they also disagree about how we should organize the teaching of thinking in schools. One school of thought holds that thinking should be a separate curricular area. Another suggests that teachers should integrate thinking into existing curricular areas. We believe that a strong middle ground exists between these two points of view. Just as we believe that teachers should teach all subject areas in an integrated fashion, we also believe that teachers should teach thinking across the curriculum.

The danger in this approach is that thinking can get lost in the pursuit of other objectives. To avoid that possibility, we believe that thinking needs to have defined objectives, strategies, and activities within the existing curriculum, and that these objectives, strategies, and activities need to be integrated with those of other curricular areas. For example, teachers should not only use science writing in their literacy development efforts, they also should use science-related thinking opportunities for the development of the skills and dispositions for thinking. Thinking objectives should be explicit lest science become simply a remembering activity. Although we use science as an example here, this approach applies equally to all curricular areas.

Much of the thinking in the curriculum is implicit in existing curricular areas. Although we believe this is important, we believe teachers also should explicitly teach thinking skills and strategies. Teachers must give students ample opportunity to practice meaningful thinking and guide them through their thinking activities. We value the power of teachers as effective instructional leaders. Adults in the children's learning environments must model the concepts and skills expected of children. Adult models must describe explicitly how they complete learning tasks such as writing, solving problems, and thinking—what Paris calls "making thinking public" (Paris, 1987).

USING TECHNOLOGY TO SUPPORT THINKING IN THE CURRICULUM

Regardless of how we organize thinking in the curriculum, technology can help us meet thinking objectives. Good thinking activities have two parts. First, they encourage students to practice their thinking skills and allow them to try thinking in new ways. Second, they engage, excite, and challenge students' thinking. Many activities achieve these goals without the use of technology. However, many of the better thinking activities are so complex as to become a management nightmare. A complex simulation that is difficult for a teacher to manage is easily handled by a computer. One of the important contributions technology can make to the development of thinking is to manage complex and engaging activities for students.

Technology also can enhance a thinking activity to make it more engaging. A teacher can add high-quality pictures, sounds, and motion video to her instruction to increase the realism of a thinking activity. She also can add a data base of factual information to give students easy access to ideas they can use in their thinking. Computer software can draw from a large data base of possible alternatives and present random suggestions to students to help spark their creativity.

Software creators have developed programs designed specifically to develop thinking strategies and skills. Some programs pose interesting problems, others assist with creativity, others require critique or judgment, and others act as tools to assist students with their thinking. Many programs also help teachers develop positive thinking dispositions in themselves and in their students. Some of these programs have obvious connections to other curricular areas, while others do not. *Logo* is one family of thinking-oriented hardware and software. *Logo* is an excellent opportunity to apply metacognition to the thinking curriculum. We discuss *Logo* at length later in this chapter.

Developmentally Appropriate Thinking Software

Software designed for the specific purpose of helping students develop their thinking spans all grade levels and covers a variety of aspects of thinking, including creativity, pattern recognition, chunking, inductive strategies, and deductive strategies. Some programs even involve social aspects of thinking, such as working with a partner or a team to produce an intellectual outcome, engage in competition, or learn cooperation.

Programs such as *Thinkin' Things* (see Figure 8-1) and *The Backyard* contain several activities that are appropriate for preschool-age children. Some of the activities in these programs require children to make decisions, discover patterns, and see relationships. The designers frame these activities as games which can be quite engaging for many preschoolers. We have observed young children playing with this software, and we believe that thinking occurs while they play. However, the use of educational games to achieve defined outcomes requires some intervention from the teacher. As with all computer learning games, many children tend to circumvent the learning to play the game. To insure learning, the teacher may need to do some explicit instruction, either whole class, individuals, or small groups. However, it is more important that the teacher monitor the students' activities and progress and intervene appropriately as their learning progresses.

Software developers have designed simulations for students of all grade levels and disciplines. Simulations not only help our students develop a deeper understanding of math, science, and social studies, but also require our students to think. *SimEarth* is a wonderful example of the marriage of science and thinking. A screen from *SimEarth* is shown in Figure 8–2. To be successful in this planetary terraform-

Figure 8–1

Screen from *Thinkin' Things*

Used with permission of Edmark

ing simulation, students must know and understand many basic scientific principles, apply this knowledge and understanding, and make decisions about which actions to take.

The simulation starts with several options. Students can start with a living planet or a dead rock. Starting from scratch has the widest learning objectives, but using a living planet can allow the teacher to focus the students on a specific aspect of the simulation. The simulation lets students work with Venus or Mars. These two options offer students a wide range of learning objectives. A student must first make decisions about how Venus or Mars is different from Earth. The distance from the sun is one of the major factors that students must consider, so the students must first learn and make judgments about the relative position of Mars or Venus from the sun. The lack of atmosphere and the minimal supply of water are other key considerations. The simulation has tools to create atmospheric gases from the planet's crust and for capturing ice meteors. These factors interact with the availability of heat from the sun and can be used to achieve certain objectives. For instance, students can create the greenhouse effect to warm up Mars or they can increase particulate matter in the air to cool down Venus.

After the students have mastered the water and atmosphere problems, they can begin adding life forms to the planet. They can add plants, animals, and microscopic organisms. Students quickly learn that if they start with animals, the animals will fail to survive for a lack of food. They also learn that beginning with plants is more difficult than beginning with microscopic organisms. These features of the simulation reinforce issues of biological diversity and interdependence. Once students have successfully populated the planet with diverse fauna and flora, they

Figure 8–2

Screen from *SimEarth*

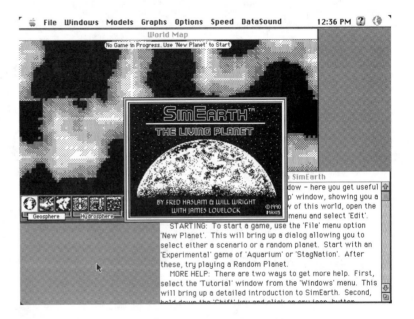

can introduce people. To ensure the survival of human beings, students must manipulate several social and political variables.

This single simulation spans the sciences: the earth and physical sciences, the biological sciences, and the social sciences. As students master each step of the terraforming process, they master important learning objectives. They also practice and sharpen their metacognitive skills: drawing inferences, questioning, arriving at the main idea, and summarizing. Students master these objectives by actively manipulating the environment in the simulation and seeing the results of their decisions.

Comparing the potential learning objectives in the simulation with the same objectives covered in a lecture makes the power of simulations evident. The simulation is much more engaging, and it requires students to think rather than passively absorb information. *SimEarth* is only one example of many simulations that teachers can use effectively to integrate thinking into their curriculum.

Creative thinking is another thinking skill. Creative thinking can occur in many areas of a child's learning, but it is perhaps most evident in children's writing. A number of programs focus specifically on creative writing, and several have creative writing as a component. Examples are *Creative Writer, Imagination Express, The Amazing Writing Machine,* and *Process Writer*. Each of these programs develops different aspects of the creative writing process. *Process Writer* focuses primarily on techniques for creative writing. *Creative Writer* provides a variety of motivational nudges and contextual connections for the young writer. The designers of *The Amazing Writing Machine* created the program for early writers. It gives examples of various forms of writing, including stories, letters, essays, poems, and journals, and requires students to fill in blanks. Students can also create their own writing from scratch. *The Amazing Writing Machine* is an example of scaffolding. It gives early writers support while they create. Once a student develops greater confidence and ability to create, the teacher can gradually reduce the support.

Although these creative writing programs have value, each seems more like a work in progress than a finished product. Software that focuses on the structural aspects of writing is rather narrow and is simply not engaging for early writers. Software that focuses on ideas and motivation is rather "thin." Not much is offered, and students quickly will exhaust the benefits that are available. A notable exception is a series called *Imagination Express*. At the time of this writing, there are four programs in the series: *Destination Rain Forest, Destination Neighborhood, Destination Castle,* and *Destination Ocean*. The software encourages students to write about some aspect of the destination. Each destination has a "fact book," a hypermedia presentation which is a rich source of information that students can use in their writing. Each program also includes story ideas. Although several creative writing programs include story ideas, the ideas in *Imagination Express* are usually expressed as classes of ideas rather than specific ideas. Story ideas that are too specific can act as a creative crutch, inhibiting rather than enhancing children's writing. Most of the ideas in *Imagination Express* force the child to make decisions about a general idea. Thus, the story ideas act more as a scaffold than a crutch. We believe *Imagination Express* is an example of creative writing software that is both helpful and engaging.

In discussing software that supports the development of student thinking, one publisher deserves special mention. Most software created by Tom Snyder Productions is designed to develop thinking skills. The software is also designed so that teachers can use it with whole classrooms organized in groups; this type of software is called "groupware." The software package includes materials that help the teacher implement lessons in the classroom. Specific titles that have a primary curricular focus include *The Graph Club* for math and *Geography Search* for social studies; these programs also encompass many multidisciplinary aspects. In addition, each title requires students to work in teams and to make decisions and judgments. To use Ennis's definition, the software asks children to decide "what to believe or do."

It is important that thinking software be engaging and challenging. If students do not connect with the activities, they will not reap the intended benefits. Most of Tom Snyder's software involves engaging situations. As an example, the program *Geography Search* involves discovering a city of gold in the New World. Teachers organize their students into teams and give each team specific responsibilities. The teams must work together to accomplish the tasks described in the initial part of the program. The computer provides information about the trip and manages all the variables, and the students keep a log book detailing their activities. A screen from *Geography Search* is shown in Figure 8–3.

Although a wide variety of software is designed to develop students' thinking skills and dispositions, we must respect the importance of the teacher in making the learning effective. Any of the great software that we have described can be a waste of students' learning time unless the teacher sets appropriate expectations, monitors progress, and provides help where students need it. Also, the software that we have described as inferior may become exactly the tool for the job in the hands of a skilled

Figure 8–3

Screen from *Geography Search*

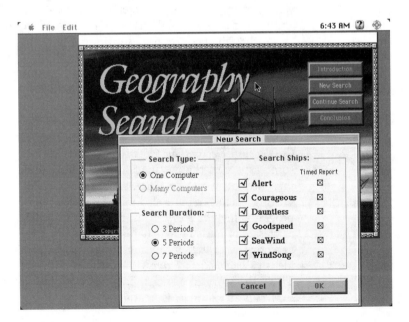

teacher who has imaginative ideas about how to use that software. To use an analogy, in the hands of a skilled and imaginative teacher, Popsicle™ sticks and empty milk jugs can be the most effective learning materials in the classroom.

LOGO AS A THINKING TOOL

The History of *Logo*

Seymour Papert developed *Logo* in the 1960s. Papert thoroughly describes *Logo* in the book *Mindstorms* (Papert, 1980). Although ancient in "computer years," the book still offers significant instructional insight and should be on the reading list of all the members of the community of leadership. Considering that Papert wrote *Mindstorms* when microcomputers were a wholly new concept, his vision is truly inspirational.

Papert developed the *Logo* concept after working at Piaget's Center for Genetic Epistemology. Piaget's constructivist thinking is evident in the writings of Papert and in the subsequent hardware and software developed by Papert and his followers. However, some distinct differences are apparent between Papert's thinking and Piaget's. In Papert's own words:

> Piaget writes about the order in which the child develops different intellectual abilities. I give more weight than he does to the influence of the materials a particular culture provides in determining that order. For example, our culture is very rich in materials useful for the child's construction of certain components of numerical and logical thinking. Children learn to count; they learn that the result of counting is independent of order and special arrangement; they extend this "conservation" to thinking about the properties of liquids as they are poured and of solids which change their shape. Children develop these components of thinking preconsciously and "spontaneously," that is to say without deliberate teaching. Other components of knowledge, such as the skills involved in doing permutations and combinations, develop more slowly, or do not develop at all without formal schooling. Taken as a whole this book is an argument that in many important cases this developmental difference can be attributed to our culture's relative poverty in materials from which the apparently "more advanced" intellectual structures can be built. This argument will be very different from cultural interpretations of Piaget that look for differences between city children in Europe or the United States and tribal children in African jungles. When I speak here of "our" culture I mean something less parochial. I am not trying to contrast New York with Chad. I am interested in the differences between precomputer cultures (whether in American cities or African tribes) and the "computer cultures" that may develop everywhere in the next decades. (1980, p. 20)

A General Description of *Logo*

Logo is a program that involves a variety of computer-related activities which involve the student in actively manipulating the computer. Some describe *Logo* as a programming language, which it is, but it is more than the typical programming language. Although children can produce a wide range of products using *Logo*, such as music or moving objects, the most common activity is working with turtle graphics. Turtle graphics is a process that involves drawing lines by directing a picture of a turtle around on the screen. The student gives the turtle a series of commands to move or turn, and as the turtle follows the commands, it draws a line.

Because the turtle is drawing lines, many people mistake *Logo* for a drawing program. In confusion, they may say, "That is the most difficult drawing program I have ever seen!" That statement, although true, is irrelevant. *Logo* can produce drawings, but the drawings are not the intended outcome. The intended outcome is the thinking that produces the drawings. *Logo* is not a drawing program but a thinking program. In Papert's words, "The Turtle serves no other purpose than of being good to program and good to think with" (1980, p. 11).

Several brands of *Logo* are available, including *LogoWriter, Logo Plus*, and the newest implementation of *Logo, Microworlds* (see Figure 8–4). All brands are quite similar. The turtle graphics commands are the most similar. The programs diverge in the area of higher level commands, such as sound commands or memory management commands.

New *Logo* Components

In the early stages of *Logo* development, Papert created robotic turtles that moved around on the floor. Once he developed the *Logo* concept, he created turtles that moved around on a computer screen. The physical turtle became something only seen in pictures. Recently, however, with improvements in robotic technology, the physical turtles have become practical for the classroom. A teacher can buy a

Figure 8–4

Screen from *Microworlds*

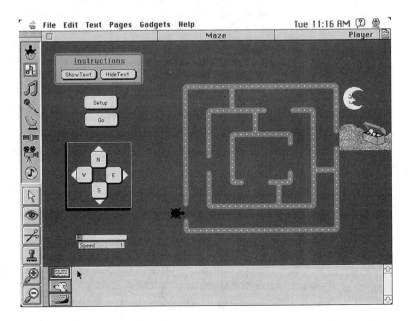

remote-controlled turtle and students can manipulate it from their computer just as they do the screen turtle. The addition of floor turtles adds an element of concreteness. This is important especially for younger children. For older children, the control of a robot can enhance their excitement with using *Logo*, which can contribute to both the development of their thinking skills and their disposition toward thinking. In short, robotic turtles can make *Logo* more exciting and challenging for children.

A more recent development is the connection of the *Lego* building block system to the *Logo* environment. The Lego Dacta Control Lab allows students to build a variety of devices that contain motors, sensors, lights, and sound devices. The students control the devices using a computer program with a graphical interface and a *Logo*-like language. A Lego Dacta Control Lab kit not only comes with all the parts to make it work—the computer program, the control box, the bricks, motors, sensor, and lights—it also comes with a teacher's guide and student design materials. A teacher can easily adapt this system to most thinking curricula. The only issue they must consider is one of gender bias. Many people perceive *Lego* blocks to be a "male" toy. Given that boys tend to be more aggressive when dealing with computers, and tend to have greater experience with *Lego* bricks, the teacher must take great care to appropriately manage the interaction of boys and girls when using this system.

Papert's Ideas and Beliefs

When Seymour Papert designed *Logo*, he brought significantly more to instructional technology than a family of hardware and software. His thinking about children, learning, and computers is powerful. He articulates much of this thinking in the book *Mindstorms* (1980). Two main ideas run through his book:

> (1) significant change in patterns of intellectual development will come about through cultural change, and (2) the most likely bearer of potentially relevant cultural change in the near future is the increasingly pervasive computer presence. (p. 216)

To set the context of his thinking, Papert relates that he had an intense interest in differential gears during his early childhood. He sees this experience as pivotal in his learning of mathematics. He calls a gear a "transitional object"—one that links the physical and the intellectual. Papert says,

> "You can be a gear, you can understand how it turns by projecting yourself into its place and turning with it" (p. xx).

Papert's own experience with gears guided his thinking in the development of *Logo*. He designed the *Logo* turtle to act as a transitional object.

Papert was trained as a mathematician, and his training pervades his thinking. He sees *Logo* as important for learning math and science, but he distinguishes between the way children learn naturally and the way they frequently learn in school:

I see "school math" as a social construction, a kind of QWERTY. A set of historical accidents . . . determined the choice of certain mathematical topics as *the* real mathematical baggage that citizens should carry. Like the QWERTY arrangement of typewriter keys, school math did make some sense in a certain historical context. But, like QWERTY, it has dug itself in so well that people take it for granted and invent rationalizations for it long after the demise of the historical conditions that made sense of it. Indeed, for most people in our culture it is inconceivable that school math could be very much different: This is the only mathematics they know. (p. 51)

Most physics curricula are similar to the math curriculum in that they force the learner into dissociated learning patterns and defer the "interesting" material past the point where most students can remain motivated enough to learn it. The powerful ideas and intellectual aesthetic of physics is lost in the perpetual learning of "prerequisite." (p. 122)

Papert does not simply criticize the existing school curriculum, he suggests that using systems like *Logo* can improve that curriculum. He contends that teachers should use engaging, inquiry-based materials and methods. Engaging activities that use transitional objects can get students back to more natural ways of learning, learning that captures rather than extinguishes a child's natural curiosity.

Our Experience with the Power of *Logo*

Adults often see children in a rigid dichotomy: smart or dumb, quick or slow, good or bad, talented or disabled. We believe these distinctions are false, socially inappropriate, potentially damaging to learning, and detrimental to development of a child's accurate self-concept. Instead, we believe that students are good at some things and not so good at others, quick in some situations and slow in others, talented in certain contexts and disabled in others. We believe all children are brilliant in their own way. One of the important duties of teachers should be to help children find ways to express and develop their brilliance.

When we watch students use *Logo*, we find numerous examples that confirm our thinking. A particularly powerful example occurred with a fourth-grade class that was in the early stages of learning about *Logo*. The class was going through a polygon worksheet, constructing the Total Turtle Trip Theorem (discussed later in the chapter). One student, Sam, was not working with the class. When we asked the teacher about him, she said he had completed the worksheet on the first day, and she had since let him work on his own, with minor help and guidance. During the time the other students had become familiar with the general movement of the turtle, Sam had mastered not only the turtle movement, but also the objectives for the next three class periods. At the time of our visit, he was creating songs using procedures for notes.

What made this most interesting was that the teacher said that Sam was one of her "poorest" students in other subject areas. It also was clear that Sam was the class nerd or outcast. However, in the *Logo* context, he was the central social focus.

Students came to him with questions. He was articulate about what he was doing, and his creativity was evident in his approach to the creation of songs. In short, *Logo* was his way to shine.

Since that early experience, we have seen numerous examples of similar situations. The way Papert organized *Logo* fits well with the learning of certain children. *Logo* helps them find their own way to be brilliant.

Another enlightening *Logo* experience occurred in a second-grade learning disabilities classroom. The teacher's initial issues were cementing the idea of left and right and of sequences of events. We were using a simplified version of the *Logo* commands that allowed the children to move the turtle and turn right angles. After spending two sessions introducing the children to the turtle and to the idea of moving the turtle, we got them started on some simple tasks. (One of these, the maze exercise, is discussed below.) Along with the tasks to be performed on the computer, we gave them a handout with some information about the commands. As we distributed the handout, the teacher became upset because she was afraid that many of the children would not be able to read it. The handout was not critical to the task, so we decided to simply see what would happen.

One red-headed young man, Charles, was particularly interested in the handout. The teacher told us Charles was her poorest reader. In fact, he was her "slowest" in other subject areas. However, Charles was also a relentless learner. He wanted to learn, and he never gave up trying. He did his *Logo* tasks somewhat more slowly than the other students, but as he was working we noticed he was using the handout. He constructed all the meaning from it and applied it to his work. When we noticed what he was doing, the teacher asked him some questions to check his understanding. She had considered Charles almost a "non-reader," yet somehow he had read the *Logo* handout completely and perfectly.

The inference we draw from our work with Charles is that *Logo* can offer a context for some children that opens doors for other types of learning. Charles wanted to control the turtle's movement, to make it do his bidding. That desire motivated him to want to read the sheet of *Logo* commands. In other words, he had a purpose for reading. The rich context of the activity gave him enough cues and connections to be able to construct the meaning of the symbols on the page. Charles' story illustrates that Papert's "transitional object" can benefit children in many ways.

We observed another interesting phenomenon while working with college students learning *Logo*, one that represents the other side of the same coin of the children's experiences above. The students in the scenarios above had trouble in other areas but found *Logo* easy. The more interesting situation is that students who seldom struggle in school sometimes have a difficult time learning *Logo*. These students frequently are leaders who are able to quickly absorb factual information and "spit it back" effectively. They also follow directions well. They are good at "doing school." Since much of their previous schooling asked little more, these students have been highly successful. When asked to create using the *Logo* commands, these students can remember the commands, and can tell the teacher what they are and what they do; however, they have extreme difficulty fashioning the commands into a desired outcome.

Many of the students who struggle also use a specific approach to design a solution: They create their solution and try it; then, if it is not perfect, they erase everything and start over. The thinking seems to go like this: "Conceive of the perfect solution, design that solution, and implement it. If it does not work, throw it out and either try again or consider the problem unsolvable and give up." These students seem to have little ability to look at an intended solution, compare it to their solution, and make modifications. What we encourage students to do in working with *Logo* is to look at their solution and engage in thinking about what they can change or modify to make it closer to the desired solution. We must teach them explicitly how to do it.

Using the problem of drawing a house as an example, the most common solution is to make a square, go forward, turn right 30 degrees, and make a triangle. Many students omit the 30-degree turn. Many students do not analyze their solution and add that turn. Instead, they delete the entire solution and start over. We must explicitly teach them to keep the useful parts of the solution, analyze what they need to change, and make only the necessary changes. In essence, we must teach them effective problem solving.

This phenomenon has some alarming implications for the thinking abilities of our students. Children who sail through school without ever hitting rough water will almost certainly run aground at some point in their adult life. For example, one of the most important thinking situations we face as adults is in our human relationships. Perfect solutions do not occur in relationships. If our marriage is not quite what we want it to be, should we analyze it to find the areas that need improvement, or should we throw it out and begin again, trying to design the perfect marriage? Far too many of us simply throw it out.

Most teachers emphasize giving children success experiences. Although success experiences are important, for some students it may be just as important to have "struggling experiences." *Logo* can be as beneficial to those students who have difficulty "getting it" as it can be to students who take to it like a fish to water (or a turtle to water). Each situation entails different kinds of learning, but each is appropriate for the child doing that learning.

Lessons from *Logo* Research

A considerable body of research is devoted to the use of *Logo*. Although much of it has been criticized for one reason or another, some tentative conclusions can be drawn. A variety of studies support the notion that using *Logo* can improve students' thinking skills. For a review of many of these findings, see Clements, Nastasi, and Swaminathan, 1993; Kafai, 1995; and Walsh, 1994.

Transfer of learning is a specific area of interest to several researchers. If a child learns to think using *Logo*, will that experience help the child think in other situations? If not, *Logo* would be a waste of our student's valuable learning time. Several studies have found that transfer does occur, although other studies contradict these findings. The contradictions led to a subsequent avenue of investigation which examined the effect of instruction on both the development of *Logo* skills and the transfer of those skills to other areas of thinking. Most of these studies indicate that explicit instruction facilitates transfer of thinking skills from the *Logo* environment to other areas of thinking.

One caution about the use of any thinking tool, and *Logo* specifically: It is important that we hold reasonable expectations for those tools. In talking about the recent backlash against *Logo*, Maddux (1992) clearly points to the dangers of becoming overzealous:

> One of the most important causes of the backlash is that early advocates of computing made the common error of making overly enthusiastic, wildly unlikely, and totally unsubstantiated claims about the benefits of using computers in teaching and learning. This has been especially true of *Logo* advocates. In fact, the "true believer" syndrome has become so advanced that I have suggested that an atmosphere of religionism has sprung up around *Logo*. The literature is replete with frenzied claims that seem based primarily on faith. . . .
>
> Most of these claims have been made by well-intentioned, if misguided individuals who were honestly attempting to gain attention and/or resources for something they believe in strongly—the implementation of *Logo*. Sometimes such efforts are successful in the short term. In the long run, however, it is usually counter-productive to promise more than can be achieved and documented. The problem is that when initial, unrealistic promises go unfulfilled, disappointment may give way to resentment, and a backlash is the result. The danger is that if the backlash is strong enough, a promising innovation may be abandoned before it has been given a fair trial. (p. 63)

One criticism of the body of *Logo* research is that much of it is anecdotal, comprising stories about individuals or small groups of children. This criticism is appropriate in a strictly quantitative world that conveniently reduces children and their learning to a series of numbers. This approach is not always the most useful to the field of practice, however. Both types of information help us make good decisions about when, how, and why to use *Logo*. The quantitative studies answer the questions related to group outcomes from using *Logo*. The anecdotal record addresses a much more compelling line of questioning relating to the possibilities. Individual case studies such as those documented by Weir (1987) tell us about children being brilliant. While we must not overstate the expected outcomes, we would also be remiss if we ignored the powerful possibilities that *Logo* presents for specific children. We must not ignore the lofty possibilities as we search for the cold, hard facts.

A byproduct of the *Logo* backlash is that many educators are replacing *Logo* with some other software, such as a hypermedia development program. They apparently believe that this substitution is akin to replacing a pencil with a pen. We contend that it is more like replacing a pencil with water colors. The outcomes students achieve with the new tool are quite different from those of *Logo*; thus, when teachers substitute the tool, they substitute the outcomes as well. *Logo* is a powerful tool for supporting a thinking curriculum. Students need a variety of tools to demonstrate their brilliance. For many students, *Logo* can be just the right tool.

THINKING IN THE CLASSROOM

Implementing a Thinking Curriculum

Undoubtedly, the most important issue in the discussion of thinking in schools is how we should organize children to be better thinkers. We would like to suggest the complete and definitive answer to that important question, but alas, we cannot. Just as we have deferred to the teacher to create lesson plans, because we lack the sufficient knowledge of any group of students and the context in which they are learning, we must do the same with a thinking curriculum. A school's curriculum is defined largely by local variables. It is the duty and responsibility of the local community of leadership to define a curriculum that meets the needs of the people served by the school. We can, however, make some broad suggestions about how we believe educators should organize a thinking curriculum. We list them in no particular order:

- The thinking curriculum should begin in kindergarten and continue through twelfth grade.
- Thinking objectives should be connected to all curricular areas, not just the main "academic" areas. (Yes, that means art, music, and PE.)
- A thinking curriculum should focus on both skills and dispositions. The affective aspect must not be forgotten.
- A thinking curriculum is necessarily active. Students do not develop good thinking skills by listening and taking notes.
- Technology should be used to support the thinking curriculum when and where technology can make a difference.
- A thinking curriculum should go beyond problem solving. Children should learn skills and develop dispositions that help them decide both what to do in a given situation and what to believe of given information.

Hardware and Software Issues

Instituting a thinking curriculum has significant implications for the purchase of hardware and software. If we want to use computers to think with, and if we want to allow students to freely explore their thinking, to "play with ideas," then we must provide them with appropriate hardware and software. Many successful classroom exercises require that each student, or each pair of students, have their own "thinking machine." Thus, we return to the debate over whether to set up a computer lab or place computers in the classroom. In an earlier chapter we discussed children's use of word processing. We described how teachers might organize their classrooms so that children can make good use of few computers. We do not believe this approach works well in a thinking curriculum. Teachers could use two or three computers in the classroom to reinforce or expand upon some basic lessons, but whole-group activities certainly are necessary.

Integrating computers in a thinking curriculum almost necessitates the maintenance of a computer lab. This could be a permanent lab, even one that teachers use for multiple purposes such as whole-group writing activities and keyboarding. It also could be a moveable or a temporary lab. As we mentioned earlier, by putting computers on wheels, a school can assemble a lab from multiple classroom computers, or can move a small lab around the building as needed.

Software is also an issue for consideration. If the school commits to a thinking curriculum, the thinking materials must be available in the classroom. This means that the software chosen must be installed as a tool on all the computers in the building. Many students today turn easily and naturally to the computer when they want to write something. They fully expect to find a word processor and are seldom disappointed. Once we fully implement a thinking curriculum, then students will turn just as easily and naturally to the computer when they need a thinking tool. When they do, that tool must be available.

STARTING *LOGO* WITH YOUNG CHILDREN

We believe that *Logo* should be introduced in the first grade. Starting children with *Logo* early has two benefits. The first is to get them familiar with the tool so that they can continue to use it as a thinking tool throughout the later grades. The second is to attain developmentally appropriate learning objectives. The main objectives we believe are important for first-graders are the idea of left and right, rudimentary estimation, sequences of events, and the idea of relativity of direction (for example, if two people are facing each other, if they both turn left they will be facing in opposite directions, not in the same direction). We also believe *Logo* can help children move to greater levels of abstract thinking.

It is helpful to couple physical activities with *Logo* activities. This is especially important with younger children. With first-graders, the teacher must introduce *Logo* by having the children act out the movement of the turtle. Students can act out the left/right and directionality by walking around and acting like *Logo* turtles. Physical turtles (toys, not live turtles) are also helpful with young children, who can manipulate the devices to explore movement and relative directions. *Logo* can reinforce these ideas and help the first-graders move toward more abstract thinking.

Our view of abstract thinking differs slightly from Piaget's rather rigid stages. We believe children develop abstract thinking in a smooth, continuous sequence. Working with a picture of a turtle on a screen is more abstract than working with a stuffed turtle on the floor. Mastering the movement of the turtle on the screen may help children develop greater abilities to work with abstract concepts.

To get young children working with *Logo*, the teacher needs to simplify the *Logo* commands. A turtle step is quite small, and children of this age are not thinking in terms of fifties and hundreds, but in fives and tens. Programming the turtle to take bigger steps is a fairly simple process.

Also, the turtle is capable of moving through an infinite number of angles. Those angles need to be simplified for young children. We recommend that the teacher start young children out with simple 90-degree angles (right angles). Just as it is fairly simple to increase the size of the turtle steps, it is also fairly simple to provide the option of working with 90-degree angles.

Given larger turtle steps and simple angles, the children need meaningful, engaging and challenging tasks. Following are several lesson ideas.

SAMPLE *LOGO* LESSONS

LESSON IDEA 1:   Maze Puzzles

In this activity, the teacher presents the children with a maze and asks them to move the turtle through it. An example is shown in Figure 8–5. The children must try to avoid touching the wall of the maze while piloting the turtle to its destination. This activity encompasses both learning about the use of *Logo* as well as directionality (left and right), relativity of direction, sequence of events, and rough estimation of distance.

Once the children have mastered the mazes and their related objectives, the teacher can add other features to continue children's learning. The next step is to decrease the size of the turtle steps, which in effect increases the size of the numbers the children must use. The teacher can also increase the number of angles available. One way is to use "clock degrees" or 30-degree angles: a half step between right angles and the full range of possible angles (360 degrees) results in 12 possible angles like the numbers on the face of a clock. A teacher could introduce this activity with a clock unit.

A useful teaching technique is to have a physical turtle with a clock face on her back. With this device a child can see how the turtle turns in relation to the numbers. When the turtle turns one number to the right, it turns from the current 12 o'clock position to the 1 o'clock position, but that new position is now 12 o'clock. This further expands the idea of directionality and gets children working with a larger range of angles.

With clock angles, children can draw a variety of pictures and figures using the turtle. This is important to give the children meaningful tasks to accomplish. Once they

Figure 8–5

A Simple Maze Puzzle

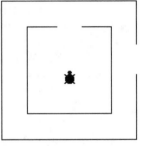

Help Turtle meet his friend fish.

have mastered the use of clock angles, they can begin working with the full range of whole-number angles (360 degrees).

LESSON IDEA 2:   The *Logo* House

Even if children do not start using *Logo* in first grade, they can begin using it in the later grades as a tool to develop thinking. The beauty of *Logo* is its versatility in the thinking curriculum. *Logo* can support virtually any approach to thinking that a teacher chooses.

One of the early problems that many *Logo* teachers pose to their students is to make a square. If the child has sufficient experience with *Logo* and is developmentally ready to complete this task, it is usually simple. Children experience right angles in their world, so they can easily handle the four right angles in a square. The next step is to use the ideas from the square to make an equilateral triangle (a triangle with all the sides and angles equal). This is significantly more difficult. The angle in a triangle is not as familiar. In addition, although all three angles are equal, drawing a triangle involves two angles: The internal angle is the inside 60-degree angle. However, the angle the turtle must turn to form the triangle is that angle's complement: an angle of 120 degrees, which represents the deviation from the turtle's previous path. The turtle must turn the complementary angle to form the triangle. Note that this is not a problem with the square because both the internal angle and its complement are 90 degrees. Nevertheless, with some help thinking about the turtle, and with encouragement to experiment, children can produce the equilateral triangle. A key metacognitive question to ask the children is this, "Compared to the square, does the turtle have to turn more or less?"

We want the children to make the steps involved in producing these figures into procedures. Just as we use word processing to capture our thoughts, the procedures created in *Logo* allow children to capture their logical thinking. The procedures for the square and triangle can be written like this:

```
to square
repeat 4[fd 50 rt 90]
end

to triangle
repeat 3[fd 50 rt 120]
end
```

These procedures produce the graphics shown in Figure 8–6.

Procedures start children on a path of constructivist thinking, beginning with small, simple pieces and producing ever larger mental constructions. Procedures get children started using "mind sized bytes" (Papert, 1980, p. 135). They start with simple procedures for figures like squares and triangles. After mastering these, they build more complex procedures using the simple ones. The process of using previous thinking (procedures) to build more complex thinking continues. Children create increasingly complex pictures that are evidence of their increasing complexity of thinking.

Figure 8–6

Logo Square and Triangle with
the Turtle

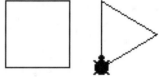

Figure 8–7

Correct House, Earthquake
House, and Hurricane House

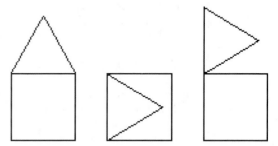

An example of this constructivist process is to use the square and triangle to form a house. The house is a *Logo* "chestnut" that Papert introduces in *Mindstorms* (1980, p. 14). Teachers do this exercise in a variety of ways. We prefer an exploratory approach, whereby the teacher asks the children to create a procedure that draws the picture of the entire house. Once children get the problem, they are free to experiment, using trial and error. Students who seem stuck or frozen must receive conceptual help or encouragement from the teacher as necessary.

To create the house, children must not only combine the square and the triangle, they must also orient them correctly. Figure 8–7 shows the correct drawing along with typical early attempts. We call the first attempt the earthquake house because the roof is caved in. We call the second attempt the hurricane house because the roof looks like it is being blown off. These names are purposeful. Many students do not see their product as a house. By calling the student's attempt an earthquake house or a hurricane house, we encourage them to see their drawing as a house that they can change and improve.

LESSON IDEA 3:   Polygons and the Total Turtle Trip Theorem

Another *Logo* chestnut involves creating a series of polygons. A teacher can use this exercise with fourth-graders in conjunction with children learning about the various regular polygons. If children have already successfully created the square and the triangle, a logical next step is to create figures such as pentagons, hexagons, and octagons. If the teacher gives children enough time and a little guidance, they can create these figures using trial and error. As they create each figure, the teacher should ask them to record information for each figure. A worksheet is shown in Figure 8–8.

Students use the series of angles and the number of sides to calculate the total degrees turned by the turtle. By doing this, students will find that to compete all the polygons, the turtle had to turn a total of 360 degrees. In *Logo* lingo, we call this the Total Turtle Trip Theorem. Teachers use the polygon examples to teach the Total Turtle

Figure 8–8

Total Turtle Trip Theorem Work-sheet

\multicolumn{5}{c}{**Logo Polygons**}
Figure Name	Number of sides (♯)	Number of angles (♯)	Degree of angles (°)	Total degrees (♯ x °)
square				
triangle				
octagon				
hexagon				
pentagon				
heptagon				

Trip Theorem. Students can then use the theorem to deduce the proper angle for any desired polygon.

Using The Total Turtle Trip Theorem, a procedure for an eleven-sided figure such as the one shown in Figure 8–9 would be written as follows:

to 11sides

repeat 11 [fd 50 rt $360/11$]

end

LESSON IDEA 4:   Drawing Stars

This lesson idea grew out of the experience of one of the authors of this book, Matthew Maurer, with drawing stars in *Logo*. This activity illustrates the utility of the tool for thinking.

Maurer developed a fixation on stars, much like Papert's fixation on gears, in early childhood, only his extended well into adulthood. As a child he had always liked the idea of the five-point stars. He learned to draw them at an early age, and could make them easily, quickly, and neatly. In college, the instructor gave Maurer's class the task of

Figure 8–9

An Eleven-Sided Figure with Turtle

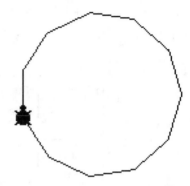

making a five-point star using *Logo*. Maurer already had a relationship with this five-point star, so he accomplished the task well before the rest of the class. The result is shown in Figure 8–10.

Maurer used the remaining time to take his thinking a step further. Since he had developed the star as an adaptation of a pentagon, he wondered whether he could also adapt other figures to look like stars. Soon he had a nice-looking seven-point star (Figure 8–11).

That led to the development of an algorithm for creating stars. The first algorithm was fairly simple. In words, it went something like this:

> A regular polygon needs a total turtle trip of 360 degrees. A five-point star needs two total turtle trips, for a total of 720 degrees. When you add two more points, you add one more total turtle trip. So a seven-point star uses 1080 degrees, a nine-point star uses 1440 degrees, and so on.

In *Logo* lingo, the procedure is written like this:

```
to star :points
repeat :points[fd 50 rt (720+(360*(:points-5))/2/:points]
end
```

This first arithmetically convoluted algorithm was the basis for "playing around" with *n*-point stars—that is, stars with various numbers of points. In time, Maurer began to wonder, "Why does my algorithm only produce an odd number of points?" Further, "What will happen if I just stick in an even number?" Maurer discovered that he could not conceive the answer without the tool, so he went right to the nearest *Logo* equipped computer, entered his algorithm, and tried working with even numbers. The results can be seen in Figure 8–12.

Figure 8–10

A Five-Point Star Drawn with *Logo*

Figure 8–11

A Seven-Point Star Drawn with
Logo

The even-point stars were only half finished. Upon analyzing the arithmetic, Maurer discovered that an even number of points always produced a certain number of total turtle trips (360 degrees) with a half trip left over (180 degrees). Maurer realized that he was not really working with total turtle trips, but with half total turtle trips. This led to the refinement of the algorithm:

> To make a star, you need at least 5 points. You also need more than one total turtle trip. To figure the number of total turtle trips, subtract one from the total number of points. The remainder is the number of half total turtle trips. If you use an even number of points, you will have a half total turtle trip left over, so the turtle will stop on the opposite side of the star, leaving it incomplete.

This led to a reduction of the arithmetic of the *Logo* procedure until it looked like this:

```
to star :points
repeat :points[fd 50 rt 180*(:points-1/:points]
end
```

The results and the arithmetic are identical, but Maurer had refined the thinking. Maurer now knew more about producing stars than he had before. Unfortunately, the original thinking that produced this algorithm clouded his thinking about stars. His misconceptions revolved around those troublesome even-point stars. If you put in an even number, you get a star that is only half finished. If you run the procedure twice, you get a completed star. Since you ran the procedure twice, you wind up with a star that has twice the original number of points. That means that the resulting stars have points that are divisible by four (twice an even number). Maurer erroneously concluded that you could not make stars that had an even number of points unless the number of points was divisible by four. Thus, a star could have 8 or 12 points, but not 10 or 14.

One day Maurer referred to the problem of even-point stars while teaching a group of college students about *Logo*. One of the students got ahead of the class and developed his own *n*-point star algorithm. As Maurer was explaining why stars could not have 10 or 14 points, this student was creating them on his computer screen. The result is shown in Figure 8–13.

Figure 8–12

Even-Point Stars of 8 and 10
Points. Note that the stars are
unfinished.

Figure 8–13

10- and 14-Point Stars Drawn
with *Logo*

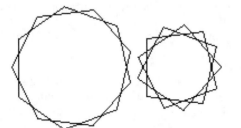 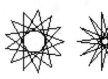

Figure 8–14

Star Family of 13-Point Stars

The student's algorithm was much simpler and yielded a much wider variety of possible starry outcomes. It looked like this:

```
to star :points :trips
repeat :points[fd 50 rt :points/360*:trips]
end
```

This is an elegant little procedure that represents a different way of thinking about the process of producing stars. The verbal description of the procedure might go like this:

To make a star, make a polygon using more than one total turtle trip (360 degrees). Try a variety of combinations of total turtle trips and polygon sides and see what happens.

This procedure not only yields all the stars the previous procedure did, but it also draws all the polygons, and even produces star families: different stars with the same number of points. Star families serve to illustrate the development of algorithms and are an example of both inductive and deductive reasoning. Figure 8–14 shows a star family of 13-point stars.

LOGO IN THE LITERATURE

Several journals publish *Logo* lesson ideas. *Learning and Leading with Technology* (formerly *The Computing Teacher*) frequently includes articles written by teachers about their successes with *Logo*. There are even publications devoted specifically to *Logo*.

The International Society for Technology in Education (ISTE) has a special-interest group called SIG *Logo* that focuses specifically on using *Logo*. The *Logo* Foundation also has a publication related to the use of *Logo,* called *Logo Update.* LCSI publishes a newsletter called *LogoLink* that has useful ideas about using *LogoWriter* in the classroom. Several books contain good ideas on how to successfully use *Logo* in the classroom (Becker, Eden, & Fischer, 1991; Clements & Battista, 1991; Goldenberg & Feurzeig, 1987; Harper, 1989; Hoyles & Noss, 1992; Maddux, 1985; Papert, 1980).

As an example of the ideas you can find, we offer a representative example. Dulsky (1993) describes a project in which the art and computer departments of a middle school worked together to develop "beautiful screen designs reminiscent of the rose windows found in Gothic cathedrals" (p. 16). These designs were radially symmetrical and rich in form and color. The teachers found that students could create an interesting design with ease, but much of their output was serendipitous and they had little ability to purposefully manipulate their designs. This necessitated some explicit instruction on the use of various *Logo* commands as well as work with concepts. The article includes a day-by-day description of the instruction, several examples of *Logo* programs, and the designs that resulted.

The author concludes the article with these comments:

> Whenever we do this project, there never fails to be that magical moment when a student spins that first shape around in a ring and a wonderful gasp of delight fills the room. As teachers we live for that moment. The *Logo* rose window project has been an interesting addition to both our art and computer curriculums. From the artistic perspective, I think it's great that we're using the computer as another creative tool. These designs would be beyond the reach of almost all the middle school students under traditional circumstances with regular art materials.
>
> So much time in computer classes is taken up by word processing and number crunching that this type of lesson adds some balance to the computer curriculum and truly enhances student understanding about the very wide role of computers in our society. This project also transcends and reinforces many traditional subjects in our schools—art history, art, mathematics, logical thinking, problem solving and computer science skills. (p. 19)

IMPLICATIONS FOR THE COMMUNITY OF LEADERSHIP

An old adage in curriculum development holds that the *what* and *how* of the curriculum is the purview of the community, and the *why* of the curriculum is the prerogative of the educators. We suggest that these differentiations are artificial. Curriculum development is the result of the interaction between the expectations of the community and the expertise of educational professionals. Curriculum development may be the best test of our concept of the community of leadership. Is it possible for the values and beliefs, vision and mission, and the school culture to produce shared and consensually adopted curricular goals? If so, then the notion of a community of leadership accepting responsibility for its children's education works.

A simple test for the community of leadership may be the mathematics or the American government curriculum. The more challenging task is the thinking curriculum. Thinking curricula are novel approaches, seem frivolous and ephemeral, and often have organized opposition. However, we can define and deliver a thinking curriculum in our schools. If the community of leadership clearly endorses the thinking curriculum, then technology can support its implementation. Thinking goals and objectives have enormous potential. We can trace much of the criticism of today's schools to difficulties with various aspects of our students' thinking skills and dispositions. We must ensure that our students are willing and able to think effectively and appropriately. Additionally, we must explicitly teach students to transfer thinking skills and dispositions from classroom settings to the adult world. If our students transfer the thinking skills they attain in school to other relevant experiences in their lives, then we have facilitated useful and meaningful learning. That is the essence of school: developing useful knowledge, skills, and dispositions toward learning.

Curricular Decisions

Most importantly, the community of leadership must decide on a format for the thinking curriculum. Two options are either to establish a separate curricular area or to integrate thinking throughout the existing curriculum. Making curricular decisions requires the community of leadership to clarify its values and beliefs about thinking and establish worthwhile, shared goals and objectives. If those worthwhile, shared goals and objectives are to infuse thinking into the existing content—that is, to contextualize thinking—then the community of leadership will implement an appropriate curriculum adoption plan. (This issue is discussed further in Chapter 11.) We believe that the thinking curriculum should have distinct curricular goals and objectives and that teachers should integrate thinking into the content areas.

A concrete example of the thinking curriculum is found in the *Logo* house activity described earlier. The objective is to help students to break problems into smaller components and attack the components individually. If a student produces the hurricane house, and the teacher responds, "Wrong," then the student may erase all her work and start again. This strategy is counter to the intended learning. If instead the teacher responds with, "That is a house, but does it look the way you wanted it to look? How might you change what you have done to make the house look the way you choose?" With this approach, the teacher guides the student toward the intended thinking. Students must analyze what they are thinking and make modifications. This activity contributes to constructivist strategy of hypothesis generation, observation, and testing.

Changes in the way we evaluate students' growth and development indicate the strength of the community of leadership. A shift must be made from summative evaluation—a judgmental approach that can do harm to the student's ego—to formative assessment—a thinking approach. This change is not trivial. The efforts of the community of leadership will need to be substantial and continuous to nurture this change in assessment. The change is worth the effort. Students' critical thinking and problem-solving strategies will blossom in the resulting supportive learning environment.

Teaching the Community

In the current "back to the basics" and "cut the fluff" educational environment, it is critically important that we educate the community about what we are doing before we implement a thinking curriculum. Informing parents after the fact would cause us to become reactors and excuse makers and would not appear professional. A proactive stance, in which we include the community in planning for substantive change in the school, is far more productive. To the lay person, having children playing with *Lego* blocks or moving turtles around a computer screen can seem to be curricular "fluff." Before implementing a thinking curriculum, we must not only explain what we are planning to do, but share the research and scholarship with our community. We must highlight the advantages of the thinking curriculum for our students. A high-profile TV news spot showing how kids are wasting time in school can do irreparable damage to a school's curricular goals. A well informed, supportive news story, on the other hand, can benefit the thinking curriculum.

Parents can become another powerful model in developing their children's thinking skills. In concert with the community of leadership, parents can learn the intentions and strategies of the thinking curriculum, how to reinforce the thinking curriculum at home, and how to encourage thinking in preschool children. Parents can also urge school policy makers to provide resources for the thinking curriculum: money, people, time, and ideas.

CONCLUSION

It is the responsibility of the school-community to determine the purpose of schooling. By including parents and interested participants in the community of leadership, all members can contribute to that purpose. We believe that the purpose of schooling goes beyond development of literacy and essential skills, and beyond preparation for the world of work. The instructional program of the future will call for teaching and learning that develop the potential of individual children, expose children to cultural diversity and individual differences, internalize essential skills, emphasize quality and beauty, and encourage critical thinking and problem solving. A quality academic program fostered by the community of leadership and supported by instructional technology defines school in the Twenty-first Century.

REFERENCES

Becker, H. D., Eden, H., & Fischer, G. (1991). *Interactive problem solving using Logo*. Hillsdale, NJ: Lawrence Erlbaum.

Bloom, B. (1956). *Taxonomy of educational objectives*. New York: McKay.

Clements, D. H., & Battista, M. T. (1991). *Logo geometry*. Morristown, NJ: Silver Burdett & Ginn.

Clements, D. H., Nastasi, B. K., & Swaminathan, S. (1993). Young children and computers: Crossroads and directions from research. *Young Children, 48*(2), 56–64.

Dewey, J. (1910). *How we think*. Boston: Heath.

Dulsky, D. (1993). *Logo* rose windows. *The Computing Teacher, 20*(7), 16–20, 22–28, 37–38.

Ennis, R. H. (1980). Rational thinking and educational practice. In J. R. Coombs (Ed.). *Philosophy of Education*. Normal, IL: Philosophy of Education Society.

Ennis, R. H. (1985). A logical basis for measuring critical thinking skills. *Educational Leadership, 43*, 44–48.

Goldenberg, E. P., & Feurzeig, W. (1987). *Exploring language with* Logo. Cambridge, MA: Massachusetts Institute of Technology.

Harper, D. O. (1989). Logo *theory and practice*. Belmont, CA: Brooks/Cole.

Hoyles, C., & Noss, R. (1992). *Learning mathematics and* Logo. Cambridge, MA:Massachusetts Institute of Technology.

Kafai, Y. B. (1995). *Minds in play: Computer game design as a context for children's learning*. Hillsdale, NJ: Lawrence Erlbaum.

Maddux, C. D. (1985). Logo *in the schools*. Redding, CA: Hayworth.

Maddux, C. D. (1992). *Logo*: The case for a cautions advocacy. *Computers in the Schools, 9*(1), 59–79.

Mason, J. M., & Au, K. H. (1990). *Reading instruction for today*. Glenview, IL: Scott Foresman.

Muth, K. D. (1989). *Children's comprehension of text*. Newark, DE: IRA.

Nisbett, R., & Ross, I. (1980). *Human inference: Strategies and shortcomings of social judgment*. Upper Saddle River, NJ: Prentice-Hall.

Norris, S. P., & King, R. (1984). Observational ability: Determining and extending its presence. *Informal Logic, 6*(3),

Palinscar, A. S. (1984). The quest for meaning from expository text: A teacher-guided journal. In G. G. Duffy, R. Roehler, & J. M. Mason (Eds.), *Comprehension instruction: Perspectives and suggestions*. New York: Longman.

Papert, S. (1980). *Mindstorms: Children, computers and powerful ideas*. New York: Basic Books.

Paris, S. G. (1987). *Making thinking public*. Lexington, MA: Heath.

Walsh, T. E. (1994). Facilitating *Logo's* potential using teacher-mediated delivery of instruction: A literature review. *Journal of Research on Computing in Education, 26*(3), 322–335.

Weir, S. (1987). *Cultivating minds: A* Logo *casebook*. New York: Harper and Row.

Winograd, P., & Paris, S. G. (1988). A cognitive and motivational agenda for reading instruction. *Educational Leadership, 46*(4), 30-36.

RESOURCE LIST

The Amazing Writing Machine, Bröderbund

The Backyard, Bröderbund

Creative Writer, Microsoft Corporation

Geography Search, Tom Snyder Productions

The Graph Club, Tom Snyder Productions

Imagination Express, Edmark

Lego Dacta Control Lab, Lego Dacta

Logo Plus, Terrapin

LogoWriter, Logo Computer Systems, Inc.

Process Writer, Scholastic

SimEarth, Maxis

Thinkin' Things, Edmark

CHAPTER 9

Breaking Down the Walls with Telecommunications

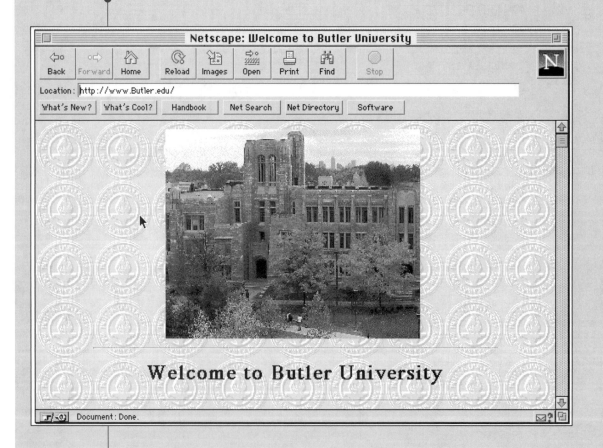

Netscape: Welcome to Butler University

Back   Forward   Home   Reload   Images   Open   Print   Find   Stop

Location: http://www.Butler.edu/

What's New?   What's Cool?   Handbook   Net Search   Net Directory   Software

Welcome to Butler University

Document: Done.

As the quantity of data and information expands, new methods of accessing data and information emerge. Technology-oriented sources of data and information challenge teachers, students, schools, and the community of leadership to engage in constant planning and decision making. We must assess the relative value of these information sources in terms of their instructional merit. Telecommunications technology may be as simple as an e-mail system within the school (a local area network) or as complicated as access to the InterNet, the World Wide Web, or distance learning.

In this chapter we describe the hardware and software requirements for telecommunications: e-mail, the InterNet, and the World Wide Web. We suggest the advantages of telecommunications, describe methods of connection, warn about the pitfalls in on-line connections, and explore leadership issues. We iterate that the value of any instructional technology, from a simple hand-held calculator to a sophisticated World Wide Web connection, lies in its ability to support a quality academic program.

INTRODUCTION

The term "telecommunication" means communicating over a distance. Typically, we use the term to talk about the ways we can use the telephone system to connect computers and computer networks. Two-way video, distance learning, distance education, or teleconferencing are other forms of telecommunications. In this chapter we focus primarily on telecommunications using computers, and discuss distance learning as a separate issue.

Telecommunications connect people to one another. We use telecommunications to talk to people, read ideas that people have written, see pictures or movies that people have made, hear music people have written and performed, and retrieve documents or programs that people have created.

ELEMENTS NECESSARY FOR TELECOMMUNICATIONS

To use telecommunications, you need three basic parts: hardware, software, and someone with whom to communicate.

Hardware

Several hardware configurations permit telecommunications. The simplest configuration is a computer, a modem, and a telephone line. A modem is a device that translates the computer's language into the telephone company's language. For two computers to communicate, a modem must be on both ends of the phone line to translate. In essence, the two modems "talk" to each other over the phone line and relay the messages to their respective computers. If you are communicating through a consumer-oriented modem, you can use the same phone line you use for voice communication. When the line is being used for telecommunications, it signals busy.

If the computers in a school building are connected to a local area network, we can use telecommunications in other ways. One way to connect the entire network to other computers or networks is to attach a network modem to a local network. This allows anyone on the network to use the network modem to communicate with other modems. Another way is to connect the network to a mainframe—a large central computer—and allow each local computer to access other networks through the mainframe. Many school districts have large central computers that they use to manage the district's information. They often connect all the district's buildings to that central computer. Once those connections exist, the next step is to connect the building's local networks to the mainframe. If the mainframe computer has access to the InterNet, then each computer on the network has the potential to access the InterNet. (The InterNet is discussed at length later in this chapter.)

Software

A modem needs software to communicate with the computer. Communications software is usually included when you purchase a modem. However, you may want to use other telecommunications software instead. For example, most integrated software packages include telecommunications software. The advantage of using the integrated package's telecommunications software rather than the modem's software is that everyone in a building or even a district can use the same software. Standardization has some management and support advantages. For example, it is easier to train the school community to use one piece of software rather than several different programs.

If you are connecting to a mainframe to gain access to other networks outside your district, you will need software that will allow you to connect to the mainframe. Once you connect to the mainframe, you may not need any other software on your individual computer; you can use the software on the mainframe to navigate the InterNet. Another option, however, is to have network navigation software on the personal computer. For example, we typically access the World Wide Web using a navigation program called a web browser. Two popular web browsers are *Netscape* and *Mosaic*.

Smaller school districts may use an amalgamation of these options. They can use a modem (or network modem) to dial the mainframe of a local telecommunications service. The mainframe computer then provides access to a wider array of network resources.

Someone to Call

Once the hardware and software are installed, you need someone with which to communicate. There are three possibilities: You can connect to a bulletin board, to a commercial service, or to the InterNet.

Bulletin boards usually are maintained on a personal computer. The computer has a modem and bulletin board software. Bulletin board software handles the incoming calls and makes the computer available to the caller. The services available on a bulletin board might include a message center or access to data.

Many organizations and individuals maintain bulletin boards. Some bulletin boards charge a user fee. The majority, however, are maintained as a part of doing business (bulletin boards maintained by organizations) or as a hobby (bulletin boards maintained by individuals). For more than a decade, bulletin boards have been a popular way for organizations to communicate with their constituencies and for computer hobbyists to communicate with one another. However, the ease and popularity of the World Wide Web may cause private bulletin boards to fade. People who once maintained bulletin boards now have home pages on the web.

You also can connect to world wide networks by using commercial services and the InterNet. Commercial services such as America On-line and CompuServe charge fees for their service. The company charges an initial fee for providing connecting software to access their network and a monthly subscription fee for using the network. Some services charge additional fees for the time subscribers spend accessing the service, or for accessing specialty information. With a commercial service, subscribers call the service's mainframe computer to access to a variety of information on the network. Most commercial services now provide InterNet access as a standard service.

The last option is to connect to the InterNet directly. The government partially funds the InterNet. The organizations that are part of the InterNet—for example, universities and corporations—provide the remaining support. Although connection to the InterNet is free, it does have associated costs. Users pay a yearly connection fee and must meet requirements about which equipment to use and how network members behave.

The popular media has publicized telecommunications. The members of the media and various politicians created the term "the information superhighway." Although vague, this term usually refers to the InterNet. Although it is difficult to predict the future of telecommunications, we believe that it will become more like the InterNet and less like commercial services.

You must not only consider to whom you are going to talk, but also your means of connection. If you are connecting directly through a modem, you will need the phone number of the modem you wish to call. If you are connecting through a mainframe, you will need an account on that mainframe and a procedure for "logging on." You may need to use a combination of these techniques—that is, you may use a modem to dial a mainframe. In that case, you will need both the phone number of the mainframe modem, an account, and a "log on" procedure.

From the description thus far, you may think of telecommunications as two computers or computer networks "talking" to each other. We think of it as connecting people together. In the case of e-mail, this is a straightforward concept; however, in many other situations, it is less so. If you use telecommunications to download a document, you are, in essence, communicating with the author(s) of that document. If you download a piece of educational software, you are communicating with the designer(s) and programmer(s) of that software. Thus, we think of telecommunications connecting people for their mutual benefit. The power of the world wide networks as they are currently evolving is that distance is not important; it is as easy to communicate with someone on another continent as it is to communicate with someone across town.

Phone line charges are an important consideration in telecommunications. If you are using a regular voice line, then you incur no additional charge to use the line for telecommunications. However, depending on how you connect, you may be incurring long-distance charges. This is particularly important in relatively isolated areas, such as rural school districts. The following scenario illustrates the problems related to phone line charges.

High Tech Community Schools is a small, consolidated district in a small town in rural Iowa serving several surrounding small towns and a local farming community. High Tech's town has its own telephone exchange, but no large computer services are available in the local calling area. To connect to the wide area network, High Tech Community Schools has to connect to a nearby community large enough to have a access to the world wide network. The cities of Dubuque, Davenport, Clinton, and Iowa City are possibilities, but each involves making a long-distance call. If High Tech Community Schools were to use a standard voice line for telecommunications, they would incur long-distance line charges each time they connected. Not only is this costly, but, more troubling, the cost is unpredictable.

Another possibility would be to lease a phone line that teachers and students can use for telecommunications. That option fixes the price, but it may be even more expensive than using the regular voice lines. This option is unacceptable because the school's telecommunications needs fluctuate unpredictably over time. This means that at times the school would be paying for an unused phone line.

This scenario shows the inequity between urban and rural school districts. Solutions may come from the public sector, the private sector, or a consortium of both. Various government entities may step in to solve this problem, or the solution may be left to the various telecommunications companies (for example, telephone and cable television companies).

TELECOMMUNICATIONS SERVICES

Commercial Services

Commercial telecommunications services such as CompuServe, America On-line, and Prodigy are in the business of providing access to world wide computer networks. Commercial services have two advantages. The first is ease of connection. Commercial services typically give the subscriber easy access to their network. Most services provide software that makes access straightforward and intuitive.

The second advantage is the wide range of services provided. Commercial services provide messaging services such as e-mail and access to archives of software from which subscribers can download free software programs. Commercial services also provide access to various data bases. One that is of particular interest to educators is the Educational Resources Information Center (ERIC), the data base that indexes most educationally related journals, annual conference presentations, and academic papers. Other data bases that might be of interest include data related to financial markets or entertainment. Additionally, users can connect to other users with a common interest through "list serves." List serves resemble bulletin boards and cover thousands of special interests: middle-level education, vintage guitars, patients with specific diseases, late-night television news, and quantum mechanics.

Many organizations provide information through the InterNet *Gopher,* a popular access program. The Weather Bureau, the Smithsonian Institution, the Library of Congress, the CIA, and Butler University all have InterNet locations on *Gopher.* (More information on *Gopher* is given later in this chapter.)

Much of the data available from commercial services also are available through the InterNet. In some cases the InterNet provides superior service. For that reason, most commercial services provide InterNet access. Some commercial services provide only InterNet access. This type of service often charges a small monthly fee for unlimited InterNet access. This can be cost effective for many school districts.

Some commercial services' offerings are not available on the InterNet. For example, most commercial services provide financial information such as stock exchange quotes, commodity prices, and currency exchange data. Commercial services do not provide this information free of charge. The InterNet does not provide this service. The World Wide Web eventually will offer "pay per use" service for special-interest data.

The down side of commercial networks is the cost. They really are designed for private use by individuals. Most of the problems schools experience with commercial services are unique to their use in the classroom. The monthly subscription fees, usually between $10 and $20, are not cost prohibitive. It is the supplemental charges that become a problem. Some services charge an additional fee for the time used on the network above a base fee; for example, if you use the service more than ten hours, you pay an additional charge by the minute. Some services assess an additional charge for a volume of messages; for example, if you send or receive more than 20 messages a month, you pay an additional charge per message. Additional charges also come from access to specific kinds of data. Most services charge an extra fee for access to a few popular data bases. Access to the New York Stock Exchange ticker and related information usually requires an additional fee.

Most of the additional fees are reasonable and manageable for an individual, but when these services are used by a building full of curious learners, the potential for incurring unmanageable and unpredictable fees is enormous. The inability to predict costs is a serious budget issue. Therefore, services that have a higher monthly fee but few (or no) additional surcharges may be preferable. Those limited services that only offer InterNet access for a single monthly or yearly fee are appealing.

As mentioned earlier, telephone line charges are another cost. If a school is located in a small town and the service does not have access to a local computer, then the connection will be a toll call. The school will be paying standard long-distance rates for students' connect time. This alone can be a "budget buster."

Recreational Telecommunications

The popularity of telecommunications created a new phenomenon: "hanging out on the net." Most commercial services provide a variety of topic-specific "chat rooms," a service that allows people to talk to each other about a specific topic in real time. ("Real time" means that communications happen instantly instead of being stored for later retrieval.) When you "enter" a chat room, you see the conversation of all those in the room on your screen. The software typically announces anyone entering a chat room by displaying their commercial identification or "handle." Chat rooms are popular among teens and singles. "Hanging out" is not a new phenomenon, it has merely shifted to a new arena. Instead of hanging out in bars or on street corners, people now hang out on their computers.

The concept of forums gives "hanging out on the net" some legitimacy. A forum is a service that allows people with similar interests—for example, coin collecting, gardening, or French cooking—to interact. Some forums are in real time, others communicate through messages. Either way, forums can be very valuable to educators, particularly when the topic is professional or connected with the curriculum, such as a Shakespeare forum or a geography forum.

A MUD, or multi-user dungeon, is a popular site for adolescents. The term comes from the adventure-gaming culture (particularly the game "Dungeons and Dragons"). Although some MUDs are similar to a chat room, the term typically refers to a group of people playing an on-line game.

Chat rooms and MUDs are gaining the attention of parents, educators, and other members of the school community because a segment of the telecommunications population spends an inordinate amount of time using these services. When young people spend much of their recreational time staring into a computer screen, that is indeed a reason for concern.

THE INTERNET

The InterNet is an alternative to using commercial services. It is superior to commercial services in many ways but inferior in others.

What Is the InterNet?

It is difficult to say exactly when the InterNet was "born" because it has evolved over time. In 1969 the U. S. government began establishing the telephone lines and computers that constitute the "backbone" of the InterNet. The infrastructure consisted of a small number of university mainframe computers located around the country that acted as regional hubs. High-speed phone lines connected these computers to one another. This infrastructure quickly overshadowed its original national security purposes and became the basis of an international supernetwork of computer networks.

A variety of organizations voluntarily join this supernetwork. Each of the local networks is unique and has special modes of operation. To join the InterNet, networks must conform to certain technical standards, but these standards have little to do with how a user interacts with the local network. The majority of the members of the InterNet are universities. Other InterNet members include a variety of federal, state, and local government organizations, school districts, and commercial organizations (with a noticeable dominance of technology companies). Figure 9–1 contains an explanation of InterNet addresses and several examples.

InterNet addresses have a similar format. In the United States, they consist of three parts with no spaces between the parts. The parts are: the individual's name followed by the "at" sign (@), the institution's name followed by a period (called a "dot") and the institution type. An individual's name can be anything that the local institution decides to use. Some use random numbers and letters; others use last names and first initials; others use combinations or variations on similar themes. Some addresses have multiple parts to the individual name, with the parts separated by periods with no spaces. The institution's name is assigned when the institution gets on the InterNet. Some addresses have multiple parts to the institution name, with periods separating the parts. The last part of the address indicates the type of organization. The three types are:

edu   educational institution

com   commercial organization (a business)

gov   a government organization

International addresses have a country code at the end. Otherwise, they are exactly the same as U.S. addresses.

Examples

Note: The first two are the addresses of the authors. The remaining addresses are drawn from real examples but are not valid addresses.

maurer@butler.edu	simple three-part addresses
gdavidson@butler.edu	
jones@inet.ed.gov	government address
green@ibm.com	commercial address
john.smith@tpoint.com	multiple parts in individual name
abc9@psuvm.psu.edu	two-part institutional name
ablack@info.curtin.edu.au	international address in Australia

Figure 9–1
InterNet Addresses

As of this writing, the United States dominates the InterNet, but its domination is diminishing. The InterNet may be responsible for the acceptance of English as the official international telecommunications and business language.

The InterNet is growing at such a rapid rate that growth itself is a defining element. Every measure of the use of the InterNet is increasing: the number of organizations on the net, the number of individuals using the net, and the number of transactions crossing the net. Probably the best indication of the growth is the volume of data that passes through the system, which increases by a staggering 30% per month. Another indication of growth is the number of on-line computers. In the first six months of 1994, the number of computers increased from 2,217,000 to 3,212,000, a growth of 81% (Internet Society, 1994).

A problem associated with the rapid growth of the InterNet is that no one knows what the InterNet will be from month to month. As an example, a university that makes information available to the InterNet community may find that access to the information overwhelms the resources of its mainframe computer, forcing the university to withdraw or restrict access. This is a common occurrence on the InterNet. Resources come and go, sometimes at a rapid pace.

What the InterNet Offers

E-Mail   One of the most popular services on the InterNet is its e-mail capability. InterNet mail has become the standard in e-mail. Most commercial services list their addresses as InterNet addresses, and they use the InterNet to communicate with one another. Through the InterNet, a message can get from virtually any person on the net to any other person, and it usually arrives instantly. E-mail can include more than we typically think of as messages. It also can contain data, pictures, movies, music, and programs. Virtually anything that can be digitized can be transmitted via e-mail, assuming both the sender and the receiver know the procedures. New applications such as *Netscape, Mosaic,* and *Java* make procedures foolproof. The e-mail capability alone is worthy of the consideration of educators around the world. However, it is only one of a series of useful applications.

Mailing Lists   Along with standard person-to-person e-mail, the InterNet also can establish mailing lists. InterNet mailing lists allow the telecommunications community to organize itself into groups with common interests. If you have an interest, for example, in alternative schedules for middle schools, then you can establish a mailing list to reach all the e-mail addresses of interested schools. Individual users can join a list temporarily to find a specific idea, such as a discipline plan, or long term to share ideas, such as an assessment list.

Any user of InterNet mailing lists can attest that mailing lists are both a blessing and a curse, much like mail that comes to our homes. Information we get from lists may be invaluable and available nowhere else. However, some percentage of junk mail is inevitable. Junk mail may be as innocuous as someone asking, "Please help me get off this list," or it can be as irritating and unethical as an advertisement.

Shareware, Freeware, and Files   The InterNet can direct teachers and students to enormous software archives. These archives contain a variety of programs that are either shareware or freeware (discussed in Chapter 3). Many of these programs have the potential to help children learn. Teachers and students can access hypermedia programs and stacks. Students can learn from the information in them; they can use them as examples in developing their own hypermedia applications; or they can publish their own stacks.

The InterNet also provides access to other types of information such as text files, pictures, sound files, and digitized video files. These files include information or resources that other people on the InterNet created. InterNet users want to share their information with others on the net.

Text files include a wide a range of possibilities. People have written documents about virtually every topic. However, the bulk of the information you will find is technology related. (This is part of a "new technology" life cycle.) InterNet users can access documents about professional organizations, documents espousing moral or political positions, documents summarizing the interactions on specific mailing lists, and more.

Picture, sound, and video files are not as numerous as text files but are plentiful nonetheless. As an example, when the *Star Trek: Deep Space Nine* television series debuted, fans digitized pictures of the space station for dissemination on the InterNet. Many different kinds of sound files are available. One of the more popular are MIDI sound files—sound files created and interpreted by a Musical Instrument Digital Interface device. Less common are video files. Because of their size, video is one of the rarer resources on the InterNet. Even so, many video clips present a wide range of activities. Clips include music videos, shots of sporting events, excerpts of cultural events, and more. A national motor oil company implemented an interesting example of how sponsors of the May 1995 Indianapolis 500 can share video. Every day of "race month," a camera crew was at the track, shooting video of the day's events. In the evening the video appeared on the InterNet.

Accessing the InterNet

Access is one of the most difficult issues posed by the InterNet. This issue is difficult to explore fully because the details will change more quickly than this book can move from the authors to the readers. Therefore, we present a picture of how access exists at this writing and attempt to predict how access is likely to change.

Today, there are four main ways schools access the InterNet: (1) rely on the good graces and generosity of a local university or business; (2) access through a commercial vendor, such as America On-line or CompuServe; (3) connect through a government organization that provides access; (4) purchase their own InterNet node. Each of these options has advantages and disadvantages.

Relying on the generosity of a local institution is certainly an attractive option. On the down side, the donor institution may limit students' access because of its own system needs and constraints. Further, the donor may withdraw its generous offer when students become more familiar with the InterNet and become more enthusiastic about the data they generate. The level of use in a school likely will mimic the rapid growth curve of the InterNet as a whole. Another problem associated with borrowing access is that the donor institution may restrict the use of InterNet tools. Students may not be able to access some of the exciting information on the InterNet because the tools for getting to this information are too costly for the donor to provide.

Borrowing access from local institutions assumes that local institutions exist. Many rural schools do not have such institutions, and the long-distance charges to connect to the nearest metropolitan area might make an InterNet connection cost prohibitive.

Commercial access requires a subscription fee, but the school can be more confident that the service will continue over time. Virtually all the large telecommunications services provide InterNet access, and some newer commercial organizations provide only InterNet access. This option typically is inexpensive, and the access is global and powerful. However, just like borrowed access, these services are not available in smaller rural areas. Furthermore, the addition of phone charges to the subscription fee may exceed a school's budget.

State governments are experimenting with providing InterNet access. The main problem with this solution is that the communication infrastructures in place are not cost effective. Most schools would have to connect to a computer at their state's Department of Education, using a modem and an 800 number. The potential cost to the state may be prohibitive. Local government organizations also are experimenting with gaining access to the InterNet and sharing that access with the local schools. Once again, schools that have no substantial government facility in their calling area are excluded from this solution. Political leaders from both parties who recognize the value of telecommunications for education are trying to legislate equity in telecommunications access for schools.

The last option is for a school district to obtain its own InterNet node. For this to be a reasonable option, several things must happen. First, the district must have a computer capable of managing an InterNet node. Although currently this restriction is substantial, it is diminishing as requirements change and as telecommunications technology improves and gets cheaper. Probably the most difficult barrier is the communication infrastructure. Each school that wants to access a node must have a connection to the node computer. In the case of larger school districts, the telecommunications lines already may be in place for management purposes. If sufficient lines are available, then the school could "piggyback" instructional uses of these lines with the district's management functions.

Connecting and maintaining a regional InterNet node usually costs several thousand dollars a year. In addition, schools must employ people to manage and maintain InterNet nodes. For larger districts that can implement some economy of scale, this may be the best option. For smaller school districts, the costs could be more than the budget will allow.

Popular Interface Tools on the InterNet

Gopher   In the recent past in human years, but in ancient history in computer years, the easiest way to access data on the InterNet was through the *Gopher* system. *Gopher* is InterNet software, designed by the University of Minnesota, that makes connections between the various mainframes easier to navigate. The software system not only aids navigation but also helps with the organization of data stored on the InterNet.

Gopher has a series of menus that help the user navigate from site to site and to find things once she arrives. If the mainframe used to connect to the InterNet has *Gopher*, then individuals have access to the system. When you get into the *Gopher* system, you will see your local *Gopher* menu. This local menu usually has some choices of items that are on the local computer and some choices that connect you to other computers. By going from menu to menu, you can navigate to any other computer with *Gopher*. Once you get to the machine you want, its local *Gopher* menu will allow you to find what you want or need.

Gopher not only lets you navigate from computer to computer and find things that are available, it also assists with retrieving the information. A group that wishes to make a series of documents available can utilize *Gopher*. Once the group establishes access, anyone looking for the documents can find them through a *Gopher* menu. When you see a title that interests you, you can download the document by simply pointing to the item and pressing the enter key. The process is the same for downloading a program.

Although *Gopher* greatly simplified downloading, the process is still rather complex. The difficulty is getting the information from your local mainframe to your computer, and in the case of programs, getting them into a usable format. The transfer from the local mainframe to an individual computer is dependent upon local software and requires that the mainframe and the computer have compatible software. The process is locally idiosyncratic, typically involving several steps that the user must follow exactly. If you are downloading a file that is not simple text, then you also have other procedures to consider. You must compress any non-text files to reduce the volume of data transfer and to avoid technical problems with transmitting non-text data through the telecommunications network. If someone compresses a downloaded file, it must be decompressed. These considerations result in enough complexity to discourage all but the most determined computer buffs. Downloading non-text files is usually the turf of the high-end computer users.

These problems notwithstanding, *Gopher* is a tremendous move forward in ease of access. *Gopher* is the first "easy" way to navigate the InterNet and download files. Ease of use is an important issue. The fewer steps required and the easier the steps to use, the greater the audience. Many InterNet users restrict their use to e-mail because of the complexity of the tools. *Gopher* allows a large segment of information producers and consumers to expand their use of the InterNet.

World Wide Web   We can draw a strong analogy between the *Gopher* system and the World Wide Web. Just as *Gopher* was a big step forward in ease of use, the web is the next step. Also, like the *Gopher,* the web offers advances in both the organization of data on the InterNet, in the form of web pages, and advances in access to data, in the form of web browsers.

People store data on the web on a screen called a web page. The web page can contain almost any data that can be displayed on a computer screen: text, color backgrounds, pictures in any resolution, video clips, and sounds. In addition, the page can contain links or connections to other web pages. One web page can link to many other available web pages. People typically make these links by creating "hot text"—a piece of text that describes the link. If the person looking at the page clicks on the hot text, the page described in the text appears. The web is, in essence, an on-line, nonlinear, hypermedia application.

The web is an advance over *Gopher*. People needed a technical expert to create and maintain a *Gopher* menu. Web pages are easy to create and easy to understand. With a page authoring program, many teachers and students can create a web page. A teacher can easily teach upper elementary school students to create web pages, and the students can take responsibility for the maintenance of their pages.

Navigating through the web is also easy. You connect to a web page using its name or Universal Resource Locator (URL). When using the web, the pages are linked together with hot text or buttons. The hot text or buttons allow movement from one page to another. With a URL, you can connect directly to any page. Many organizations are listing their URLs so you can connect to their web page. For example, most of the television news programs list their web addresses.

Not only has the organization of the data taken a giant step forward, but access to data has become easier. Web browsers simplify access to web pages. *Mosaic* was one of the earliest browsers. Software developers soon created a second browser, *Netscape*. *Netscape* has become the most popular browser for accessing the web.

The beauty of *Netscape* lies not only in its ability to move around the web smoothly, but also in its on-line help. So much data exists on the web that just keeping track of what data each item represents and how to access it can be a nightmare. *Netscape* manages much of that. For example, if you wanted to download a program from the web, the necessary steps would be similar to the steps described for the *Gopher* system. The difference is that *Netscape* completes all the steps for you. The only thing to do is tell *Netscape* where to put things. *Netscape* has a system for helper applications. Helper applications are all the decompression, sound, and video driver programs. When you need them, *Netscape* automatically accesses them.

Prior to *Netscape*, we could get all the same information, but we had to keep track of several complicated procedures. The ease that *Netscape* affords puts use of the web into the hands of the average early-elementary student. *Netscape* is easy enough that even most adults can use it with relatively little frustration.

Another feature of the World Wide Web/*Netscape* combination is simple messaging. On a web page you can define hot text that initiates a short message sequence that the software will send to a specific e-mail address. This feature does not eliminate the need for a separate e-mail system but integrates e-mail into the web.

The ease of creating, navigating, and maintaining web pages has created an explosion of web-based data and information. Although the system is only a few years old, it represents the largest collection of data ever known. Every conceivable kind of data is available on the web. You can find data about ostriches and beach-front real estate. You can find data about baseball and sail boats. You can find data about technology planning and gardening. You can see real-time video of places around the world, from Oxford University to a Hollywood bus stop. We have yet to seek data about any topic area and fail to connect. You may not be able to find exactly the data you are seeking, but you can certainly find information related to it.

The ease of creating web pages has moved us into a new era in computing and telecommunications. Until recently telecommunications was the exclusive domain of computer experts. Although computer fanatics still dominate the web, a large population of regular users now have their own web page. Some may argue that anyone who has a web page is by definition a fanatic, but if that is the case, the world population is rapidly turning into computer fanatics. The implication is clear: new telecommunications technologies will evolve, solving yesterday's concerns and creating tomorrow's problems.

The ease of web use and the sheer volume of available data makes the web a most impressive telecommunications system. When an adult first experiences the web, you will be sure to hear "Oh Wow!" An especially interesting phenomenon is the lack of reaction by technology-savvy children. We recently worked with a group of knowledgeable children creating hypermedia presentations about baseball. They had never seen the World Wide Web or *Netscape*, and they came armed with questions. Throughout the entire day, the children never said a single "Oh Wow!" From the teacher, yes. From the children, no. For example, one group was looking for a picture of Yankee Stadium. We found a picture of our local team's stadium, along with three or four other stadium pictures. The children's response to the pictures was, "I want Yankee Stadium." In one case, the system even allowed them to pick a section of a major league stadium and see what the field looked like from that section. That stadium was far from these children's homes; they were relatively uninterested.

The missing "Oh Wow!" reaction gave us reason to pause and reflect. Our assumption was that the web is no more impressive to these children than, for example, automobiles are to us. The children would no more say, "Oh Wow, look at that web page!" than we would say, "Oh Wow, look at that horseless carriage." Tools like the World Wide Web are rapidly becoming natural parts of young people's lives.

We believe that the InterNet is the most likely route to the future of telecommunications, and that the World Wide Web is the main path. While school reform has failed to lessen transmission teaching, the InterNet and the web may make traditional teaching obsolete.

THE POSSIBILITIES AND CAPABILITIES OF TELECOMMUNICATIONS IN SCHOOLS

Many people are talking about telecommunications' ability to "break down the walls" of our schools. Through telecommunications, we can connect our schools to the outside world more easily and intimately. We can use telecommunications to bring people together. Schools can use e-mail, information data bases, software and document archives, and the multiple possibilities of the world wide web. New possibilities continually emerge. The field is changing so rapidly that we can only paint the possibilities in broad strokes. Capabilities will continue to expand, producing even greater possibilities, and people in the telecommunications community will certainly explore those possibilities creatively.

E-mail

E-mail is an application that has enormous potential in schools. It will benefit the entire learning and leading community. Consider the relative isolation of a teacher in a classroom. A typical teacher spends much of her day in a classroom with children. When the teacher has a break from the children, she may spend this time attending to issues within the classroom—grading papers and other instructional or management activities. The time a teacher spends interacting with peers in the building is often short. The time a teacher spends interacting with others outside the building is even shorter. If the teacher is a specialist, such as an art teacher, or has special interests and talents, such as an interest in elementary science, then she may have no peer in the building. Teachers have minimal opportunities to interact with peers with similar interests. Telecommunications can reduce that problem. E-mail within the building can give teachers another means of interacting with peers. Connection to the world wide e-mail system can lessen teachers' isolation.

E-mail within the building requires that each teacher have access to a computer. As technology advances, a computer for every teacher becomes less a luxury and more a necessity. Just as we accept that a teacher needs a desk, chalkboard, and chalk, we also should accept that a teacher needs a computer, software, and computer supplies. The potential for e-mail within a building is substantial. Once teachers start using e-mail, they begin to "talk" to each other more. An important strategy is to get them to start. A straightforward way is to require teachers to use e-mail to send and receive information to and from the principal's office. They can use e-mail to send attendance and lunch counts and receive announcements.

An added bonus of using e-mail is that it eliminates most of the interruptions over the public address system. Interruptions like, "Mrs. Smith, Billy's parents called and want him to take the bus home tonight," can be conveyed as an e-mail message instead of a blaring announcement that interrupts student learning.

For communication outside the building, a teacher can subscribe to a mailing list that relates to her special content area and have daily interaction with others. To use a technology-related example, an art teacher looking for a tessellation (patterning) program to use with her children could post a message to the list asking her peers for recommendations. Within a couple of days, she is likely to receive many suggestions. As an additional benefit, others on the list may use the discussion of tessellation programs as their first step in deciding to use these concepts in their own art classes. E-mail becomes an informal staff development strategy.

Individual e-mail can be quite useful to teachers. The people with whom we choose to communicate define the value of that communication. A teacher may communicate regularly with a state Department of Education's social studies consultant to discuss ideas about the school's social studies curriculum. She may communicate with individuals at the national science laboratories to get answers to troublesome science questions. She may communicate with another teacher who can become part of her thinking, planning, and support network.

One of the advantages of international e-mail is that it can help us meet people. If teachers subscribe to several active mailing lists and regularly read the posted messages, in time they will get to know some of the people on the list. It is common for people to reply to many messages from the list, or to the individual rather than to the entire list. These e-mail communications can be the start of a professional relationship.

We should not think of e-mail as the exclusive domain of the adults in the school, however. Students can also use e-mail. Some of the same issues that are important to the teachers—for example, communicating with individuals with like interests—also apply to our students. In addition, communicating with "key pals"—the e-mail equivalent of pen pals—can add authenticity to our instruction. Many people have implemented this idea successfully. In foreign language instruction, for example, e-mail effectively can replace postal pen pals. The advantage of e-mail is that it is quicker. With standard letters, children may only be able to send and receive a dozen or so letters in a semester. With e-mail, a student can send and receive one or more messages a day.

Another example comes from social studies. If your children are studying Europe, the teacher can establish e-mail connections between her children and European children. The children in both countries could tell each other about their cultures, and both groups benefit. In current events, students could link with other students who are in the news. For example, they can communicate with children in an area that has just experienced a major hurricane or a military conflict. If students study the rain forest in science, the teacher could link her students with students who live near a rain forest. Through the resulting communication, both groups can learn what it is like to live within a different biome. Teachers across the country have successfully implemented all of the examples cited above.

Another example of a powerful use of e-mail is to connect students with experts. Many experts are on the net and are willing to communicate with children. Some experts communicate as part of their defined responsibilities. For example, the National Science Laboratories, funded by the National Science Foundation, have education as a defined responsibility and make experts available to teachers and students. Many businesses also make experts available to educators. E-mail is an effective way to interact with experts.

Information Services and Data Bases

In Chapter 6 we discussed the process by which students collect data and construct meaning to create information. The next step is for students to put the information into action and construct knowledge. Telecommunications is an excellent tool for turning data into information and information into knowledge.

The amount of data available through the combined resources of commercial telecommunications services and the InterNet is staggering. In the past we thought of libraries as our greatest collections of data. Libraries, although sacred institutions, are being overshadowed by electronic resources. When we want our students to find data, the library should not be their only resource. They should also investigate various telecommunications services. Teachers and students may find different and more current data from telecommunications sources than from a library. While publication is a lengthy process, updating data through telecommunications can be immediate. Consider, for example, country names and boundaries. A student who looks in the encyclopedia might get geographic information that is years old. In today's ever-changing political environment, outdated information is worthless.

Another advantage to data collection through telecommunications is the data's scope and detail. The typical library available to students is relatively small. But when students go on-line, they have access to the combined resources of the Library of Congress and dozens of large public and university libraries. Through telecommunications, our students can expand and supplement that data.

One weakness of on-line data is that it is not finely focused for educational purposes. Many services are designed for professionals or the home/entertainment market. However, teachers can adapt the data and information for classroom use. For example, a teacher could use a service intended for constitutional lawyers in a government class. Another teacher could use a service intended for medical doctors in a biology class. Another could use services intended primarily for entertainment, such as book reviews, in language arts classes. As networks continue to grow, so will classroom applications.

Sharing Software or Documents

The amount of "free" information and software available for schools to download to their computers is greater than ever. People around the world have created documents and programs on a variety of topics and have published their work over the InterNet. Not only is more material available than ever, it has become easier to access. With modern telecommunications tools, almost anyone can download information or programs. The community of leadership can overcome technical impediments. We must overcome the problems of inappropriate sites and individuals to get our teachers and our students using this unique resource wisely.

Web Pages

The use of web pages in our schools is perhaps one of the most exciting technology-related innovations. We believe the World Wide Web will become a supplement to the library of the future. The volume of data on the web already rivals all but the largest libraries. If our students have access to the web, then they have access to enormous stores of data. The data itself is not what makes the web exciting; it is the potential for that data to become information and then knowledge. For example, with gardening suggestions (data) from the web, students can create a data base (information) from which they can learn how to plant seeds for hydroponic farming (knowledge).

Not only does the web allow us to bring information into the school, it allows us to send out information. Many schools have created web pages describing their school and informing the public about school activities. An exciting aspect of publishing this information on the web is that it is immediately available across the entire web—that is, world wide. Schools everywhere can learn from one small, local school.

Another rich area schools can explore is the publication of student writing. If, for example, we have our children write a story that describes a day in their life at school, we could publish that story on the web. In essence, we can let the world know what a day in our children's life is like. This not only provides a large audience for children's writing, it has other possibilities. For example, children can publish their stories as a community service, giving the teacher the opportunity to discuss service with her children. The "community" we are discussing is the telecommunication's community, which is rapidly becoming the world community.

On-Line Projects

A number of on-line projects are discussed in the professional literature. However, because of the relative slowness of publication and relative speed of technological advances, much of this information may be dated. Most of the published projects involve students' use of e-mail. This will change as publications begin to reflect the current state of technology. Nevertheless, these published accounts can form the basis for new ideas. They also can help us avoid problems others have already solved. The following two accounts are samples of solutions published in the literature.

McCullen (1995) describes a project called "MidLink Magazine," which was designed to help middle school students learn about and connect with students in other parts of the world. The project was an attempt "to use the InterNet in a new way: as collaborative cyberspace" (p. 8). The students played a large role in shaping the project; it has been highly successful in meeting its goal.

Smith (1995) describes exploration projects for students on the InterNet. She describes how students "around the country, are connected directly through the InterNet or via commercial on-line services to the ongoing adventures of scientists and explorers on expeditions such as a bike trip across Africa, a dogsled crossing on the North Pole or a sailing voyage around the world" (p. 26). The article lists seven specific exploration projects and describes how to contact their organizers.

In addition to publishing accounts of K–12 projects, many education journals include a monthly feature on networking on the InterNet. One example is the monthly column "Mining the InterNet" in *Learning and Leading with Technology*. As an example of this column, the November 1995 issue described how a school can create a web site. This column and similar monthly features in other journals can contribute to the completion of exciting school projects.

IMPORTANT CAUTIONS

The unfortunate reality is that nothing as powerful as telecommunications can come to us without unique problems. Although we do not believe the problems, dangers, and concerns are sufficient to abandon the use of this powerful tool, we do believe that the community of leadership must explicitly address these issues. It is the obligation of the community of leadership to insure that the new tools and methods introduced into the school are actually a step forward, not a half step forward and a full step backward.

Avoiding Pornography

A controversial issue in telecommunications is the accessibility of pornography. Pornography exists in our culture. It exists as an electronic representation of our culture. The social reasons pornography is available through telecommunications are the same as print media. We may abhor the existence of pornographic materials, but we value freedom of speech so highly that we defend it over other social concerns. This is not a new debate; it simply has spread to a new arena.

When we open up our classroom to the world, which is the appeal of telecommunications, we open it to both the good and the bad. We can control what children read, view, and hear through telecommunications in much the same we control it in the print environment: by monitoring what our children are doing. If we send our children into the world without supervision, many of them will end up at inappropriate places. Another way to think about monitoring telecommunications is to relate it to the typical school field trip. We would not consider sending our children on a field trip without supervision. Likewise, we must not send them on a virtual field trip without supervision. Teachers and parents must learn about telecommunications to monitor their children's safety.

Another solution used with print is to remove inappropriate material from our schools. Blocking undesirable material from entering our schools through telecommunications is a difficult problem from a technical standpoint and can be labor intensive. Individual networks are fluid and the InterNet is the most fluid. How can technologists block material when the environment changes so rapidly? Many bright and talented minds are working on this problem. The Telecommunications Act of 1996 advocates the V-chip as a technological solution. Over time, the ability to block or filter data entering the school will improve and become easier to manage.

The debate over freedom and its reasonable restriction will continue to be fundamental to our culture. However, until a remedy is found, we must protect our children from inappropriate material.

Protecting Children from Pedophiles

Another problem is the use of telecommunications by pedophiles to connect with unsuspecting children. Most e-mail systems attach the return address to any mail it sends. When our children send messages, some of the people responding to those messages may have malevolent intentions. Once such people have an e-mail address, they can use innocent messages to access a vulnerable child. This is sad and shocking, but, once again, when we open the school to the world, we take risks. One of the things we want our children to do with telecommunications is meet people and make positive social connections. Nevertheless, we must not risk our children's safety.

One solution is to monitor children's e-mail messages. It pains us to make this recommendation, but we believe it is necessary. Teachers and parents should monitor student e-mail to know with whom our children are speaking and the topics they are discussing. Any discussion with strangers that is unnecessarily personal or of a sexual nature is cause for intervention. Also, we should stop any requests to meet in person. Many pedophiles cleverly disguise themselves as peers to lure children. If we monitor e-mail and keep the potential dangers in mind, we can better protect our children.

Another safety solution is to educate our children to the potential dangers. If we were to stand on the adage, "Don't talk to strangers," our children would not be able to talk to anybody on the net. We need to update that thinking to, "Be careful what you tell a stranger." If our children know the potential dangers of "talking" to strangers over the InterNet, they can avoid dangerous people and become part of the solution by identifying and reporting such people.

Another possible solution is currently being debated. Some consider it to be the government's responsibility to monitor the Net and stop "bad people." Such policing activity generally is intended to stem the distribution of child pornography. This issue is so sensitive to all of us that it requires no discussion. However, as policing activities develop, a significant debate does arise: If government officials are checking the net for child pornography, what else are they monitoring? Is "big brother" watching us when we are on the net?

This issue has launched a raging debate about our right to privacy. Is that right superseded by the potential harm that could befall vulnerable children? The debate escalates as well-meaning individuals and groups initiate vigilante activity. For example, the Guardian Angels, a group originally formed to protect people in the streets of large cities, has begun to monitor the InterNet to seek child pornographers. The ethics of this activity are questionable, and many officials who are working in this area oppose the aggressive involvement of private citizens. A person who purports to be trying to catch pedophiles could be a pedophile himself. As mentioned earlier, the implications of individual freedom in telecommunications will continue to be a topic of heated discussion and debate.

Protecting Children from Other Dangerous Influences

Pornography and pedophiles are clearly a problem, but there are other concerns that we also must consider. If our children are connected intimately to the net, and that net represents our world, then children can be exposed to every negative aspect of our world. For example, there have been reports of significant drug-related activity on the net. We must monitor the activities of our children on the net to minimize such exposure, just as we monitor their activities outside the school or the home.

Violence is another potential danger. Devious people can plan violent activities over the net. However, the violence is seldom to a person but to parts of the net itself. The perpetrators are called hackers. People use this term in different ways. Some use it to describe a telecommunications zealot, one with skill and daring. Others use it in a more narrow way, to describe someone who tries to damage the net.

Although security across the net is significant, it is seldom perfect. Certain individuals make breaking existing security their own personal challenge. Only a few do this with malicious intent, but the distinction is sometimes difficult to see. Such people usually do some damage to demonstrate that they have breached the security. It is difficult to tell whether that damage is done maliciously or as an overzealous demonstration of individual skill. Regardless of the intent, the damage occurs. Hacking, as described here, is a criminal activity. It has become one of our newest crimes. To ensure that our children are not involved in this or any other criminal activity, we must monitor their net use at school and at home.

Preventing On-Line Addiction

Just as television created the "couch potato," the net has created its own addicts. Some experts argue that an on-line addict is not as bad as a television addict because being on-line is active while watching television is passive. This may be true, but anything overdone can be problematic. A few people are so deeply involved in the net that the virtual world begins to overshadow the real world. These concerns are passionately described in the book *Silicon Snake Oil*. Although we believe the concerns as expressed in this book are somewhat exaggerated, the basis for concern is certainly real.

It is our position that teachers and children should use the net to augment and enhance current learning strategies and curricula. Once we use these capabilities to replace traditional activities, we start moving from the real world into the virtual world. To return to a previous example, we can use various telecommunications activities to take a virtual field trip to the zoo. This means that we can visit a zoo any time we choose, which is positive. But if it means that children never really visit the zoo, but only see animals on their classroom monitor, that would be a step backward. Just because we have a technological tool does not mean that we should use it. High-tech solutions are not always the best. Instead, we should expose children to both real-world and virtual activities. We should show children that the real world has a richness that cannot be imitated in the virtual world.

DISTANCE LEARNING

Distance learning is one of several terms that describes a process of connecting two or more locations via an interactive audiovisual link. Other terms used to describe this method of telecommunications are teleconferencing, distance education, interactive video, and two-way video. Although distance learning technology has been available for many years, its use in schools increases.

Technologists have used several strategies to implement distance learning. Most of these methods involved some sort of video connection. The delivery of that video connection was sometimes a one-way connection, such as a class televised over a satellite. In other cases, delivery was via a two-way connection, with no interaction between the two sites. Today's technology makes two-way interactive video connections both possible and reasonably priced (depending on what you consider reasonable!). Two-way interactive video equipment is becoming more plentiful, easier to operate, and easier to connect to other similar sites. With these changes, the term "distance learning" is becoming almost synonymous with two-way interactive video.

The minimum equipment necessary to implement two-way interactive video includes a large screen monitor, a camera and microphone at each site, and a special telephone line to connect the sites together. A video signal contains much more information than a standard voice signal, so special broad-band telephone lines are necessary to carry the larger signal. Many distance education sites also include other devices, including document cameras, additional cameras and microphones, and data connections to enhance the capabilities of the site. A document camera is used to show papers or small objects to students at the other site. Data connections allow students to share information from computers at both sites. Additional cameras and microphones give the other location a variety of views of the room and the people assembled there.

Because the equipment to deliver distance learning is becoming more common, distance learning activities have begun to increase. A typical example is the small high school that has few classes in specialty areas such as foreign languages. These small schools are forming a partnership with larger schools or a collection of other smaller schools to deliver combined classes using two-way interactive video equipment. This allows smaller schools to have a wider range of course offerings without incurring the associated staffing expenses.

Although potentially exciting, this technology is still in its infancy. The implementation of new technology often follows a predictable cycle, and the technology that enables distance learning is no exception. The early stages involve using the technology to do what schools have always done, but to do it better, faster, or cheaper. Much of the thinking that underlies distance learning is still operating at this stage. Another indication that implementation of this technology is still in its early stages is that schools often engage in experimental activities that are not philosophically grounded and are not connected to the school's vision and mission. Such activities are usually launched with the idea, "Now that we have this equipment, what can we do with it?" In other words, distance learning equipment is a solution in search of a problem.

The later stages of the implementation of a new technology are characterized by the development of new ways of accomplishing the school's goals. Rather than doing the same thing faster, cheaper, or better with new technology, schools instead find new ways to use the unique elements of the technology. Little work has been done in this area in distance learning, but the potential is enormous. Two-way interactive connections between people and groups of people can dramatically change the way we organize children to learn and can expand the opportunities for learning we bring into our classrooms.

Distance learning equipment raises some major cautions, however. This equipment has great potential to enrich our children's learning, but also to impoverish their experiences. Children's distance learning experiences need to be balanced with face-to-face interactions with real people. For example, after a distance learning presentation given by a scientist in another part of the country, the teacher can ask a local scientist to visit the class, or can take the class on a field trip to a nearby university or government research facility to interact with scientists at work.

GOVERNMENTAL AND SOCIETAL TELECOMMUNICATIONS TRENDS

Government has been involved with the development of the net as it currently exists. The future of that involvement is uncertain. The need to insure equitable access is the best reason that government should remain engaged with telecommunications. We believe that the net is, and will continue to be, one of the most powerful ways a child can learn, develop, and grow. The issue of equitable access is important to us because we believe that every child should have the opportunity to improve her life. To truly achieve equitable access is a costly proposition, but cost must not be the qualifying issue. All the constituencies involved in education must work toward compromise, but that compromise must not relegate some children to a life of ignorance and poverty.

If we are to continue moving toward equitable access, then the federal government must continue its support of a national infrastructure for the InterNet or its successor. However, the infrastructure is not the only area of concern. Inexpensive local access to the InterNet is another problem. We can solve local access problems in several ways. These solutions can involve federal, state, and local government agencies, private funding sources, and for-profit business and industry. Who provides access to the net is less important than that all schools have equitable access.

As society uses telecommunications to a greater extent, it is likely that the commercial telecommunications companies will integrate with the InterNet. Commercial companies will always be needed because it is unlikely that the government will support all the demands of the public. Individual users will have to pay for many services. This payment can be either through subscriptions or "pay for view." It is likely that some combination of these options will emerge. The integration of commercial services and the InterNet has already begun; many commercial companies now offer InterNet access. The next step will enhance user access to the InterNet through commercial telecommunications services.

Technologists and educators have discussed how the "information superhighway" or the "national information infrastructure" will evolve. The positive involvement of the community of leadership must continue. We need to be major players in these discussions or risk letting people with special interests, unique philosophies, or profit motives determine the future of telecommunications.

IMPLICATIONS FOR THE COMMUNITY OF LEADERSHIP

The community of leadership bears the responsibility for managing and leading instructional technology environments. The community of leadership must maintain an interest in and knowledge of technological developments. If we ease our vigilance or vacillate in our commitment to technology and quality academic programs, then all the previous work will have failed.

The community of leadership must persevere at two major efforts. The first is to constantly assess and improve its academic program, including reviewing instructional strategies, increasing clinical supervision and peer coaching, and developing and implementing quality staff development. The second is to maintain interest and knowledge about innovations in instructional technology. Some efforts require continuous learning about hardware, software, connectivity, and telecommunications. Although some efforts require educated guesses, knowing what the school needs to successfully support its instructional program makes guessing less uncertain.

The community of leadership must monitor our children's on-line activity, show interest, and stay in touch with our children's network activities. We also must model the appropriate use of telecommunications, being careful not to overuse this powerful technology but instead to use it to expand, enhance, and enrich our children's world. In addition, the community of leadership must keep in touch with the future of telecommunications. The InterNet, the World Wide Web, and distance learning have potential to influence our schools, and the nature of that influence must be a prime concern. We should not be passive recipients of technology; instead, we should participate in shaping its development so that it meets our educational goals. To do this effectively, we must look at the past and predict the future.

PREDICTIONS FOR THE FUTURE OF TELECOMMUNICATIONS

We predict continued growth of nonlinear access to a greater variety of data. The World Wide Web will continue to add nodes and connections among nodes. Public Broadcasting System's library of nature videos and recordings of cultural events are examples. The special knowledge of a wide variety of individuals is available also. We believe our perspective of an international electronic information web will continue to grow at a rapid pace. We also believe more people will begin using the web, and that they will use it for an increasing number of reasons. The international information web will become more interactive.

We believe that federal involvement will increase, but not to the extent that most educators wish. We believe that federal, state, and local government initiatives will provide all schools access to the net. Others in the community will have more limited access.

The kind of data that will be available on the net will continue to evolve. Data will continue to become more reality-based, with more detailed pictures, more access to motion video, and higher quality sound. Access also will continue to influence both hardware and software development. The tools available today seem easy to use for those of us who have struggled for years with complicated applications. This trend will continue, making net access simpler and therefore available to an even wider audience. The increase in the size of the net makes the ease of access important because as the net gets larger, it becomes more difficult to navigate. For example, finding an audio clip of whale songs is difficult because of the large amount of available data. Teachers will need powerful machines with powerful searching software to easily and conveniently access the data they wish to use in their instruction. We believe this powerful hardware and software is forthcoming. When we mention whale songs in a biology lesson, we will be able to easily and quickly "punch up" whales, so that our children can see the humpbacks swimming and hear their songs.

The effect of changes in telecommunication on the classroom will be multifaceted. We will interweave our instruction with realistic examples and illustrations. Beyond that, our classroom cultures will undergo many changes. Teachers will use less direct instruction. The possibilities telecommunications afford will allow learners to take greater control of their own learning—to be more constructivist. Society will always need teachers to guide the learning process, but we will not need teachers who follow the transmission model and simply pass information to a passive audience. The information will be available on the net, and it will be the teacher's job to help each individual student find that information and use it to create knowledge. If we consider children's minds simply another hierarchical node on the net, the teacher's job will be to decide what, how, and where data should reside. Some data must surely be in the node that is the child's mind. The teacher will plan the access and activities that will transfer certain data from the electronic net of the computer to the biological net of children.

CONCLUSION

Telecommunications, whether a local area or an international network, is a part of today's instructional program. Students and teachers need access to data and information available on-line, from simple e-mail to the more complex World Wide Web. It is now possible for teachers and students to interact and learn with people from around the world. It is possible for teachers and students to conduct research involving other schools across the city, state, country, and world. It is possible for teachers and students to obtain data and information inaccessible from anywhere else. For example, teachers and students can access the libraries of most of the major universities world wide. Teachers and students can access data and information about a thematic instruction topic from primary sources. Through e-mail, teachers and students can contact the individuals and organizations they are studying.

Lest we believe that teachers and schools will be replaced by an inexpensive computer, a modem, and an InterNet connection, remember a major issue of instructional technology. Technology can help us find data: raw bits of facts. Technology can help us manipulate the data into useful information through charts, graphs, distributions, and sorts. Only teachers and students can hypothesize, connect ideas, and problem solve using data and information. Only teachers and students can turn data into information and information into knowledge.

REFERENCES

Internet Society. (1994). *Latest internet measurements reveal dramatic growth in 1994.* (Press Release.) Reston, VA: Author.

McCullen, C. (1995). World Wide Web in the classroom: The quintessential collaboration. *Learning and Leading with Technology, 23*(3), 60–63.

Smith, M. (1995). The new "trekkie". *Electronic Learning, 14*(5), 26–30.

Stoll, C. (1993). *Silicon snake oil: Second thoughts on the information highway.* New York: Anchor.

RESOURCE LIST

America On-line (telecommunications service)

CompuServe (telecommunications service)

Gopher (InterNet navigation software), developed by the University of Minnesota Microcomputer and Workstation Networks Center

Mosaic (web browser), National Center for Supercomputing Applications

Netscape Navigator (web browser), Netscape Communications Corp.

Prodigy (telecommunications service)

III

The Community of Leadership

10.

Staff Development:
A Community of Learners,
A Community of Leaders

Staff development is a process for guiding improvement of instruction. There is no question about the importance of quality staff development efforts. There is a question, however, about the value of current instructional technology staff development. Instructional technologists and the community of leadership often believe that teachers will use technology after more training. We believe, however, that instructional technology will not become an instructional tool until teachers and administrators engage in specialized staff development.

The current workshop/course and "teachers as trainers" models to staff development have not worked. We propose a different strategy which includes preparing teachers in their own classrooms, during the school day, using their instructional goals and objectives, and working with their students. Included in this model is a strategy for continuous learning after the "trainers" have left the school or district. Clinical supervision and peer coaching are essential elements of a successful model for improving instruction. This new model for staff development may be more labor intensive, but it will be more successful.

In this chapter we describe the current state of staff development efforts; how to improve staff members' knowledge, skills, strategies, and attitudes; how experts influence staff development; new models of teaching and learning; how leaders support staff development; background issues in staff development; interactive staff development; models for teacher evaluation, supervision, and peer coaching; and successful programs for staff development in instructional technology.

INTRODUCTION

There is little disagreement that schools must continue to improve. Our schools have to produce better educated students who achieve higher standardized test scores and more productive educational outcomes. If we think about schools as a system, the critical part of the system that can cause change in student outcomes is the teacher. If we improve the teacher's ability to help children learn, then we will drastically improve the school as a system. We see the teacher as the most powerful and malleable variable in the school improvement effort.

School administrators and teachers who devote one evening a month or one day a semester to staff development perceive staff development as unimportant. If we are to change schools by changing teacher behavior, then our staff development efforts cannot be only a small part of what happens in the school, but must be the heart of our efforts to continually improve our schools. For our staff development to be effective, we have to view it as central to the success of the school.

THE TECHNOLOGY TRAIN

A moving train serves as a useful metaphor for thinking about staff development in instructional technology. Technology is the train. Unlike the trains we know, this train never stops. It never even slows down. Instead, it keeps going faster and faster. Teachers who ride the train reap the benefits. Those who run along the platform experience the frustrations of not being on the train and find it increasingly difficult to gain sufficient speed to jump aboard.

We see technology-oriented staff development as getting teachers "up to speed" so they can jump on the train. Some experts see this as a major problem as schools become more technologically rich. Others minimize the problem, believing it will disappear through staff attrition. Although we are improving the technological knowledge, skills, and dispositions of our new teachers, the change in the total population of teachers is small. Considering the acceleration of the technology train, we may only be holding steady rather than moving forward.

While teacher preparation programs are ensuring that new teachers board the technology train, many experienced teachers are disembarking. The improvement of teacher preparation programs, although critical, is only a small part of the solution. We must help the existing skilled and experienced teachers jump on the technology train.

COMMON MODELS OF STAFF DEVELOPMENT: WE CAN DO BETTER

The standard model of technology-oriented staff development is to hire an expert—either someone external to the school system or a school employee, bring her in after school or for a teacher in-service day, and let her deliver her prepared program. Afterwards, teachers continue their practice as though nothing has happened. Two issues have caused us to question this model. The first is an experience we had with more than one technology-rich school whose teachers had many hours of staff development. The formal administration waited for the staff development to evolve into changes in classroom activities. Instead of using the new knowledge, the teachers replied, "If I only had a little more training, then I would do it in my classroom." It seemed that no matter how much training they had, they felt that they needed more preparation before they could transfer the skills to their instructional practice. They were getting up to speed but were reluctant to jump on the train.

The second issue stems from our own experience facilitating technology-oriented staff development. We have delivered many training sessions using the standard model. The teachers learned in most of those training sessions, and what they learned was potentially useful to them and to their children. However, when we returned to the school months later, we saw no evidence of that learning. The staff was still on the platform. They had not gained any speed. This is a common frustration among teachers, administrators, staff development professionals, and students.

For staff development to be beneficial, the learning has to transfer to the classroom. The teachers must take action based on their learning. That action should be noticeable as a positive change in the school. The fact that staff development efforts seldom produce meaningful change caused us to examine possible problems with the traditional approach. Many elements of the approach are questionable:

1. When we do after-school skill development, we are catching the teachers at a poor learning time, when they are tired and have their minds on other issues of the day.

2. Most staff development happens after the children have left the building. The children are the largest part of the context of the learning, yet they are not a part of the staff development experience.

3. Most staff development happens outside the classroom, and often outside the school building, although the classroom is an important part of the context in which the learning should be applied.

4. Staff development programs often are prepackaged. Experts arrive on the scene with the answer to the school's problems. Many of those experts know nothing about the school but try to apply a generic solution to unknown problems. Thus, technological staff development becomes a solution in search of a problem.

5. Many staff development experts do not recognize the existing knowledge and skill of the teachers being trained. They come into the school with the attitude that they are going to "fix" the teachers, when in fact, most of the teachers are not broken; they simply need help getting up to speed in a specific area. Their lack of knowledge and skill in technology does not diminish their knowledge of a wide variety of other instructional issues. The experts do not have all the

Adults and children learning together.

answers; they only have elements of the answers, which must be combined with the elements that teachers hold.

6. Much staff development happens in one session. For example, teachers who want to learn to use spreadsheets in the classroom typically attend a one-day workshop. From this single experience, it is expected that the teachers not only will use spreadsheets but will generalize that knowledge and do other technology-oriented activities as well. This is like giving a first-grader a day's worth of instruction and then expecting her to read. We know that learning usually takes time and practice, yet we expect teachers to be exempt from this reality.

7. Staff development often is disconnected completely from the instructional program within a school. We teach the instructional staff specific technological skills without explicitly connecting the skills to the existing curriculum. We thereby fail to provide teachers the opportunity to develop schemata and form mental models.

8. Standard models of staff development seldom include any mechanism for the staff to continue to improve after the initial learning. Without this mechanism, teachers quickly lose the new knowledge and return to their standard practice.

9. Many teachers see experts as possessing knowledge and skills that they cannot possibly attain. This belief tends to diminish teachers' self-esteem and becomes a disincentive in the learning environment rather than an incentive.

Most schools are using weak staff development models. We have the knowledge and skill to improve these models. We can spend our time more effectively and produce more meaningful changes in the operations of our schools. We can only do this, however, if we are willing to rethink our staff development paradigm.

Staff developers commonly notice that teachers gain some speed, then lose some speed. The staff development task is to help teachers steadily gain speed over time until they are ready to jump on the train. Jumping on the train suggests that teachers have become independent, lifelong learners. The goal of the community of leadership is to empower its members to supervise their own learning.

IMPROVING CONCEPTUAL KNOWLEDGE

Possibilities and Capabilities

If teachers are to use technology effectively to improve learning, then they must first learn the possibilities and capabilities of new technology. They must assume a technologist's view of new technology applications. This is an effective way to use the one-shot experiences we have for staff development. The difference between the staff development model we are suggesting and the current model, however, is that this experience is only a starting point. It is important also that the teachers know that the goals of this activity are merely to inform.

Another way we can help our teachers learn the possibilities and capabilities of new technology is to subscribe to technology-oriented journals and make them available to teachers. In addition, if someone in the building is responsible for reading each issue and routing appropriate information to teachers, then a subscription can help influence the instructional program.

A third way we can help teachers learn possibilities and capabilities is to send them to conferences. We tend to send our most technologically advanced teachers to technology conferences. However, these conferences can be useful to other teachers also. Sending a technology expert and a technology novice to a conference together is a way to help the novice join the expert on the train.

IMPROVING SKILL

What It Takes to Develop Skill

Much of technology-oriented staff development is devoted to skill development. Using a word processor, for example, is essentially a skill. Skill development requires practice over time. As our staff development efforts evolve, we must keep this principle in mind. For the skill to develop, the learning that happens in a staff development session must be applied to the work in the classroom, and it must be applied repeatedly. This means that if we want the time, effort, and expense we devote to staff development to pay off, then we have to expect that teachers will use the new knowledge and skill in the classroom with children.

For example, to teach spreadsheet operations we may begin by having a staff development session. For that learning to become a skill, the teachers must practice using spreadsheets. The principal could require that all budget requests, grades, and attendance be submitted on a spreadsheet. In this way we help teachers achieve automaticity (Samuels, 1988).

Just-in-Time Training

In the just-in-time manufacturing process, all the raw materials for a product arrive at the factory as they are needed. This keeps the investment in raw material to a minimum and reduces storage and handling expenses. This same thinking has been applied to business training for many years: In business, training seldom is delivered if it is not immediately necessary. Training relates only to necessary knowledge and skill. Many business training programs require that learners attend when they demonstrate a need for the training.

The just-in-time concept also could be applied to staff development in schools. Under the existing staff development paradigm, all teachers must attend, and many teachers resent having to participate. We deliver information and hope wonderful things will happen in the classroom. Instead, we could target staff development; only those people who demonstrate an immediate need for the knowledge need attend.

The voluntary aspect of just-in-time preparation means the principal can no longer report that "64 teachers were trained" on her yearly performance evaluation. Issues of school improvement displace statistics on the number of teachers educated. Volunteerism also raises questions about teachers who refuse to participate:

How long should the school wait? How should the untrained be supervised? This issue is deeply imbedded in the school culture. It can only be answered by examining the context of each individual situation. The advice we offer is that every teacher does not have to be "on the train." It is possible for a teacher to be great—that is, to be a powerful influence on positive student learning—without using the latest technology. Numerous examples spring to mind of nurturing and caring individuals who make strong connections with children and their learning. However, technology is becoming integral to our society, so we cannot afford to have many untrained teachers in our schools.

This paradigm shift requires a different relationship with experts. The necessary experts also must be available just in time. Booking an expert will be more difficult in a just-in-time environment. These issues can be resolved if we are willing to invest the necessary planning.

BACKGROUND ISSUES AND DEFINITIONS OF STAFF DEVELOPMENT

Staff development or in-service education is an integral part of the teaching and learning process. Just as the school's vision and mission influence implementation of learning theories and determine a school's culture, the school's values and beliefs about teaching and learning should direct the focus of the staff development program. New educational ideas and strategies that teachers study and practice should reflect both the school's goals and objectives and the issues and needs that arise from the supervision of instruction. As the principal or the community of leadership observes teaching in action, she or they may recognize, for example, that certain teachers have not increased the frequency of higher order questions in classroom discussions. Questioning strategies, then, become a part of the staff development plan for several teachers.

All staff development plans have elements in common. Whether the school's goal is to introduce teachers to cooperative learning, advisor-advisee programs, or hypermedia, the same goals, objectives, procedures, planning, and assessment processes apply. In the discussion below, we first consider the generic issues of staff development or in-service education and then apply these elements to staff development and in-service education plans in instructional technology.

Lieberman and Miller (1991, p. 244) make a distinction between two definitions of in-service education: In-service education can be (1) "any effort to engage individuals or groups of teachers with improvement exercises," or (2) "a serious and systematic effort to engage a group of professional educators who work together, a staff, in activities designed specifically to increase the power and authority of their shared work." Clearly, the second definition is the one that meets the spirit of the community of leadership.

Values and Beliefs about Staff Development: The State of Georgia

Just as participants in the school must decide on their worthwhile shared goals about leadership, teaching, and learning, the community of leadership must establish its set of values and beliefs about staff development. Without consensus, a program to improve teaching and learning and to encourage lifelong learning would become confused and fall prey to superficial educational trends and the "hot topics" of the season.

In 1983–84, the State of Georgia (cited in Wiles & Bondi, 1991) developed and published its values and beliefs about staff development. These ideals reflect the State's philosophy and become the expectations for all staff development programs. In Georgia, educators' dispositions toward staff development are the need for esteem, interest in new knowledge, positive attitudes and beliefs, continuous growth and lifelong learning, and collaboration. Staff development programs include needs assessment, comprehensive plans for change, individual teacher and school-based plans, decision-making autonomy, and certification renewal accreditation. Administratively, staff development programs are a high priority of the school and district; they are designed to improve instruction and school services; they are connected to the school's vision and mission and to the school's curriculum; they take full advantage of employees' internal and external expert resources; and they are a primary responsibility of the community of leadership. Although this description is a snapshot of one state's values and beliefs at one moment in time, it serves as a foundation for a quality staff development plan.

Conditions for Successful Staff Development

Rubin (1989) continues our consideration of the elements of effective staff development. He suggests eight conditions for successful staff development activities, conditions which meet the State of Georgia's general values and beliefs about staff development. Rubin's conditions consider several universal themes in staff development or in-service education. His conditions represent a concern for improving instruction through changing teacher behaviors and through participant collaboration and empowerment. Although these are general conditions for all staff development programs, they clearly represent what "ought to be" in instructional technology.

1.   The educators closest to the instructional problem should determine or at least participate in the selection of staff development topics. An example of a staff development topic deriving from teachers working with instructional problems might be the use of spreadsheets in mathematics—converting data into graphical information into knowledge.

2.   Thinking about staff development topics should be a continuous process among the community of leadership, faculty, and staff. As we meet to discuss how technology can support an effective academic program, teachers should express their areas of concern and need for increased skills and knowledge. Teacher evaluation, clinical supervision, peer coaching, and curriculum discussions should influence the selection of staff development topics and problems. For example, teachers' discussions about their needs to integrate telecommunications into content area curriculum would influence a staff development plan.

3. Empowerment should be about real educational issues important to the community of leadership. Staff development training fits Rubin's prescription. We no longer can accept the selection of staff development topics by administrators outside the instructional loop. For example, teachers' subjective judgments about expository writing, supported by writing samples and standardized test scores, may indicate the need for process writing skills and word processing. In other words, just because brain-compatible learning is a hot topic, it should not replace the teacher's perceived, real needs.

4. Staff development leaders and committees must create a cadre of specialists among the community of leadership who can deliver instruction, help with transfer of learning to the classroom, and become a resource for continuing practice. The traditional model of public education's staff development program relies on a one-day training session taught by an outside expert consultant; although learning does occur, little is transferred to the student's learning. Preparing teachers and children with these skills—creating a team of experts—may increase the probability of transfer of learning.

5. It is not enough that the participants select the topics for staff development; they must also help plan, implement, and assess the experience. Assessment should involve an understanding of the usefulness and immediacy of the skills and knowledge for the classroom rather than meaningless frequency distributions about the numbers of persons attending or the length of a session. Participants should hold follow-up sessions to consider issues of quality, efficacy, and future learning. For example, once *Logo* is introduced into the thinking curriculum, additional curriculum planning must determine the future direction of students' thinking and problem-solving culture.

6. Staff development training should derive from two important sources of assessment: an evaluation of the quality of the school's teaching and learning, and information gathered from the supervision or coaching of classroom teachers. Teachers who are struggling to integrate science, mathematics, and social studies in a middle school need specialized skill development in their in-service education programs. Listening to an outside expert in strategic planning will not improve the seventh grade's integrated curriculum.

7. The staff development program should be viewed as an ongoing, open system that invites adjustments or changes through formative assessment. For example, as the need for skill development in thinking lessens, work in publishing student writing may increase. Flexible staff development plans can adapt to curricular growth and change.

8. Staff development topics and programs should be individually planned and implemented for specialized segments of the teaching and learning environment. For example, the early childhood staff might need additional knowledge about cognitive psychology and child development, while the secondary vocational educa-

tion program might need skills in computer-aided design. An effective staff development program must be malleable enough to meet all the teachers' real needs. The community of leadership should reject school or district-wide staff development activities or presentations which do not reflect its values and beliefs and vision and mission.

Additionally, Rubin (1989) cautions the community of leadership and staff development participants that well-developed content area knowledge, reflective practice, and a disposition toward lifelong learning are critical principles for successful staff development and in-service education practices. Rubin ends his discussion with this admonition:

> In the final analysis, fine teaching stems from a well-informed mind, a repertory of finely-honed skills, and a passionate desire to excel. (p. 181)

INTERACTIVE STAFF DEVELOPMENT

The instructional strategies that the community of leadership chooses to institute must be consistent with its values and beliefs about leadership and teaching and learning. Staff development activities must reflect the guiding principles of the school's moral position, its vision and mission, and the school's cultural conditions of collaboration, empowerment, and worthwhile shared goals.

Griffin (1991) proposes an interactive staff development model which meets the premises of this book. Interactive staff development suggests that individual and school values and beliefs are continuously in motion and must be understood to reach the desired improvement in instruction. Additionally, interactive staff development implies a continuous process toward goals and objectives in a systematic effort while considering the developmental level of the faculty—the movement from novice to expert teaching. This is not a static process. Interactive staff development requires the community of leadership to envision staff development practices beyond the current boundaries of delivery.

Assumptions Underlying an Interactive Staff Development Model

Griffin (1991) suggests seven assumptions which underlie an interactive staff development model and which are directed toward devising a successful, generic staff development program. We can extrapolate these ideas to describe a quality academic program supported by instructional technology.

"Assumption 1: Teachers, more often than not, are perceptive about their shortcomings and strong points" (p. 247). Historically, formal leadership established processes to make summative judgments (statements of rightness or wrongness or goodness and badness) about teachers' performance independent of teacher input. Over time, this process resulted in assumptions that teachers were not reflective practitioners, could not assess their own performance, and were not lifelong learners. Quite the opposite may be true. Teachers are interested in analyzing their strengths and weaknesses and developing strategies for change. Current discussions about

teacher empowerment and a review of McGregor's (1960) classic Theory X, Theory Y research, support teachers' concern for quality.

"Assumption 2: Teachers value highly their interactions with students" (p. 248). A positive and successful way to view the work of teachers and the processes by which they learn begins by legitimizing teachers' feelings about their interactions with children. Respecting teachers' affective connections with children should produce conditions for improvement and change in teaching and learning. We believe, for example, that teachers will learn more technology skills and will better understand a specific technology's possibilities and capabilities when staff development occurs in the teacher's classroom with her children.

"Assumption 3: Teachers' worklives are enhanced by professional interactions with other adults" (p. 249). The community of leadership advocates collaboration and empowerment because it believes that the people who do the task know the task best. Another condition, seldom mentioned, is that collaboration and empowerment, even the simple co-planning and co-teaching of lessons, lessens the teachers' sense of isolation and frustration. Teachers will perform better when they work in collaborative dyads and teams.

"Assumption 4: School leadership, as currently conceptualized, is an increasingly impossible task and must be reconstructed to include teacher leadership" (p. 250). Griffin's fourth assumption suggests that current models of school leadership are inconsistent with the goals and objectives of public education and the demand for accountability. The concept of the community of leadership advocated in this book expands on Griffin's warnings and presents a viable solution.

There are many reasons that today's principalship places inordinate responsibilities and pressures upon leaders. Most notably, the principal suffers from the institutionalized conflict between her role in status maintenance—ensuring that the organization is stable and operates smoothly—and her role as the change agent—ensuring that the organization adapts, improves, and grows. The need to keep staff morale high, which is a status maintenance task, is in direct conflict with the need to implement program change, which is a change agent task. This conflict between stability and change creates ambiguity which contributes to personal stress and professional paranoia.

"Assumption 5: The success of interactive staff development must be a consequence of ongoing reconceptualization of responsibilities for school and student success" (p. 252). Griffin not only suggests that staff development strategies must change, but also that the school's organizational practices must adapt to changing social, economic, and political conditions. He recommends that the community of leadership focus on individual school's expectations, standards, and accountability. He proposes that schools rather than the district be the focus for accountability. School-based technology resources, connected to the curriculum, will serve students better than district-wide or centralized technology services. According to Griffin, "the proof of any 'reform' in public education will lie in the degree to which what was changed has some positive bearing on the purpose of schools, helping students become knowledgeable, skillful, and thoughtful citizens" (p. 253).

"Assumption 6: Participating in interactive staff development will require new knowledge and skill on the part of all involved and will be accompanied by considerable anxiety,

stress, tension, and conflict" (p. 253). Assumption 6 is self-evident and is lessened by the staff development changes advocated by the community of leadership. As Watson (1967) suggested in his research on the change process, leadership must understand the reasons that participants fear change and must honor those fears. Peer coaching (Joyce & Showers, 1982) is a strategy of staff development and improvement of instruction which helps release and diffuse these stressors.

"Assumption 7: Despite the problems associated with learning new knowledge and skills, participants in interactive staff development will be more fully and productively engaged in teaching and schooling than is typical" (p. 255). Griffin cites several examples of teachers expressing feelings of joy and success in staff development activities, even when faced with ambiguity and chaos. For example, although teachers often find *Logo* difficult to understand and master, they are excited by its usefulness in the thinking curriculum. We argue that the demand for accepting the challenges of thinking and problem solving, of conquering ambiguity and chaos, moves teachers upward in Maslow's (1954) hierarchy of needs towards esteem and self-actualization.

The community of leadership is a response to each of Griffin's concerns about staff development. The community of leadership reflects his recommendations for strategies and practices which reduce the stress between participants and the school context, his demands for member empowerment, and for change in teaching and learning consistent with the school's vision and mission. The shift from the generic issues of staff development to technology-based staff development should be self-evident.

TEACHER EVALUATION, SUPERVISION, AND PEER COACHING: THE IMPROVEMENT OF INSTRUCTION

Directly connected to staff development and in-service education are processes for determining teachers' contribution to the improvement of instruction, lifelong learning, and the school's moral leadership and culture. School leaders employ three processes to clarify the teachers' commitment to the school and the profession: teacher evaluation, clinical supervision, and peer coaching. Each can produce interesting results. However, we consider peer coaching—a model for learning new strategies and for the improvement of instruction—as the preferred method to reinforce staff development programs. Coaching, then, is a collaborative process for teachers (peers) to continue to grow and improve their instruction.

Teacher Evaluation

In this book we make an important distinction between teacher evaluation and the supervision of instruction. Teacher evaluation is a summative rating system of teacher behaviors, often in checklist form, which seeks to rank the quality of an individual teacher's performance. Evaluations are used often to determine tenure, personnel decisions, and job retention. Many of the issues of teacher evaluation are not related directly to instruction but to conditions of the position, such as attendance and punctuality, accuracy in completing paperwork and budgets, and relations with staff and parents. Evaluations are completed by an administrator after observation(s) and typically do not include a systematic model or program for continuous improvement. Teachers rated as excellent often do not receive improvement suggestions and are not evaluated regularly.

Wiles and Bondi (1991) detail eight categories often cited in teacher evaluation instruments or checklists: dependability, human relations skills, managing the classroom, planning instruction, implementing instruction, knowledge of subject matter, assessing and evaluating students, and professionalism. (See Figure 10–1.) Although these categories rate teaching and learning, ratings usually are phrased as yes/no, or "superior," "meets expectations," or "needs improvement." The evaluation characteristically is clear; the strategies for improvement are not.

A teacher who receives superior ratings in each of the categories and subcategories may feel elated initially, but soon wonders how she can improve. In such teacher evaluation systems, rarely do teachers receive meaningful suggestions for improvement, alternative strategies, or information about newly published instructional methods. The evaluation may improve teachers' esteem initially but is not likely to improve their instructional practices.

Clinical Supervision

Clinical supervision is a formative assessment alternative to summative teacher evaluation systems. Clinical supervision is a model solely for the improvement of instruction. In clinical supervision, the teacher and a supervisor, often an assistant principal or principal, work together to improve the teacher's performance. Glickman, Gordon, and Ross-Gordon (1995), proponents of developmental models, define supervision as "a school function that improves instruction through direct assistance to teachers, curriculum development, staff development, group development, and action research" (p. xvii).

Clinical supervision is a hierarchical, power-based relationship between teacher and administrator. Even though the supervisory relationship (referent power and authority) is built on trust, there remains the superordinate-subordinate relationship (legitimate power and authority) which can interfere with the process. Teachers might be reluctant to share their instructional concerns and their desire to improve.

There are many variations on the basic format of clinical supervision. The Teacher Concern Model (Tracy & MacNaughton, 1993) represents a collaborative process dependent upon a trusting, open relationship between the teacher and the supervisor. The model's purpose is to help determine the teacher's instructional concerns and apply strategies to improve the teacher's performance. Tracy and MacNaughton describe this model:

> The focus of this model is the teacher's concerns. The supervisor assists the teacher in clarifying uncertainties about his/her teaching, then observes instruction and gathers data related to the teacher's area of concern. Following an analysis of the

I.   Dependability
    A. Punctual
    B. Fulfills duties
II. Human Relations Skills
    A. Helps development of positive self-images in learners
    B. Demonstrates skills in various kinds of communications
III. Managing the Classroom
    A. Maintains a safe environment
    B. Manages disruptive behavior appropriately
IV. Planning Instruction
    A. Selects appropriate learning goals and objectives
    B. Demonstrates skill in evaluating the instructional plan
V.   Implementing Instruction
    A. Relates instruction to the world of the learner
    B. Demonstrates skills in questioning and responding
VI. Knowledge of Subject Matter
    A. Demonstrates adequate general academic preparation
    B. Demonstrates knowledge of areas of specialization
VII. Assessing and Evaluating Students
    A. Recognizes individual personalities/learning styles
    B. Skillful in providing feedback to students and parents
VIII. Professionalism
    A. Seeks to improve own professional competence
    B. Demonstrates skill in professional decision making

Figure 10–1

Teacher Evaluation Categories

Source: Wiles, J., & Bondi, J. (1991). *Supervision a guide to practice* (pp. 306–310). New York: Merrill/Prentice Hall.

data, the supervisor and teacher work together to identify strategies that will help alleviate the problems and achieve the desired changes. This is usually followed by additional observations and conferences to monitor progress. (p. 17)

Most clinical supervision models are based upon the process whereby a supervisor and a teacher determine the instructional strategy to be observed and the characteristics of the lesson, followed by observation, application of an objective data-collection tool, and an analysis of the observation (lesson). Classic clinical supervision and peer coaching models use a combination of these elements.

Clinical supervision is a model of continuous improvement of instruction rather than merely conducting one or two teacher evaluations. The three parts of the model include:

1. *A planning conference.* The teacher and the supervisor determine which teaching and learning process to observe and what objective feedback to provide.

2. *Classroom observation.* The supervisor observes the lesson and uses an objective data-collection tool to describe the teacher's modeling of the agreed-upon teaching strategy. For example, the objective data collection tool may be a written record of teacher and students' higher order thinking questions and responses, a frequency chart of the teacher's recognition of girls' and boys' comments and questions in science or mathematics classes, or a seating chart representing proximity control—the pattern of teacher movement around the classroom during a lesson.

3. *Analysis.* The supervisor provides the teacher with an analysis of the objective data, assists the teacher's self-analysis, and helps the teacher adapt new strategies or behaviors. It is important that the teacher recognize and accept the analysis of the objective data and participate in the discussion of improvement practices. Additionally, the supervisor and the teacher review the clinical supervision process and its affective impact: how the process has influenced both participants.

Selected Objective Data-Collection Formats   The creation of an objective data-collection tool is essential to the clinical supervision process. An objective data-collection tool gives the teacher authentic information about the teacher's classroom behaviors unscreened by a supervisor's interpretation. Several clinical supervision scholars suggest specialized objective data-collection tools. Pajak (1993) describes eight objective data-collection tools and their advocate(s).

1. *Selective Verbatim* (Goldhammer): Goldhammer recommends "written verbatim" (p. 31) or written notes about the teaching including a record of the classroom activity and the behaviors of the teacher and her observable body language.

2. *Frequency Distribution:* Supervisors can use charts documenting the number of times a teacher or student responds in an expected or unexpected way.

3. *Decision-Making Model* (Hunter): The supervisor or coach records teacher and student behaviors through a form of shorthand note taking called "script taping" (p. 192). Hunter believes that teachers will understand their behaviors best in the context of a formal lesson.

4. *Videotaping What Teachers and Students Say and Do* (Mosher & Purpel): "As the act of teaching becomes public instead of private, the study and modification of its processes and outcomes are made possible" (p. 57). This is another scripting

tool using audiotaping and/or videotaping to help teachers recognize the effects of their instructional behaviors.

5. *Interaction Analysis* (Cogan): Cogan, an original proponent of developmental supervision, suggests helping teachers match their emerging teaching styles with their personality, using reflective practices. He recommends four data collection tools: verbatim transcript, videotaping, audio taping, and interaction analysis.

6. *Artistic Approach* (Eisner): Eisner diffuses the more objective aspects of supervision. He suggests that supervision is more like artistic criticism than a science. The supervisor or coach depicts the observation in vivid and perceptive terms and interprets the teacher's lesson using existing educational theory.

7. *Eclectic Approach* (Atcheson & Gall): Atcheson and Gall recommend a diverse approach to collecting objective data using several tools. They suggest using selective verbatim, seating charts, verbal flow, audio and videotaping, anecdotal records, checklists, and time codings.

8. *Developmental Approach* (Glickman): Glickman believes in a developmental approach that views the improvement of a teacher's instruction as an emergent process that takes the teacher from a novice to an expert. Glickman uses eclectic data collection tools similar to Atcheson and Gall.

Peer Coaching

Clearly, clinical supervision is an improvement from teacher evaluation. However, peer coaching is an improvement from clinical supervision. The difference is the trusting relationship, free from judgment and consequences to job status, offered by peers or equals. Peer coaching and clinical supervision are similar and often use the same strategies. The difference is in the relative power and authority of the supervisor/coach and the teacher. In clinical supervision, the supervisor has a super-ordinate (boss) relationship with a subordinate (worker). The supervisor-teacher tie is tainted by the inevitable unequal power and authority relationship. In peer coaching, the coach and the teacher are peers and have equal power and authority. The coaching relationship depends upon trust and knowledge.

Peer coaching, as a process, has several purposes which improve upon clinical supervision. First, peer coaching creates a community of leadership that studies the art and craft of teaching. Second, peer coaching provides a common language and a shared bond for learning new strategies. Third, peer coaching encourages teachers to increase their professionalism—their dedication to lifelong learning and the improvement of instruction. Lastly, peer coaching affirms teachers and celebrates their professionalism and real accomplishments.

Joyce and Showers (1982) advocate a model to help teachers learn new strategies and to encourage one another to improve. They suggest that six-member teams practice and master the peer coaching model. Joyce and Showers' four-stage model includes: study, demonstration, practice and feedback, and coaching.

The first stage, study, encourages teachers to read about a new strategy and learn about its theoretical base and philosophy. For example, the six-teacher team may learn *ClarisWorks'* word processor as an aid to children's writing.

The second stage, demonstration, uses an expert (live, audiotaped, or video-taped) to show the team the best uses of the strategy. For example, the expert may apply process writing to word processing by using the potato exercise or progressive writing (see Chapter 4).

The third stage, practice and feedback, helps teachers learn the strategy by co-planning practice mini-lessons and co-planning authentic classroom lessons which are then taught and coached. The teacher plans a classroom lesson with a partner who helps students select topics and begin their writing. For example, the teachers may explore different story-starters to encourage students' writing. They may ask students to create a series of drawings about a topic. The drawings then become main ideas for creative writing.

The fourth stage, coaching, allows teachers to risk using the new strategy in the safety and security of their own classrooms, with team members providing suggestions, alternative ideas, and affirmation. The teacher's partner, using subjective observation and objective data-collection tools, can support or scaffold the teacher and provide praise for real success.

Transfer of Learning

Transfer of learning is one of the key issues in staff development, teacher in-service, and supervision or peer coaching. Transfer infuses the new strategies into the teacher's regular teaching repertoire and promises the successful use of the strategy in the teacher's classroom. Transfer of learning may be inhibited by the difference between the way the team learns a new strategy and its authentic classroom context. The teacher may revert to her previous and trusted strategies due to her legitimate feelings of ambiguity and uncertainty about using the new strategy. Team membership during peer coaching should help teachers overcome these constraints to change. However, teachers and peer coaches must practice transfer of learning strategies within their classrooms. Transfer of learning will not happen serendipitously.

SPECIALIZED STAFF DEVELOPMENT IN INSTRUCTIONAL TECHNOLOGY

We have presented several models and strategies of generic staff development. The ideas were applicable to staff development for instructional technology. In this section we present several ongoing, influential instructional technology staff development projects.

The Whole Language/Technology Connection

The authors of this book headed an instructional team of consultants which worked with a technology-rich, urban school whose teachers wanted more preparation in whole language and the instructional technology to support the constructivist, whole-language philosophy. Based on our experience as instructional technology consultants, we agreed that staff development programs that met for one-day sessions; required the attendance of the whole school or district; were expert-based, administrator neutral, and offered minimal transfer of learning opportunities; and were without a process for continuous improvement were insufficient and unethical (Maurer, Davidson, & Pirkle, 1995). The instructional team resolved to implement and test a strategy that converted these weaknesses into strengths. The resulting staff development occurred over time (a semester), involved the principal, required volunteer teachers, mentored teachers during their school day, used real students in real learning situations, provided methods for transfer of learning, and instituted a model for continuous learning: peer coaching.

The instructional team designed a staff development model in which three professors would work with ten teachers one morning a week for ten weeks. The general approach was to present new knowledge or theory during the group's 30-minute preparation period at the beginning of the day, before the students arrived. The rest of the morning would be used for a variety of activities including modeling new information, observing the teachers implementing the strategies, co-planning the implementation of the strategies, and peer coaching.

A liaison from the school helped our instructional team create two schedules for working with teacher dyads. The first schedule, Plan A, allowed the instructional team to meet with the dyad without their students. Plan A utilized the dyad's usual planning time to meet the dyad's individualized needs, to present new ideas, to model co-planning, to coach, and to debrief the instruction.

The second schedule, Plan B, allowed the instructional team to meet with the dyads and their students. In Plan B we modeled, observed, and introduced the use of whole-language strategies and new applications of technology with the dyad and their students in the classroom. In some weeks the instructional team modeled effective practice; in other weeks the teachers practiced or demonstrated their learning. Whenever the instructional team or the teachers modeled instruction, we always conducted an observation, a peer coaching experience, and a debriefing of the process and content. On several occasions an instructional team member supervised a teacher's classroom so that the teacher might be available to co-plan, co-teach, or peer coach.

Our instructional team decided that peer coaching was the missing element in staff development. Peer coaching gave the teachers a strategy to continue their learning after the experts left. Peer coaching solved many of the problems we identified with unsuccessful staff development models.

The cognitive issues of staff development were not enough to convert the knowledge into action in the classroom. Our instructional team also concentrated on the affective side of learning. We believed that teachers did not receive reward or praise for their real accomplishments. We required that affirmation or celebration of teachers' successes become a part of the ongoing peer coaching strategy. We believed that experts often approached teachers with a sense of intellectual superiority, and that this approach was dysfunctional to learning. Foremost among our objectives was the affirmation of teachers' knowledge and skills. Affirmation of teachers rarely occurs. Teachers do not experience constructive feedback on the skills and strategies they do well. We affirmed the teachers in two ways: We included as much affirmation as possible in the 30-minute meetings, and we affirmed the teachers often in our coaching sessions.

Because the instructional team decided to make affirmation a positive part of the workshop, we were attentive to how teachers viewed their own knowledge and skills. We found that many teachers did not have an accurate view of their own performance. Many teachers did not know how good they really were. An underlying or hidden purpose of the workshop was to give our instructional team ample opportunity to affirm the teachers' good skills and strategies and to praise strengths in the teachers' knowledge and use of whole-language methods. Additionally, peer coaching gave us an opportunity to conduct a nonthreatening formative assessment which would help teachers determine how they might improve their own performance.

Implementing Joyce and Showers' Model of Peer Coaching   The instructional team adapted Joyce and Showers' (1982) peer coaching model to provide teachers with a continuous process for the improvement of instruction. The four-part model informs teachers' practice by:

1. *Study.* The teachers learned about a new skill or strategy.
2. *Demonstration.* The instructional team or a member of the school's faculty modeled the skill or strategy.
3. *Practice and Feedback.* Teachers practiced planning artificial mini-lessons to develop fluency, and then co-planned and taught authentic lessons.
4. *Coaching.* Teachers planned authentic lessons for their classrooms, taught them, and participated in peer observations and peer coaching.

Our instructional team did not use Joyce and Showers' recommended groups of six but organized the teachers into one group of ten. Also, our instructional team modeled skills and strategies both in the 30-minute sessions and in the teachers' classrooms with their students. For example, we demonstrated schema activation (Anderson & Pearson, 1984) and process writing (Graves, 1983) using the word processor during the 30-minute sessions and during the morning in the computer lab with first- and second-grade students. We emphasized creating lessons based on the teachers' natural context (curricula, classrooms, technology, and students).

An exciting outcome of the combination of schema activation and peer coaching came from a dyad's concern about whole-language techniques. Two of the teachers were reading a children's story about a camping trip. They found that many of their children had little prior knowledge about camping. Prior knowledge or schema is essential to reading comprehension (Anderson & Pearson, 1984). Teachers must assess prior knowledge and then explicitly teach students their missing schema. The two teachers combined their classrooms and held an all-day camping trip within the classroom. The teachers and students brought tents and sleeping bags. For lunch they ate crock-pot hot dogs that the students "roasted" over a flashlight camp fire. Throughout the day they completed thematic lessons and used many whole-language/technology strategies. The experience was challenging and exciting for the teachers and children and was supported enthusiastically by the principal and the parents.

In a formal session at the end of each morning's staff development, the instructional team debriefed the progress of the learning and formatively assessed our performance, the teachers' growth, and the students' learning. We coached one another through our successes and difficulties. We constantly reaffirmed with one another our belief that we were doing righteous work. We sought ways to improve by asking, "No matter how good we are, what would it take to get better?"

Staff Development in Rural Schools: The *Enlist Micros* Model

Long-term continuous staff development is not always possible. Rural schools, for example, have special needs that urban and suburban schools do not. We fail to consider needs when we advocate models which they cannot adopt. There are other models which can help teachers grow. Several of the problems associated with staff development in rural schools include distance, budget constraints, distance from resources, and the use of one-day staff development sessions.

Borchers, Shoyer, and Enochs (1992) studied *Enlist Micros,* a staff development model developed specifically for rural schools. Their research suggests that the *Enlist Micros* staff development process, in fact, does increase the use of microcomputers in science in rural schools and does change teacher beliefs. The investigators conclude that, "This study also demonstrated that 1-shot workshops are not as effective in changing teachers' behaviors and beliefs as continuous and comprehensive staff development projects are" (p. 389).

Enlist Micros is a three-year project, funded by the National Science Foundation. The process is one in which experts train a group of district-based trainer-experts, who then return to the districts to teach their peers. During year 1 teachers are taught "microcomputer usage in science teaching" (p. 385). During year 2 trainees are introduced to "leadership skills, cooperative learning, and peer coaching" (p. 385). During year 3 the expert teachers are returned to their districts, where they undertake the tasks of "administering, and providing training to other teachers" (pp. 385–386).

During the Fall Semester, preparation consisted of a two-day workshop with the objective of instructing teachers to design action plans for their schools. The Spring Semester program consisted of four half-day workshops taught monthly on Saturday mornings. The experts made site visits and remained in contact with the teachers as needed. Additionally, the program provided printed resources and a curriculum guide.

The results indicated increases in teachers' use of microcomputers and in their feelings of self-efficacy: that they can teach and children can learn. The authors argue that *Enlist Micros* does help teachers change. They also indicate that the process was adapted for rural schools, with conditions that could not be changed. The investigators end their presentation with this statement.

The phrase "staff development" implies a program of professional growth and evolvement of teacher behaviors and beliefs. Staff development is not an easy task since educational change is a complex process. Staff development should, however, be an integral part of the long-range plans and visions of all school involvement projects. In education, all of the above must be taken into account when planning a successful staff development project. (p. 390).

Staff Development Responsibility of the Technology Industry

Boe (1989) suggests that the producers of the hardware and software in which school districts lavishly invest also should provide staff development for schools. Further, the producers must apply staff development strategies that are appropriate to schools rather than simply import business or governmental models. He presents a list of reasons why schools have bought computers and the objectives schools wish to meet:

> ... to improve student content mastery; to improve student thinking skills; to increase individualized instruction opportunities; to prepare students for a technology-oriented world; to increase teachers' job satisfaction; to increase the cost-effectiveness of instruction. (p. 39)

As early as 1989, technologists and administrators were concerned about the efficacy of the purchase of computers for schools. The problem, as Boe states, is the lack of appropriate staff development for teachers.

According to Boe (1989, pp. 40–42), the Office of Technology Assessment (OTA) describes four conditions critical to staff development that brings "the power of teachers and technology together" (p. 40):

1. *Staff Development and Technology Skills.* Many teachers are intimidated by the computer. Preparation must start at an elemental level so that teachers can find personal uses for the computer. Then, teachers should be taught simple programs useful in their classroom, such as *Kid Pix* and *Print Shop*. Learning these applications should help teachers see the power and possibilities of the computer to support their instructional goals and objectives.

2. *Educational Vision.* The unfortunate message that computers and their applications are easy to use has led to an assumption that teachers do not need much staff development, that they can learn the skills themselves. This, unfortunately, is not accurate. Teachers must not only learn how to make the hardware and software work, but they also must reconsider, relearn, and reevaluate how the computer can influence learning in their classrooms. Teachers must consider new roles, new teaching strategies, new forms of self-assessment, and new forms of student assessment. Boe calls the act of accepting new teaching and learning roles for teachers and students "revisioning" (p. 41).

3. *Support for Experimentation and Innovation.* The district administration and the school's community of leadership must give teachers the opportunity and the permission to take educational risks while "revisioning" instructional strategies, roles, and curricula. Teachers must understand that this is a collaborative function, both in risk-taking and emotional and educational support for change.

4. *Time (and Resources) for Learning and Practice.* The OTA warns us that teachers need time to practice the skills learned in technology-based staff development. They need time provided by the school or district either during the school day or paid time outside the school day. Also, teachers need access to the very hardware they are encouraged to use. Teachers must have computers available on their desks at school and at home. State and federal agencies, manufacturers, and foundations have been flooded with requests to provide teachers with hardware and software to enhance their technology skills for the classroom.

The OTA suggests the use of the Concerns-Based Adoption Model (CBAM) to plan for educational change designed to help the staff use new technology. The model has three steps that ease teachers' concerns about change: " . . . from self-concern, through task implementation, to the final stage, where major instructional impact and innovation can occur" (p. 42).

Three elements must accompany the CBAM model. The first is a realization that change occurs over a long time, often three to five years. The second is that teachers' concerns move from personal uses to instructional strategies. The third is a collaborative model of change much like the community of leadership. The implementation of a CBAM model of staff development should include plans to increase the teachers' belief in their own efficacy or esteem. Change in beliefs, strategies, and curricula are weakened without changes in the personal and professional development of teachers.

This appears to be a powerful responsibility of the producers of educational hardware and software. So far, we do not see strong evidence that the manufacturers and software providers have accepted the challenge. However, much of what Boe and the OTA have advised is applicable to our own consideration of staff development.

A Chapter One and Learning Disabilities Metacognitive Model: HOTS

HOTS is a thinking and problem-solving program designed to improve the metacognitive strategies of Chapter One and learning disabled students. Designed by teachers of Chapter One and learning disabled children, HOTS is a pull-out supplement to the regular school program, is used in over 2,000 schools, and targets the 60–80 percent of children identified with metacognitive deficiencies (Pogrow, 1995a). Although HOTS is heavily technology-based, the program focuses on several non-technological issues. Pogrow describes HOTS as a program that is not organized to help teachers learn to manipulate hardware and software, but to create an appropriate set of teaching strategies and to provide state-of-the-art staff development in the area of curriculum and teacher-student interactions. According to Pogrow, the objective of the HOTS program is to

> ... emphasize the development of new talking and listening reflexes around the use of the curricular materials [an element of the program] as opposed to training in the philosophy and theories of teaching, or how to use the materials. The teaching techniques and training must develop skills in talking and listening to students in new ways. (Pogrow, 1995a, p. 21).

HOTS' success has been documented in a recent research study. Darmer's (1995) results indicate that HOTS students make twice the gains on standardized tests of reading and mathematics and three times the gains in reading comprehension compared to Chapter One and learning disabled students with metacognitive deficiencies in remedial classes. In non-standard measures, HOTS students outperform companion students in writing development, selected IQ scales, metacognition, transfer to novel tasks, and the more subjective classroom grade point averages. Additionally, Pogrow (1994) suggested that "gains produce a form of transfer that enables the students to learn classroom content more effectively" (p. 62).

The HOTS program has evolved into a significant learning environment with specialized teaching characteristics. The learning environment consists of the use of computer technology and what Pogrow calls a "social interface" to produce measurable learning gains. The social interface is a curriculum designed to integrate Socratic dialogue with staff development. The objective is to redirect the teacher's instincts away from traditional teaching strategies to the new teacher behaviors of "probing and acting puzzled" (Pogrow, 1995b). Staff development becomes preparing teachers with new ideas about questioning students—posing questions that help students explore the consequences of their ideas. As a consequence of their staff development, teachers develop new talking and listening skills with students.

The staff development process is key to the success of the HOTS program. HOTS is not organized in a unique way and does not even suggest non-traditional staff development practices. It is inquiry-based, with a strong emphasis on co-planning and co-implementation followed by debriefing by the teachers and the HOTS facilitators. The model does encourage an initial period of instructional ambiguity and chaos which is eased systematically by practice, feedback, and reflection.

Schools and districts which are interested in obtaining the HOTS combination of commercially prepared and HOTS-prepared software, curriculum guides, networking, staff development, and continuous resource assistance must apply for acceptance into the HOTS network. HOTS will not sell or license the materials without acceptance into the network and staff development for each teacher using the program. Typically, in-service education occurs on a neutral site with ten teachers from schools throughout the country. The teachers receive cursory background in the hardware and software. This, however, is a minor part of the one-week training. The majority of the staff development is the co-planning, co-implementation, and feedback of lessons prescribed in the HOTS curriculum.

Over the course of three efforts at planning and implementation, teachers emerge from the ambiguity and chaos with carefully considered ideas for their new teacher behaviors. The facilitators do not model best HOTS practice, but urge, provoke, and cajole teachers to hone their skills. Feedback sessions and debriefing of lessons taught to "practice students" [other teacher participants] help teachers organize their schemata or mental models about how HOTS changes the interaction between teachers and children. An additional, optional day of training is available to teachers after their initial experience with teaching the HOTS program.

HOTS is an expensive and labor-intensive program which demands a commitment from the entire school-district organization. Yet it is a successful program designed for a specialized group of students. HOTS works with fourth- through seventh-grade Chapter One and learning disabled students with metacognitive deficiencies. Reading Recovery, another successful program, works with first-graders identified as students with a potential for being at risk for educational failure.

SUMMARY

Staff development is one of the elements of a quality academic program; the improvement of instruction is a significant part of teaching and learning. In this chapter we described the importance, the purposes, and several models of staff development. We connected the development of staff development to teaching and learning, quality academic programs, skill development, the community of leadership, generic components of staff development programs, and examples of staff development experiences specifically created for instructional technology.

Staff development must have a strategy for continuous or lifelong learning. We described three processes for the evaluation and assessment of teachers' performance: teacher evaluation, clinical supervision, and peer coaching. We described the purposes and implications of each process. The three models differed in their use in ranking teachers for employment decisions and in the significance of their relative power and authority. Teacher evaluation was high on ranking and high on power and authority. Clinical supervision was low on ranking but high on power and authority. Peer coaching was low on ranking and low on power and authority. We believe that peer coaching is the most effective model for improvement of instruction and for lifelong learning.

Staff development programs have few rules. The requirements of the school's academic program, coupled with the school's values and beliefs and its vision and mission, become the moral minimum for staff development. We believe that quality staff development programs are those that promote continuous learning, emerge from the needs of the teachers, occur during the teachers' day, apply real learning situations with real children, are monitored and assessed by the community of leadership, and are taught by school-based facilitators.

The Whole Language/Technology Connection and the HOTS programs described in this chapter approach staff development in entirely different ways. The former is a complete staff development program designed to increase the teachers' ability to use technology to support a whole-language curriculum. The latter is a simple one-week workshop to introduce teachers to a different way to facilitate children's learning. However, both involve teachers in learning new strategies and applying technology to support a quality academic program, and both practice co-planning, co-implementation, and coaching strategies.

Staff development is too important a component of the teaching and learning environment to be relegated to second-rank status. Staff development should be considered by the community of leadership as an important responsibility. We believe that staff development is as much of a requirement of existing or new curricula or programs as planning, implementing, and assessing. Staff development should be a function of the initial planning of any educational change, not an afterthought to fulfill the State's requirement for teacher in-service education days.

REFERENCES

Anderson, R. L., & Pearson, P. D. (1984). A schema-theoretical view of basic processes in reading comprehension. In P. D. Pearson (Ed.), *Handbook of reading research*. New York: Longman.

Boe, T. (1989). The next step for educators and the technology industry: Investing in teachers. *Educational Technology, 29*(3), 39–44.

Borchers, C. A., Shorter, M. G., & Enochs, L. G. (1992). A staff development model to encourage the use of microcomputers in science teaching in rural schools. *School Science and Mathematics, 92*(7), 384–391.

Darmer, M. A. (1995). *Developing transfer and metacognition in educationally disadvantaged students: Effects of the HOTS Program*. Unpublished doctoral dissertation, University of Arizona, Tucson.

Glickman, G. D., Gordon, S. P., & Ross-Gordon, J. M. (1995). *Supervision of instruction: A developmental approach*. Boston: Allyn and Bacon.

Graves, D. (1983). *Writing: Teachers and children at work*. Exeter, NH: Heinemann.

Griffin, G. A. (1991). Interactive staff development. In A. Lieberman & L. Miller (Eds.), *Staff development for education in the '90s* (pp. 243–264). New York: Teachers College Press.

Joyce, B., & Showers, B. (1982). The coaching of teaching. *Educational Leadership, 40*(1), 4–10.

Lieberman, A., & Miller, L. (Eds.). (1991). *Staff development for education in the '90s*. New York: Teachers College Press.

Maslow, A. (1954). *Motivation and personality*. New York: Harper & Row.

Maurer, M. M., Davidson, G., & Pirkle, S. (1995, June). *Technology and teacher in-services: A peer coaching model*. Paper presented at the annual meeting of the National Educational Computing Association, Baltimore, Maryland.

McGregor, D. (1960). *The human side of enterprise*. New York: McGraw-Hill.

Pajak, E. (1993). *Approaches to clinical supervision: Alternatives for improving instruction*. Norwood, MA: Christopher-Gordon.

Pogrow, S. (1994). Helping students who "just don't understand." *Educational Leadership, 52*(3), 62–66.

Pogrow, S. (1995a). Making reform work for the educationally disadvantaged. *Educational Leadership, 52*(5), 20–24.

Pogrow, S. (1995b). Personal communication, December 20.

Rubin, L. (1989). Curriculum and staff development. In M. F. Wideen and I. Andrews (Eds.), *Staff development for school improvement* (pp. 170–181). New York: Falmer.

Samuels, S. J. (1988). Decoding and automaticity: Helping poor readers become automatic at word recognition. *The Reading Teacher, 41*, 756–760.

Tracy, S. J., & MacNaughton, R. H. (1993). *Assisting and assessing educational personnel*. Boston: Allyn and Bacon.

Watson, G. (Ed.). (1967). *Change in school systems*. Washington: Cooperative Project for Educational Development.

Wiles, J., & Bondi, J. (1991). *Supervision: A guide to practice*. Upper Saddle River, NJ: Merrill/Prentice Hall.

Planning Today, Insuring Tomorrow

Successful implementation of educational technology requires a structured planning process. The process must involve all significant participants and encompass the school community's values and beliefs, the community of leadership's vision and mission, and the educational administrators' management skills. Without effective planning, technology will remain a "solution in search of a problem." In this chapter we explain the basic planning knowledge base and describe several technology plans. Leadership may apply these ideas to create an implementation plan for its district and schools.

The planning process takes many forms and uses many discrete processes. Planners often follow a three-part process which includes strategic, tactical, and operational plans (Lunenburg, 1995). The keys to successful planning are the school community's vision and mission, which are outlined in the strategic plan, and its objectives, which are found in the tactical plan. The operational plan is the method of accomplishing tactical objectives in a school or classroom. Strategic, tactical, and operational plans generally follow a four-part planning process: Needs assessment, planning for implementation, implementation, and evaluation.

Instead of using strategic, tactical, and operational planning, we believe strategic, curricular, and operational are more pragmatic categories for school technology planners. Strategic planning encompasses the vision and mission for the use of technology in the school. Curricular planning involves all the learning issues associated with the use of technology in schools. Operational planning encompasses all the practical considerations of using technology in schools as well as all the management aspects of using technology in schools. As originally conceived, strategic, tactical, and operational planning were hierarchical, one following the other. In our adapted understanding, strategic planning occurs first followed by curricular and operational planning concurrently and interactively. Ultimately, these three parts come together as a single planning document called the technology plan.

In this chapter we discuss traditional planning models, rational planning models, planning for cultural change, and management and leadership perspectives. We then present the actual technology plans of three states.

INTRODUCTION

Why Plan?

An important starting point for a discussion of planning is to answer the question, Why do we plan? Through the planning process we test our moral position as stated in the school's vision and mission statements. The completed plan should represent an implementation of the school's vision and mission.

Planning also helps us act in unison. Without a clearly stated plan, each individual in the school would be operating independently, potentially leading her students in decidedly different directions. A technology plan gives the technology experts, those independent high fliers, a common direction to follow. It also aids those with less expertise, helping them gain altitude and guiding them in the direction set by the community of leadership.

Another reason we plan is to better allocate our scarce resources. Without advance consideration, there is a great potential for wasting time and money. School personnel may purchase hardware and software that is not effectively used. Poor technology decisions waste teachers' instructional and preparation time. More importantly, poor technology decisions may waste students' learning time and cognitive abilities. A good technology plan guides the community of leadership toward the wide use of resources.

Thinking of planning in more poetic terms, we might say that planning is designing the future. In the planning process the community of leadership makes critical decisions about the paths to the future and the final destination. The plan becomes the road map. The implementation of the plan becomes the trip. The assessment of the plan is our opportunity to adjust and correct our journey in flight.

The Planning Muddle

Many critics of education focus their criticism on the use of technology. Their complaints suggest wasted money, wasted time, and promises that have not been fulfilled. We believe that much of this criticism is valid. Promises have been great and accomplishments have been modest. We believe planning is the strongest means to correct this problem.

As we have assessed technology plans and planning processes locally, regionally, and nationally, we find that most plans are less than ideal. One central problem with plans and planning processes is a lack of clarity. In short, they are muddled. The planning process is muddled with the planning document; the operational elements of the plan are muddled with the curricular elements of the plan; the learning objectives are muddled with management issues. The result is that the community of leadership cannot effectively implement the plan because they do not understand it. We believe separating planning into its component parts will improve clarity.

The first distinction we believe will clarify planning is to distinguish between the planning process, the planning document, the implementation of the plan, and the assessment of the plan. The most common confusion is between the planning process and the planning document. The document is the road map, and the process is our means of creating the document. Additionally, the planning process informs the community of leadership about the plan and establishes their ownership. For the community of leadership to effectively implement any plan, they must understand it and own it. An effective planning process will accomplish all these purposes.

Most planning processes begin with the establishment of a planning committee. However, there are formal leaders who take the position that it is more efficient to assign the technology plan to a specific individual or small group. Some plans are written by formal leaders or their subordinates; others are written by technology consultants. While this may be an efficient way to create a document, it is seldom effective in creating effective learning decisions. More importantly, if the plan is created by an individual or small group, it is impossible for the community of leadership to know and own it. The committee should serve the obvious purposes of creating a document and enriching it with their technology and curricular expertise. The committee should also serve the less obvious purpose of increasing the community of leadership's knowledge and ownership of the plan.

The next distinction is to clarify the difference between the curricular and the operational portions of the document. Many of the plans we have examined are strong in the strategic and operational areas and weak in curriculum. Technology planners tend to be good at vision and mission. They can dream big dreams. They also tend to be good at the operational elements. They can prepare budgets, design implementation strategies, make decisions about placement of equipment. All these operational issues are, however, only the means of reaching the students' learning goals. The curricular components are the ends, and they tend to be weak or missing.

We believe the learning issues should be at the center of the planning process. As the focal point, the curricular elements of the plan have a dual purpose, first to clearly identify learning issues and second to guide the community of leadership to use technology to improve teaching and learning.

The curricular plan is quite tricky to create. The plan should not be so specific that it impedes the technology experts, or so vague that it is of no value to the novice. Finding useful middle ground will be an important function of the planning process. The act of finding middle ground helps the community of leadership own the plan.

The last distinction that we believe will help technology planners is to separate management from learning issues. This is another common error that confuses those who try to implement technology plans. We believe all the learning issues should be clearly defined in the curricular portion of the plan, and all the management issues should be relegated to the operational portion of the plan. This is not to say that we do not value management issues. We separate them simply for the sake of clarity, to avoid confusion. For example, if we plan to implement automated attendance, that becomes part of the operational plan. Teachers can clearly see that there are no intended learning issues related to automated attendance. This will help teachers focus their efforts on the other elements of the plan that are intended to directly help students learn. We need curricular plans and teaching and learning decisions that are crystal clear.

Expert Planning Advice

The Book Report (Martinsen, 1993) describes several helpful considerations for technology planning. These points apply to most strategic, curricular, and operational technology plans.

- Appoint people who have a stake in the results to the initial planning group. Administrators must be a part of and supportive of the planning process.
- Develop a realistic plan.
- Delineate clearly why and how technology will be used in the curriculum.
- Make staff development a component of the plan.
- Monitor implementation continuously. A plan cannot implement itself.
- Review and revise the plan annually. A technology plan should be an evolving, working document that guides district personnel to agreed-upon goals.
- Emphasize that technology requires more than a single capital expenditure.
- Adopt new technologies cautiously.
- Acknowledge that proposed changes may cause fear and resistance. Some individuals see change as an opportunity and a challenge; others dread and may oppose or obstruct change. Good communication and slow, easy implementation efforts can do much to reduce the opposition. (p. 26)

TRADITIONAL PLANNING MODELS: THREE EXAMPLES

The literature on planning is largely anecdotal in that it describes what individual schools have done to plan for instructional technology. As with any plan, the quality of a technology plan depends on many factors, including the planners, the resources, and the school's culture. The unifying characteristics of the planning process are its three basic categories: strategic planning, curricular planning, and operational planning.

A GENERIC PLANNING MODEL

Many school district plans follow the strategic, tactical, and operational planning models. We present two of many examples of strategic plans from the literature, one simple and one complex.

A State-Wide Model

The Executive Summary of *Vision 91 of 21st Century Schooling for Indiana* (Indiana Curriculum Advisory Council, 1991) describes and prescribes a plan for curriculum change. The plan is intentionally formative to allow individual school districts the flexibility to apply the model. This state-wide model has six stages:

- Develop Vision Statement
- Assess Needs
- Examine State Proficiencies
- Set Program Objectives
- Implement Program
- Evaluate Program. (p. 14)

A School-District Model

This is a generic model for individual schools to plan curricular change. In their anecdotal report, Wepner and Kramer (1987) describe a district's proposal for using computers to teach reading. This model is applicable to almost any curricular change. The model has four stages: needs assessment, planning, implementation, and evaluation. The model is intentionally more prescriptive, inclusive, and structured than the previous state-wide model. Elements of the plan are as follows:

I.   Needs Assessment (p. 53). Needs assessment tools discover the current condition of the school or district in relation to the desired outcome of the goal or problem. For example, how much word processing and process writing does the school currently expect of its middle-grade students? Within the needs assessment stage, the model considers:

   A.   District Goals

   B.   Personnel

   C.   Budget

   D.   Facilities

   E.   Board of Education Support

   F.   Central Office Mandates

   G.   Government Mandates. (pp. 54–58)

II. Planning (p. 58). Planning suggests that a small group of the community of leadership should make comprehensive curricular decisions based upon the results of the needs assessment. Curricular decisions in this plan may include:

   A.   Purpose of Computer Implementation

   B.   Location of Computers in the Schools

   C.   Student Assignments

   D.   Computer Hardware

   E.   Software

   F.   Staff Development

   G.   Evaluation Procedures. (pp. 58–63)

III. Implementation (p. 63). Implementation is the stage in which "plans are put into action" (p. 63). In this plan for using computers to teach reading, the implementation includes scheduling, in-service education, monitoring computer use, hardware maintenance, and software purchasing.

IV. Evaluation (p. 64). The purpose of evaluation is to determine how well or to what extent curricular goals have been met. Evaluation, in this case, includes program, personnel, and student assessment. The school sets its own specialized assessment procedures according to its unique context and based on its vision, mission, and shared goals.

The two models described above represent the schema or mental model invoked in most planning processes often called the rational model. In the next section we describe the rational model and its implications.

THE RATIONAL MODEL

Description of the Rational Model

We believe that the process of planning and decision making are so similar as to be two sides of the same coin. At best, planning is the process of continuously making small decisions to reach a goal. At the extreme, decision making is a process of implementing a plan. Regardless, planning and decision making share many activities and implications. In decision making and planning, the term "rational" connotes that decision makers and planners select among options with clarity, certainty, and precision. Rational, in this context, does not mean sane or logical.

Traditionally, a rational process includes these four conditions.

1. *Identify the problem*. In a rational decision-making process or a systematic planning model, the decision maker or planner can identify and articulate the problem with clarity, certainty, and precision. In our previous school-based planning model, the problem was how to improve student reading skills.

2. *Know the alternatives*. A rational planner must have the knowledge and resources to understand all of the potential alternatives for solving a problem or implementing a solution. In our reading example, alternatives might include process writing, phonics approaches, or comprehension skills, and how technology supports these strategies. The rational model, by definition, requires that the decision maker or planner have enough resources to know *all* of the possible alternatives.

3. *Know the consequences of each alternative*. A rational planner must be able to describe *all* of the possible consequences, helpful and harmful, of each alternative. If the planner fails to uncover any consequence of an accepted alternative, then the plan may cause unforeseen consequences. The dilemma of unforeseen consequences is that by the time they are discovered, it is often too late to correct the decision or plan.

In his seminal work, *The Unanticipated Consequences of Purposive Social Action,* Merton (1936) argued that when decision makers only use rational processes and they may fail to identify or misidentify alternatives and their consequences, the resulting decisions are destined to have unforeseen effects. The same principle applies to planning. As a simplistic example, suppose a school district formulating a technology plan decides that keyboarding should become an alternative to handwriting. Without complete information or knowledge of technological trends, the school could spend thousands of dollars and hundreds of hours on special keyboards, keyboarding software, keyboarding consultants, keyboarding curriculum plans, and student learning time. Relatively quickly, voice-recognition software could replace the keyboard as the standard input device. The unanticipated consequences of the school district's keyboarding decision could be serious and irreparable.

4. *Establish a valuing mechanism for making the right decision.* Even when the decision maker or planner understands the problem exactly, knows each alternative, and understands all of the consequences of each alternative, she still needs a set of values and beliefs and a vision and mission against which to measure the correctness of her decision. Our values and beliefs about instructional technology focus on the use of technology to support a quality academic program. The quality of the educational program is more important to the success of the decision than the wizardry of the technology. If the participants do not have shared goals or an established school culture, then any decision, no matter how inappropriate or inconsistent, may be acceptable.

The Limits of the Rational Model: Bounded Rationality

"Bounded rationality" is the term the Nobel-prize-winning economist Herbert Simon (1977) coined to describe the limits of human decision making. He stated that rational decisions will always be limited by our inability to know *all* the possible alternatives and *every* consequence. Individuals and schools lack the time and resources to gain that knowledge. People seek less complicated and quicker decision processes. Simon suggests that, instead of seeking the perfect solution, decision makers and planners should use one of several "bounded" processes.

Bounded or limited rationality includes the processes of satisficing, heuristics, intuition, and incrementalization. These four processes are preferences or predilections that decision makers and planners use in a bounded or limited rational system.

Satisficing. The act of satisficing lets the decision maker or planner select the first right decision among alternatives rather than the best or the value-maximizing alternative. The first right decision prevails until a problem arises. Then, decision makers or planners move to the second right decision. Satisficing often is described as selecting the first needle in the haystack, not the best needle in the haystack.

Heuristics. Heuristics are a set of premises that individuals believe affect decisions. Lunenburg (1995) describes them as "rules of thumb" and cites such examples as the "Golden Rule" and "When in doubt, punt" (p. 124). In teaching and learning, a traditional heuristic is, "Technology supports good teaching!" Heuristics may have limited utility because of the possibility that a rule of thumb is not accurate, true, or useful.

Intuition. Decision makers and planners who rely on intuition use their past experience to influence their problem-solving practices. For example, decision makers and planners whose experiences have caused them to doubt teachers' commitment to change may not select curricular or technological solutions that obligate teachers to accept and master new teaching strategies. The use of intuition tied to theory and practice is wisdom. Without theory and practice, intuition is unreliable.

Incrementalizing. Lindbloom (1959) describes incrementalizing—seeking small, successful, step-by-step solutions—as "muddling through." Instead of referring to shared goals or value-maximizing alternatives, incrementalizers or muddlers must take small steps to reach a successful decision or plan. Muddling through is similar to the psychological notion of "successive approximation or shaping" (Cooper, 1973)—the process that is used to help reacclimate school-phobic children to the classroom. Incrementalizing, often, is the slow and steady pace that prevails.

Decision makers and planners use rational systems to describe how problems ought to be resolved in schools. However, the limits of our knowledge, capacity, and resources inhibit the goal of "value maximizing" or seeking the best possible solution. Bounded or limited rationality more closely resembles the way that decisions and plans actually are made in organizations, especially schools. Decision makers and planners simply do not have the intellectual, financial, and temporal resources to achieve value maximization. A refusal by decision makers and planners to accept the boundaries of rational models exposes problem solvers to conditions and consequences that restrict successful decision making and planning. Rigid reliance upon the rational model to the exclusion of other models, such as the political model, often leads to inadequate planning and imperfect implementation.

A powerful historical example of the nature of limited rationality was the early use of Apple IIe computers. Decision makers and planners reviewed the literature, considered instructional implications, and surveyed the school community. Yet schools did not value-maximize learning using Apple IIe computers. Because of a lack of experience with technology, the relative newness of computers in schools, and the educational learning models developed using previous technological "break-throughs" such as the 16mm movie projector, the overhead projector, and the television, computer implementation often was superficial. In most cases, the computer was disconnected from what happened in the classroom, was used mainly for low-level learning objectives (e.g., reinforcement of skills using games), and was used as a reward when children achieved appropriate learning and behaviors.

One specific characteristic of a problem does suggest a rational model solution. Rational processes are more likely to be successful when the planned task is simple. Non-rational models, such as limited rationality or political models, are more likely to be successful when the planned task is complex. Simple or structured tasks are those tasks that are completed the same way each time. Complex or unstructured tasks are tasks that are solved differently each time. An example of a simple task is using a specialized program to compile daily attendance. An example of a complex task is deciding why and how to implement an Integrated Learning System or constructing an on-line library catalogue. As a rule of thumb, or heuristic, we should not apply rational processes to complex, unstructured problems.

PLANNING FOR TECHNOLOGY: CREATING CULTURAL CHANGE

The Management Perspective

Planning is an essential element of good administration. Planning is no less essential to the administration of computers. Plans for all aspects of computer use are needed: to determine what kind of hardware and software are needed, to make sure that implementation goes smoothly, and to insure that proper budgets are submitted. Such plans result in policies that guide decisions and procedures to be followed in daily management (Kearsley, 1990, p. 85).

A Management Plan

Kearsley (1990) describes the managerial perspective in technology planning. Management, as described in Chapter 1, is "doing things right." Quality management is basic to good leadership. In a poorly managed school, schools do not thrive and students do not learn. Kearsley proposes a specific process for planning technology change and managing implementation (pp. 86–98):

1. Identifying Goals and Objectives

[Kearsley suggests several general or global goals:]

- to better prepare students for jobs or college
- to improve the efficiency of administrative operations
- to deliver better quality education to all students
- to achieve more accurate budgets and controls of funds
- to give students and teachers more classroom options.

[Kearsley lists specific objectives that arise from general goals:]

- to increase reading and writing skills in second grade
- to reduce the costs/time required for attendance tracking
- to get more minority students to take science and math
- to send out more detailed progress reports to parents
- to provide better vocational counseling to graduates.

2. Acquiring Hardware/Software

3. Implementation Scheduling

[Kearsley presents a timeline for planning tasks:]

- Create a computer advisory committee.
- Develop a school/district computer plan specifying goals and objectives.
- Conduct pilot study.
- Identify training needed.
- Make facilities changes.
- Field test hardware and software.
- Evaluate first term/year results.
- Review/revise computer plan.

[Kearsley suggests a schedule for implementation tasks:]

- Develop plan for computer use.
- Present plan for discussion/review.
- Establish computer advisory committee.

- Develop budget and proposal for planned computer activities.
- Obtain funding for computer plan.
- Develop specifications for hardware/software.
- Acquire and install hardware/software.
- Develop implementation plan and schedule.
- Pilot test and evaluate.
- Proceed with full scale implementation (p. 92).

4. Evaluation (p. 93)

[Kearsley suggests appropriate evaluation criteria:]

- achievement scores
- grades
- attendance
- graduation
- disciplinary actions
- student esteem
- teacher/parent satisfaction.

5. Establishing Policies and Procedures.

[Kearsley suggests policies and procedures for hardware and software management:]

- software piracy and privacy of data
- scheduling
- back-up of data
- staff computer competencies
- incentives and compensation
- equal access to computers for all school students.

Kearsley's plan is for the selection and management of technology. It does not consider, except in global terms, the role of technology in teaching and learning. On the other hand, Pogrow's planning process, discussed in the next section, suggests a process for infusing technology into the curriculum. Kearsley's procedural plan may be the management stage and Pogrow's curricular plan may be the leadership stage in preparing a successful strategy for the adoption of instructional technology.

THE LEADERSHIP PERSPECTIVE

Pogrow's (1983) planning process represents the leadership perspective in technology planning. As defined in Chapter 1, leadership is "doing the right thing." For

Pogrow, the right thing is the use of technology to support a quality academic program. Pogrow states:

> What is important is that these decisions should be made as part of a conscious, highly participative process [involving the community of leadership] in which the computer is viewed as a curricular device rather than a piece of capital equipment, and in which there is a conscious effort to identify the best software for a predefined, specific, appropriate instructional objective. (p. 123)

Criteria for Technology Adoption

Pogrow (1983) suggests three criteria for incorporating technology in the curriculum to enhance academic effectiveness.

Pogrow's first criterion for purchasing technology and implementing it into the school's curriculum is to improve student learning: "Direct gains will thus be considered the first criterion for appropriate computer use for effectiveness improvement" (p. 102).

Pogrow's second criterion is efficiency of instruction: How the computer can save valuable time which can be used for other instructional purposes: "Thus, the second criteria . . . is the extent to which a particular application can save personnel time by automating the delivery of a set of instructional transactions so that personnel may increase the time they devote to other tasks" (p. 102). The use of an insect data base, for example, may free teachers from some direct instruction responsibilities. The additional time saved may be given to students with special needs or to students who are completing individual research.

Pogrow's third criterion relates to the efficiency of costs: "As a result, the third criterion of appropriate effective computer use is the extent to which a computerized application can reduce costs without impairing learning" (p. 104). This third criterion may be the least significant. Although technology can save teachers' time and, as a result, save money, in terms of actual dollars spent it may increase the costs of instruction. Nevertheless, estimates of the costs of instruction are essential to planning for technology.

Criteria for Effectiveness Enhancement

Pogrow's first concern is technology's role in the improvement of teaching and learning. He calls this criterion "effectiveness-enhancement" (p. 106). This criterion includes:

(a) directly improve learning outcomes,

(b) create the potential for improving effectiveness by reducing the amount of personnel time that would otherwise be required for delivering a given activity (so that more instruction can be provided for a different objective), and

(c) reduce the cost of a set of instructional transactions without impairing learning effectiveness. (p. 106)

Implementing the Effectiveness-Enhancement Plan

Pogrow describes criteria for implementing technology as an instructional support for a quality academic program. He believes that the key is perceiving the school's purpose for including technology in the curriculum. He asks, "What is the best plan for linking instructional objectives to the acquisition of computers?" (p. 112). The steps for implementing effectiveness enhancement are:

> The first step in resolving these issues is to link them to a set of differentiated instructional objectives such as (a) remediation, (b) reinforcement, and (c) the development of specific computer skills. (p. 114)
> The second step in the process of developing a structure for the centers [computer clusters] is to identify the types of students that will be involved with each of the objectives along with the mode of involvement. (p. 114)
> Once costs have been projected, the next stage is to plan the phasing-in process, since it is unlikely that there will be sufficient funds or expertise to implement the plan all at once. (p. 116)

Pogrow believes that implementation is a three- to five-year process.

LINKING MANAGEMENT AND LEADERSHIP MODELS

Cox, a technology practitioner, suggests that two important and divergent technology issues demand planning. The first, content planning, is the process of using technology to obtain instructional facts. The facts, then, change from data to information and from information to knowledge. Content planning is a leadership function. The second, infrastructure planning, is the process of creating a method of delivering the facts. Infrastructure planning is a management task (Cox, 1994).

Fullan (1994) argues that the decision and planning processes—the traditional top-down approach and the increasingly popular bottom-up approach—are flawed. Top-down change is too complex to be centralized. Bottom-up change lacks outside pressures for change, is difficult to manage, and incurs problems with continuing quality standards and maintaining innovation. According to Fullan:

> When two alternative positions—opposite solutions, really—are both found to be basically flawed, it normally means that a paradox lies behind the problem. A shift in mindset is required—from either/or to both/and thinking. (p. 191)

Taken together, these two models are an excellent starting place for planning for technology. The ability to adapt these models to the culture and context of a particular school is effective leadership. Developing plans for technology implementation is the responsibility of the community of leadership, supported by technology and instructional specialists.

PLANNING FOR CHANGE: TECHNOLOGY AND SCHOOL RESTRUCTURING

Although much of the decision making and planning for instruction is related directly to curricular change, technology has become an important part of the school restructuring effort. Discussion of the purposes of technology implementation must precede all planning efforts. Ray (1991) conducted an 18-month project to study how technology affects school restructuring. Ray muses:

> It seems significant that, although all the restructuring schools involved in the study are unique organizations with unique cultures, they do share very similar, emerging visions of new educational and organizational directions. They are all somewhere on the cusp between two educational paradigms, reexamining and reconsidering the content and methods of education. They are also on the cusp of two organizational paradigms, attempting to democratize decision-making with the school, to flatten the hierarchy, to improve communication, and to share the responsibilities of education among all the stakeholders. (p. 10)

Clearly, Ray is supporting the concept of the community of leadership that we have outlined in this book.

As an outcome of the study, Ray lists 16 trends in technology and restructuring (pp. 11–19). Each trend is an important reason to consider or justify implementing technology in support of a quality academic program. Several trends may be a starting point for garnering a vision, mission, and shared goals.

1. *Higher Order Cognitive Skills.* Technology implementation is an excellent model to turn data into information and information into knowledge. Technology can support a thinking, problem-solving curriculum, teach library/research skills, organize complicated data, and increase communication skills.

2. *Past-Present-Future Focus.* Students must be able to think about solutions to today's problems, but also consider an ambiguous future. A focus on the future that incorporates higher order thinking skills might include simulations (for example, *Geography Search*) as a strand to integrate content area learning.

3. *Whole-Person Education.* In planning to restructure education to include technological support, planners must consider the individual development of the learner. The computer, for example, is an interactive device which may improve pedagogy—the instruction of children—and andragogy (Knowles, 1980)—the instruction of adults—and prepare individuals for lifelong learning.

4. *General Education.* Ray suggests that learners become generalists. That is, students should consider larger educational issues and integrate their learning around a theme (for example, urban living using CD ROM reference books). The principles of constructivist thinking fit Ray's prescription.

5. *Transdisciplinary Education.* One of the themes of restructuring is creating a holistic curriculum. Transdisciplinary education, similar to interdisciplinary models and thematic instruction, is a problem-centered process. Traditionally, holistic curricula include learning tools such as word processing, data bases, and spreadsheets which are used across curricula and thus support transdisciplinary education.

6. *Education for Collaboration.* School restructuring recognizes the real-world skill of collaboration. Many advocates of change argue that students no longer should be isolated learners. Good curricula create ideas and problems that can be studied or solved by a learning team. Examples of education for collaboration include Cooperative Learning (Slavin, 1995) and the Project Approach (Katz, 1989). Several software applications and technology approaches support collaboration; telecommunications is a powerful example.

7. *Education for Communication.* Learning designed for communication increases literacy skills to include reading, writing, speaking, and listening. Additionally, learners must understand how to interpret and assess text, speech, and graphics. Some educators believe that education for communication must reflect globalization and include the study of a second language. A variety of word processing, telecommunications, and foreign-language programs support education for communication.

8. *Education for Metacognition, Reflective Practice.* The reflective practice of metacognition (Baker & Brown, 1984)—that is, learning how one learns—is a goal of many school reformers. Metacognitive skills offer learners more flexibility and independence for their own learning. Examples of metacognitive strategies include self-questioning, finding the main idea, and summarizing (see Chapter 1). These skills can be taught through methods such as Reciprocal Teaching (Palinscar & Brown, 1984) and *Logo* (Papert, 1980). Each requires that the learner think about how she solves problems and reflect upon her learning strategies.

9. *Education for Global Stewardship, Social Ecology.* Restructuring in education suggests that teachers and learners create new learning roles. One of these roles is that of membership in the global society. Several simulation, CD ROM, and laser disk programs direct the learners' interest toward globalism and help teachers and learners integrate curriculum content around issues such as pollution, overpopulation, or global warming. Software available from documentary producers such as Nova and National Geographic support education for global stewardship.

10. *Human Values.* A controversial issue in restructuring is values education—teaching children about beliefs, ethics, and moral responsibility. CD ROMs and laser disks from producers such as ABC News include topics such as drugs, sexuality, war, politics, and government. The critical issues impacting values education are: Who is to decide what values are important, and what form will values

instruction take? Clearly, technology can assist the presentation of values and beliefs, both overtly and covertly, but instructional technology cannot decide questions about values and beliefs. The community of leadership is the appropriate body to begin the discussion.

11.   *Active Learning.* Restructuring has at its core several basic premises. One of these is the movement from traditional or transmission models of teaching to constructivist or student-active models of learning. Whether through active or interactive (technology-based) learning, learners eventually must take responsibility for their own learning strategies. A variety of technological applications offer the students opportunities to be active learners. Teachers must continue to make sound institutional strategy decisions based on the objectives of the learning.

12.   *Service Learning.* Service learning—learning by participating in the life of the community—may be as simple as tutoring classmates in the school or as complex as working in social welfare agencies or with governmental projects outside of school. As a first step, telecommunications can connect children to the community. A key controversy in service learning is whether it should be required or voluntary.

13.   *Education for Lifelong Learning, Andragogy.* Andragogy is the study of adult learning. Adult learners are more independent and self-directed than children. Andragogy is the goal that many school reformers have for lifelong learning. Schooling should not end after high school or college. Individuals must learn continuously for employment, for maintaining essential life skills, and for self-fulfillment. The mastery of technology-related skills such as searching a data base or writing with a word processor are strategies to begin lifelong learning.

14.   *Personalized Learning.* With the advent of computerized data collection and data analysis, the question of homogeneous or heterogeneous learning may become moot. Teachers can use technology to monitor each student's progress, create a prescription or individualized educational plan, and implement individualized learning within an integrated and collaborative learning environment. The management of each student's individualized learning plan may be mastered by teachers using basic desktop computers and simple data base and spreadsheet applications. However, the knowledge and judgment of experienced and professional teachers cannot be replaced by computers or specialized applications.

15.   *Process and Inquiry Approaches.* Ray suggests that "educators in restructuring schools agree that learners must become engaged in the process of learning and inquiry rather than focus only on the products [outcomes] of learning" (p. 19). Process and inquiry approaches are assumed in constructivist thinking. Technology can assist learners to master these skills. Currently, learning to read through writing and process writing, the use of mathematics manipulatives, and thematic teaching exemplify the process-inquiry models.

16. *Master-Apprentice Approach.* The master-apprentice approach views the learner as a novice who becomes independent or an expert through the process of Cognitive Apprenticeship (Collins, Brown, & Newman, 1989). The teacher's role is to model appropriate expert behavior for the novice, to provide support or scaffolding in the early learning stages, and then to step back or fade when the novice becomes expert. Additionally, the teacher's role is to provide a learning environment with appropriate learning experiences to guide a student's movement from novice to expert.

Ray's sixteen trends for restructuring schooling represent most, if not all, of the concerns educators have for change and cover many of the fractious issues and controversies currently hindering educational reform. Concerned coalitions of private citizens and organized constituencies battle over who will control the values and beliefs and the vision and mission of school districts and individual schools. Technology cannot resolve this conundrum. A responsible community of leadership must merge divergent opinions into shared goals. The community of leadership can and should encourage the school's emerging culture.

OPERATIONAL PLANS: SHARED GOALS AND COMMON THEMES

Above, we reviewed many international, national, state, and local technology planning efforts. In discussing the original three-step model of strategic planning, tactical planning, and operational planning, we concentrated on operational plans. Almost all of the operational plans followed the classic model: needs assessment, planning, implementation, and assessment. However, no district's plan resembled another because of local issues such as participants, budget, instructional vision, decentralization, and technology expertise.

In our review, several themes or commonalities emerged. The commonalities among the several operational plans included shared goals, risk-taking, leadership, teaching and learning, curriculum action planning, quantitative and qualitative measures, access, attitudes and anxiety, cost models, and assessment.

Shared Goals

All of the technology plans expressed the district's shared goals. Huh (1993) described the shared goals of the Korean nation's school community. Huh stated succinctly and definitively that Korea needed more computer professionals in education, research, business, and industry. Additionally, the Korean government indicated that computer education in elementary and secondary schools was necessary to increase the population's entry into the information age. From these two shared goals, Korea developed a medium- and long-range operational plan for implementation of technology. The operational plan had at its core three major objectives: "(1) Improvement of the teaching-learning process. (2) Improvement of science education. (3) Preparation for an information society" (p. 43).

Risk-Taking

Bruder (1990), capturing the essence of the Central Kitsap school district's operational plan for implementing technology, emphasized the risks involved and the need for the community of leadership's involvement in the vision and mission statements. Central Kitsap's mission was to created enjoyable and challenging learning in which children and adults "eventually become ethical citizens in the world at large" (p. 16). Risk-taking is encouraged as a process to reach quality. Bruder subtly supports constructivist thinking when he reflects the thoughts of a principal: "It's OK to take risks and possibly fail; then you can think through what you've done and adapt your approach" (p. 16).

Leadership

In an interview in the journal *Technos,* Linda Roberts, Special Advisor on Educational Technology in the United States Department of Education, was asked about leadership in technology and educational reform. Roberts believes that technology and educational reform or restructuring are inexorably linked. She is a passionate spokesperson for the involvement of the greater school community while understanding the nature of the change process necessary for reform. Roberts, in her unique role as the recognized leader for the national government, asserts that merely placing technology into schools did not and cannot cause educational reform. She believes that technology must recreate the classroom. She states:

> If we really think about technology and its full potential in education, we begin to realize that we are actually redefining education and the classroom. We all become a community of learners. And we don't need to be within the confines of a school to learn. The classroom may be our homes or our libraries or our workplaces. (p. 5)

If we consider leadership only at its basic level—as doing the right thing—then Roberts is advocating the right thing in educational reform or restructuring.

Teaching and Learning

Almost all of the operational plans that we reviewed recognized the need to adapt the roles of teachers and students in changing classrooms. Many of the operational plans included the tenets of constructivist thinking. Teachers and children became responsible for their learning, projects emerged as longer term assignments, failure was valued for its learning potential, and technology was a constant support for a problem-solving, thinking curriculum (Huh, 1993; Larner & Timberlake, 1995; Roberts, 1994).

Curriculum Action Planning

Mendrinos (1987) describes her curriculum action plan in a small school in Massachusetts. Mendrinos' vision and mission was the integration of content areas within a grade level. As the media specialist, she assumed the responsibility to formulate a five-step plan of action.

The first step in Mendrinos' plan was to assess "the weaknesses and strengths of each curriculum and the role that microcomputer software could fill in meeting those needs" (p. 272). She created non-threatening learning sessions for the faculty which included copies of computer magazines by content area. Eventually, she succeeded in having the faculty come to her to implement change.

The next step was to conduct an in-service workshop that was "focused on word processing applications within the curriculum, not separated from it" (p. 272). She involved the principal and made teachers comfortable with the friendliest and easiest application to use and to recognize its instructional implications.

The third step was to introduce word processing applications: "Once comfortable with word processing, the teachers wanted to try it with their students. Working as a team to plan lessons, the teachers and the library media specialist introduced word processing" (p. 273). The school realized increases in student writing, creativity, and editing and revising. These increases occurred across the ability spectrum, from gifted and talented children to children with special needs. Increasingly, content-area teachers, beyond language arts, used word processing as a part of their regular instruction. These children, teachers, and classrooms became fundamentally different.

Once teachers recognized the power of word processing, they were ready to proceed to the next step. "The fourth step to successful curriculum integration is implementation" (p. 273). Teachers investigated and used on-line information services for the generation of data. They joined CompuServe, purchased the *Grolier's Encyclopedia*, accessed information providers such as *NewsNet*, computerized their library's card catalogue, and used an electronic version of the *Reader's Guide to Periodical Literature*.

The fifth step in Mendrinos' plan was "continuous and ongoing evaluation. Teachers should not be intimidated but learn to evaluate the effectiveness of the tool and its impact on the student and the course of study" (p. 274). Mendrinos advocates that teachers recognize technology's importance to their content area before proceeding, completing a needs assessment, initiating staff development, participating in continuing curriculum development projects, using and analyzing specialized assessment tools, and documenting successes while integrating them into the emerging school technology culture.

Sharp (1992) describes an operational plan a New Jersey high school created to integrate technology into its content areas. Sharp reports on the five-year study of that implementation. Among the objectives of the planning process were that "integration and multimedia were provided for teachers in the district" (p. 1). This section of Sharp's report did not seem to be a powerful declaration of vision and mission. The planning team may not have had enough information, time, people, or resources to develop effective strategic plans.

The technology committee of the high school believed that its objective of curriculum integration would occur best in a teacher center: "It was also promised that the center would organize computer instruction around critical and creative thinking, cooperative learning, inter-disciplinary learning, information and knowledge processing and active learning" (p. 90). Clearly, the planners promised too much and prepared too little. After less success than hoped for, several iterations of basic rules evolved into a final plan:

1. Technology use would be focused on areas where it provided a direct benefit to students based on a definite need.

2. The critical elements of staff training for implementation and ongoing support would be interwoven with the integrated plan.

3. Bridges would be developed, or at least addressed, that would connect instruction in the various disciplines of the high school curriculum.

4. Because the time frame for implementation spanned five years, the committee would plan with an eye toward the future. Tomorrow's needs would be envisioned before the committee's plans were implemented today. (p. 94)

Finally, after much discussion and rereading of the literature, the technology planning committee settled on several important goals. The superior goal was integration, which was "to improve the teaching-learning process through the maximization of educational technology, primarily through the integration of computers into the total K–12 curriculum" (p. 95). The integration of technology into the content areas, then, became a shared goal of the entire school community not just the high school. The effort would not have been successful otherwise.

Quantitative and Qualitative Measures

Several of the operational plans included information gathering in both quantitative and qualitative terms. Quantitative measures answer questions about "How many?" and "How often?" Examples are: "How widespread is . . . ?" and "How much access do students have to . . . ?" Qualitative measures ask "Who?" "Why?" and "When?" questions (Huh, 1993). Examples are: "What type of projects . . . ?" and "What are the prospects for . . . ? Each of these categories of measures are important for providing useful data for decision makers. Biggs' (1988) notion of a technology audit would include essential decision-making information collected from both quantitative and qualitative measures.

Access

A key issue in the development of technology plans is to factor equity into the plan at the outset rather than adjusting for equity after implementation. It is clear that different segments of the student population are systematically advantaged and disadvantaged by technology access. Smart, well-behaved boys tend to get more computer time. With these students, the computer is used as a reward for completion of work and for compliance with desired behaviors. Girls have fewer opportunities to use the computer and apparently use the computer less for problem-solving and critical-thinking activities. White students use the computer more frequently than minority students. Urban/suburban students use the computer more frequently than rural students. Regular education students use the computer more frequently than special needs students.

Martinsen (1993), a district administrator in Wisconsin, noted these anomalies and conceded:

> I realized that while we had purchased a large amount of equipment, there were inequities in access to computers and in the quality of instruction in computer skills. These inequalities were due to differences in the comfort levels of teachers using computers and teaching computer literacy skills. A computer lab for kindergarten-grade 8 students was empty for much of the day because we did not have staffing in the lab. (p. 25)

The issue of equity among students was a minor focus in Martinsen's report. (See Chapter 12 for a more detailed discussion of equity.)

Attitudes and Anxiety

Larner and Timberlake (1995) conducted a survey of teachers and found that teachers' anxiety level correlated most strongly with computer use by teachers with limited technology knowledge. Larner and Timberlake list six variables which seem to justify effective, ongoing technology staff development:

> A review of the literature reveals that six of the most important variables in determining the degree to which teachers integrate computers into their instruction and planning are knowledge, anxiety, personal attitudes, professional attitudes, school support, and school resources/set-up; with knowledge being the most critical. (p. 1)

In a review of the computer anxiety literature, Maurer (1994) "found a relationship between computer experience and computer anxiety" (p. 374). This finding suggests that the strongest course of action to reduce teachers' computer anxiety is to give them opportunities to gain experience with computers.

It must be noted, however, that the study of the treatment of computer anxiety is in its infancy. Many writers offer detailed prescriptive solutions to the problem, but seldom are these prescriptions based on research. As Maurer states, "The only valid conclusion that can be drawn from the existing body of literature is 'we do not know what to do about computer anxiety' (p. 374)".

Cost Models

Radlick (1994) looks to a state-wide cost model for implementing technological support for instructional objectives. The New York State model is a starting point for a discussion of implementing technology. State education officials advocate a three-stage local, state, and federal plan. This plan is clearly managerial; it demonstrates how to do things right. Radlick calculated the costs in three stages: in stage one, the costs to establish work centers in a school district's libraries; in stage two, the costs to expand computer work centers into each classroom; in stage three, the costs to increase the number of work centers in each classroom and to add InterNet access.

Radlick provides the spreadsheets, projected costs, and the number of school libraries and classrooms in the State of New York in 1994. The data reveal that the costs of implementing technology are staggering. Radlick suggests six considerations about the costs and implementation of technology:

> First, no technology implementation could, or should, be implemented in a single year. . . . Second, the model has different stages of deployment, with the first stage reflecting the lowest total cost [to get a minimal level of adoption]. . . . Third, the models make no assumptions about funding sources or new funding, particularly from the State or the Federal government to support technology. . . . Fourth, wealthy school districts are already implementing the vision in their schools, thereby advantaging their students. . . . Fifth, the cost model . . . reflects a complete, life cycle view that includes all the critical components of technology planning and implementation. . . . Sixth, the cost model is based on list prices, and assumes no discounting. It is likely that substantial discounts could be negotiated for most of the components of the model. (pp. 10–12)

Assessment: Schools and Student Learning

Losak and MacFarland (1994) assessed the Florida Model Technology Schools Project. The project's mission was to design and implement plans to use technology for management and teaching and learning. Additionally, the project personnel were charged with the model's evaluation and dissemination.

This essentially qualitative study generated findings which indicated that technology motivates students; that technology increases information for managers, teachers, and students; that teachers view technology instruction as an excellent preparation for graduates; and that technology provides tools to help equalize instruction for special needs children.

Losak and MacFarland report that in Florida during 1994, students were using computer resources between one and ten hours per week. After implementation of the Model Technology Schools project, students in the five participating schools had greater access to computers than other students throughout the nation. Teachers reported increases in "enthusiasm, improved time on task, and collaborative behavior" (p. iv). Student behavior improved. Teacher communication improved using electronic mail. And the findings from the Model Technology Schools Project suggest that gains may occur even when students use second-generation computers (p. iv).

Losak and MacFarland view the Model Technology Schools project favorably and advise the initiation of a formal research study. They offer several recommendations based upon their assessment:

- Continue funding for the five schools currently participating in the MTS program.
- Broaden the scope and diversity of the MTS Program.
- Expand the project to incorporate a formal research phase.

- Develop assessment tools that reflect how technology is used in the curriculum.
- Expand parent and community involvement in the MTS Program.
- Develop a training model for use by non-Model Technology Schools in incorporating technology into the curriculum.
- Develop mechanisms to ensure flexibility in the application of project components.
- Ensure a primary focus on learning outcomes. (pp. v–vii)

Although this study was a specialized assessment of a unique technology program, the type and kind of analysis can be applied to other technology plans. The findings and recommendations may differ, but the assessment and evaluation procedures measure school effectiveness and student achievement.

THREE STATE TECHNOLOGY PLANS: THE LONG VIEW

North Carolina

State-sponsored planning tools are often global, strategic plans that are based on sound visions but lack tactical and operational plans for implementation. North Carolina's technology plan (Superintendent of Public Instruction, 1994) provides both a strategic look at shared goals, vision, and mission and a guide to the tactical and operational plans for their accomplishment. Although the document includes challenges, benefits, objectives, and strategies, it also includes advantages for participants in the school community, case studies for implementation, and lists of statewide resources. In the section entitled "Plan Purpose," the authors describe the State's responsibility:

> The second purpose of the plan is to indicate the commitment of the Department of Public Instruction to provide all schools a technology framework. . . . " (p. 2)

Education's Challenges   One of the three significant sections of the document lists eight challenges to today's schools. Many challenges can be mitigated for teachers and students by an enlightened academic program supported by technology. The list includes:

1. Students poorly equipped for personal well-being.
2. A changed state economy and job market.
3. Goals from the future, tools from the past.
4. Inequities among school districts and student populations.
5. Teachers in need.
6. Principals in need.
7. Weak school-home and school-community relations.
8. Increased school violence, inadequate security systems. (pp. 3–7)

Many of these challenges appear in documents decrying the state of public education. The North Carolina plan is a model for acknowledging these challenges and suggesting solutions at the individual district, school, and classroom level.

Objectives for Change   The strategic plan for North Carolina is a global vision. Individual educators or communities of leadership cannot institute change from these goals. At the tactical plan level, the North Carolina planning team creates objectives that can translate into action: creating improved academic programs and educational opportunities.

First, the objectives seek to change the nature of schools "to create an active, flexible environment, open to the community" (p. 17). Second, the objectives correspond to constructivist thinking by making school a more active, collaborative, and personally meaningful experience with a powerful emphasis on communication skills. Third, the objectives seek to change the responsibilities of teachers toward facilitation—"the guide on the side"—with a disposition to teach all students. Fourth, the objectives seek to change the role of educational administrators to a balance of management and leadership with an emphasis on school-community relations. Fifth, the objectives seek to transform assessment into a diagnostic and prescriptive tool and then as an accountability measure. The purposes of the objectives, according to the state plan, are:

> To achieve tomorrow's learning community—where all students reach high standards and where all teachers, school staff, and administrators are effective in reaching their goals. . . . (p. 17)

Strategies for Action   The final section of note in North Carolina's strategic plan is "Strategies for Action" (p. 29), which details a method of meeting the state's objectives and establishes the shared relationship between the Department of Public Instruction and the individual districts and schools. Each of the five tactical or operational strategies has a structured and outlined process:

1. Establish an *ongoing* planning process at both state and local levels.
2. Provide ongoing funding for building state and local technology-schooling infrastructures.
3. Develop technology-based networks and other means for ongoing communication of ideas and collaborative problem-solving among those using technology to improve instruction and administration.
4. Develop a human resource base of individuals who are skilled in the use of technology and comfortable leading teachers and administrators . . . to meet objectives outlined in this plan.
5. Adopt an ongoing, cyclical evaluation-revision process at state and local levels that finds success and builds on it, encourages innovation, and uses the opportunities of failed efforts to learn, improve, and make appropriate changes. (pp. 29–32)

North Carolina's ideas are not unique to technology planning. What appears different is the covenant that the state makes with the local school districts to nourish change and the positive spirit in which the planners offer that bond.

Wisconsin

Most of the previous discussion of technology planning considered the computer as the dominant technological tool. The State of Wisconsin's *Instructional Communication: A Resource Planning Guide* (State Superintendent of Public Instruction, 1995) elected to address other, equally intriguing, technology tools: telecommunications.

Today, an information superhighway of global dimensions is being developed, one that is capable of linking people around the world more intimately than television images ever could. This superhighway is not only an express lane to the future, but a means of changing the present and shaping the future itself. As expressed in the Wisconsin guide:

> The path of this electronic highway is paved not with asphalt or concrete . . . but with new forms of telecommunications capable of transporting information between people around the world. (State Superintendent of Public Instruction, 1995, p. 1).

Wisconsin's vision of the telecommunications revolution specifically considers the instructional application of telecommunications tools: transmission methods, radio, broadcast, microwave, and cable television, video and teletext, satellites, and fiber optics. The purpose is to explore instructional delivery systems unavailable to most Wisconsin school districts.

Wisconsin's telecommunications planning document resembles other state planning documents except that it does not appear to begin at the strategic planning stage. The planning process begins with tactical planning at the state level and moves to operational planning at the local level. Wisconsin relinquishes the vision and mission elements of strategic planning to the local school districts rather than forcing Wisconsin's Department of Public Instruction's values and beliefs about telecommunications.

Anderson (1987), the author of the curriculum guide for the Wisconsin plan, presents a graphic representation of the recommended State tactical plan. Anderson envisions the plan as an ongoing planning cycle. First, she recommends creating a district plan which includes "a planning process, philosophy and rationale, curriculum integration, facilities/resources, and budget considerations" (p. 57). Second, she recommends a plan for implementation which includes both staff development and selection, purchasing, and administration. Third, she recommends an evaluation based upon an overview and a checklist. Fourth, she advocates a review and revision procedure that includes "planning for change, analyzing/interpreting program evaluations, setting priorities, implementing change, and evaluating impact" (p. 57). Within the closed system of planning, implementation, evaluation, and review, the school-community provides analysis and support at each stage.

The Wisconsin document helps school districts and schools operationalize their planning to include a needs assessment, which includes identifying existing information, data to be collected, vision, timelines, and a needs report. Additionally the operational plan details sections about "creating an instructional telecommunications plan . . . articulating curriculum . . . calculating costs . . . identifying financing options including a cost-benefit analysis" (pp. 60–66).

Maryland

The Maryland state-wide strategic planning document (Office of Administration and Finance—School Facilities, 1991) encourages local school districts to plan for electronic communication systems to support their other forms of technology. The statements of beliefs resemble many visions and missions in other state and local planning documents with one exception. Maryland specifically perceives its relationship with the school-community as a model of two-way communication, not just information and requests from the district to the community. Belief four of the planning document states:

> Every school facility is a community resource. As such, it both serves and takes advantage of the community's human and technological resources. (p. 5)

Elements of the Maryland Report   *Electronic Communications Systems.* Electronic communications systems are forms of telecommunications. They comprise three separate categories: voice, video, and data. Voice includes two-way communication using telephone messaging between the school and the community and a public-address system (p. 7). Video includes all forms of television and radio produced both internally and externally. Data incorporates two-way communication via local and wide area networks including the InterNet and the World Wide Web.

Building Components. Building components include the infrastructure necessary to support technology in schools. Engineering concerns include structural issues of cable and wire installations and building integrity, sufficient electrical power, adequate lighting for technology, climate controls, acoustics, heating, ventilation, and air conditioning (HVAC), and wall, ceiling, and flooring materials.

Operational Plan Format. Additionally, the Maryland plan presents a unique section in its planning document. The plan includes telecommunications planning criteria, local area network overviews, specifications for buildings and grounds descriptions, hardware specifications, and an appendix for an educational format. The plan considers design and review processes. The outline of the generic format includes:

Section I. Project Rationale
    Introduction
    The Community
    School Board Policies

Belief Statements

Scope of Work, Budget, and Schedule

Section II. Educational Plan

Curriculum Component

Instructional Method Component

Staff Support Component

Technology Component

Section III. Project Design Factors

Site Conditions

Building Systems

Section IV. Activity Areas

General Overview

Program/Service Function

Section V. Summary of Area Relationships

Section VI. Summary of Space Requirements

In a description of the overall plan within the sections, the Maryland planners suggest operational subplans to help school districts and school officials implement their instructional technology vision and mission.

Activity Areas. School facilities planners, influenced by operational technology planners, must create learning environments conducive to instructional objectives and technology needs. The Maryland document makes this case:

> Traditional labels for a school's activity areas may be no longer appropriate and the traditional groupings no longer acceptable in cases where instruction and classroom management are supported by a technology infrastructure. As the belief statements suggest, it is not only appropriate but desirable to think non-traditionally when planning "technology-friendly" spaces. (p. 38)

The plan lists several activity areas in which technology-supported instruction occurs: "the generic classroom, career and technology education, art, music, physical education, science, the library media center, computer clusters, the computer lab, interactive TV classroom, and a TV production facility" (pp. 45–65).

SUMMARY

The planning process is at once complicated and simple. Many technology plans follow a characteristic model: develop vision statement, assess needs, examine state proficiencies, set program objectives, implement program, evaluate program. Many organizations at the national, state, and local levels follow a strategic, tactical, and operational planning process. The plans and processes presented in this chapter are merely guidelines and suggestions. Actual strategic, tactical, and operational plans for specific local districts and attendance centers must reflect the school's values and beliefs, vision and mission, and culture. Planners must temper these guidelines with the wisdom of theory and practice.

Change in each organization begins with the completion of one element. A local school may begin with a discussion of how technology can support the academic program, or with a survey of current computer use. Either way, the community of leadership must take the first step into a new future. As we argued in a paper about peer coaching in whole-language and technology (Davidson & Maurer, 1995), implementation of technology requires "an intellectual and leadership paradigm shift . . . from which there can be no retreat" (p. 24).

REFERENCES

Anderson, M. E. (1987). A guide to curriculum planning in computer education. (Eric Document Reproduction Service No. ED 287 469)

Baker, L., & Brown, A. L. (1984). Metacognitive skills and reading. In P. D. Pearson (Ed.), *Handbook of reading research.* New York: Longman.

Biggs, P. (1988). Create ownership in your long range plan with a technology audit. *The Computing Teacher, 16*(2), 31–33.

Bruder, I. (1990). Restructuring: The Central Kitsap example. *Electronic Learning, 10*(2), 16–19.

Collins, A., Brown, J. S., & Newman, S. E. (1989). Cognitive apprenticeship: Teaching the craft of reading, writing, and mathematics. In L. B. Resnick (Ed.), *Knowing, learning, and instruction: Essays in honor of Robert Glasser* (pp. 453–494). Hillsdale, NJ: Erlbaum.

Cooper, J. A. (1973). Application of the consultant role to parent-teacher management of school avoidance behavior. *Psychology in the Schools, 10*(2), 259–262.

Cox, C. (1994). Strategic planning for the future. *School Executive, 31*(2), 58.

Davidson, G., & Maurer, M. M. (1995). Leadership in instructional technology. *TechTrends, 40*(3), 23–26.

Fullan, M. G. (1994). Coordinating top-down and bottom-up strategies for educational reform. In R. F. Elmore & S. H. Fuhrman (Eds.), *The governance of curriculum. The 1994 ASCD Yearbook* (pp. 186-202). Alexandria, VA: Association for Supervision and Development.

Huh, U. (1993). The impact of computing in education in Korea. *Educational Technology, 33*(9), 42–47.

Indiana Curriculum Advisory Council of the Indiana State Board of Education and the Indiana Department of Education. (1991). *Vision 91 of 21st century schooling for Indiana: Executive summary.* Indianapolis, IN: Author.

Katz, L. (1989). *Engaging children's minds: The project approach.* Norwood, NJ: Ablex.

Kearsley, G. (1990). *Computers for educational administrators.* Norwood, NJ: Ablex.

Knowles, M. S. (1980). *The modern practices of adult education: From pedagogy to andragogy.* Englewood Cliffs, NJ: Cambridge Adult Education.

Larner, D. K., & Timberlake, L. M. (1995). *Teachers with limited computer knowledge: Variables affecting use and hints to increase use.* (Report No. SP 038 095). Charlottesville, VA: University of Virginia. (ERIC Document Reproduction Service No. ED 384 595).

Lindbloom, C. (1959). The science of "muddling through." *Public Administration Review, 19*(2), 79–88.

Losak, J., & MacFarland, T. (1994). *An evaluation of Florida's Model Technology Schools program: 1988 to 1993: (You can't go home again).* (Report No. IR 017 044). Fort Lauderdale, FL: State of Florida, Department of Education. (ERIC Document Reproduction Service No. ED 381 129).

Lunenburg, F. C. (1995). *The principalship concepts and applications.* Upper Saddle River, NJ: Merrill/Prentice Hall.

Martinsen, K. (1993). Creating a district plan for technology. *The Book Report, 12*(2), 25–26.

Maurer, M. M. (1994). Computer anxiety correlates and what they tell us: A literature review. *Computers in Human Behavior, 10*(3), 369–376.

Mendrinos, R. B. (1987). The educational media specialist: Training the trainer. *Library Software Review, 6*(5), 272–275.

Merton, R. (1936). The unanticipated consequences of purposive social action. *American Sociological Review, 1,* 894–904.

Office of Administration and Finance—School Facilities. (1991). *Model educational specifications for technology in schools.* Baltimore, MD: Maryland State Department of Education.

Palinscar, A. S., & Brown, A. L. (1984). Reciprocal teaching of comprehension-fostering and comprehension-monitoring activities. *Cognition and Instruction, 2,* 117–175.

Papert, S. (1980). *Mindstorms: Children, computers, and powerful ideas.* New York: Basic Books.

Pogrow, S. (1983). *Education in the computer age.* Beverly Hills, CA: Sage.

Radlick, M. (1994). *A cost model: Implementing technology in New York state public schools.* (Report No. IR 017 113). Albany, NY: New York State Education Department. (ERIC Document Reproduction Service No. ED 382 176).

Ray, D. (1991). Technology and restructuring part 1: New educational directions. *The Computing Teacher, 18*(6), 9–20.

Roberts, L. G. (1994). Interview. *Technos, 3*(1), 4–7.

Sharp, G. F., Jr. (1992). *The development and implementation of a five-year plan for the integration of computers through a total school curriculum.* Unpublished doctoral dissertation, NOVA University.

Simon, H. A. (1977). *The new science of management decision.* New York: Harper and Row.

Slavin, R. E. (1995). *Cooperative learning: Theory, research, and practice.* Boston: Allyn and Bacon.

State Superintendent of Public Instruction. (1994). *A technology plan for North Carolina public schools.* Raleigh, NC: North Carolina Department of Public Instruction.

State Superintendent of Public Instruction. (1995). *Instructional telecommunications a resource and planning guide* (Bulletin No. 95171). Milwaukee, WI: Wisconsin Department of Public Instruction.

Wepner, S. B., & Kramer, S. (1987). Organizing computers for reading instruction. *Computers in the Schools, 4*(1), 53–66.

CHAPTER 12

Funding Technology Projects

The tragic reality of funding for education remains that resources are limited for many school districts. This means school districts cannot fully fund instructional technology. When the community of leadership commits to a program of instructional technology, including the purchase of hardware and software, systematic maintenance and upgrading of assets, staff development, and assessment, they must seek alternative funding. For many schools, this means that the community of leadership must enter the competitive world of external funding. They must learn the special language of grants, how to win a grant, which are the appropriate granting agencies, why proposals are funded, and why and how to collaborate with businesses and universities.

In this chapter we describe the realities of school funding; the external funding arena, including the grant cycle; the criteria for selecting grant recipients; the structure of a grant proposal; the sources of funding; the projects that are funded; and the people and organizations that are funded.

INTRODUCTION

Completing a grant proposal is similar in many ways to constructing a house. If you want to build a house, you begin with an idea for that house. The next step is to flesh out the basic idea by hiring an architect to formalize your original ideas. You go through a similar process when you create a grant proposal. Just as you need a team of people to build a house, you need a team of people to produce a successful grant proposal. The house has specific parts: a foundation, walls, windows, plumbing, and a roof. All these parts are necessary. If one is missing, the house falls down or does not function properly. Likewise, a grant proposal has several parts, and if one is missing, the proposal is not successful.

To extend the metaphor, think of the ideas of the proposal as the foundation of the house. The proposal itself forms the walls of our house. The funds are the roof: Once we place the roof on the house, we can begin living in it. Many members of the community of leadership view the funds as the end of the process. This is analogous to building a house that no one will live in. Grant proposals should fund projects that enhance student learning. We build a proposal only for the purpose of student learning.

THE REALITIES OF SCHOOL FUNDING

The realities of school funding can be sobering at times. The bumper sticker that suggests that we fund schools fully and hold a bake sale to buy armaments speaks directly to this issue. While the requirements placed on schools are expanding, most school budgets are either stagnant or shrinking. Year by year, we expect schools to do more with the same or less money.

Very few educators entered the field with the idea that they would bear responsibility for coming up with the funds to do their jobs. That, however, has become the reality of the field. Not only must we generate the ideas for great learning, we also must find ways to fund those great ideas. Many technology-related learning innovations are relatively costly. Given a climate of flat or shrinking budgets, we must find additional funding to turn great teaching ideas into great learning activities for children.

To alleviate these problems, many schools turn to external funding sources. Unfortunately, in most schools, the community of leadership is relatively unskilled at fund raising. This deficiency will have to be corrected unless funding improves. Our advice to anyone who is counting on improved funding for schools is: "Don't hold your breath." Even well-meaning legislation for special projects or mandates is often not fully funded. Funding for technology and staff development often reimburses only a part of the necessary costs.

Many educational leaders take a flawed approach to securing external funds. They search for grant opportunities and try to develop projects that will secure those funds. We disagree with this approach both philosophically and practically. We believe that the community of leadership should view external funding as a means of accomplishing specific outcomes. They should begin with great ideas to help children learn and seek funds to make those ideas a reality. Starting with a grant opportunity is much less likely to be effective. Further, this approach transforms our community of learners into a community of opportunists. We believe the field of education and the people in it have far too much dignity and importance to be reduced to mere opportunists.

Some educators even believe that it is wrong to use external funds for something as fundamental as technology. This view was put forth in a short article in a special issue of *Electronic Learning* devoted to external funding for technology projects (McCarthy, 1993):

> Goeff Fletcher, Assistant commissioner at the Texas Education Agency, is a thoughtful proponent of educational computing. He believes, however, that the money to buy computers for schools should come from state departments of education and local school taxes—not local fund-raising efforts.
>
> "Computers and software are necessary classroom materials," he says. "Therefore the state education department, or the locals school district, ought to be supplying them. Those monies shouldn't be used to fund something as essential as technology" (p. 13).

THE EXTERNAL FUNDING ARENA

To be successful in garnering external funds, the community of leadership needs to know many things. First, they need to be conversant in the language of external funding, to understand what is required in various grant applications. Second, they have to understand that virtually all grants are competitive. Third, they have to understand the general processes of a funding cycle. Lastly, they have to understand various criteria for selection of grant recipients. Understanding all these issues will help the community of leadership shift its focus from grant writing to grant winning.

The Language of External Funding

A number of terms used in the external funding arena can be confusing. Three terms relate to the specific details of a grant opportunity: priority, initiative, and request for proposal (RFP).

The issues that a funding organization addresses are their *priorities*. These issues are usually rather broad, long-standing, and stable. In the case of government agencies, the legislature has mandated most of the priorities by law. Specific funding programs that an organization undertakes to accomplish their priorities are its *initiatives*. The publication of the specific details of an initiative is called a *request for proposal,* or RFP. The RFP usually contains all the specific details for preparing a grant proposal. It conveys the focus of the initiative, the application rules, and any restrictions the organization may place on the project or the recipients of the funds.

Although each term has a different focus, the terms are often used interchangeably as shorthand for the announcement of the funding opportunities for a specific organization. This may be because the priorities of an organization often are not stated explicitly, but are implicitly defined by the organization's initiatives. The only place we find out about the initiatives of many funding organizations is through their RFPs.

Two terms frequently used in the preparation of a grant proposal are assurances and disclosures. The term *assurances* can mean different things to different funding organizations. In general, the term refers to a section of the document in which the applicant promises to meet the qualifications of the published opportunity. The variation in the use of the term occurs in specifying the qualifications. In some cases, the assurances state that none of the people involved with the grant (even people whose names may not appear in the document, such as the chief financial officer of the applying institution) has been convicted of a crime relevant to funding. In other cases, the assurances state that the applying institution will expend the funds as detailed in the proposal. The assurances may even specify that the funds will not be spent in some specific way, such as to harm animals or to lobby Congress.

A *disclosure* is an affirmation that the applicant has told the funding organization everything. In some grant applications, assurances make disclosures unnecessary. In others, disclosures are a separate section. Federal agencies often require the disclosure of any lobbying efforts by the personnel involved with the project.

Two terms that describe people in the grant writing arena are principal investigator and program officer. The *principal investigator,* often called the PI, is the main person in charge of carrying out the project. The term comes from the research arena, where the PI is the main person investigating a research question. In the case of a project proposal, the PI is the person who investigates the feasibility and effects of a project. The *program officer* is the person at the funding agency who is in charge of an initiative or group of initiatives. For example, a large foundation may have one program officer in charge of all education initiatives. If you have questions about an initiative, or if you want to run an idea past someone at a funding organization, the program officer is usually your contact person. If you are planning to submit a large grant application, it is advisable to contact the program officer in charge of that initiative before you submit the proposal.

The word "winner" describes people who are successful at obtaining a competitive grant. We are disturbed by that word because it implies that those who do not get funds are "losers." If you apply for a grant and do not get the money, you are not a loser. There are many reasons why you did not receive the funds. You may have proposed a great project and presented it well, but the funding organization's funds were so limited that your great project fell just below its financial cutoff. Another common reason is that your proposal did not match the priorities of the funding organization as closely as another proposal. Instead of thinking in terms of winners and losers, we prefer to think in terms of great projects that have been funded and great projects that are still seeking funds. If we call people "losers," we encourage them to quit. By calling them "people still seeking funds," we encourage them to persist.

The Nature of Competitive Funding

Competitiveness is one issue that escapes many educators who are entering the external funding arena. Virtually all grant opportunities are competitive because more people need funding than there are funds available. It is very common to hear the first-time grant writer speak of a grant as "a done deal." Because their grant conforms to all the rules described in the application materials, they believe the organization will fund the project. This thinking is seldom realistic. Many granting organizations receive more than ten times the number of applications than they are able to fund. Many of the proposals they accept are from people who have previously been successful at procuring grants. It is difficult for the first-time grant writer to break into the field—difficult, but not impossible.

Because grants are so competitive, the application processes are important. The grant administrators are looking for ways to reduce the field of applicants. One quick way to eliminate an applicant is on a technicality: If an application is late or does not meet the requirements of the application procedure, it is quickly eliminated. Hence, it is important to get your grant application in on time and to make certain it conforms precisely to the application specifications. Excuses and rationalizations will fall on deaf ears.

Grant Cycles

Not all funding organizations follow a strict cycle. Small, local foundations may simply receive applications, fund those that are worthy and that they can afford, and ignore the rest. Local businesses may allocate a certain amount of money annually to philanthropy and give money to certain kinds of causes until that money is gone. In these cases, the implicit cycle is their fiscal year. Because the amount of money is limited and is gone by the end of the fiscal year, it is important to know when the fiscal year begins. It is also important to know roughly how much the organization generally has to donate and any internal rules they may use. As an example, suppose a local business allocates $10,000 a year and splits it evenly between health care and education. Knowing "when" and "how much" gives you an advantage in the competition. If you submit a good proposal early in the year, and if the request is for something that is within their budget, your chances are good.

Information on smaller foundations and businesses may be difficult to discover. However, because they are local, you can rely on your local contacts. This is one more reason why our community of leadership should be all-inclusive. If your community includes people who work in that business, they will be very willing to share this kind of information with you. Otherwise, those opportunities may never come to light, and the local hospital (for example) may get all the business's money every year.

Many funding organizations, particularly larger organizations and national organizations, follow a specific cycle in awarding their grants. The grant cycle is instituted from the point of view of the granting agencies or organizations. To be successful in getting money from these organizations, the community of leadership must understand the grant cycle. The five stages of the cycle are: announcement of grant initiatives, receipt of proposals, review of proposals, notification of grant recipients, and receipt of final reports.

Announcement of Grant Initiatives   The cycle begins with the announcement of the opportunities for the year. Some organizations announce their opportunities in specific publications. For example, all U. S. government agencies announce their grant opportunities in the *Commerce Business Daily* and the *Federal Register*. Most large funding organizations (and some smaller ones) publish their grant opportunities on the Internet. The World Wide Web can be a great place to find out about grant opportunities.

Large funding organizations have a very predictable cycle, so you can watch for the funding opportunities at regular intervals. Smaller funding organizations may announce their programs through other means, such as a web page, local publications, or specific national publications. Another way to find funding opportunities is by reading articles in professional journals that track grant opportunities. Many professional journals have a column or periodic feature that summarizes grant opportunities pertinent to the field covered by the journal.

Receipt of Proposals   The second stage of the grant cycle is receipt of the proposals. The vast majority of funding organizations have strict deadlines for the receipt of proposals. If you are late, do not even bother sending your application because the organization will not consider it. You may, however, be able to resubmit your application for the next deadline, provided a later deadline is set for the same initiative. A few organizations, usually smaller funding organizations with a specific focus, accept applications continuously. You can apply for funds related to the priorities of these organization at any time.

Once a funding organization receives the grant proposals, its staff assesses the appropriateness of each proposal. If your proposal does not fit the stated priorities of the funding opportunity, it will be eliminated. Some funding opportunities have very specific application procedures. For example, the number of pages may be limited (e.g., "Include a narrative description of your project, not to exceed five pages"). A specific requirement may need to be met (e.g., your school must have a high percentage of minority students). The funding organization will have a procedure for dealing with violations of the application rules. The procedure is often to simply remove the proposal from consideration. Some funding organizations that impose page limits will not eliminate the entire proposal. Instead, they will remove any pages from the proposal that exceed their limits. It is important to follow the rules when putting together your application.

Review of Proposals   The third stage of the cycle is the review of grant applications. Even organizations that accept applications continuously usually have a specific time frame for the review of proposals (e.g., quarterly). The review of proposals with strict deadlines usually begins shortly after the deadline. Most national funding organizations use subject-matter experts to evaluate their proposals—that is, people with expertise in the priority area. The majority of these people are university faculty, but the group may also include parents and business leaders. The agency may mail a group of proposals to a small group of reviewers, or they may convene a group of reviewers at their headquarters. The reviewers typically only make recommendations to the staff of the agency. The agency may not be bound by reviewers' recommendations. However, since the review process is time consuming and expensive, the agency usually follows the reviewer's recommendations very closely. In some cases, the reviewers actually make the final determination of the rank order for the funding of proposals. In the case of local or regional grants, some funding organizations have an internal review process while others use local experts as a review panel.

The important issue to consider in the review process is your audience. Your audience is usually composed of experts with specialized knowledge in the priorities of the funding organization. Hence, it is important that your proposal be correct and accurate. One of the reviewers is likely to catch any errors, omissions, or misstatements.

Every review situation is unique, but our experience tells us that, once a proposal makes it to the review process, passion beats technical excellence every time. The reviewers usually are people who care about the priority being funded. Your proposal must capture the essence of the results of the project clearly and with passion. The effects on children are important. All too often, when a professional grant writer prepares a proposal, the proposal is technically strong but lacks the passion that wins the competition. (Professional grant writers are discussed later in this chapter.)

Another important issue to consider is brevity. Virtually all funding organizations receive a flood of requests, which means reviewers must read a large number of proposals. Most of the reviewers read the proposals very quickly out of necessity. Hence, they appreciate brief, clear, and effective writing. Padding your verbiage will irritate the reviewers.

Notification of Grant Recipients   The fourth step, the notification of the grant recipients, is the joyful part of the process for those who win the grants. However, if you are like most grant recipients, the elation of winning a grant will be quickly followed by the sobering realization that you now have to do all the work promised in your proposal. Most winning proposals are ambitious, and so work involved is usually monumental.

Receipt of Final Reports   The last step involves reporting. The reporting requirements vary significantly among funding organizations. Typically, the larger the amount of money you receive, the more reporting you will have to do. Most larger funding organizations require ongoing financial reporting. They may also require periodic reports on the progress of the project. On the other end of the continuum, small, local grants may not require any reporting at all; the check arrives and that is the last contact with the granting agency. Most often, however, the organization requires some form of summary report showing whether or not the project achieved the intended outcome.

Knowing you will have to submit a summary report implies that you will have to assess the effectiveness of your project. Depending on the nature of your project, this undertaking can be simple or complex. For example, if the intended outcome of your project is to increase school attendance, your summary report will simply need to report the change in student attendance. However, if your project is designed to increase young women's interest in science, assessing the outcome of your project will be much more complex. If your community of leadership does not have a lot of assessment expertise, it is a good idea to expand the community to incorporate that expertise.

Continuation Funding   Some larger grants may have later stages that involve continuation funding. If this is the case, these funds are usually still competitive, but you are competing against a much smaller pool of applicants. In essence, the cycle begins again with continuation funding. If continuation funding is available, it is seldom long term. Virtually all grant opportunities expect the receiving organization to continue the project with internal funding. One common type of continuation funding is a dissemination grant. If your project was highly successful, the funding organization may give you additional money to help you make your project known to others.

Determining Priorities and Initiates   There is one more stage in the grant cycle that precedes the first stage. Once your community gains experience and reputation in the external funding arena, it may become involved in helping funding organizations determine their priorities and initiatives. For example, how does the U. S. Department of Education determine the exact nature of the programs it funds? Legislation outlines the general parameters, but experts in the field fill in the specific details. Your community of leadership may be able to advise the government agencies that determine the initiatives. By becoming politically active, they may also be able to influence the priorities mandated by Congress.

Returning to a previous example, how do executives of a local company decide how to spend their philanthropic fund? Perhaps a better question would be, How can we persuade them to change their minds? As our community of leadership gains expertise, we hope to apply our expertise more widely. Our ultimate goal is to do our best to help children learn, develop, and grow. A powerful way to accomplish this goal is by influencing grant priorities and initiatives.

Keep in mind that most grants follow a cycle, and that when one cycle is completed, another begins. This means that if you miss one opportunity, another is just around the corner. If your proposal is rejected, you can resubmit an improved version next time.

Criteria for Selecting Grant Recipients

The criteria for selecting a grant recipient varies from one funding agency to another. A grant from a private corporation will probably have different expectations than a grant from a government agency. For example, a grant from the National Endowment for the Arts will have different selection criteria than a grant from the National Science Foundation. Private foundations each have specific areas of interest, and their selection criteria reflect those areas of interest. However, most grants have some common criteria. Following are some questions most grant reviewers ask as they read grant proposals:

1. In my professional opinion, will this project achieve the desired outcomes?
2. Do I fully understand what these people are going to do?
3. Can they really carry out this project?
4. Will the results of the grant continue after the grant money runs out?

The funding agency usually asks the grant reviewers to score the proposals. That means that they not only ask the above questions about each proposal, but they compare the results among proposals. Thus, the above questions become:

1. Which proposals have the best chance of achieving the desired outcomes?
2. Which proposals are clearest?
3. Which proposals have the best people?
4. Which proposals have the best chance of continuing results after the funds run out?

Budget considerations also vary from one funding opportunity to another. Some organizations ask their reviewers to examine the budget and make decisions based on the money requested. Others ask the reviewers to omit financial considerations and review only the substance of the proposal. In the latter situation, the staff of the granting agency reserves the right to make all financial decisions. What this means to the grant writer is that the money will certainly be a consideration, but who considers it may vary.

Even when reviewers are not charged with considering budget issues, they will. In the case of government grants especially, virtually all grant reviewers care how our hard-earned tax dollars are spent. In the case of private funding, we all would like to see those meager funds go to the people who will use them most frugally. Most reviewers are painfully aware that once we grant the money, it is gone forever. Anyone who is involved with schools is used to pinching pennies and has a very low tolerance for financial waste. The advice is obvious: Do not inflate your budget. Keep it reasonable. If there is a cheaper way to achieve the desired results, use it. On the other hand, make sure the budget is adequate. Although inflated budgets are most common, it also is not unusual to find a grant proposal that has budget omissions. Thus, ask for what you need to complete the project and not a penny more.

As mentioned earlier, one of the strongest criteria is passion. Although funding agencies do not mention passion in their request for proposals, remember that most reviewers are people who care about children. Your proposal should capture the hearts and imaginations of the reviewers. If your proposal causes reviewers to imagine good things happening for children, your proposal will rise to the top of the pile. As an example, a group of local grant reviewers looked at a collection of proposals, and one clearly stood out above the rest. The project focused on a local community resource, and the proposal made it clear that the community shared significant pride in their unique resource. The resource acted as a theme for a variety of important learning activities. The way the proposal writers talked about the resource in the proposal, and the way they organized the learning activities around that resource, captivated the reviewers. Although many other proposals were technically superior, the group of reviewers was unanimous in its support of this particular proposal. Because the passion of the authors was evident, the proposal rose above others that were better written, better organized, and better prepared.

In most cases, but not all, the agency will send you the reviews of your proposal. This is helpful whether or not they funded your proposal, but particularly when they did not. The reviews help you know what you did well in the proposal and what you did poorly. By maintaining your strengths and learning from your weaknesses, you can improve subsequent proposals.

THE STRUCTURE OF A GRANT PROPOSAL

The structure of grant proposals varies from organization to organization. Smaller foundations may simply send a letter detailing the project. At the other extreme, federal agencies have a specific, complex format that must be followed before a proposal will even be considered.

SOURCES OF FUNDING

Many sources of funding for technology-related projects exist. There are national, regional and local sources, and government, foundation, corporate, and organizational sources. At one time, grant money was relatively plentiful. In today's world, however, the funds are shrinking. This means that, to make a project happen, you may have to do more work than ever before to secure the funding. In the past, it was easier to find sources to fully fund a great project. In today's environment of tight grant funds, you may have to put a package of donors together to fund that same great project. For example, if your project requires staff, hardware, travel, and supplies, you can get the hardware from a local hardware vendor, the travel from a local travel agency, and supplies from a local business. Then, when you ask a foundation or government agency for the money to cover the staff expenses, not only is the required funding less, but you are showing existing support for the project. This is the reason to be aware of the full range of funding opportunities available to K–12 institutions.

National Funding Sources

There are a number of national funding sources. Several are described in the sections that follow. National grants tend to be larger than regional or local grants. They are usually the most difficult grants to win because the field of competition is so large. As you should expect, the bigger the pool of money that is available, the stiffer the competition. However, you should consider entering the competition if your community of leadership has a strong idea, one that will help children learn, develop, and grow.

Federal Grants   Agencies of the U. S. Government have a number of grant programs aimed at education. You can get program information from one of the Federal Information Center regional offices. You can also keep tabs on new Federal grant opportunities by watching for the announcement of grants in the *Federal Register* or the *Commerce Business Daily*. Documents detailing specific funding opportunities, as well as documents describing the rules for preparation of a grant application and the management of a grant, are all available from each agency, free of charge. Some government agencies and government-sponsored organizations that commonly grant money to education include the U. S. Department of Education, the National Science Foundation, the National Endowment for the Arts, the National Endowment for the Humanities, and the U. S. Department of Energy.

The community of leadership should track possible opportunities to garner funding for the learning opportunities the community would like to implement. Many of these opportunities are not directly available to the K–12 community, but are designed to benefit the K–12 community. Many grant opportunities are available only to the university community. For example, most research priorities are open only to university applicants. Other funding opportunities do not limit the applicants to university personnel, but the structure of the process is biased in favor of university recipients. At first this may sound discouraging, but there is a positive solution to this bias. If a K–12 community forms a partnership with a university community, the resulting proposal can be stronger and more compelling than either community could produce separately. In addition, this partnership can produce an even larger and stronger community of learners and community of leadership.

Just as there are educational grant opportunities specifically available to universities, there are also opportunities specifically available to the business community. These are often economic development opportunities for small companies that are in the business of education. As with grants open only to universities, a partnership between a business and a K–12 institution has two positive outcomes: It improves the grant proposal, and it provides an opportunity to draw these disparate communities together toward a common goal.

Some grant opportunities are specifically designed by the funding organizations for K–12 institutions. The management of federal grants is no simple task. There are usually requirements for reporting prior to the receipt of a grant (e.g., demographics of your school or district, lobbying efforts of the people involved, previous federal funding). The organization may require ongoing financial reports and a final report summarizing the results of the project. The complexity of the management of large grants is one reason many organizations' opportunities are biased toward universities. Most universities, unless they are very small, have an administrative structure for handling all sorts of grants.

Most K–12 institutions do not have such a structure, although that is changing. Given the management aspects of a federal grant, it is virtually impossible for an individual school to apply for one. School personnel can write a proposal, but it must be submitted by the district. The granting agency must have assurance that the moneys will be managed properly. The reporting requirements of federal grants has a built-in bias against small districts. Again, the solution to this dilemma is a partnership, either with a university or with a larger district. The larger district could assume responsibility for the management of the grant. This not only gets a smaller school community into the external funding arena, it helps our learning and leading communities grow by drawing districts together to work toward a common goal.

Large Foundations   A number of large foundations offer funding opportunities for education. These foundations are listed in *The Foundation Directory* (Faczko & Rich, 1995). This book has important information about over 7,000 foundations and is updated yearly. The information includes a brief financial summary of the foundation, the priorities of the foundation, and the name and address of a contact person. Because of the large number of foundations included in this volume, the information about each foundation is brief. Other resources, such as *Corporate Foundation Profiles* (Jones, Lewis, & Toth, 1994), have more detailed information about specific types of foundations. Many states have a foundation organization that publishes a state directory containing specific information on the foundations that primarily serve that state. These books, and the organizations that produce them, can be very helpful in locating a suitable foundation to fund your projects.

Foundations account for a significant percentage of the grant money that is available to education. Each foundation has some areas of interest. Many share education as one of those areas. They may have other, more specific areas of interest, such as technology-oriented projects or projects that benefit women or girls. Many of the rules that apply to federal grants also apply to these larger foundations. The bottom line is that the granting organization wants assurance that the money will be spent wisely and in their area of interest. As with federal grants, a strong bias toward universities exists in foundation grants because universities are better able to make those assurances.

Large Corporations   Most larger corporations have philanthropic efforts. Some larger corporations have created foundations to organize and consolidate their philanthropic efforts. However, many corporations that have a corporate foundation also have direct funding programs. There may be distinctions between the activities of the foundation and the direct programs. For example, the foundation may have different priorities than the direct corporate programs. Many foundations operate for the greater good of society, while the direct programs usually have some clear benefits to the corporation. Your proposal to a corporation should subtly answer the question, "How will the corporation benefit by supporting this project?"

Typically, corporate philanthropic efforts have a connection with the corporation's business. For example, computer companies will donate equipment to a few schools that will demonstrate the value of that equipment to the educational community. This is a typical win/win situation: The school gets the computers, and the corporation looks good for being generous and for producing a product that benefits children. Many times all the corporation gains from their philanthropy is a good name. At other times the corporation realizes direct advertising benefits. Suppose, for example, that you become a test site for new software. This means that you will have some additional responsibilities. The corporation may ask you to submit a review of their products, or may ask to send prospective customers to your school to see their product in action. Once again, this is a win/win situation because schools need positive advertising as much as corporations do.

There was a time in technology-oriented corporate history when grant opportunities were numerous and attractive. Profit margins were relatively large, which meant money was available for philanthropy. In today's highly competitive market, with its relatively small profit margins, corporations have less money to spread around. This does not mean that grant opportunities are not available, only that they are fewer, smaller, and more competitive.

National Organizations   Most national organizations, such as The International Society for Technology in Education and the National Reading Association, have small grant opportunities that are available either to their members or to individuals in the specific area of interest to the organization. These are much less competitive than larger grants because of the limited audience and the smaller size of the grants. However, some of these grants can be part of making a specific project happen. The publications of these organizations are your best source of information about these grants.

Regional and Local Funding Sources

Educators who have been in the field for a while are typically familiar with local funding sources. These sources can be a large part of how we fund many of the projects that make our schools vital learning places. For those newer members of our learning and leading communities who are not yet familiar with local funding sources, we describe various sources in the sections that follow.

State Agencies   Most of us think of our state department of education when we think of state government funding. However, just as federal funds are available from a variety of agencies, funds are also available from several state organizations. Your state department of transportation may be a source of funds for transportation-related projects. Your state department of energy may be a source of funds for school projects related to energy issues. To stay abreast of these opportunities, you can seek out the appropriate contact person at your state's department of education, or locate a state publication that lists all state grant opportunities. If members of your community of leadership (parents, for example) work for these organizations, they may be able to get you the information more quickly. They can also keep you informed of opportunities that you might otherwise overlook. This is yet another reason to keep your community of leadership all-inclusive.

Local Foundations   Local foundations are usually organized and run by local people who have a stake in the local community. These may be business people who have been highly successful and have organized a foundation to share their success with the local community (while enjoying the tax benefit). Sometimes an heir to a large fortune will set up a foundation to meet a local need, such as sheltering and feeding the homeless. These kinds of foundations often operate with ongoing local donations. Regardless of the reason for the foundation, they can be enormously helpful in making smaller projects happen.

Although large foundations account for the greatest share of the money that is available from foundations, smaller foundations account for the greatest share of the grants. Small, local foundations give many small grants. For example, if you need a scanner for a multimedia project, you may be successful in getting a local foundation to provide the funds to purchase that piece of equipment. For projects that do not require big money, local foundations may be the answer. In addition, some larger projects may be possible through a smaller local foundation. Suppose, for example, that a small foundation annually gives $200,000 to education in 400 grants of roughly $500. If you have a powerful project that very closely matches the priorities of the organization, you might be able to persuade the program director to give most of their money in a particular year to your project.

Local Businesses and Merchants   Your local business community can offer significant support to a good project. There are many good reasons for local businesses to support the local school system. These reasons are obvious to many, and you can easily persuade the rest once you have drawn them into your learning community.

In the past, many local branch offices of large corporations have controlled a local philanthropic fund. In today's tight economic environment, many large corporations have abandoned this policy.

In many arenas, including external funding, rural schools in smaller communities are at a disadvantage. Funding from local business is one shining exception. When educators from a large city try to contact a business directly to request funds, they are frequently snubbed because of the large number of requests that the business gets. Rural communities are different. If your school is the only school in the community (as is usually the case), the local businesses are your exclusive fund-raising domain. That does not mean, however, that business will simply throw money at the schools. Proposing good projects that have a positive impact on children is still the best way to garner funds.

Local Organizations   Most communities have several local organizations, such as fraternal organizations, unions, charitable organizations, special-interest clubs, and professional organizations. Many of these groups use part of their dues for philanthropic purposes. Many also have philanthropy as part of their charter. They may hold an annual event to raise money for specific purposes. These groups can be useful not only for funds to accomplish projects, but also for the "people power" needed to get things done. For example, if you are creating an outdoor science laboratory as a project, the local garden club may be a good source of help in doing necessary landscaping. The local Chamber of Commerce may help you organize a group of people with heavy equipment to excavate the site. These are tasks that would be very expensive if you had to hire professionals.

PROJECTS THAT ARE FUNDED

Before you should even consider seeking money from a potential funding source, you should have a good project in mind. What makes a project "good" is highly subjective and can vary significantly from situation to situation. It is easier to describe "bad" than "good." Do not seek external funds to support regular school activities. These should be paid for with regular school funds. Do not seek external funds for large, expensive, ongoing projects. As mentioned earlier, funding organizations seldom support projects that will require an ongoing expenditure of funds.

Program officers and grant reviewers seldom favor projects that do not directly impact children. For example, it would be easier to sell a telecommunications project that gets children communicating with people in a local retirement community than it would be to sell a telecommunications project that gets the district principals communicating with the district office.

The idea for a project should be educationally and philosophically sound. It should be one that other educational professionals think will work. It should be in line with the vision and mission of the school, and with the objectives of the organization providing the funds.

Lastly, the idea should be morally sound. It should not have negative implications over the long term, and it should help those who really need help. Ideas that help "the rich get richer" tend to be unsuccessful. Most successful ideas fill important needs or shore up significant weaknesses.

A grant proposal should convey your vision of the value children will gain from the project.
Photo courtesy of Edmark.

Beyond having a good idea, two issues need to be addressed for potential funding source to consider your proposal. First, you must correctly prepare your proposal. If the funding organization has specific proposal requirements, follow the guidelines to the letter. The second is a match with the funding organization's priorities. The funding organization has to care about the project you are proposing. Most grant programs that state their priorities will eliminate your proposal from the review process if it does not fit. Look for a good match between your project and potential funding sources. For example, if you are developing a project on water pollution, contact your state department of natural resources. If you are developing a project on finance, contact your local banks and brokerage offices. The people you contact may not be able to fund your project directly, but they may be able to tell you whom to contact. For example, your local food bank may not have funds to support your nutrition project, but they may be willing to share their funding sources so you can get the funds elsewhere. These activities involve expanding your learning community.

The next issue to consider is feasibility. After reading your proposal, reviewers ask themselves, "Given the existing resources, plus the requested resources, can the applicant complete this project?" This means that you need to be sure you have the necessary physical resources to complete the project, such as space, equipment, and supplies. Carefully consider what you will need to complete the project, and make sure that you either have or are requesting everything you need.

Often the most important resource reviewers consider is the people. Do you have the people with the proper talent and time to accomplish the project? If you have human resource weaknesses, consider a partnership to strengthen them. For example, if you are considering a telecommunications project and you have no one on staff with expertise in that area, you may be able to find a telecommunications expert in a local business or university. Adding that person to your implementation team will tremendously strengthen your proposal.

A common weakness in many proposals is the evaluation of the project. You may be able to collaborate with a local university to get help with the evaluation component. The partnership could provide an opportunity for a graduate student to complete a required research project. As a side benefit, the entire community profits from adding these people to your learning community.

Reviewers also consider the self-sufficiency of projects. Can you continue the project after the grant money runs out? Funding agencies give money to schools to encourage good things to happen for children. Once the funding organization plants the seed, you are expected to nurture the tree to full maturity. For example, suppose you receive a grant from your state department of education for a project aimed at increasing school attendance. The grant money enables you to institute a new program, develop new approaches, or organize children differently to increase attendance. Once you complete the project and the grant money runs out, the state department of education expects you to continue the successful program indefinitely.

Reviewers favor projects that do not require a large, ongoing influx of money. As an example, reviewers would not favor a project that involved hiring teacher's aides in every classroom to increase the one-on-one opportunities for children. A project that instead involved revising the curriculum to make it more engaging for children would be more likely to be funded.

As you put your proposal together, consider how others might implement your project. If your situation is totally unique, and if your project can only be conducted in your unique situation, that is a drawback. A project that a large number of schools could implement has a better chance of being funded. The best projects are those that require no additional funds to implement elsewhere. Once the grant money has been used to perfect an idea, others can implement it with their local resources. Next on the list are projects that only require a modest influx of external funds. Few schools can implement a project that requires a lot of money, since funds are usually so limited.

The last issue, and one that pervades all the others, is clarity of the proposal. Have you made your idea clear? Have you clearly communicated all the elements described above? Have you sufficiently described how your idea matches the priorities of the potential funding organization? Have you let the reviewers know that your idea is educationally sound? Have you explained any potential ethical pitfall involved in your project? Have you clearly described the need for the project or the weaknesses the project will correct? Have you clearly described the existing resources that are necessary to complete the project? Have you described the people, their talents, and the time they have to devote to the project? Have you explained how others might be able to implement your ideas? Last but not least, is your budget clear and accurate? An incomplete or inaccurate budget will significantly hamper your prospects of obtaining a grant.

In preparing your proposal, as you try to cover all bases, meet all the requirements, and strive for maximum clarity, remember one thing: Do not work all the passion out of the document. Your proposal should touch the heart and soul of the caring human beings who will be reading it.

Many funding organizations will provide specific advice for new grant writers preparing a proposal. For example, the National Science Foundation (1993) publishes guidelines for grant writers. When recommendations such as these are provided, they are tremendously helpful. You should consider them carefully.

CHARACTERISTICS OF PEOPLE AND ORGANIZATIONS THAT RECEIVE FUNDING

If you pay attention to external funding, you will quickly notice that certain people and organizations tend to get a lot of grants and others do not. What are the distinguishing characteristics of the successful individuals and organizations? We have observed nine characteristics that seem to distinguish the people and organizations who are continually successful in finding external funds for their projects:

1. *They have ideas.* The highly successful people and organizations are those that frequently try new things. Ideas are the foundation of a successful grant proposal. Applicants who build their proposal around an idea usually surpass those who build their proposal around a funding opportunity. If we think of a funding opportunity as the final stage of implementing a good idea, it seems clear that the successful grant writers will start with the foundation rather than the roof.

2. *They keep in touch with funding opportunities.* Once you have a good idea that needs funding, the next step is to find a funding source. There are many ways to keep in touch with funding sources. Many larger districts have a grant writer or even a group of people involved with external funding. If your district has people like this, they probably have the responsibility to keep the community of leadership informed of possible opportunities.

Many professional journals have a column that announces grants. However, by the time they publish a grant in a journal, the deadline is often very short. It is usually helpful to have more time to prepare your proposal. Professional journals are also the place to find the grant opportunities provided by the professional organization associated with the journal.

We recommend that individuals take responsibility for keeping track of opportunities within specific areas. For example, the art, music, and physical education teachers should each be responsible for grants that come from their professional organizations. If a school has people (as most schools do) who have strong interests in a specific subject area, they can be responsible for keeping track of funding opportunities in those specific areas and of organizations that provide those funding opportunities.

A publication that deserves special mention is *Educational Grants Alert*. A subscription to this publication can be helpful in keeping you up to date on new funding opportunities.

3.   *They have a team.* There are so many elements to a good proposal that one person is seldom able to cover all the necessary bases. Successful organizations usually have a grant-writing team. This team may be somewhat fluid, bringing in different people for different responsibilities. Having a grant-writing team in place in a school or a district can be a powerful way to become successful at obtaining funding.

It is important that the members of the grant-writing team have sufficient time to participate in grant-writing activities. You may have an opportunity to seek significant funds for a project, but if the grant-writing team does not have sufficient time to work on it, you are unlikely to produce a successful proposal. The formal leadership should consider ways to buy the necessary time of the critical members of the grant writing team. For example, if a project is the brainchild of a committed and passionate teacher, that teacher is necessary to the preparation of a winning proposal. Hiring a substitute teacher for a few days (or even half days) would give that teacher the time to participate in the writing of the proposal. Another solution could be for members of the formal leadership to take over a class or two to give the teacher time to participate in preparing the proposal.

4.   *They can respond quickly.* Once you have an idea and a funding source that matches that idea, you frequently must respond quickly or you will lose it. The way many grants are announced and the way we find out about them often means that much of the available time has elapsed before we even learn about the opportunity. Having an experienced grant-writing team already in place can be an important element of quick response. Another way to hasten the process is to compile a packet of previously published information: the demographics, values and beliefs, and vision and mission of the school or district. With the grant-writing team already in place and basic information readily accessible, you can use most of the limited time available gathering necessary information and writing the proposal.

5.   *They have a good writer on the team.* As we pointed out earlier, the clarity of your proposal is a critical issue. Your good idea can be lost in a confused presentation. In addition to clarity, the proposal must also have a logical organization. A person or people who are skilled at organizing a piece of writing will vastly improve a proposal. In addition, your proposal must be persuasive. The objective of your proposal is to persuade the reviewers to recommend that you get the money. Therefore, you should view a grant proposal as a piece of persuasive writing.

Many districts employ a professional grant writer. Grant writers can be helpful, but, as mentioned earlier, the danger in using them is the loss of the passion of your proposal. For this reason, a good professional grant writer must have talents that go beyond technical writing. It is important that the document be clear and accurate, but to win a competition it must also capture the reader. We believe the best of both worlds is to use the people with the ideas to write the proposal and use a professional grant writer to ensure the accuracy and proper organization of the final document. Inherent in this partnership is that the professional grant writer has to understand that she cannot alter the persuasive elements of the writing without collaborating with the idea person. Ideally, every participant should own every idea and every word in the proposal.

6. *They are passionate.* Educators are often passionate people. They have passion for learning, passion for helping children, or passion for their subject area. These passions frequently produce powerful projects. It is important that this passion come through in the proposal. Nothing can persuade a grant reviewer more than a passionate presentation of a project that will benefit children.

7. *They are relentless.* Grant-winning teams are persistent to the point of being relentless. This characteristic is necessary due to the fierce competition for grant money. Dozens of proposals are written for every grant opportunity. No team, regardless of how good it is, wins every time. Most funding organizations give you feedback on your failed proposal. This feedback can be useful in rewriting your proposal for resubmission. If you do not get feedback automatically, a member of the grant-writing team should contact the program officer and ask for feedback.

In addition to resubmitting your proposal to the same funding organization, there are several other alternatives. You can find another source to fund the idea, try other ways to get the funds, or try breaking the project up into smaller pieces and seeking funding from a group of sources.

Virtually everyone who has been successful in this endeavor has also experienced failure. Most have failed many more times than they have succeeded. Once you have developed your foundation—your good idea—funding is merely a matter of putting a roof on your house. Keep trying different roofs until you find one that fits.

8. *They are experienced.* It is very easy to get emotionally involved in a grant proposal. This may be the reason why so many "green" grant writers write their first proposal and then talk as though they have already won the grant. The best thing experience does for a team of grant writers is help them understand that the chances of winning a grant are small. Thus, they get emotionally involved in the idea but not the grant; they see the grant as merely a means to an end. Getting emotionally involved with a particular funding source is almost certainly a guarantee of great disappointment. It is hard to be disappointed and persistent at the same time. Experienced grant-writing teams realize that if their grant does not win, they can rework it and resubmit it, either to the same funding source or to a different source. They may approach it differently. Instead of dreaming about how they are going to spend the money when they get it, they dream about the next most likely place to get the money to make their good idea a reality.

9. *They can follow directions.* The preparation of a winning proposal begins with a good idea and ends when you send that proposal off to a funding organization. Many funding organizations have specific requirements that you must follow. Certain sections may be required, and each may have a required length. A specific number of copies may be required. There is usually a specific deadline. An error in any of these details can send your proposal to the rejection pile. It is important that your proposal conform precisely to the directions of the funding organization. The best idea people are seldom the best at following directions, which is one more reason to have a grant-writing team. One or more people on the team should be responsible for the correctness of the proposal.

RECOMMENDATIONS

From the information above, it should be clear that our first recommendation is that you form a grant-writing team. It should be a team that stands ready to take advantage of opportunities. Many funding opportunities are "one-shot deals." If you miss the deadline, you miss the opportunity.

Your grant-writing team should include the following talents: a good writer— someone whose writing is clear, correct, organized, and persuasive. Your team should also include an idea person and a detail person. It is also helpful to have a person or people with experience in getting grants as part of the team. A member of the formal administration can be part of the team, but that is not necessary. As a minimum, the team should report to someone with formal authority because your proposal will require her signature. You may also need other information or assurances that can only be provided by the formal leadership, such as an assurance of matching funds.

You need to have two kinds of idea people on your grant-writing team: specific idea people and general idea people. The specific idea people originate the idea for which you are seeking funds. They are a necessary part of the team, and they change from proposal to proposal. The general idea people have the ability to develop a good idea. They are people who can take the vague elements of a good project and mold them into a cohesive proposal. They often see additional elements of the project or additional connections to other constituencies. Such people can turn a good idea into a great idea. General idea people can be standing members of the team.

As an example of specific idea people and general idea people, a specific idea person may be a science teacher who wishes to increase the hands-on biology experiences of her children by adding a greenhouse to the school building. This person is essential to the grant-writing team because she holds much of the knowledge and passion for how the greenhouse will be used to help children learn. A general idea person may come up with ideas such as having an Industrial Arts class design the structure. She may see ways to involve the local community in the preparation of the site. She may suggest the addition of an extracurricular horticulture club. She may see possible community connections, such as having the local garden club join

with the horticulture club in using the greenhouse to grow annuals for city beauti-
fication. In this example, the specific idea person created an idea that would benefit
her students, while the general idea person expanded the idea to benefit a much
larger community. The original idea may not have been sufficient to win a competitive grant, while the expanded idea is. What is important is that the original intent
of the idea has been retained, and all the additional elements of the project benefit
children's learning.

Our second recommendation is that tangible rewards be provided to grant
writers. Many times the formal administration sees the receipt of a grant as
enough reward, and feel that a warm pat on the back and a hearty "thank you" are
all that the grant writers require. We do not want to diminish the importance of
the affirmation, but it is simply not sufficient. You must reward those members of
your grant writing team for their extra effort. The people with the ideas are even
more critical. Without a tangible reward for their efforts, their only reward for
their hard work—preparing and submitting the grant—is more hard work—doing
the proposed project. This is how grant-writing can become a self-extinguishing
process. The formal administration must build in tangible rewards for those individuals who are making special and unusual contributions to the total efforts of
the unit.

Some organizations make the mistake of rewarding only successful grant writers. This ignores the fact that it is just as much work to apply for a grant and lose
as it is to apply and win. Your organization should reward the effort, not the success. Given the highly competitive nature of external funding, rewarding only success may extinguish the effort before your grant-writing team develops expertise.

We also believe that there should be tangible rewards for the completion of a
project. Many times the formal administration sees external funding only as an
input to the total funding picture. From this view, the process is complete when
the check arrives. However, in terms of the benefit to the school and the children,
that is when the process begins. The community of leadership should reward the
people who make special effort to complete the project, either when the project is
complete or at critical points along the path to completion.

Most larger school districts have an existing infrastructure for managing
grants. If your district does not, some structure is necessary. Without a structure,
certain types of grants are out of the question. To seek a federal grant, you must
have someone who can administer that grant. The same is true of many grants
from large foundations. In addition, it is very helpful to have a "grant watcher"
who keeps tabs on grant opportunities and informs interested people. Having a
grant watcher in your district can buy the grant-writing team some necessary
time. If you find out about a grant a month sooner, you have another month to
prepare the proposal.

A third function of an external funding infrastructure is a central repository
for experience with securing external funding. The old phrase "nothing succeeds
like success" was never more true than in external funding. The more experience
you can bring to bear on a proposal, the better. Many school districts employ a
grant writer who drafts all the proposals. This can be helpful, but it can also be a

detriment. It is not uncommon for a professional grant writer to prepare correct, proper proposals that lack the passion and vision of the people with the idea. Unless you are lucky enough to have an extraordinary grant writer, we believe it is preferable to have the idea people heavily involved in the writing, and to have a central office person act only as final reviewer.

Excellent and successful grants are the result of passionate ideas and well-written proposals. Experienced grant-writing teams are basic to successful grant writing. Schools must nurture and train teams for action just as hospitals nurture and train emergency medical teams. Another ongoing, nurtured, and trained team, ready to interact with the grant writing team is the planning team (see Chapter 11). Consistent and ongoing assessment of the school community's shared goals, vision, and mission can improve the proposal and shorten the preparation time.

REFERENCES

Directorate for Education and Human Resources. (1993). *Elementary, secondary and informal education: Program announcement and guidelines* (NSF93-131). Washington, DC: National Science Foundation.

Faczko, M. M., & Rich, E. H. (Eds.). (1995). *The foundation directory, 1995 edition*. New York: Foundation Center.

Jones, F., Lewis, K., & Toth, G. (Eds.). (1994). *Corporate foundation profiles*. New York: Foundation Center

McCarthy, B. (1993). Fund-raising. *Electronic Learning Special Edition, 12*(5), 11-13.

National Science Foundation, Directorate for Education and Human Resources. (1993). *Elementary, secondary, and informal education: Program announcement and guidelines* (NSF93-131), pp. 7–9. Washington DC: Author.

Solomon, G. (1993). All about grants. *Electronic Learning Special Edition, 12*(5), 14-23.

RESOURCE LIST

Educational Grants Alert,

Science, Mathematics and Technology Education Sourcebook 1990–1991, by B. J. Calinger & B. Walthall. Available from the American Association for the Advancement of Science, P. O. Box 753, Waldorf MD 20604. (ERIC Document Reproduction Service No. 347 049)

Guidelines of the National Foundation for the Improvement of Education, available from Shirley Nelson, NFIE, 1201 Sixteenth Street, NW, Washington DC 20036. Phone (202) 822-7844.

CHAPTER 13

Toward a Brilliant Future

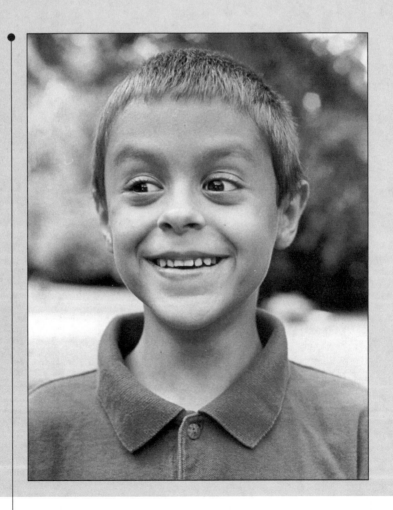

Teachers and principals from the 1940s, the 1950s, and the early 1960s describe that era as their "golden age" of education. We think that their golden age was the age of compliance, the time when students did as they were told and when parents supported the school. We believe that the golden age of education is taking place now and in the immediate future. Our golden age is the age of teaching and learning—the age of instructional technology in a context of community. We base this conclusion upon the collaboration between our new vision of teaching and learning and the power of the community of leadership. The new vision of teaching and learning can be illustrated by instructional models that help students turn data into information and information into knowledge. The new vision of community of leadership is a cultural change in classrooms and schools predicated upon "doing the right thing": following values and beliefs, vision and mission, and shared goals and objectives.

In this chapter we characterize our vision of the golden age of education by describing trends in technology and leadership, teaching and learning at the forefront of educational leadership, changes in teachers and administrators, and building a future.

INTRODUCTION

Predicting the future is never easy. Unforeseen social events, new inventions, and major acts of nature can have such dramatic effects that no one can predict the future with any level of certainty. However, if we do not focus our efforts on shaping the future, we may find ourselves living in a present that is significantly less than we would wish.

Trends in Technology

If there is one thing everyone can agree upon, it is that technology is changing rapidly. Year by year, computers get logically bigger, physically smaller, cheaper, faster, and easier to use. We are seeing various technologies merge. Television and computers interact with digitized video and audiovisual computers, creating the prospect of computer networking through the cable television infrastructure. The telephone and the computer, joined by fax modems and automated voice mail, create the prospect of networking through the telephone infrastructure.

In the past, all computers were text based. Today, we are steadily moving toward a more graphical computing world. We use more graphics in our work (for example, illustrations) and in our interfaces (the way we interact with the computer). The use of color is steadily increasing. Color monitors are now the standard. Cheap, high-quality color printing is the next evolution. Sound capabilities parallel color capabilities. We are able to integrate more sound into our work. Programs include much more sound, and that sound is of increasingly higher quality. We have moved from a few beeps and buzzes through simple music and mechanical speech to a world where we can talk to computers and computers can respond.

Networking is a third element in the evolution. Computers are linked together in an increasing variety of ways. Most office computers, and even some home computers, are linked in a local area network. Most computer systems have the capability to link to a wide area network. The move toward wireless communication is starting to have a profound effect on telecommunications possibilities.

We expect all these trends to continue. The result is that computers will continue to get easier for the average person to understand and operate, and their capabilities will continue to increase. If we were to dream just a bit, we could imagine a world in which instead of a car displaying a little light to indicate an oil change, it could put a note on a "to do" list. We could imagine a world in which we talk to computers instead of using the keyboard. We can imagine a world in which instead of taking our pictures to the photo lab, we take a disk into our den and print our own pictures. All these dreams are possible today, but they are expensive. In time, mass production will reduce the cost to a reasonable level and these dreams will be reality. We only have to look to movies and television programs to find these dreams. The "Star Trek" model indeed may be the case: a future in which only a handful of people do the things people do today, while the majority tend the technology. Our future can finally be realized, with the majority of our population engaged in the pursuits of beauty and brilliance.

> I must study politics and war, that my sons may have the liberty to study mathematics and philosophy, geography, natural history, and naval architecture, navigation, commerce, and agriculture, in order to give their children a right to study painting, poetry, music, architecture, statuary, tapestry and porcelain.—*John Adams*

In conjunction with the technical trends, expanding technology has social implications. Computers are being used in more places. More people are adopting the computer as their tool. The machine that was once the exclusive domain of scientists, accountants, military specialists, and statisticians has become the tool of the common person. Computers pervade the working world and are found in an increasing percentage of homes. Many professionals have three computers: one at work, one at home, and one in their briefcase. Children are adopting the computer as a device of particular interest. Even senior citizens are beginning to log on as one of the fastest growing segments of the computer market.

Not only are more people using computers, but computers are being integrated into more places in our world. We probably do not know how many computers we own because they are in places we might not expect. We have computers in our cars and thermostats. We have computers in our kitchen appliances, stereo equipment, and video equipment. We are making all our tools more intelligent by adding microprocessors.

In addition to all the trends that can be examined and projected, new inventions must be considered. The invention of the transistor and the subsequent invention of the microchip are examples. Before they were invented, there were

Many children have computers in their bedrooms.

practical limits to what we could do with computing equipment. These inventions broke barriers. We are due for similar ground-breaking inventions. Unfortunately, new breakthroughs may take longer than in the past because the funds for research are shrinking. Federal funding is more scarce today than it was in the past. The money that large corporations spend on research also is declining, due to shrinking profit margins. Although we enjoy the advantage of full computer systems costing less than $2,000, we also suffer the disadvantage of the slower development of radically new technology.

With shrinking funds for research and development in corporations, an increasing percentage of the research and development budget is focused more heavily on near-term problems and issues rather than on new discoveries. However, there are people in our world for whom innovation and invention are their life blood. They may not have the funds that were once enjoyed in technology development, but they retain the drive to innovate and invent. New inventions will continue to occur, and they will radically alter our world in ways that are impossible to predict.

Our overall view of future technology is that we will integrate it more universally into our lives. It will become a more powerful and helpful influence. There are trends that we can reasonably suggest, and there are changes that are impossible to predict. The only certainty is that the future will be different from the past.

Trends in Leadership

A theme we have woven throughout this book is the community of leadership. We believe this idea encapsulates future trends in leadership. We believe leadership will become more a shared endeavor than a hierarchical structure. We believe leadership roles will become less rigid, with responsibilities shifting to those most capable of the greatest success. As this community evolves, we believe it will focus on leadership issues such as vision, mission, planning, staff development, instruction, and supervision. We believe the management functions often associated with formal school leaders will be carried out by professional managers, leaving the community of leadership free to pursue leadership tasks and carry out leadership responsibilities.

The Conjunction of Leadership and Technology in the Classroom

Some forecasters suggest that classrooms and teachers will be unnecessary in a technology-rich future. We do not agree with this prediction. In the foreseeable future, we believe society will reap sufficient social benefit for the expense of maintaining school buildings. We also believe that the teacher, as the director and facilitator of learning, will always be necessary. The teacher's role will continue to evolve, as it has in the last few decades. There will always be a need for human guidance in making learning decisions. There will always be the need for human encouragement and affirmation. And there will always be the need to celebrate human accomplishment.

The overarching role of teachers in the future will be the same as it was in the past: to care about children and their development. It seems absurd to envision a future in which we eliminate people who worry about an individual child's development. It is true that school buildings as houses of knowledge dissemination will be unnecessary. However, they will always be necessary as houses of social dissemination. Our school buildings will continue to be an important place where our young people learn how to become happy, successful, productive members of our society.

THE GOLDEN AGE OF EDUCATION

We believe that technology is improving our lives. If this is true, then bringing more technology into our schools should create positive changes in the teaching and learning environment. Many scholars of education have described elements of a better learning environment. We believe that technology will continue to be instrumental in making these possibilities a reality.

Learning Issues Move to the Forefront

Much of what defines a school today has little to do with learning. The bus and lunch schedules play a large part in defining the management of the school. The summative evaluation (standardized testing) of learning often takes precedence over learning itself. We focus on testing rather than on learning. The simple management of the children and the curriculum (the data and information) defines much of our organization of a school. We believe technology will allow us to refocus our attention on issues of learning (knowledge). Schools will become places that single-mindedly focus on helping and guiding children's learning.

The specific changes we believe will be possible with the increased use of technology include:

1. a continuous move toward greater individualization of learning.
2. a more fluid arrangement of children for group learning experiences (multi-age grouping).
3. the integration of once-isolated disciplines.
4. a movement away from Carnegie units toward authentic learning.
5. a movement away from discipline-driven environments and toward social modeling.
6. a shift toward more powerful learning strategies.

Technology has already allowed us to move in the direction of individualization of learning. However, we are two steps down a road that is miles long. In the future we hope that each child will have an Individual Educational Plan (IEP) that is agreed upon by the child and the people who care about that child's development. These plans will be detailed and specific, focusing on authentic learning outcomes, prescribing strategies and authentic assessments, and guiding the organization of the learning. These plans will involve the whole child, not just cognition. Everyone who cares about the child's development will have a role, not just the child and the teacher.

In recent history we have seen the dissolution of nuclear families, the separation of extended families, and the diminishing role of church and community organizations. These events suggest that fewer and fewer people care about a child's development. We hope that the use of technology can repair some of this damage, by enabling us to increase the participants who can guide of the development of each child.

Today, we organize children's learning based on age. This organizing principle is troublesome; the most significant problem is a reliance on efficiency. Much of what we teach in our classrooms today is either above or below the ability level of the learners in the classroom. Either the children are not yet developmentally ready to learn the topic of the day, or they already know it. We organize children to learn this way because it is efficient given our resources. If technology gives us significantly more options, then we can consider better ways of organizing children for learning.

Much of what we do today is done in large groups. We do things this way because of tradition and because we lack the resources to change. In many learning activities, working with a large group is not only ineffective, it is detrimental. For example, consider worksheets that drill math facts. Every child gets the worksheet and must complete it. One child does it in two minutes because that child already knows the math facts. Another child struggles with the worksheet and gets every problem wrong, which reinforces the child's poor strategies and adds to a sense of failure. In the golden age of education, children will concentrate only on the facts they need and do not already know. Further, they will not be asked to drill facts until they are developmentally capable of learning them.

Many school activities, however, do require that children work together. Social interaction is important to the learning process. In our current organization of children's learning, the assumption is that, by virtue of having lived a certain number of years, all children are ready to learn the same things. This is clearly nonsensical. In the golden age of education, children will be formed into *ad hoc* groups so they can learn together according to their learning interests and needs, not their age or ability. We do little of this today because it is too difficult and expensive to organize. We believe that the power of technology can be used to organize children more fluidly for the sake of their learning.

More individualized learning will make some of our current systems seem absurd. The labeling of certain children as gifted and talented or as learning disabled will cease. We will be able to acknowledge every child as having talents and gifts. Similarly, we will be able to identify, monitor, and remediate the individual learning problems each child faces.

Technology can help us manage the curriculum. Many educators espouse interdisciplinary teaching and learning, integrated units, and thematic teaching. Most educators would agree that teaching is more powerful when the specific disciplines are taught together rather than as decontextualized skills. However, the move away from isolated disciplines has been erratic at best. We believe that one reason these efforts are not dramatically successful is that they are more difficult to plan, implement, and manage. In an integrated curriculum, children still must learn math, language, science, and social studies. Technology could mediate this problem. Computer applications could be used to help manage the full range of important learning objectives that are prescribed for each child.

Similarly, the way we organize children from year to year may change. The management of children through their entire learning process is easier if we simply dictate that a child must attend school for 13 years and complete a certain number of credits. However, this is not the most effective way to help children learn. In fact, many children today are choosing not to complete the entire process because they see it as unnecessary and irrelevant. A system in which a child constructs important and useful knowledge rather than passing to the next grade would be an important improvement. In such as system, the child, the community of leadership, and others who care about the child agree on the knowledge, skill, and dispositions that the child must construct. When the child can demonstrate achievement of the prescribed learning, the child "graduates." Part of children's individual learning prescription would include how they demonstrate their learning, probably using primarily authentic assessment. Today, much of the management of the learning process is for the convenience of adults. In the golden age of education, the management of learning will be single-mindedly focused on children's individual development.

Another change that we expect to see in the golden age of education is a change in the culture of schools. Many schools are behavior-management facilities first and learning environments second. We expect to see discipline problems minimized as a precept of school. Discipline is unlikely to remain a dominant goal in a learning environment in which children are continually engaged in learning that they agree is important, doing activities that are challenging and engaging, and working with others to construct important learning. If school is a place that children value and want to be, then behavior problems should be a minor consideration. Behavior management should be part of the prescribed learning for each child, not apart from it. In the golden age of education, children are not forced to behave in an appropriate manner; they adopt developmentally appropriate behavior as part of their individual prescribed learning.

We dream of one last change in schools that would define our golden age of education. We envision a move toward more powerful learning. Today, most of the curriculum is focused on factual learning. Facts are easily garnered in today's world. Learning facts, alone, is of little value. Procedural learning is far more valuable. Procedural learning is doing, and most procedures require some facts.

We suggest a third type of learning: strategic learning. We want children to develop a variety of strategies. Strategies require facts and procedures. The difference between procedures and strategies is that procedures apply to a narrow set of circumstances, and strategies can be applied universally. Strategies can be applied to new and novel situations, whereas procedures cannot. Effective education should vest children with a variety of powerful and effective strategies for accomplishing what children wish. Wise and caring adults should guide children's wishes. The development of these strategies should become the fabric of the academic program. Some educators talk about designing successful learning experiences for children. We suggest aiming higher. Rather than helping children have isolated successful experiences, we should help children develop successful strategies so they can experience success more continuously. These success strategies become the important shared goals of the school. We can replace isolated success experiences with continuous bursts of brilliance.

Changes in the Teaching Profession

Most of the changes in the teaching profession that we envision are implied by our recommended changes in the learning environment. However, we envision additional changes that would further strengthen the schools of the future.

We previously suggested that technology could help us manage a more complex organization of children and learning. We hope that quality instructional systems will develop along with quality management systems. We do not necessarily envision automated instruction. This may be one possibility, but beyond that, we envision vast and easily accessible data bases of instructional assistance. If a teacher needs help guiding a child or group of children in the construction of some specific knowledge, the teacher should have a wide variety of assistance available. Not only should resources (including text, video, people, and places) be at the teachers fingertips, but also ideas. We have data bases of ideas and learning solutions, but they are not easily accessible. In the golden age of education, all the teaching and learning resources, including good ideas about alternative instructional strategies, would be easily accessible.

We also envision a more fluid arrangement of the learning environment. Although we believe the school building will remain an important part of the educational system, we do not believe it will be as central to learning as it is today. We know that much of a child's learning happens outside the classroom. In the golden age of education, not only will this fact be acknowledged, it will be integrated into the learning process. Children will learn where it is most effective to learn, with the obvious considerations of learning and cost. We also expect that the priorities about learning follow this order: first learning, then cost. But then, we are optimists.

The last change in the teaching environment that we envision is a more effective move toward career paths in education. Here we are using an old term to describe something we believe has new elements. In our vision of career paths, educators will have different functions. Today, the choices are few. There are classroom teachers, specialists (for example, speech therapists, special education teachers), and formal leaders. We believe each of these jobs still will be necessary, but we envision additional positions that will strengthen our ability to help individual children attain important strategies. Just as we see the organization of children becoming more fluid, we see the organization of teaching naturally following the same path. We expect to see strategy-specific specialists who work only with children who are ready to attain a specific goal or objective. We also expect to see problem-specific specialists: teachers who are particularly adept at helping children overcome specific learning problems. Problem-specific teachers will be similar to our special education teachers today, but their activities will be more broad-based, applying to all children, not just those identified as at risk for academic failure or categorized by artificial labels.

In addition, we envision super teachers: teachers whose talents are most strongly focused on helping teachers help children. This role may subsume much of what is contained today in graduate teacher education programs. The super teachers may help teachers improve on the job in a high-context environment as opposed to the low-context college classroom.

One last thought: Each role in the school of the golden age will have corresponding status and remuneration. It is our hope that the "top" jobs in the school of the golden age will be those jobs that directly assist children. If we truly value our children as the most precious product of our society, then it follows that we should value most highly the people who guide the development of our children. People who cannot effectively work with children will have to opt for lower-status jobs, such as doctors and attorneys. People in the school systems who are less effective at working with children will have to be demoted or removed. Once again, we are clearly optimists.

BUILDING A FUTURE

Some of our predictions about the future of education may seem grandiose and "outside the box." The pessimistic educator may decry, "It can never happen!" We believe that we are all shaping the future through our actions in the present. The daily newspaper provides us with a continuous stream of concerns about the present we have constructed. Violence is increasing while our ability to control our world is diminishing. Our schools are our last, best hope to shape a future in which we can all feel happy and safe, be brilliant and productive, and show concern, care, and love for one another. Just because things are the way they are does not mean that is the way they have to be. If we do not actively shape our schools' present, we will live with a lesser future.

Name Index

Subject Index